CRITICAL CONVOY
BATTLES OF WWII

The Stackpole Military History Series

THE AMERICAN CIVIL WAR
Cavalry Raids of the Civil War
In the Lion's Mouth
Witness to Gettysburg

WORLD WAR I
Doughboy War

WORLD WAR II
After D-Day
Airborne Combat
Armor Battles of the Waffen-SS,
    1943–45
Armoured Guardsmen
Arnhem 1944
The B-24 in China
The Battalion
The Battle of France
The Battle of Sicily
Battle of the Bulge, Vol. 1
Battle of the Bulge, Vol. 2
Battle of the Bulge, Vol. 3
Beyond the Beachhead
Beyond Stalingrad
The Black Bull
Blitzkrieg Unleashed
Blossoming Silk Against the Rising Sun
Bodenplatte
The Breaking Point
The Brigade
The Canadian Army and the Normandy
    Campaign
Critical Convoy Battles of WWII
A Dangerous Assignment
D-Day Bombers
D-Day Deception
D-Day to Berlin
Decision in the Ukraine
The Defense of Moscow 1941
Destination Normandy
Dive Bomber!
Eager Eagles
Eagles of the Third Reich
The Early Battles of Eighth Army
Eastern Front Combat
Europe in Flames
Exit Rommel
The Face of Courage
Fatal Decisions
Fist from the Sky
Flying American Combat Aircraft of
    World War II, Vol. 1
For Europe
Forging the Thunderbolt
For the Homeland
Fortress France
The German Defeat in the East,
    1944–45
German Order of Battle, Vol. 1
German Order of Battle, Vol. 2
German Order of Battle, Vol. 3

The Germans in Normandy
Germany's Panzer Arm in World War II
GI Ingenuity
Goodbye, Transylvania
The Great Ships
Grenadiers
Guns Against the Reich
Hitler's Final Fortress
Hitler's Nemesis
Hitler's Spanish Legion
Hold the Westwall
Infantry Aces
In the Fire of the Eastern Front
Iron Arm
Iron Knights
Japanese Army Fighter Aces
Japanese Naval Fighter Aces
JG 26 Luftwaffe Fighter Wing War Diary,
    Vol. 1
JG 26 Luftwaffe Fighter Wing War Diary,
    Vol. 2
Kampfgruppe Peiper at the Battle of
    the Bulge
The Key to the Bulge
Kursk
Luftwaffe Aces
Luftwaffe Fighter Ace
Luftwaffe Fighter-Bombers over Britain
Luftwaffe Fighters & Bombers
Luftwaffe KG 200
Marshal of Victory, Vol. 1
Marshal of Victory, Vol. 2
Massacre at Tobruk
Mechanized Juggernaut or Military
    Anachronism?
Messerschmitts over Sicily
Michael Wittmann, Vol. 1
Michael Wittmann, Vol. 2
Mission 85
Mission 376
The Nazi Rocketeers
Night Flyer / Mosquito Pathfinder
No Holding Back
Operation Mercury
Panzer Aces
Panzer Aces II
Panzer Commanders of the
    Western Front
Panzergrenadier Aces
Panzer Gunner
The Panzer Legions
Panzers in Normandy
Panzers in Winter
Panzer Wedge, Vol. 1
Panzer Wedge, Vol. 2
The Path to Blitzkrieg
Penalty Strike
Poland Betrayed
Red Road from Stalingrad
Red Star Under the Baltic
Retreat to the Reich

Rommel Reconsidered
Rommel's Desert Commanders
Rommel's Desert War
Rommel's Lieutenants
The Savage Sky
The Seeds of Disaster
Ship-Busters
The Siege of Brest 1941
The Siege of Küstrin
The Siegfried Line
A Soldier in the Cockpit
Soviet Blitzkrieg
Spitfires & Yellow Tail Mustangs
Stalin's Keys to Victory
Surviving Bataan and Beyond
T-34 in Action
Tank Tactics
Tigers in the Mud
Triumphant Fox
The 12th SS, Vol. 1
The 12th SS, Vol. 2
Twilight of the Gods
Typhoon Attack
The War Against Rommel's Supply Lines
War in the Aegean
War of the White Death
Warsaw 1944
Winter Storm
The Winter War
Wolfpack Warriors
Zhukov at the Oder

THE COLD WAR / VIETNAM
Cyclops in the Jungle
Expendable Warriors
Fighting in Vietnam
Flying American Combat Aircraft:
    The Cold War
Here There Are Tigers
Land with No Sun
Phantom Reflections
Street without Joy
Through the Valley
Tours of Duty
Two One Pony

**WARS OF AFRICA AND THE
MIDDLE EAST**
The Rhodesian War

GENERAL MILITARY HISTORY
Battle of Paoli
Cavalry from Hoof to Track
Desert Battles
Guerrilla Warfare
The Philadelphia Campaign, Vol. 1
Ranger Dawn
Sieges
The Spartan Army

CRITICAL CONVOY BATTLES OF WWII

Crisis in the North Atlantic, March 1943

Jürgen Rohwer

STACKPOLE
BOOKS

Copyright © 1977 by Jürgen Rohwer

Published in paperback in the U.S. in 2015 by
STACKPOLE BOOKS
5067 Ritter Road
Mechanicsburg, PA 17055
www.stackpolebooks.com

Printed in the United States of America

10 9 8 7 6 5 4 3 2 1

FIRST STACKPOLE EDITION

Cover design by Wendy A. Reynolds
Translation: text by Derek Masters
Appendix 10 by A. J. Barker
Photo captions by T. Phelps Penry

Library of Congress Cataloging-in-Publication Data

Rohwer, Jürgen.
    [Geleitzugschlachten im März 1943. English]
    Critical convoy battles of WWII : crisis in the North Atlantic, March 1943 / Jürgen Rohwer.
        pages cm. — (Stackpole military history series)
    Includes bibliographical references and index.
    ISBN 978-0-8117-1655-0
1. World War, 1939–1945—Campaigns—Atlantic Ocean. 2. World War, 1939–1945—Naval operations—Submarine. 3. World War, 1939–1945—Naval operations, German. 4. Naval convoys—North Atlantic Ocean—History—20th century. I. Masters, Derek, translator. II. Title.
    D771.R6313 2015
    940.54'293—dc23
            2015020114

Contents

Preface

For some thirty years books and articles about the Battle of the Atlantic have been appearing regularly in both Germany and Britain. It is obvious why there has been great interest in this subject in Britain: there everyone knows what part the Royal Navy's command of the sea routes and its victory over the U-boats played in the country's survival in two world wars. But even in the much more continentally-minded Federal Republic of Germany books on this subject have got onto the best-seller lists in recent years. After so many publications it might justifiably be asked whether there is now anything new to be said about the U-boat war of 1939–45 which has not already appeared in one form or another elsewhere.

Today it is much easier to answer this question affirmatively than it was a short time ago. Now that the British thirty-year rule no longer affects documents relating to the Second World War, the historian is in the fortunate position of being able to reconstruct the events of the Battle of the Atlantic far more precisely than was hitherto possible. This applies not so much to questions of grand strategy which have been adequately dealt with already in official British and Allied works and in various source publications, as in the memoirs of the leading commanders on both sides. It concerns much more the interplay of forces on both sides in the sphere of operational command with its many technical aspects, particularly in the field of radio control and intelligence and of surface and underwater location. And it also applies to the presentation of the tactical course of individual actions. Hitherto it was necessary to restrict this mainly to a description of events as seen or experienced by one side. The incomplete nature of such observation and assessment of what was really happening on the other side necessarily involved inaccuracies. Now, in most cases, it is possible to compare the War Diary of one side with the no less detailed battle reports of the other.

The study of a large number of convoy operations and their individual tactical actions shows that many current theories cannot stand up to detailed investigation. Frequently exaggerated successes claimed by both sides have to be corrected and the causes of the faulty appreciation found. In addition, many assumptions about the efficacy of particular techniques, equipment and weapons systems are shown to have been oversimplified and must be seen in the context of factors such as the impact of other sensors and weapons, and weather, human error, luck and coincidence. It emerges that the existing picture of events is based too much on a pattern of individual and frequently depicted operations where special circumstances were often untypical of the time. Inevitably both in the larger surveys and the description of individual operations the convoy battles which were selected were generally those which were eventful, while the far greater number of convoy journeys and U-boat patrols which produced nothing of note were forgotten.

For this reason an attempt has been made in this book to describe one of the most famous convoy battles of World War 2, that against convoys HX.229 and SC.122 in March 1943, not, as hitherto, in isolation and divorced from the "uneventful" operations going on at the same time, but in the overall context.

After reviewing the development of the strategic conceptions of both sides in the various phases of the Battle of the Atlantic from 1939 to 1943 and describing, in particular, the problems of operational control, an attempt has been made to present the convoy and U-boat operations in the whole of the North Atlantic in the first twenty days of March 1943 and to indicate them on maps.

This work would not have been possible without the generous and patient cooperation of the historical departments of the navies which took part in the Battle of the Atlantic and the help of their archives, as well as numerous participants on both sides, from commander-in-chief to formation commander, captain and sailor, including the civilian technician. It is not possible to thank them all here; but some names may be mentioned on behalf of all:

Rear-Admiral P. N. Buckley, Mr. J. D. Lawson and Mr. H. C. Beaumont of the Naval Historical Branch, Ministry of Defence, London;

Group Captain E. P. Haslam and Mr. J. P. McDonald of the Air Historical Branch (RAF), Ministry of Defence, London;

Mr. F. F. Lambert of the Public Records Office, London; Rear-Admiral Ernest McNeill Eller, Captain F. Kent Loomis and Mr. S. L. Morison of the Division of Naval History, Office of the Chief of Naval Operations, Navy Department, Washington; Dr. Dean C. Alland, Mr. Cavalcante and Mrs. Lloyd; Dr. G. N. Tucker, Mr. E. C. Russell, Mr. S. F. Wise, Commander W. A. B. Douglas and Mr. Philip Chaplin of the Directorate of History, Department of National Defence, Ottawa;

Kapitän zur See Dr. F. Forstmeier and Korvettenkapitän H. Horkisch of das Militärgeschichtliche Forschungsamt der Bundeswehr, Freiburg;

Dr. G. Maierhöfer of the Bundesarchiv-Militärarchiv, Freiburg;

Flottillenadmiral Dr. W. Schünemann and Fregattenkapitän W. Brost of the Embassy of the German Federal Republic, London.

Mrs. Pain of the Public Records Office, London.

They all gave me generous support in my work, going well beyond their official duties.

Of the Allied participants in the Battle of the Atlantic, my thanks for help are due to the following, who have themselves published work on this subject: Vice-Admiral B. B. Schofield, who was part of the Allied Command in the Trade Division of the Admiralty, Vice-Admiral Sir Peter Gretton and Captain Donald McIntyre, who were outstandingly successful Escort Commanders, and Capitaine de corvette Pierre de Morsier and Captain John M. Waters, who respectively spent the spring of 1943 in the North Atlantic as Commander of the Free French corvette *Iobelia* and as Officer on the US Coast Guard cutter *Ingham*.

On the German side I would first like to thank the Commander U-boats, Grossadmiral a.D. Karl Dönitz, for many lengthy discussions of the problems of the U-boat war, also Konteradmiral a.D. Eberhard Godt, Fregattenkapitän G. Hessler (who, sadly, died all too early), Korvettenkapitän a.D.A. Schnee and Kapitän zur See a.D.H. Meckel of the B.d.U. Stab, the experts in the field of the Naval Intelligence Konteradmiral a.D. Stummel, the Kapitäne zur See a.D.A. Bonatz, H. Giessler and H. Möller and the many U-boat commanders who survived the Battle of the Atlantic and who, over nearly thirty years, have imparted to me the various details of their experiences. I have received valuable information about German radar and W/T from Dieter Berenbrock, Dr. Frank Reuter, Dr. Ing. Wachtel and Fregattenkapitän Grundke; and from Dr. Hüttenheim and Fregattenkapitän Singer for information about the German encoding machines.

Nor must I forget my historian colleagues, Rear-Admiral Professor Dr. Samuel Eliot Morison and Captain Stephen W. Roskill, the authors of the official American and British histories of the war at sea, to whom I am indebted for many suggestions and details.

Finally, I would like to thank my dear wife, Evi, and my two sons, who showed great patience and consideration during my work in the evenings and weekends, and to my two secretaries, Frau Kasper and Frau Niggl, who typed the manuscript.

Stuttgart   *J. Rohwer*

PREFACE TO THE ENGLISH EDITION

Since the appearance of the German edition in autumn 1975, two events during 1976 have necessitated certain alterations and additions to the text:

1. The release of information about the British efforts and successes in deciphering German Naval ciphers in World War 2.
2. The publication of Martin Middlebrook's book, *Convoy: The Battle for Convoys SC.122 and HX.229* (London: Alan Lane 1976).

Thanks to the friendly assistance of Commander Patrick Beasley, who was assistant director of the British Admiralty's Submarine Tracking Room from January 1942 until the end of the war, it has been possible to work into the text some of the more important facts about the effects of the British deciphering of German radio messages in the different phases of the Battle of the Atlantic, above all in March 1943. The major points are also briefly described in an appendix (Appendix 10) which also includes acknowledgments of other help received. For technical reasons only a few isolated cases could be worked into the text from the findings of Martin Middlebrook's book. Mr. Middlebrook had been able to draw on the records of both the Allied naval and merchant shipping and of the U-boats, as well as upon the personal accounts of many survivors of the battle on both sides. In Mr. Middlebrook's book the emphasis is on the comparison of the experiences and the fate of the participants in the battles on both sides, while this book deals more with its strategic and tactical leadership problems. In this way the books complement each other very well. We shall try to solve the few remaining contradictions or inconsistencies in friendly cooperation in later editions.

J. Rohwer

CHAPTER 1

Introduction: Prewar Considerations

The Battle of the Atlantic was the longest battle of the Second World War. It began on September 3, 1939 and ended on May 8, 1945. What were at stake in this battle were Britain's vital supplies from overseas. In addition to the actual battle in the Atlantic many other factors played a role in this war of supplies: the sea and air offensive against shipping off the British coast; the mine war conducted by aircraft; the activities of surface ships and submarines on British shipping routes; the air attacks on British harbors; and the policy of isolating Britain from the European continent by the German occupation of Norway, Denmark and France. Apart from this, there was the naval and air war in the oceans and coastal seas of Europe and the Far East insofar as this was directed against Allied and neutral shipping which could be used in the Allied cause. But this war of supplies was decided in the Battle of the Atlantic in which the German U-boats, occasionally supplemented by battleships, cruisers, auxiliary cruisers, long-range bombers and Italian submarines, had to bear the main brunt in a contest that lasted nearly 69 months.

By the spring of 1943 the Battle of the Atlantic had reached its dramatic climax. In the first 20 days of March 1943 the U-boats came nearest to their aim of interrupting the lines of communication between the Old World and the New when they sank 39 merchant ships out of four successive convoys. But only eight weeks were to elapse before the picture changed and the convoys got the upper hand over the U-boats. By May 24 the Commander U-boats had to abandon the fight against the convoys in the decisive areas of the battle—the waters of the North Atlantic between Newfoundland, Greenland, Iceland and Northern Ireland.

Many books and articles have been written since about the greatest of these convoy battles, involving SC.121, HX.228, SC.122, HX.229 and ONS.5 etc. In most of these books it is the experiences of the crews in the U-boats, the merchant ships and escort vessels which form the core of the accounts. In order to incorporate as much action as possible into these accounts it is inevitable that convoy battles have often been chosen which ended with the

1

maximum losses on the one side or the other. It is rare in all this literature to find details of the movements of convoys whose passages were more or less uneventful and which accordingly did not provide material for dramatic descriptions. In the case of the eventful convoy battles the emphasis has been on tactical leadership. But the details about the control of operations on both sides have not really been adequately dealt with. For this reason the first part of the present book proposes to deal largely with the operational problems on both sides which led to the biggest convoy battle of the Second World War, that against convoys HX.229 and SC.122 from March 16 to March 20, 1943. We shall examine the system of convoy control in March 1943 on the one side and the U-boat operations on the other. In doing so, we shall devote special attention to the development of new weapon systems and technical equipment because they particularly influenced the outcome of the Battle of the Atlantic.

It is generally believed that the technological turning-point of the U-boat war in the Atlantic was connected with the successes of Allied radar. This equipment, which allows its user to "see" by night and in fog and is therefore such a fascinating source of inspiration to the human imagination, has gripped the attention of writers, whether they be seamen who partici-pated in the battle, historians or journalists; the result has been that they have tended to underestimate the significance of other factors.

This applies particularly to another field in the "war of the ether": wire-less telegraphy. This was the means by which ships and U-boats taking part in operations were able to exchange information and to receive orders from the tactical commanders at sea and from the operational commands on shore. Without it neither the German Commander U-boats could have directed the operations of his boats nor could the Allied commands on both sides of the Atlantic have controlled the convoys and shipping.

The fact that radio waves are used to transmit information means that this information can be heard not only by the intended recipient but also by the enemy. Accordingly, from the time of the First World War, navies have sent their radio information and orders in cipher to prevent them being intercepted by the enemy. Naval intelligence services, therefore, tried to learn the procedures to encode radio messages and to render them intelli-gible for their own commanders. Increasingly complex ciphers and, eventu-ally, the use of cipher machines were designed to make this task more difficult. To complicate the work of the enemy cryptographic service still more, the growing radio traffic was divided up into particular spheres depending on operational, tactical or geographical factors. They were allot-ted special frequencies and the frequencies and codes were changed with increasing rapidity.

But it was not merely the cryptographic service which provided the enemy with the possibility of acquiring information from radio traffic. It was possible to take bearings of the places whence the radio messages were being transmitted from two or more stations on shore and so to determine their position. If the radio intelligence service could identify the places transmitting, by interpreting the call signs at the beginning or the end of the message, it was possible from the radio picture obtained, to get an idea of the composition and disposition of the enemy forces without actually being able to decipher the message. To make it difficult for the enemy to obtain such a radio picture it was usual for units at sea to maintain radio silence and only to transmit their own messages if they had, in any case, been discovered by the enemy or if the situation made it absolutely necessary. Finally, efforts were made to mislead the enemy by carefully prepared radio decoy systems.

To understand the significance of these techniques for the decisive phase in the Battle of the Atlantic in the spring of 1943 it is necessary to look back briefly at the methods employed by the German and Allied commands.

RADIO CONTROL AND WOLF-PACK TACTICS

In 1935 Fregattenkapitän Karl Dönitz, as he then was, was entrusted with the task of building up and training the new German U-boat arm. He was soon convinced that, in the event of war, Britain would again resort at once to the well-tried convoy system she had adopted in the First World War to protect her trade. On the basis of his own experiences as a U-boat commander in the First World War, and after considerable thought, exercises and experiments, Dönitz adopted the so-called group, or wolf-pack, tactics as the central concept for the deployment of German U-boats against this convoy system. In this way he hoped to pit a concentration of U-boats in a tactically closely coordinated group against a concentration of enemy ships and a convoy's defense.

We can see the beginnings of these wolf-pack tactics in the First World War. In 1917 when the initial experiences with British convoys showed that a single U-boat had only slender chances against the strong defense, the Officer Commanding U-boats in the High Seas Fleet, Commodore Bauer, suggested that several U-boats should operate jointly. For this purpose he wanted to put a flotilla commander on one of the submarine cruisers of the *U 151* class, converted as a command U-boat, and to allow him as tactical commander to coordinate by radio an attack by several U-boats on a convoy. But after Bauer was relieved as Officer Commanding U-boats this proposal was not put to practical test and U-boat commanders were left to make their own improvised attempts to operate in unison against convoys.

The ideas of wolf-pack tactics, developed between 1935 and 1939, had some similarity with the plans already described, although they were modified by progress made in signals technique. The development of shortwave transmitters and receivers had reached a stage when the U-boats could receive radio messages from command headquarters in every part of the ocean with regular repeats of messages at fixed times and a choice of suitable frequencies. The efficiency of the shortwave transmitters on the U-boats had been so improved that it was now also possible to receive the U-boat radio messages in Germany. The use of very long-wave transmitters even enabled the U-boats to receive radio messages with the help of mast aerials at periscope level. In this way it was possible to control the operational deployment and the movements of the U-boats directly from command headquarters in Germany. If the approach of enemy convoys was known, the U-boats could then be concentrated in a suitable area and deployed in an appropriate formation with a view to intercepting one. If the convoy was found, the flotilla commander on one of the U-boats was to take over the tactical leadership of the pack and see that contact with the convoy was maintained until the other boats in the pack came up. If contact was lost, the tactical commander had to give the appropriate orders to find the convoy again. The exercises carried out before the war in the Baltic and also in the Atlantic seemed to indicate that this procedure was practicable. Because most of the U-boats envisaged for the convoy war were Type VII, where space was generally restricted, it was proposed to equip some of the Type IXB and IXC boats being built in 1938–39 as communication boats with additional transmitting and receiving equipment and to keep particularly suitable boats for command duties.

It was obvious that the use of U-boats in groups would make it necessary to violate the rule of radio silence at sea in certain circumstances. The deployment of the group was only likely to be successful if the U-boats were able to pass, by means of radio messages, information that was important both for the Command and the other U-boats. Since the transmission of any message brought the risk of the enemy being able to take a bearing and therefore the loss of its position, care had to be taken that this was reduced to a minimum. Accordingly, there were basic instructions which laid down the circumstances when U-boats had to ignore orders to preserve radio silence. The following kinds of information had to be transmitted, in principle, by the U-boats at the earliest possible opportunity:

1. Reports about the enemy which would make possible the deployment of other U-boats.
2. Warning reports about enemy submarine positions or mine barriers.

3. Reports about the situation in the operational area, traffic, the possibility of offensive action and the type and strength of the escort.
4. Weather reports.
5. Reports on positions and sightings, if they had been ordered or their transmission appeared vital for the command.
6. Reports made at the request of the command. The operational order laid down what reports were to be made.

To reduce, as far as possible, the danger of being located, a short signal manual was produced in the winter of 1939–40 which allowed most reports to be sent in a short signal form containing a few code signs. The signal could not readily be located in the light of experience at the time. To limit the use of a bearing to the enemy, the U-boats received instructions to send their messages—if they were not, as in the case of a report about the enemy, tied to a particular time—as far as possible in the evening, or at night, or before major changes of position, so as to make it difficult for the enemy to react. The U-boats were informed that the enemy had a highly developed and efficient network of direction-finding stations round the Atlantic and that, despite the constant change of frequencies used by the U-boats, it must be expected that there were always several enemy D/F stations concentrating on those frequencies. Since the effectiveness of a direction-finder depended, apart from reception conditions, very much on the length of the beam and the angle cut by several beams, it was particularly dangerous for the U-boats to send medium length or long radio messages, near or in the English Channel, near the North Channel or east and west of the Orkneys. In this area, a very rapid deployment of anti-submarine forces was to be expected once a bearing had been obtained. On the other hand, it was believed that more than 200 kms from the coast less importance should be attached to the danger of counteraction based on D/F.

THE BRITISH CONVOY SYSTEM

For the British the U-boat danger was not the most pressing problem for the Admiralty between the wars. First, there were no U-boats capable of interrupting Britain's only vital sea routes—those in the North Atlantic. Secondly, the agreement of all the major naval powers to the London submarine convention of 1930 appeared to rule out unrestricted U-boat warfare and only this represented a serious danger. And, thirdly, the rapid development since 1927 of the underwater sound-locating equipment, asdic, promised to be a successful method of fighting submerged U-boats. So, at first, the British limited themselves to ensuring that, in the event of war, the entire merchant marine would come under, and be controlled by, the Admiralty. In this way, the merchant ships could be brought together at dangerous traffic concentration points and better protected. It was assumed that, in the event of war, shipping would be endangered more from surface ships harassing merchantmen than from U-boats.

Nor was this view at first radically altered when in 1935 the Germans began to rebuild their U-boat arm: this was because the strength of the German U-boat force was restricted to 45% of the not very powerful British submarine force and because Germany also signed the London submarine convention. British planning still did not change in 1937 when Germany took advantage of the clause which allowed the German U-boat force, in certain circumstances, to be brought up to 100% of the British. It became apparent in the talks that year between the Admiralty and the Air Ministry on the future deployment of aircraft at sea and the role of RAF Coastal Command that the Admiralty proposed, if there should be a new U-boat war, to fall back on the convoy system which had proved itself so well in the First World War. Although the Air Staff regarded the great concentration of ships in convoys as very exposed to air attack, the Naval Staff succeeded in persuading the Committee of Imperial Defence on December 2, 1937 that in the improbable event of unrestricted warfare the advantages of the convoy system greatly outweighed the dangers of air attack. Only when, with the Sudeten crisis in autumn of 1938, there were clear dangers of a European war, did the Admiralty send Rear-Admiral Sir Eldon Manisty, the organizer of the British convoy system in 1917–18, on a tour of the centers of the shipping routes vital to Great Britain. His task was to investigate the question of merchant shipping control and the possible needs to establish a convoy system. On the basis of his recommendations the Trade Division of the Admiralty was greatly expanded in 1939 with the result that on August 26, 1939 it was in a position to assume control of all British merchant shipping. All the station commanders responsible for the individual sea areas had received their instructions about taking over and controlling traffic, as well as about the possible need to introduce convoys with their routes and cycles.

Because the German U-boats had in fact originally received orders to conduct U-boat warfare according to international law, the British would not at first have gone beyond controlling shipping through the Admiralty and guarding the concentration areas. But the *U 30*, on the mistaken assumption that it had seen an auxiliary cruiser, sank the passenger ship *Athenia* without warning on the first day of the war. This caused the Admiralty to think that Germany had already embarked on unrestricted U-boat warfare and the order was given to introduce the convoy system. Apart from the convoys in coastal areas, the most important convoy routes for the Battle of the Atlantic came into use in the course of September. On September 7 the convoy OA.1 from the Thames via the English Channel and the convoy OB.1 from

Liverpool via the Bristol Channel set out westward. These convoys were commanded and escorted by the Commander-in-Chief Western Approaches in Plymouth. At first at longitude 12°30'W but soon at 15°W, these convoys were relieved of their escort. The ships proceeded on their own and soon after went on to their destinations individually. To begin with, these two convoys ran every two days.

On September 9 the C-in-C South Atlantic in Freetown ordered the first convoy SL.1 to set out for Britain. On September 15 the convoy KJ.1 put to sea from Jamaica from the command of the C-in-C America and West Indies Station. On September 16 the HX.1, controlled by Naval Service Headquarters Ottawa, set out from Halifax to Britain on the most important North Atlantic route. On September 26 there followed from the command of the C-in-C North Atlantic in Gibraltar the first Gibraltar convoy HG.1, while simultaneously from October 1 an OG.1 section was split off from the westward-bound convoy, which escorted the southbound traffic as far as latitude 47°N. These last-named convoys went at seven or 14-day intervals. Parallel with this, the French Navy organized convoys from Oran on the French North African Mediterranean coast (RS) and from Casablanca (KS): these were, to some extent, linked with the British Gibraltar convoys.

While the individual C-in-C's task was to ensure the safety of the convoys in his own command areas, it was the responsibility of the Trade Division of the Admiralty to prepare the convoy timetables and fix the routes in outline: this was because, with its Trade Plot based on information coming in from all over the world, it was able to plot the positions of the 2,500 merchant ships at sea on an average day and to ensure that they were integrated into the convoy system at the right time.

CHAPTER 2

1939–41: The Experiences of the First War Years

The main problem for the Trade Division and the C-in-Cs in the first phase of the war was to coordinate the convoy timetables and the routes in such a way that the Escort Groups, having left the outward-bound convoys, could meet the homeward-bound convoys in the area with the least possible delay. The meeting points for the units at sea had to be indicated by radio from shore headquarters. As early as September 11 the German radio cryptographic service (the "B" Service) was able to decode the first radio messages on convoy meeting points near the Bristol Channel and to pass them to the Officer Commanding U-boats. Four days later *U 31*, which was operating in this area, sighted the first convoy, the outward-bound OB.4. In the expectation of encountering convoy traffic the Officer Commanding U-boats had previously ordered the most modern and powerful U-boats back to their bases, so that they could be jointly deployed with resounding success against such a convoy in October. But the number of U-boats which Dönitz was able to concentrate in October and November 1939 and February 1940 west of the Bay of Biscay and the Iberian Peninsula in his first attempts at group operations against convoys was too small. The contact-keeping U-boats were able to bring up other U-boats over great distances to the convoy, but the successes were few, particularly because of torpedo failures. Nevertheless, these operations showed that radio control was practicable. After a pause, due to the operations in Norway and the campaign in the West, new attempts were made in the area west of the English Channel and the Bay of Biscay in June 1940. But the U-boats of the two packs formed had so many targets that they had generally expended their torpedoes in a very short while and before there was an opportunity to carry out an operation against a convoy.

On the other side, the experiences of the first months of the war confirmed the Admiralty's belief that it had been right to introduce the convoy system. Of 5,756 ships proceeding in escorted convoys up to the end of 1939 only four, or 0.07% had been sunk by U-boats. Against this there had been 114 losses of merchant ships proceeding independently or in unescorted groups.

Having secured and established bases in Norway and France, the German U-boat arm was in a much better position to begin the second phase in the Battle of the Atlantic from the middle of July 1940. In spite of the fact that, in absolute terms, there were less front-line U-boats, more of them could be kept in the operational area because their outward and homeward routes had become much shorter. Two other factors helped the U-boats at this time. Because of the great danger to shipping in the English Channel all convoys from the east coast had to be routed round Scotland with the result that there was a strong concentration of traffic near the North Channel. At the same time, the losses and casualties off Norway and Dunkirk and then the defection of the French Navy and the fact that many destroyers were committed to repelling an invasion (the planned operation *Seelöwe*) resulted in a great weakening of the Escort Groups for the convoys. The situation was made even more difficult because, since the U-boats had extended their operational areas, a decision had to be taken in July to escort the convoys to 17°W and in October to 19°W. The heavy losses of slower ships proceeding independently led to these mainly small and old ships being assembled in Sydney, Nova Scotia, and being sent from August 15 eastward in a new, slow convoy SC.1, etc.

Normally the HX and SC convoys, on leaving Newfoundland, were accompanied only by one or two auxiliary cruisers, cruisers or even battleships against the expected German surface raiders until they got their anti-submarine screen. The surface raiders actually made their appearance on the North Atlantic convoy route at the beginning of November. Because of the weak A/S forces and also since there were hardly ever more than 10 German U-boats in the operational area at the same time, the best hope the C-in-C Western Approaches (CINCWA) had of preventing the loss of ships lay in trying to avoid the changing U-boat formations off the North Channel by getting the convoys to take evasive action.

In these efforts he could rely on the work of the Submarine Tracking Room of the Operational Intelligence Centre in the Naval Intelligence Division of the Admiralty; it worked closely with the Trade Plot Room situated next door. Under Paymaster Commander Thring, who had the same duties in the First World War, information coming in on the British side about the German U-boats and, in particular, the results of the radio D/F service were collected and made to form a current U-boat situation picture. On the basis of this situation picture the Head of the Trade Plot, Cdr. Richard Hall, RN, the son of the first Director of Naval Intelligence of the First World War, and, then, CINCWA could recommend evasive action for the convoys. In his headquarters in Liverpool these convoy movements could again be coordinated with those of the escort forces and the operations of No. 15 Group,

RAF Coastal Command and formulated in instructions about new courses and meeting points. These were communicated to the units at sea by radio.

But this technique, largely based on radio instructions, could not prevent several convoys being found in the summer and autumn of 1940 and sustaining losses in fighting off U-boats which attacked in packs on the surface by night. On the German side, too, radio intelligence provided a substantial basis for successful operations. The British results came predominantly from the shore-based D/F stations (Y stations). But in the German case at this time it was the "B" Service under Capt. Bonatz which was repeatedly able to decode details of the altered course instructions and the new meeting points with the escort forces and passed this on, in time, to the Commander U-boats, as he became in October 1939, instead of Officer Commanding U-boats. In August it had already become clear that the Allied Command was trying to reroute the convoys away from the known U-boat positions. In any planned deployment of the U-boat groups it was therefore important to make the premature locating of the U-boats by the enemy more difficult. So they were again instructed to maintain radio silence at all costs except when convoys were sighted. The result was two convoy battles in September followed by two successive convoy operations in the middle of October against the convoys SC.7 and HX.79, in which eight U-boats sank 31 ships totaling 152,000 tons without loss to themselves.

It was not surprising that the Commander U-boats and his staff saw further confirmation in these very successful operations of the correctness of their prewar concepts of carrying out U-boat group operations against the convoys with the aid of W/T. Experience had shown that it was not necessary to appoint a tactical commander for the U-boats making up a pack at sea. It repeatedly happened that in decisive phases the tactical commander was forced by the defense to submerge and so was eliminated as a leader. On the other hand, it was clear that signal communication between shore headquarters and the U-boats worked so well that it was possible for headquarters in Germany or Western France, which had the best overall picture, to provide tactical command of the U-boats with the convoy. But a precondition was that the U-boats stationed near the convoys should send contact reports. The danger of U-boat radio messages being located by D/F, which had at first seemed a possibility, appeared not to be so serious in the light of experience. U-boats, which had been sent far westward as "weather boats," in preparation for the operation *Seelöwe*, to send regular weather reports by radio were repeatedly run into by the convoys. Clearly, the D/F bearings from shore posts over several hundred miles were not sufficiently exact to determine the position of a signaling U-boat and so to avoid it with certainty. Once the battle had begun and the first attacks made, the presence of the U-boats was known to the enemy. If there was, in principle, objection to all unnecessary radio signaling, it was natural, on the other hand, that the tactical commanders on shore should welcome every bit of information about the scene of operations to fill out their situation picture.

Their favorable experiences in the first year of the war certainly contributed to the German's failure to cope promptly or adequately with possible Allied countermeasures against this form of radio control of the U-boat war.

THE BRITISH REACTION TO WOLF-PACK TACTICS

For the British the supposedly new German tactics of wolf-pack U-boat attacks was an unpleasant surprise. The escorts had had to look on at the attacks helplessly. Their asdic underwater equipment was ineffective against the U-boats because they attacked on the surface. The escorts still had no radar equipment. Often the faster ships—the destroyers and sloops—remained behind to cover the torpedoed ships and to rescue survivors. The new corvettes, which remained with the convoy and still had no fighting experience, were unable to recognize the approaching U-boats in the dark. The difficulties the escort commander (Senior Officer Escort, SOE) had in communicating with his ships made tactical control and teamwork within the Escort Group impossible. The only available means of communication at night and in bad visibility, W/T, was too slow since every message had first to be encoded and then decoded when it was received. Accordingly, the SOE and his commanders had no alternative but to act independently, often without knowing what was happening on the other side of the convoy.

The solution was the VHF radio telephone which made direct communication possible between the SOE and his ships in the immediate vicinity of the convoy.

From the end of 1940 onward the necessary equipment was built into the escort ships with all possible speed so that the SOE could then deploy his few ships tactically even at night. In doing so the British sought to counter the danger of the U-boats listening in where possible by the use of code names, letters and figures. But for the purposes of tactical leadership the U-boats, which could hardly be recognized in the dark nights, had to be made visible. There were two ways to do this. Attempts could be made to illuminate the darkness by the use of star shells and other pyrotechnical devices. That risked attracting distant U-boats to the scene.

Radar appeared to provide a better solution. The ASV-II equipment, which had been developed with a view to being installed into aircraft of RAF Coastal Command and which operated on a wavelength of 1.4 meters, was adapted to become the naval model 286 M. The first experimental model was ready in September 1940 and from November 1940 a start was made to installing it into destroyers of Western Approaches Command.

But, initially, this equipment did not satisfy the high hopes of the commanders. To obtain the greatest possible range, the aerial had to be installed on the mast top: this did not improve the stability of the ships which were already top-heavy with additional gear. At first the aerial was fixed and could only cover a sector of 50° ahead on each side. But, in addition, strong echo interference was received in this angle from the stern. The range in the case of a surfaced U-boat was hardly more than two to three miles in calm seas and this was sharply reduced when the sea was only moderately rough. The result was that in most cases the range was less than the visual range from the conning tower of a U-boat operating against escorts and even merchant ships.

Some improvement was provided by the rotating equipment, operating on the same wavelength, such as the British model 290 M, the Canadian SW1C and SW2C and the American version, SC1. This equipment could be rotated in every direction but could only look for a target in one direction at a time. Looking back, we can see that this equipment, which was standard for all Allied escort vessels until the end of 1942, was of greater use in helping the escorts keep station with the convoy on dark nights. This released many of the lookout personnel who could now be detailed for the task of spotting U-boats.

However, developments in Britain were not confined to this equipment. Parallel with this there was being developed a panorama model operating on a 9 cm wavelength, the 271 M. With this equipment, transmitter, receiver and aerial were contained in a cylindrical-shaped scanner screen and placed over the bridge. The scanner rotated uniformly and indicated on the plan position indicator screen the situation around the ship as shown by radar. With this equipment it was possible to locate bigger ships up to eight to 10 miles away, U-boats under normal conditions up to about four miles and a little further under favorable conditions, particularly smooth seas. On the other hand, performance fell off considerably in rough weather because the wave echoes appeared on the screen. The radar echoes enabled the Escort Commander or the captains to see at a glance both the position of most of the ships in the convoy, as well as U-boats approaching the area from outside. In March 1941 the first corvette was equipped with a prototype of this device. In July 1941, 25 ships were converted, and in September 1941 a start was made to building the equipment into all escort vessels. But owing to the large number of units involved this went on until 1943.

However, it was not only in the technical field that the British looked for improvements. In the summer of 1940 a suitably equipped merchant ship was sent out to the Atlantic to observe German radio traffic and the weak point in the German wolf-pack tactics was quickly recognized: the need for intensive use of W/T. The success or failure of a convoy operation depended on whether the U-boat, which first approached the convoy, was able to transmit its initial enemy situation report and send out over a period regular contact signals that made it possible to determine more precisely the speed and general course of the convoy. It was, therefore, important for the defense to find this contact-keeper as early as possible, to drive off and to prevent it sending more reports or bearing signals for the other U-boats.

It was fairly easy for the British signals intelligence service to see that a U-boat was keeping in contact with a convoy. The reports about the enemy and the brief signals sent by the shortwave transmitter began with the sign alpha (— — . — —) which corresponded to a barred "e" in the British morse code. When such an "e-bar" message was encountered by the British radio listening posts (X stations) and located by the Y stations, a comparison between the position located by D/F and the map in the Trade Plot Room showed with which of the convoys the U-boat was probably in contact. The convoy could then be warned and take appropriate evasive action. But as long as the Escort Commander did not know on which side of the convoy the U-boat was keeping contact, it was always a risky business for him to allow his generally much too few escorts to make sorties in this or that direction at a critical moment before a turn in the hope of trying to force the U-boat to submerge. It happened too often that the escort ships were not available in those decisive hours of the night when the U-boats made their attacks. This problem could only be solved by the development of a shortwave D/F device with which the escort vessels could directly locate the radio messages of the U-boats.

THE DEVELOPMENT OF SHORTWAVE RADIO D/F

The principle of radio D/F had been generally known and adopted in all navies and merchant navies before the Second World War. But the long-waves which were particularly suitable for purely D/F purposes attracted most attention. On board ship reception generally was by means of a rotatable frame aerial. After the appropriate tuning-in this frame aerial was turned manually until the minimum signal was found, that is to say, the frame aerial was at right angles to the oncoming beam. The D/F bearing could then be read on a circular scale. Even before the war the newer British destroyer and flotilla leaders had been equipped with this D/F which, apart from navigational purposes, could also be used to obtain bearings of ships transmitting on long-wave. The frequency range of this long-wave D/F equipment was, however, not sufficient to receive the frequency used by the U-boats to give their bearings on long and very long waves.

Research on shortwave D/F transmitters had cost a lot of effort before the war. Frequent use was made of a fixed aerial system named after the British inventor Adcock. This consisted usually of four single aerials whose receiver voltages were connected in opposition so that the difference in the voltage gave the bearing voltage which, then, with the aid of a connected goniometer, made it possible to read the D/F relative bearing in degrees. This equipment was being operated on shore before the war; but in Germany, at least, it was thought that it could not be accommodated on ships, particularly small escort vessels, because of its size and weight.

But in 1938 the technological department of the French Navy had come to realize that in a future war operational radio traffic at sea would be sent by means of new codes and other procedures with very short transmission periods. For this reason the existing D/F methods would be inadequate to locate the transmitters more precisely because they required too much time. Accordingly, the department commissioned a study group under the French research scientists, Deloraine and Busignies, who had concerned themselves since 1928 with the problems of automatic D/F procedure, to develop a shortwave D/F which would make it possible to locate a distant transmitter precisely, even when the transmission period was very brief. By May 1940 the two scientists had succeeded in producing four experimental models of automatic high- frequency visual D/F. The German attack on France, however, interrupted this work; the experimental models were dismantled and hidden. In the autumn of 1940 Deloraine and three of his colleagues escaped to America with the help of the French Navy. They arrived there on December 31 and were then asked by the US Navy to resume and complete their work on a large scale. By April 1, 1941, the first new experimental model of their radio D/F was ready.

The equipment consisted of an Adcock aerial system with two pairs of vertical aerials and a fifth aerial to determine the sense of the bearing. The voltages received by the aerials were conveyed by a feeder to a so-called stantor. This was a cross-coil arrangement which produced a field in a small insulated space corresponding to the electromagnetic field received by the aerial. A third coil, a rotor performing 20 revolutions a second, which revolved inside the space insulated from the two coils, was provided with a high frequency electric current that with each turn produced two maxima and two minima for each received impulse. Their direction was determined by the direction of the voltage field inside the space encircled by the coils. The electric current was transferred to a highly sensitive reception device. When tuned in to the desired wave, the impulse was amplified and rectified in the reception device, then conveyed to a coil which revolved synchronically with the high frequency rotor round the neck of a cathode ray oscillograph. The rotating field created by this coil deflected the spot of light on the screen of the tubes. In traversing the field through the zero point, corresponding to the classical minimum of the former acoustic procedure, the spot of light was no longer deflected. It now showed the bearing directly on a 360° scale which, through a transparent mirror, was represented on the screen of the oscillograph. If the direction of the located transmitter was uncertain by 180°, the precise position of the second direction could be ascertained by using the fifth and central aerial. A few turns of the rotor, i.e., some 1/10th seconds, were sufficient to receive the diagram. A bright screen prepared with persistent fluorescent material ensured that, even after brief signals had ceased, the D/F direction was indicated with adequate accuracy.

The French research scientists were able to build a laboratory on Long Island and were asked to produce a copy of their D/F equipment. On April 1, 1941, the team working in association with the American company ITT received an order for four prototypes. This was increased on October 10, 1941, to 15 more models of this type. They were at first intended for the construction of a shore-based automatic shortwave radio D/F network.

Parallel with this Franco-American development the British had been busy improving radio D/F equipment since the beginning of the war. In 1926, the subsequent father of radar, Sir Robert Watson-Watt, had, in dealing with meteorological problems, worked on the use of cathode ray tubes to determine the direction of distant storms. Later these studies were discontinued. But at the beginning of 1940 the papers referring to these researches were rediscovered in the archives of the Signals School. When asked, Sir Robert pointed out that the combination of cathode ray tubes and an Adcock D/F aerial would probably make possible the development of an automatic shortwave D/F for a wide frequency band. This equipment could perhaps be made on such a small scale as to enable it to be accommodated on an escort vessel.

Attempts to produce a shortwave D/F for smaller ships with the old methods of direction finding had led to a prototype of the FH 1 model being installed on the destroyer *Hesperus* on March 12, 1940. But the equipment was still unsatisfactory. Major improvements were necessary before this equipment which operated with an acoustic reproduction produced results. In July 1941 an improved FH 2 was ready and it was installed in August. A little later, the FH 3 model, developed in accordance with Sir Robert's suggestions, was ready as a prototype. The sloop *Culver* was equipped with it in October 1941, but she was sunk, while escorting convoy SL.93, by the U-boat *U 105* on January 31, 1942 before she was able to acquire any practical experience.

RADIO CONTROL AND THE OPERATIONS OF 1941

In the first three months of 1941 the British were increasingly successful in rerouting the convoys in the North Atlantic round the German U-boat formations. One reason for this was, that as a result of a change in the British cipher procedure, the German "B" Service had for a time fewer successes. The Commander U-boats hoped to make this deficiency good by the deployment of the long-range reconnaissance aircraft, FW 200-Condor, which became available from January. They were meant to find convoys on their flights from France, westward round Britain to Norway, report them and then bring up the U-boats by transmitting D/F signals. But usually the aircraft could not maintain contact with the convoy long enough for a U-boat to approach. In addition, the operations were made more difficult by the inaccurate navigation of the aircraft. Another reason was that the Allied D/F stations were easily able to locate by cross-bearings the messages and D/F signals from the aircraft with the result that the convoys could be ordered to take evasive action. Conversely, however, U-boats repeatedly found convoys in this phase of the battle and were able with their D/F signals to guide the Condor aircraft of KG 40 to these convoys. Although, toward the end of February, most of the outward-bound convoys were found either by aircraft or U-boats, the U-boat attacks became constantly more difficult. The Escort Groups of the convoys no longer consisted of individual vessels brought together on an ad hoc basis, but of destroyers that remained in their units and newly arrived corvettes which gained increasing experience. The loss of the three most successful U-boat commanders, Prien, Schepke and Kretschmer, in March prompted the Commander U-boats to move the formations further to the west and northwest so as to be able to attack the convoys where they had no A/S protection. The intention was to avoid the danger of new and unfamiliar weapons of defense. In fact, it was only in Schepke's sinking that new equipment played a part: then the only destroyer with the convoy HX.112 which was equipped with the first radar model, 286 M, the *Vanoc*, found *U 100* at a range of 1,000 meters and sank the boat by ramming before it could submerge.

But it was not so much this new radar equipment, which at first was only available in a few escorts, that largely rendered the U-boat operations ineffective between June and August 1941. The main reason was an important break into the German cipher system.* In April 1940 the British had succeeded in recovering from *U 49*, sunk off the Lofotens, a bag containing several operational documents such as grid charts and a map on the location of German U-boats off Norway. Despite the fact that the British cryptanalysts at

*See also Appendix 10, p. 254.

Bletchley Park had solved the secrets of the German "Enigma"-cipher machine used by the Army and Air Force, the similar Navy cipher machine "M" could not be cracked. Also when in March 1941 some of the additional cipher cylinders of this machine were captured from the patrol vessel *Krebs*, the machine resisted all attempts to decipher the enciphered messages. Only the capture of a complete "M" machine and its cipher documents could solve the problem. The daily changing settings for the cipher were on one sheet of soluble paper. If cipher documents seemed to have been compromised, it was possible to send a code word known only to the commander, and which would prompt him to change their cipher settings.

In spring 1941 the British learned of an opportunity to covertly capture a cipher machine and cipher documents. The study of radio traffic showed that German trawlers had set out from Norway and France for the Atlantic and, in particular, for the waters north of Iceland, to send back weather reports vital for the operations by the heavy German naval ships in the North Atlantic. Although the positions of these weather trawlers were still not located very accurately by D/F, it was hoped to find one of these vessels in the poor visibility of the European Arctic with a reconnaissance patrol of cruisers and destroyers. At the beginning of May reports from the German weather observation ship, *München*, which had already set out for the proposed operation of the battleship *Bismarck*, were located by D/F and at once a squadron, comprising the cruisers *Edinburgh, Manchester* and *Birmingham* and four destroyers, was deployed. On May 7 the weather observation ship was sighted at a distance of 6,000 meters and the *Edinburgh* at once opened fire. The crew took to the boats after destroying the radio equipment and the cipher machine. But, before the ship could be scuttled, as was the intention, the British destroyer *Somali* was alongside and the British were able to salvage important maps and cipher material which were brought to Scapa Flow by the destroyer *Nestor*.

It happened by chance that this material could be substantially supplemented. On the same day, May 7, *U 94* had found the outward-bound convoy OB.318 south of Iceland and was able to direct several U-boats to it. At midday on May 9 the *U 110* succeeded in sinking two ships from this convoy in an underwater attack. But the boat was so badly damaged by the depth charges from the corvette *Aubrietia* that the commander had to surface. While the crew was abandoning the slowly sinking boat, the commander of the destroyer *Bulldog* saw his chance and put a boarding party on it who were able to close the opened sea-valves in time. All secret documents, the cipher machine and other papers were intact and were taken aboard the destroyer before the *U 110* sank while under tow.

The documents captured from the *München* in combination with the D/F locations of German radio messages by shore stations, played a substantial part in uncovering the Atlantic supply system devised for the operation *Rheinübung.* Those from *U 110* were to have their effect on the U-boat operations. But it was not only the German supply system which was fully uncovered. In addition, the British succeeded in capturing the tanker *Gedania* on June 4 and the U-boat supply ship *Lothringen* on July 15 and so were able to get hold of more documents. Finally, on June 25, a small squadron, comprising the cruiser *Nigeria* and three destroyers, was able to locate the weather observation ship *Lauenburg* with the help of shortwave D/F equipment on the destroyer *Bedouin* and to surprise her in poor visibility. Once again valuable cipher documents and maps were captured. With these materials Bletchley Park was able to read the German messages "on time." The OIC (Operational Intelligence Centre) was able up to the beginning of August to reroute all convoys round the U-boat formations which were known from the radio instructions. From then until January 1942 the U-boat signals also could be deciphered, but during this period the deciphered messages were available at the OIC only after time lags of up to four days.

The Commander U-boats tried to counter this development, the cause of which he did not know, by ordering the U-boats in the area of the Britain/Gibraltar route to operate against the convoys there with the help of air reconnaissance and sailing reports from agents stationed on Spanish territory opposite Gibraltar. Although it had partial knowledge of these German orders, the Admiralty was only able to take limited evasive action against these operations with the result that there was a series of hard-fought convoy battles. But success in terms of tonnage was insignificant due to the fact that the ships were small.

CONTINUOUS CONVOY ESCORT IN THE NORTH ATLANTIC

In the summer of 1941 the Allies made considerable changes in the organization of the convoy system. The penetration by German U-boats from the middle of March into the North Atlantic as far as the waters south of Greenland and several U-boat attacks on convoys before they received their A/S screen, persuaded the Allies of the desirability of providing the convoys with continuous A/S protection from their departure harbors on the west coast of the Atlantic until they reached Britain. The large number of corvettes which had now been delivered from British and Canadian yards made it possible to form the necessary Escort Groups, although the inadequate ranges meant that at first the groups had to be relieved several times. On May 27, 1941, the first continuously escorted convoy, HX.129, set out from Halifax. A Canadian

Escort Group from the Newfoundland Escort Force, stationed at St John's, escorted the convoy to the Mid-Ocean Meeting Point (MOMP) about 35°W. After it had been relieved by an Escort Group of the Iceland Escort Force, stationed in Hvalfjord, the first Escort Group proceeded to Iceland to take oil and then went back to MOMP to take over a westward-bound convoy there. The Escort Group from the Iceland Escort Force was relieved at the Eastern Ocean Meeting Point (EASTOMP) by an Escort Group of the Western Approaches Escort Forces from Liverpool or Londonderry.

From July it was possible to give the outward-bound convoys from Britain continuous protection. For this purpose the westward-bound convoys were also divided into fast ON and slow ONS convoys. In the North Atlantic the Escort Groups generally consisted of one to two destroyers and four to five corvettes. For the continuous protection of the Gibraltar and Sierra Leone convoys new Escort Groups were formed with the sloops, which had a greater range, in combination with some corvettes. The Sierra Leone convoys were escorted by the Londonderry Escort Force as far as 20°N, NW of the Cape Verde Islands, and then taken over by corvettes of the Freetown Escort Force.

During these summer weeks the number of front-line German U-boats in the North Atlantic exceeded 30 for the first time. This meant that the Commander U-boats was able, in addition to the packs operating on the Gibraltar route, to concentrate another group with up to 15 and more boats in the area south of Iceland. With this he could "rake" toward Greenland and Newfoundland in a wide-ranging search movement. The first of these groups found the convoy SC.42 south of Cape Farewell at the beginning of September and sank 20 out of 63 ships in what was until then the biggest convoy battle before the onset of fog prevented the complete destruction of the convoy. This success encouraged the Commander U-boats to form more groups in the following weeks from the new boats coming from Germany. Up to the beginning of November they crossed the North Atlantic in four successive waves, each finding a convoy and attacking, although there was no repetition of the success against SC.42. Clearly this was largely due to the fact that the Bletchley Park could no longer read the U-boat radio traffic "on time" by using the captured cipher settings. Solving the daily settings took up to four days.

THE INTERVENTION OF THE USA IN THE BATTLE OF THE ATLANTIC

It was during these operations that there occurred the first serious incidents with American warships. President Roosevelt's "short of war" policy was designed to give Britain the most effective possible support and found its clearest expression so far in the destroyer-naval base deal of September 1940 and the Lend-Lease Act of March 1941. In line with this policy the American

Fleet tried to relieve the Royal Navy everywhere where its duties could be taken over without direct participation in the war. To justify the presence and activities of American warships in the Western Atlantic the boundary of the Western Hemisphere which, until then, had lain in the Pan-American security zone up to 60°W, was advanced on April 18, 1941, to 30°W and on June 14, to 26°W. West of this line American forces had instructions to shadow all Axis vessels that were sighted and to report their positions continuously in clear. On July 7 American troops were landed in Iceland to relieve the British forces stationed there. On July 15 the Icelandic waters were also included in the Western Hemisphere. A powerful Task Force 1, comprising battleships, cruisers, aircraft carriers and destroyers, was moved to Hvalfjord in Iceland to guard the Denmark Strait. At the same time, Task Force 4, which had been formed on March 1, 1941 and which consisted of three destroyer squadrons and four air reconnaissance squadrons, took over the task of escorting supply convoys to Iceland. Neutral merchant ships were able to join the American transports in these convoys.

At the Atlantic Conference between Roosevelt and Churchill in Argentia Bay, Newfoundland, in August 1941 it was decided to integrate the American escort ships fully into the defense of the North Atlantic convoys. From September 15 the American Task Force 4, based on Argentia with Escort Groups sometimes consisting of five destroyers, assumed the task of escorting the fast HX and ON convoys from Newfoundland to the Mid-Ocean Meeting Point brought forward from 30° to 26°W. There the convoys were relieved by Escort Groups of Western Approaches Command and the American ships proceeded to Iceland to take on oil. On September 24 an Escort Group, coming from Iceland, escorted an ON convoy for the first time. Simultaneously the Canadian Newfoundland Escort Force, based at St John's, with its Escort Groups of, in all, eight destroyers and 21 corvettes (including three Free French) started escorting the slow SC and ONS convoys between Newfoundland and the Mid-Ocean Meeting Point.

In spite of Hitler's instructions to avoid incidents with American ships and, then, the orders of the Commander U-boats that destroyers should only be attacked in self-defense, it was hardly possible to avoid naval action between German U-boats and American warships after this reorganization of the convoy system in the North Atlantic. The first serious incident occurred on October 17 when the American destroyer *Kearny*, which, with her Escort Group, had taken part in a 36-hour convoy battle involving SC.48, was torpedoed by *U 568*. A fortnight later, *U 552* sank the American destroyer *Reuben James* which was part of the escort of convoy HX.156. Further incidents were only avoided because the situation in the Mediterranean in November made it necessary to transfer a powerful U-boat group there and to assemble the remaining Atlantic U-boats in the area west of Gibraltar. This concentration off Gibraltar resulted in there being no boats available to start a prompt U-boat war off the American coast in December 1941 when the German Command was surprised by the Japanese attack on Pearl Harbor. It was to take five weeks before it was possible to start the fourth phase in the Battle of the Atlantic with the first five U-boats.

CHAPTER 3

1942: The Strategy of the Economic Deployment of the U-boats

As part of his strategy for the economic deployment of the U-boats, Dönitz thought the ultimately decisive criterion was the quickest possible sinking of the largest possible amount of enemy shipping and shipping of potential use to the enemy. He wanted his U-boats to be deployed from the point of view of economy where, in given circumstances, they could sink the maximum amount of shipping with the least waste of time and where losses could be kept as low as possible. His concern was their degree of effectiveness, i.e., the amount of tonnage sunk for each day at sea.

Because of the inexperience of the American defense and the fact that shipping was moving in almost peacetime conditions along the American coast, that area seemed to be then the most favorable operational one in spite of the great distances involved in getting there. It was there that the boats which cruised individually over vast operational areas were able to achieve considerable success up to May. It was some help to the Commander U-boats that the first supply U-boats were now ready: this meant that the smaller Type VII boats could now enter these waters. Only when the Americans, after constant pressure from the British, started to assemble the shipping on the American coast in convoys at the end of April and beginning of May did the sinkings decline.

In this period the convoy battle in the North Atlantic was pushed into the background. There were occasional convoy operations in the spring of 1942 when boats proceeding from Norway to France or to the American coast happened to encounter a convoy and were then able to bring up other boats in the area. These operations and, once more, the increasing successes of the German "B" Service showed that the Allied Command had now started to send their convoys across the North Atlantic on the shortest great circle route. On the one hand, there was no greater danger of encountering a U-boat there than anywhere else in the Atlantic. On the other, by shortening the route much time could be saved on each ship's run and the very scarce shipping space could be better used. When this was realized, the Germans considered the possibility of forming a group with the boats proceeding to the American coast and using it to "rake" the great circle route. If the group found a convoy, it was to attack and then take on fuel from a U-boat tanker south of the Newfoundland Bank and continue toward the American coast.

But before such an operation took place the successes off the American coast declined in number; as a result the Commander U-boats left the *Hecht* group on the North Atlantic route after it had located the first convoy in the middle of May. This group was followed at the beginning of July by the *Wolf* group and, with it, the convoy operations in the North Atlantic were resumed in the middle of the month and the fifth phase of the U-boat war began.

The experiences of the first new convoy operations and the need for the economic deployment of the U-boats in this situation produced the following strategy which was to become the operational basis for the fifth phase in the Battle of the Atlantic from August 1942 to May 1943. It was proposed to collect in a group the U-boats setting out from Germany and France, at first on the eastern side of the Atlantic, just outside the range of enemy air reconnaissance based on Iceland and Northern Ireland, and to have it proceed slowly westward as a patrol line. The boats were to cover the recently observed convoy routes and those which were expected on the basis of other information, particularly that from the radio intelligence service. The intention was to find a westward-bound convoy as early as possible, to follow it over the entire North Atlantic and then refuel the U-boats from a U-boat tanker stationed outside the traffic routes northeast of Bermuda. The replenished boats would form a new patrol line in the area of the Newfoundland Bank and its task would be, if possible, to find eastward-bound convoys and to attack them. After breaking off the convoy battle on the eastern side of the Atlantic, the U-boats with sufficient fuel could join a new group. Those which had expended their torpedoes, had little fuel or were damaged were to return to their bases in Western France.

THE ALLIED CONVOY SYSTEM IN 1942

In the first half of 1942 events led the Allies to make a number of changes in the convoy system. The demands of the war in the Pacific and the losses in the Western Atlantic had made it necessary to withdraw some of the American destroyers from the original eight American Ocean Escort Groups in the North Atlantic. They were partly replaced by American Coast Guard cutters and, above all, by new Canadian corvettes coming into the front line. This nationally-mixed composition of the Ocean Escort Groups created, however, some problems and, accordingly, the Americans proposed a reorganization which came into force from March 13, 1942.

The entire control of the convoy operations in the area west of 26°W was handed to the former Commander of Task Force 4, the American Vice Admiral Le R. Bristol (later Vice-Adm. R. M. Brainard), in Argentia. All the escort forces deployed in the western part of the North Atlantic were put under his command and given the name Task Force 24. The Canadian Western Local Escort Force which was deployed by the Canadian Commanding Officer, Atlantic Coast (COAC), Rear-Adm. L. W. Murray, RCN, in Halifax and which consisted of 13 British and 25 Canadian destroyers and corvettes, became Task Group 24.18. It was responsible for escorting the convoys from Halifax to WESTOMP at 49°W after the departure point for SC convoys had also been transferred to Halifax. The Mid-Ocean Escort Force, based on St John's in the west and Londonderry and Liverpool in the east, now formed Task Group 24.1, to which belonged seven British, four Canadian and one American escort groups. Their task was to escort the HX, SC, ON and ONS convoys as far as EASTOMP at about 20°W, where they were then replaced by the Eastern Local Escort Groups. To escort the ships proceeding to Iceland which turned off at about 25°W (ICOMP) the Americans made available two escort groups as Task Group 24.6. In addition, the escort vessels deployed on the Sydney–Greenland stretch, mostly old ships of the Coast Guard, were put under the command of Task Force 24 as Task Group 24.9. There was also the possibility of forming Support Groups for endangered convoys from Task Group 24.12 from the available destroyers in the Western Atlantic.

With the setting up of the American coastal convoy system, the Interlocking Convoy System, it became necessary to connect the North Atlantic convoys with this system which extended to New York. At first there was an independent feeder convoy system BX-XB between Halifax and Boston. From September 1942 the departure point for all transatlantic convoys was moved to New York so that there was direct connection there with the American Interlocking Convoy System. This made a new arrangement necessary in the Western Atlantic since the escort forces, as constituted so far, were not sufficient for the stretch between New York and WESTOMP. Accordingly, a new relief point, HOMP, was created in the Halifax area at 61°W. Here the Western Local Escort Groups could be relieved; their number had to be increased to 12 Escort Groups within the framework of Task Group 24.18.

The composition of the individual Escort Groups of Task Group 24.18 and the various feeder escorts was constantly changing. But from April 1942 efforts were made to keep the Ocean Escort Groups together as a unit wherever possible in order to achieve a well-functioning defense. The need to send British escort vessels to the Caribbean as a result of U-boat attacks in the area led to EASTOMP being moved closer to the North Channel in the summer of 1942. The consequence was that the British Escort Groups B 1 to B 7 were based permanently at Londonderry and Liverpool and the Canadian

Groups C 1 to C 4 and the American A 3 at St John's. But these groups were continuously deployed as convoy escorts on the whole North Atlantic stretch between EASTOMP and WESTOMP, irrespective of the area where the convoy was. West of 26°W the operational control of the convoys came under the C-in-C of the American Navy (COMINCH) and in the person of the Commander of Task Force 24 (COMTASKFOR or CTF 24) and east of that the Admiralty in the person of CINCWA.

West of the Change of Operational Control (CHOP) line the Convoy and Routing Section with the Chief of Naval Operations under Rear-Adm. M. K. Metcalf, USN had responsibility from July 1, 1942. Some eight days before the departure date of an eastbound convoy the Trade Division of the Admiralty sent suggestions for the convoy route to this office on the basis of the existing U-boat situation picture. After checking, and possibly adopting suggested modifications, the convoy route was then agreed between these two authorities. The convoy route consisted of four or more points indicated by letters, with their geographical position according to longitude and latitude, through which the convoy had to pass. In these course instructions the various relief points HOMP, WESTOMP, ICOMP and EASTOMP were given with probable dates and times. To facilitate long-term planning and to achieve a uniform circulation, as well as to make the best possible use of the available forces, a cycle was fixed for the departure dates of each convoy. From time to time this was altered to meet operational requirements. Originally, the HX convoys set out weekly and the SC convoys fortnightly. When the departure point for all convoys was moved to Halifax the cycle was changed to one of six days, so that a convoy set out every three days.

In 1942 the individual convoys became larger and the interval between them was extended to seven, eight and finally 10 days. One of the most important duties of the commands on both sides was to ensure that the feeder convoys were punctual, so that the ships needed to spend as little time as possible in harbor. This was particularly important in New York where, until the spring of 1943, the entire transatlantic traffic concentrated. At the end of March it was decided to let the SC convoys leave again from Halifax. When the details had been fixed COMINCH and the Admiralty informed the following authorities of the convoy route, including the stragglers' route and the meeting points:

Commander-in-Chief Atlantic Fleet (CINCLANT)
Commander Eastern Sea Frontier (COMESF) New York
COMTASKFOR 24 Argenia (CTF 24)
Canadian Naval Staff Headquarters (NSHQ) Ottawa
Commanding Officer Atlantic Coast (COAC) Halifax
Flag Officer Newfoundland Force (FONF) St John's

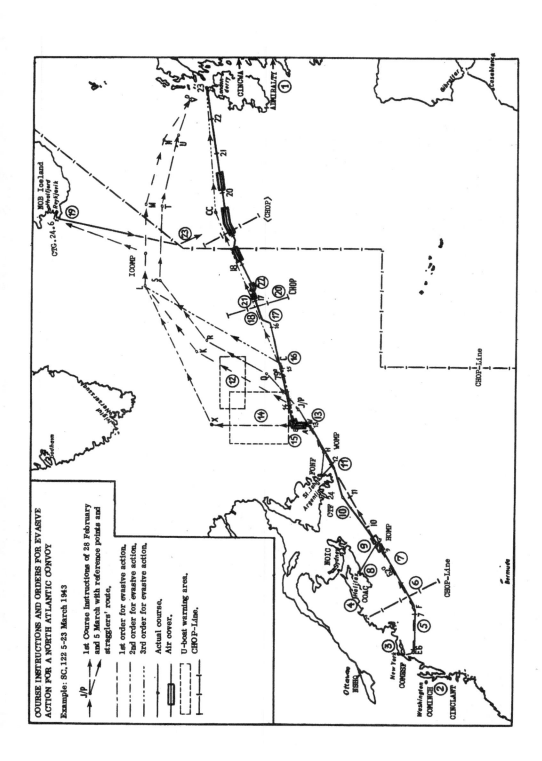

COURSE INSTRUCTIONS AND ORDERS FOR EVASIVE
ACTION FOR A NORTH ATLANTIC CONVOY

Example: SC.122 5-23 March 1943

J/p

1st Course Instructions of 28 February
and 5 March with reference points and
stragglers' route.

1st order for evasive action.

2nd order for evasive action.

3rd order for evasive action.

Actual course.

Air cover.

U-boat warning area.

CHOP-Line.

Course instructions and orders for evasive action for a North Atlantic convoy (Example SC.122 in March 1943)

#	Date/Time	Description
1	Feb 26	Convoy and Routing Section of the Admiralty issues course suggestions for SC.122 to Convoy and Routing Section of the Commander-in-Chief US Navy (COMINCH).
2	Feb 28	COMINCH (C & R) issues provisional course instructions to relevant authorities: Admiralty; Commander-in-Chief Western Approaches (CINCWA); Commander-in-Chief (US) Atlantic Fleet (CINCLANT); Commander Eastern Sea Frontier (COMESF); Naval Service Headquarters (RCN) (NSHQ); Commanding Officer (RCN) Atlantic Coast (COAC; Naval Officer in Command (NOIC), Sydney; Commander Task Force 24 (CTF 24); Flag Officer Newfoundland (RCN) (FONF); Commander Task Group 24.6 (CTG.24.6). The Commanders of the US Naval Air Groups, the US Army Air Force, the RCAF and the RAF Coastal Command, who have orders to co-operate, are informed.
3	Mar 4	Convoy Commodore (CDRE) holds convoy conference in New York.
	Mar 4 2300 hrs	Port Director New York announces by radio the departure of convoy SC.122 fixed for Mar. 5.
	Mar 5 1230 hrs (local 0730 hrs)	SC.122 sets out from New York.
	Mar 5 2130 hrs	PD New York issues sailing telegram by radio. Final course instructions go to those concerned. Reference points E, F, G (Halifax Ocean Meeting Point HOMP), H (Western Ocean Meeting Point WOMP), I, K, L, Iceland Meeting Point ICOMP, M, N, O (Eastern Ocean Meeting Point EASTOMP). Stragglers' route P, Q, R, S, T, U, V. Change of operational control (CHOP) probably on Mar. 19.
4	Mar 6	COAC announces by radio feeder convoy HSC.122 with 14 ships from Halifax.
5	Mar 6-7	SC.122 encounters severe storm. Out of 50 ships which set out, 11 stragglers, 2 return to New York, 6 put in to Halifax, 1 missing, 2 close up. Escort Group W.1.
6	Mar 7 2000 hrs	After passing CHOP line between COMESF and COAC CDRE gives situation report.
7	Mar 8 1500 hrs	CDRE gives position report.
8	Mar 8 1800 hrs	COAC sends sailing telegram by radio for HSC.122 with 14 ships and Escort Group W.8.
9	Mar 9	RCAF provides air cover for SC.122.
	Mar 9 1600 hrs	CDRE releases 2 ships to Halifax with 2 escorts.
	Mar 9 1900 hrs	SC.122 at HOMP. EG.W1 relieved by EG.W8. Feeder convoy HSC.122 joins up. Convoy has 51 ships.
10	Mar 10-11	Actual course deviates to N of course instructions.
11	Mar 11 1330 hrs	Feeder convoy from St John's (1 merchant ship, 1 escort) sets out. FONF issues sailing telegram.
	Mar 11 1400 hrs	Ocean Escort Group B.5 sets out from St John's.

#	Date/Time	Event
	Mar 12 0730 hrs	1 merchant ship from SC.122 released with 2 escorts for St John's.
	Mar 12 0930 hrs	SC.122 at WOMP. Western Local North EG.W8 relieved by Escort Group B.5.
	Mar 12 1000 hrs	1 merchant ship sent to St John's with damage. Feeder convoy met. Convoy proceeds with 50 ships and EG.B5 plus US destroyer Upshur.
12	Mar 10-12	Allied shore-based D/F stations obtain several bearings from U-boat signals (Raubgraf group) on course between reference points J and K.
13	Mar 12 1416 hrs	COMINCH orders evasive movement for SC.122. From new point W 360 to new point X, from there direct to L leaving out K. Corresponding change of stragglers' route (omitted here, points Y, Z).
14	Mar 12 (afternoon) -Mar 13 (midday)	Allied shore-based D/F stations obtain bearings on new U-boat signals (Raubgraf group) between 50°-54′ N and 43°-49° W, as well as contact signals from 1336 hrs on Mar. 13 from area of approaching ON.170.
15	Mar 13 1602 hrs	COMINCH orders new evasive movement for SC.122, from 1900 hrs on Mar. 13. A course of 67° from new point A. But convoy has already passed point A. Accordingly changed to 73° from new point B to point C and then on 31° to old point L. RCAF Coastal Command provides convoy with air cover.
	Mar 13 1900 hrs	SC.122 proceeds on new course of 73°. Plotting soon shows course 79° necessary to reach point C.
16	Mar 15 morning	Because of severe NW storms convoy cannot change to course 31° at point C. CDRE suggests maintaining course.
		Senior Officer Escort (SOE) requests by radio new instructions for direct course to North Channel.
17	Mar 16 morning	Admiralty proposes to COMINCH request be granted. But because of transmission difficulties new order only arrives in evening; accordingly SC.122 now proceeds on course of 31.°
18	Mar 16 1330 hrs	COMINCH orders new evasive course: from point C to new point CC or D at 55° N 22° W, from there direct to North Channel.
19	Mar 16 1845 hrs	USS Babbitt and USCGC Ingham set out from Reykjavik to meet the Iceland part of SC.122 with USS Upshur at ICOMP and to escort them to Reykjavik.
20	Mar 16 2000 hrs	SC.122 passes new CHOP line. Operational control passes from COMINCH to CINCWA.
21	Mar 17 0200 hrs	U 338, which is one of the U-boats of the Sturmer group deployed against HX.229 following closely behind, locates SC.122 and attacks. Bearings are received from the contact signals. SOE now independently orders emergency turns in agreement with CDRE.
22	Mar 17 morning	The Air Officer Commanding (AOC) 15th Group, RAF Coastal Command provides air escort for SC.122 at request of CINCWA. It is again provided on the following days.
23	Mar 18 1831 hrs	CINCWA orders USS Babbitt to proceed to the more sorely pressed HX.229, instead of to SC.122 and USCGC Ingham to remain together with the Iceland section with the main body of the convoy.

The harbor masters of New York, Halifax, Sydney and St John's were informed, as were the headquarters of the US Navy Air Force and RCAF in Newfoundland. On the eastern side of the Atlantic the headquarters of CINCWA and No 15 Group, RAF coastal command in Liverpool were informed. CTF 24 and CINCWA informed the senior commands about the distribution of the escort forces and these at once received their preparatory deployment orders. On the morning of the departure day the convoy commodore held a conference in the harbor at which all masters of the merchant ships and the Local Escort commander were present. At this conference the masters were given their individual course instructions and general procedure rules were discussed, such as the need to keep as exact a route order as possible, the black-out of the ships, instructions on how to proceed in the event of losing contact with the convoy, as well as the need to maintain strict radio silence. The Escort commander gave the necessary instructions on how to proceed in the event of U-boat attack and what signals were to be used in such a situation.

Usually the convoy set out in the early afternoon from the assembly point in the harbor roads in order to have sufficient time to establish the route order before the onset of darkness. The convoys were arranged, depending on the number of the ships, in seven to 14 columns, each of which had three to five ships in a line. The space between ships was about 500 meters fore and aft and 1,000 meters on the beam. The convoy had a specific call sign (mostly two-letter) and all ships were given a tactical number. The number, counting from port and ahead, indicated the column with the first figure and the position in the column with the second. With eastbound convoys care was taken to put ships proceeding to harbors en route on the port side of the convoy so that they could easily pull out. Their positions were then taken by ships from these harbors at the ocean meeting points. For westbound convoys the opposite procedure was adopted.

The convoy commodore, usually a retired admiral or captain recalled to service, was embarked on a merchant ship at the head of a central column. Ideally this ship would have suitable accommodation and possess the necessary intelligence and signals installations. The convoy commodore was responsible for seeing that the general course was maintained and the merchant ships kept formation. The Escort Commander assumed tactical command in the event of a U-boat attack. He was usually a fairly young destroyer commander with the rank of Lt. Cdr. or Cdr. He was himself empowered to change the course of the convoy on the basis of his appreciation of the situation within a 40-mile area and he could make the appropriate recommendation to the convoy commodore. In the case of bigger diversions he had to send reports by radio to the commands in Washington or London. Conversely, COMINCH and the Admiralty were able, on the basis of their fuller information about the disposition of German U-boat formations, to order the convoys by radio to take evasive action, by changing the geographical coordinates of the reference points and replacing them with new ones.

GERMAN RADIO INTELLIGENCE

The detailed information required for the control of convoy traffic was naturally communicated, as far as possible, by line or teleprinter. But as it often happened that units taking part in an operation were still at sea after an earlier operation or had already set out for a new one, much information had to be passed by radio. This included, for instance, reports from the New York harbor master; orders about meeting times or the ending of the air and sea escort of homeward- and outward-bound convoys, which had been delayed in weather conditions or other factors; instructions about changes of convoy or stragglers' routes; and escort meeting points, etc. These routine messages provided the German radio intelligence and cryptographic service with important clues for their work, since they were presented in very similar outward form and were recognizable by certain features, like the contact signals of the German U-boats. It was often possible to guess the contents of these routine radio messages. By constantly comparing these messages, the German cryptographic service was repeatedly able to establish changes in the cipher and code book and to keep the code book up to date because the Allies, with remarkable inflexibility, often used it for a long time.

When in August 1940 the British Admiralty changed its cipher, the German "B" Service was at first unable to produce results. This was a disadvantage, particularly in the period of British radio intelligence successes in 1941. But in 1942 the German "B" Service was again able to make some important breaks in the Allied ciphers, particularly in respect of individual ships and stragglers. It went on to have increasing success in breaking the Allied ciphers, although it was not always able to decode the material in time for operations to be based on the deciphered messages. Nevertheless, it was possible in this way, with the dates provided by the "B" Service, for the staff of the Commander U-boats to reconstruct the cycle of the convoys and to work out the Allied convoy timetable very precisely. It was therefore usually possible, when a contact report came in from a U-boat, to identify the sighted convoy correctly. It was a great achievement when the "B" Service was able, in the spring of 1943 to decipher the U-boat situation reports sent out daily by radio from the British Admiralty and COMINCH. Often the reference points of convoy routes or instructions on evasive action were deciphered in time. Frequently, too, the radio traffic of the air cover was promptly deciphered.

In making use of enemy radio traffic to plan operations, the Germans also experimented, in the second half of 1942, with putting "B" Service personnel on the U-boats themselves in order to intercept the VHF radio telephone traffic of the escorts. On December 4, 1942, for example, *U 524*, which was equipped with a device to listen in to the British VHF traffic, heard conversation, for the first time, on the suspected escort speech wavelength. Some 10 participants could be heard. It turned out to be the talk of the British Escort Group B 6, the escorts of convoy HX.217. Two days later the convoy was located as a result of *U 524*'s reports by the U-boat group which came up quickly and attacked. Further listening in to the traffic by *U 524* revealed that the beginning and end of the message was in plain language with the use of code names, but the text was in letter groups and numbers which could not be decoded quickly enough with the resources at the U-boat's disposal. Since, with the existing equipment, the traffic could only be heard up to about 30 miles and could not be located by D/F, this method seemed to offer only limited possibilities.

As the German radio intelligence service produced such good results, particularly in the climactic period of the U-boat war, it may seem strange that since 1940 hardly any fundamental changes had been made in the procedure by which the U-boats were controlled by W/T. There was virtually no direct contact between the U-boats of a pack. The VHF telephone equipment which had been used during the working-up period in the Baltic and had a range of about 10 miles was regarded as useless and was normally disposed of before the first operation against the enemy began. At sea the U-boats, when they surfaced, used their shortwave receivers to listen to the radio messages of other U-boats and to receive those of the Commander U-boats. When a group of U-boats operated against a convoy, cooperation between the boats was maintained because the boats were ready to receive on the prescribed frequency on shortwave and to send their own messages on this wavelength. The messages from the U-boats were regularly repeated by shore headquarters at fixed times so that all U-boats could receive them, irrespective of whether they had, or had not, already heard the first signal from the contact-keeper. If the other U-boats deployed could not find the convoy, they could ask for bearings from headquarters. The Commander U-boats then ordered a contact-keeping U-boat to send D/F signals on long or very long wave and, at regular intervals, it transmitted these signals which could be received at about a range of 100 miles.

To obtain information about the situation at sea, the Commander U-boats could put questions to a commander in a radio cipher exchange. This was done on shortwave in a special code and at a time determined beforehand by radio. But it was relatively seldom used because the U-boats were very exposed to the danger of being located by D/F.

GERMAN NAVAL GRID MAP
North Atlantic

THE ROLE OF THE ALLIED D/F SYSTEM

The Allies took full advantage of intercepted radio traffic. During the "black out" of "special intelligence" from January to December 1942, the radio location picture, derived from D/F-locating the U-boats sending messages, was the most important source to the Submarine Tracking Room in preparing the daily U-boat report. This was the basis for routing and rerouting orders, which in 1942 had still to be restricted to a narrow area both sides of the great circle route because of the number of available escorts and the fact that the principle of their refueling at sea had not yet been generally introduced, making it necessary to avoid delays in order to economize on resources. At the beginning of 1943 the difficulties of refueling at sea had been overcome and every convoy had with it a suitably equipped tanker to provide oil, and the numbers of the escorts were slowly increasing. Only then did it become possible to disperse the convoy routes over the whole expanse of the North Atlantic. But then this advantage was partly canceled out by the fact that, for the first time, the Germans had some hundred U-boats at sea, the figure the Commander U-boats had asked for in 1939. The result was that the evasive movements in face of an identified U-boat frequently meant that the convoy ran into the jaws of another group, particularly since, thanks to the work of the German "B" Service, the Commander U-boats was repeatedly able to move his formations to the right area before the arrival of the convoy.

Nevertheless, Commanders Hall and Winn in the Admiralty and their American counterpart, Capt. Knowles, managed, out of a total of 174 North Atlantic convoys proceeding according to timetable between the middle of July 1942 and the end of May 1943, to reroute 105, or about 60%, round the German U-boat formations, without them being located. Of the 69, or approximately 40%, which were partly located by the waiting U-boats according to plan and partly sighted by chance, 23 escaped without loss, 40 sustained minor losses, sometimes only stragglers. Only 16 of the convoys lost more than four ships.

The radio direction finding of the U-boat traffic from the shore was generally decisive for the control of the convoys. But, to a large extent, the convoys' own successful avoidance of the German U-boat formations was the result of progress made in developing the automatic visual D/F equipment (HF/DF) which from 1942 onward was installed in an increasing number of escorts. After the loss of the sloop *Culver*, a start was made to equipping the rescue ships, which sometimes accompanied the convoys in the North Atlantic, with the HF/DF FH 3 model.

On February 21, 1942 *U 155* established contact with a convoy ONS.67. Its first contact signal was intercepted by the rescue ship *Toward*, equipped with the FH 3; she was proceeding in the center and at the rear of the convoy. The Commander of the American Escort Group deployed the destroyer *Lea* on to the D/F bearing. But her radar was out of order and her commander broke off the sortie prematurely with the result that *U 155* was able to submerge in time when the destroyer was visually sighted.

Because the main operations at this time were taking place off the USA, it was not until June 1942 that there was further practical experience. On June 16 *U 94* (Oblt Ites) reported the convoy ONS.102, but its own contact reports and those of five boats of the *Hecht* group were located by the FH 3 of the Canadian destroyer *Restigouche*. The Escort Commander, the American Cdr. Heineman, was able to drive off all the U-boats with his two Coast Guard cutters, *Campbell* and *Ingham*, the destroyer *Leary* and four Canadian corvettes. *U 94* and *U 590* were damaged by depth charges.

At this time also the American HF/DF equipment, developed by the French research scientists mentioned above, became available. It was installed for the first time in the new destroyer *Corry* in May 1942. After favorable experience and as a result of Commander Heineman's report and recommendations, the two Coast Guard cutters, *Spencer* and *Campbell*, were first equipped with this new model, which went by the name of DAJ, In October 1942.

The further development of this equipment led in 1943–44 to the installation of a British version, FH 4, and an American DAQ, invented by Dr. Goldstein. With these it was possible to secure accurate automatic bearings even from very brief signals of less than a second's duration.

This HF/DF equipment was particularly important for the convoy escort because of the transmission properties of shortwaves. The energy from a shortwave transmitter is largely deflected upward and disappears into space. The waves are only reflected at certain angles to the ionosphere. They then continue to bounce off at a distance of 100 kilometers and more almost endlessly. Between the transmitter and the first bouncing wave there is a dead zone which can, however, be filled by the so-called ground wave for a distance of about 30 miles. There therefore exists a relatively broad dead zone between the extreme range of the ground wave and the smallest range of the reflected wave. With proper equipment and well-trained personnel it is possible to distinguish between the ground waves and the space waves. If a bearing was intercepted by an escort in the range of the ground waves it meant that a U-boat must be within 30 miles of the convoy and the bearing gave the direction of the U-boat from the escort using the D/F.

A precise analysis of the convoy operations from the autumn of 1942 to the spring of 1943 shows that in a considerable number of cases the operations failed, in spite of a U-boat locating and reporting the convoy, because the escort was able to locate the U-boat's messages by D/F and to force it to submerge shortly after its first report. In the meantime the convoy took evasive action and contact was lost. Because, after the start of a convoy battle, i.e., after the first sinkings, the U-boats were no longer inhibited from sending contact reports and other radio information, the escorts were often able to locate the U-boats transmitting messages, even during the operation, to force them to submerge and to drive them off.

In the beginning of December 1942 Bletchley Park succeeded in solving the problems of the big "black out" with the U-boat cipher circuits, possibly by the capture of new cipher materials from a U-boat which was forced to surface and boarded in October–November 1942. From then on U-boat signals could again be deciphered sometimes very quickly, sometimes only with time lags of up to seven days and a few times not at all. With this "special intelligence" available the Submarine Tracking Room again could effectively reroute the convoys in January and February 1943. But then a new difficulty had to be overcome.

## CHAPTER 4

Forces at the Beginning of March 1943

THE ALLIED ESCORT FORCES

March 1943 brought some changes in the Allied convoy timetable. First, with the convoy RA.53, which returned from Murmansk in the first half of March, the northern convoy route to Russia was suspended for the summer of 1943. It was felt that in the bright summer months, on the basis of experience during the previous summer, this route was too seriously exposed to attacks by German surface ships, U-boats and aircraft. The units of the Home Fleet deployed on these operations were therefore released for the operations planned for early summer in the Mediterranean. In addition, it seemed essential to use the fleet destroyers, which were hitherto employed to protect the convoys against surface ships, to build up Support Groups for the North Atlantic. The A/S groups of the Arctic convoys, the 20th Escort Group with eight older destroyers and escort destroyers and the 22nd, 23rd and 24th Escort Groups, each consisting of four corvettes, were at first earmarked for overhaul in the yards at the end of the convoy operations on account of their heavy duties.

The increasing traffic made it necessary to shorten the convoy cycles in the North Atlantic in March 1943 and the ensuing months. From then onward an HX and an SC convoy were to leave New York every week. Twelve Ocean Escort Groups were necessary for the protection of these convoys. They were to consist of three destroyers, a frigate and six corvettes, although it was assumed that from time to time one or two ships would be in the yards for overhaul. Seven of these groups were British (B 1 to B 7), four Canadian (C 1 to C 4) and one American (A 3).

But the demands made by the southern routes from Britain at the beginning of March caused some bottlenecks. There were not only the fast MKF and the slow MKS convoys proceeding from Gibraltar to Britain, which took the place of the old HG and OG convoys, but also the KMF and KMS convoys in the opposite direction to be protected. In addition, there were the Sierra Leone (SL and OS) convoys which had been suspended since November, but were now resumed, and the new tanker convoys from Britain to the Caribbean (UC and CU convoys). The Escort Groups 37, 38, 39, 40, 42 and 44, consisting of sloops and corvettes, were not sufficient for this purpose; so some changes had to be made. At the same time, the fast UGF and the slow UGS convoys with their counterparts, GUF and GUS, operated on the route USA–Morocco/Gibraltar. They were from time to time escorted by the American Task Forces 32, 33, 34, 35, 36, 37 and 38 and consisted mainly of destroyers.

The following table shows the composition and operational state of the Allied Ocean Escort Groups employed on March 1 on the convoy routes USA–Britain, Britain–Gibraltar and USA–Gibraltar:

Escort Group B 1 (Task Unit 24.1.15) (Cdr. E. C. Bayldon, RN)
Destroyers: HMS *Hurricane* (leader), HMS *Watchman,* HMS *Rockingham*
Frigate: HMS *Kale*
Corvettes: HMS *Dahlia,* HMS *Meadowsweet,* HMS *Wallflower,* HMS *Monkshood*
(In the yards: the corvette HMS *Borage* in Belfast)
The group had escorted convoy SC.119 until February 22 and was waiting in Londonderry to pick up convoy ONS.171 on March 6.

Escort Group B 2 (Task Unit 24.1.16) (Cdr. Donald Macintyre, RN)
Destroyers: HMS *Vanessa,* HMS *Whitehall*
Sloop: HMS *Whimbrel* (L) (temporarily attached from the 2nd E.G.)
Corvettes: HMS *Gentian,* HMS *Clematis,* HMS *Heather,* HMS *Sweetbriar*
(In the yards: destroyer HMS *Hesperus* in Liverpool and corvette HMS *Campanula* in Liverpool)
The group had escorted convoy SC.118 until February 2 and lay in Liverpool waiting to pick up convoy ON.170 on March 4.

Escort Group B 3 (Task Unit 24.1.17) (Cdr. A. A. Tait, RN)
Destroyers: HMS *Harvester* (L), HMS *Escapade,* ORP *Garland,* ORP *Burza*
Corvettes: HMS *Narcissus,* FFS *Roselys,* FFS *Aconit,* FFS *Renoncule*
(In the yards: corvettes HMS *Orchis* in Liverpool, FFS *Lobelia* in the Clyde)
After the relief of convoy ONS.167 the group arrived in St John's on March 2 and was to take over convoy HX.228 on March 8.

Escort Group B 4 (Task Unit 24.1.18) (Cdr. E. C. L. Day, RN)
Destroyers: HMS *Highlander* (L), HMS *Vimy,* HMS *Beverley*
Corvettes: HMS *Pennywort,* HMS *Anemone,* HMS *Abelia*; HMCS *Sherbrooke* (attached)

DEPLOYMENT OF THE OCEAN ESCORT GROUPS April 1942 to May 1943

Top table

ESCORT GROUP	APRIL	MAI	JUNI	JULI	AUGUST	SEPTEMBER	OKTOBER	NOVEMBER	DE
B.1		HX 187	HX 193	ONS 108	ON HX 119 120	ONS 124	ONS 134	HX 215	
B.2		SC 81	SC 86	HX 198	SC 92	HX 128	HX 138	ONS 206	ONS 148
B.3		HX 188	ONS 98	ONS 107	ONS 118	ONS 126	ONS 136	ONS 146	
B.4		SC 82	ON 99	SC 87	SC 93	HX 130	HX 207	HX 214	HX 150 217
B.6			HX 101	ON 111	HX 200	ONS 132	SC 104	ONS 144	HX 216
B.7		HX 186	ONS 100	ONS 106	SC 117	HX 205	SC 103	ONS 142	
C.1		ONS 189	HX 192	HX 195	SC 94	SC 99	HX 211	ON 143	SC 110
C.2		SC 84	ON 103	SC 89	ON HX 201 119	SC 102	ON 139	SC 108	SC 149
C.3		ON 93	ONS 104	ON 113	SC 98	ON 129	SC 139	SC 109	
C.4		HX 91	ON 105	HX 197	ON 115	ON 131	HX 210	ON 141	ON 147
A.3	HX 185	ONS 92 190	ONS 102	HX 196	ONS 116	SC 127	ON 137	HX 107 212	SC 145 111

Bottom table

TASK UNIT	DEZEMBER	JANUAR	FEBRUAR	MARZ	APRIL	MAI	JUNI	JULI	AU
B.1	ON 151	SC 114	SC 119	ONS 171	ON 178	SC 236			
B.2	HX 218 148	ON 159	SC 118	HX 228	ONS 123	ONS 129	ONS 9		
B.3	ONS 150	HX 157 220	ONS 167	HX 174	HX 232	HX 181	HX 241		
B.4	HX 217	ON 161		ONS 169	HX 234	ON 183			
B.5				ON 168	SC 126	ONS 7			
B.6	ON 155	SC 116	ONS 165	HX 227	SC 25	SC 131			
B.7	ON 153 216	HX 222	ON 164	SC 120	ONS 1	SC 130		SC 133	
C.1	ONS 154	ONS 160	HX 225	ON 173	HX 231	ON 184			
C.2	SC 113 149			SC 121	ONS 2	SC 127			
C.3	ONS 152	HX 221	ONS 163	ON 172	ON 179	HX 237	ONS 8		
C.4	SC 112	ONS 156	HX 224		HX 180 235	HX 238	HX 240		
C.5	—				ON 177	ON 182			
A.3	SC 111	HX 223	ON 166	HX 229A	HX 233	ONS 3	SC 128		
EG.40	—								

(In the yards: destroyer HMS *Winchelsea* in Hartlepool, corvettes HMS *Asphodel* and HMS *Clover* in Belfast)

The group was with ONS.169 on the way to WOMP, where it was to be relieved on March 10. After staying in St John's it was to take over convoy HX.229 on March 14.

The destroyer *Vimy* was detached to Reykjavik.

Escort Group B 5 (Task Unit 24.1.19) (Cdr. R. C. Boyle, RN)
Destroyers: HMS *Havelock* (L), HMS *Volunteer*
Frigate: HMS *Swale*
Corvettes: HMS *Saxifrage*, HMS *Godetia*, HMS *Pimpernel*, HMS *Buttercup*, HMS *Lavender*
(In the yards: destroyer HMS *Warwick* in Dundee)

The group was with convoy ON.168 on the way to WOMP, where it was to be relieved on March 6. After a stay in St John's it was to take over convoy SC.122 on March 13.

Escort Group B 6 (Task Unit 24.1.4) (Cdr. R. Heathcote, RN)
Destroyers: HMS *Fame* (L), HMS *Viscount*
Corvettes: HMS *Acanthus*, HNoMS *Eglantine*, HMS *Vervain*, HMS *Kingcup*
(In the yards: destroyer HMS *Ramsay* in Grimsby, frigate HMS *Deveron* in Middlesbrough, corvettes HNoMS *Rose* in Cardiff, HNoMS *Potentilla* in Liverpool)

The group was with convoy HX.227 on the way to EASTOMP, where it was to be relieved on March 5. After waiting in Liverpool it was to take over convoy ONS.1 on March 18.

Escort Group B 7 (Task Unit 24.1.5) (Cdr. P. W. Gretton, RN)
Destroyer: HMS *Vidette*
Frigate: HMS *Tay* (L)
Sloop: HMS *Woodpecker* (attached from 2nd Escort Group until March 3)
Corvettes: HMS *Alisma*, HMS *Pink*, HMS *Loosestrife*, HMS *Snowflake*
(In the yards: destroyers HMS *Duncan* in Tobermory, HMS *Ripley* in Liverpool, corvette HMS *Sunflower* in Belfast).

The group was with convoy SC.120 on the way to EASTOMP, where it was to be relieved on March 2. After a stay in Londonderry it was to take over convoy ON.173 on March 16.

Escort Group C 1 (Task Unit 24.1.11) (Lt. Cdr. A. H. Dobson, RCNR)
Destroyer: HMCS *St Croix* (L)

Corvettes: HMCS *Shediac*, HMCS *Battleford*, HMCS *Kenogami*, HMCS *Napanee*

(In the yards: destroyer HMCS *St Laurent* in U.K. from March 4 after arriving with EGB 6 with convoy HX.227; HMS *Burwell* in Londonderry; frigate HMS *Itchen* in Tobermory; and corvettes HMCS *Agassiz* and HMCS *Pictou* in Liverpool)

The group was with the convoy KMS.10 on the way to Gibraltar, where it was then to take over convoy MKS.9 on March 8. A Canadian E.G. of the Mediterranean Escort Force (MEF), comprising the corvettes HMCS *Baddeck*, HMCS *Regina*, HMCS *Prescott*, and the minesweepers HMCS *Fort York*, HMCS *Qualicum* and HMCS *Wedgeport*, was attached as a Support Group.

Escort Group C 2 (Task Unit 24.1.12) (Lt. Cdr. E. H. Chavasse, RN)
Destroyers: HMS *Broadway* (L), HMS *Sherwood*
Frigate: HMS *Lagan*
Corvettes: HMCS *Drumheller*, HMCS *Morden*, HMCS *Chambly*, HMS *Primrose*, attached HMS *Snowdrop* and aviso FFS *Savorgnan de Brazza*
(In the yards: HMS *Polyanthus* in the U.K.)

The group had escorted convoy HX.225 until February 14 and lay in Londonderry waiting to take over Convoy KMS.11 on March 13.

Escort Group C 3 (Task Unit 24.1.13) (Cdr. R. C. Medley, RN)
Destroyer: HMS *Burnham* (L)
Frigate: HMS *Jed* (temporarily attached from 1st Escort Group)
Corvettes: HMCS *Bittersweet*, HMCS *Eyebright*, HMCS *Mayflower*, HMCS *La Malouine*
(In the yards: destroyers HMCS *Assiniboine* in the U.K., HMCS *Skeena* in Halifax, corvettes HMCS *Sackville* in Liverpool, HMCS *Galt* in Halifax)

The group had escorted convoy HX.226 until February 24 and then lay waiting in Londonderry to meet convoy ON.172 on March 11. The corvettes HMCS *Alberni*, HMCS *Port Arthur*, HMCS *Summerside* and HMCS *Woodstock* were allocated as Support Group for this purpose from the MEF.

Escort Group C 4 (Task Unit 24.1.14) (Cdr. G. N. Brewer, RN)
Destroyers: HMS *Churchill* (L), HMCS *Restigouche*
Corvettes: HMCS *Amherst*, HMCS *Brandon*, HMCS *Collingwood*, HMS *Celandine*
(In the yards: corvettes HMCS *Trent*, HMCS *Baddeck*, HMCS *Orillia*)

The group had left the convoy HX.224 on February 7 and after a stay in Londonderry was to take over convoy KMF.10 B on March 2.

Escort Group A 3 (Task Unit 24.1.3) (Capt. P. Heineman, USN)
Destroyer: USS *Greer*
Cutter: USCGC *Spencer* (L)
Corvettes: HMS *Dianthus*, HMCS *Rosthern*, HMCS *Trillium*, HMCS *Dauphin*
(In the yards: USCGC *Campbell*, corvettes HMCS *Chilliwack*, HMCS *Arvida*, HMCS *Wetaskiwin*)
The group had handed over convoy ON.166 on February 26 and, after a short stay in St John's, was to take over convoy SC.121 on March 2.

1st Escort Group (1st Support Group) (Cdr. J. G. Gould, RN)
Sloop: HMS *Pelican* (L)
Cutter: HMS *Sennen*
Frigates: HMS *Rother*, HMS *Spey*, HMS *Wear*
(In the yards: HMS *Jed* which, when work was completed, was temporarily attached to E.G. C 3.)
The group was with convoy OS.43 on the way to Freetown, where it was to take over convoy SL.126 on March 12.

2nd Escort Group (2nd Support Group) (Lt. Cdr. Proudfoot, RN) (still in process of formation)
Sloops: HMS *Wren* (L), from March 3 HMS *Woodpecker* (temporarily attached to E.G.B.2)
(In the yards: HMS *Cygnet*. In "work-up": HMS *Kite*, HMS *Wildgoose*)
Temporarily attached: destroyer HMS *Douglas* (from E.G.20), "Hunt" destroyers: HMS *Eggesford*, HMS *Badsworth*, HMS *Whaddon*, HMS *Goathland*, ORP *Krakowiak*.
With *Wren* and *Woodpecker* and the attached destroyers it was escorting convoys KMF.11 and WS.28 from March 15.

3rd Escort Group (3rd Support Group) (Capt. J. W. McCoy, RN)
Formed in the middle of March from destroyers of the Home Fleet: HMS *Offa*, HMS *Obedient*, HMS *Oribi*, HMS *Orwell*, HMS *Onslaught*.

4th Escort Group (4th Support Group)
Formed at the end of March from destroyers of the Home Fleet: HMS *Inglefield*, HMS *Icarus*, HMS *Eclipse*, HMS *Fury*.

5th Escort Group: Formation planned for April 1943.

North Atlantic Convoys and their Escort Groups in March 1943

ROUTE	CONVOY KONVOI	FEBR. 26 27 28	MARCH / MÄRZ (1–28)
U.K. ← U.S.A.	ON.166	A.3 w w	H W S — New York
	ONS.167	B.3	w W 10 — H W.3 — New York
	ON.168	B.5	w W 2 — H W 8 — Cape Cod
	ONS.169	E B.4	w W.5 — H W.3 — Cape Cod
	ON.170	Liverpool	E B.2 — w.W 6 — H W 10 — New York
	ONS.171	Liverpool	E B.1 — w W.7 — H W.5 — New Y.
	ON.172		Liverpool — E C.3 — w W.1 — H W.6
	ON.173		Liverpool — E B.7 — w W 4 — H
	GNS.1		Liverpool — E B.6
U.S.A. ← U.K.	HX.227	B.6	E — Liverpool
	SC.121	H W.5	w A.3 — E — Liverpool
	HX.228	N.Y. W.7	H W.6 — w B.3 — E — Liverpool
	SC.122		New York — W.1 — H W.5 — w B.5 — E — Liverpool
	HX.229		New York — W.9 — w B.4 — E — Liverpool
	HX.229A		New York — W.10 — H W.1 — w 40. — E — Liv
	SC.123		New York — W.8 — H W.4 — w B.2
	HX.230		New York — W.5 — H W.8 — w B.1
U.K.→GIBR.	KMS.10	Liv	E C.1 — Gibraltar
	KMF.108	Liverpool	E C.4 — Gibraltar
	OS.44	Liverpool	E 39. — Gib — Freetown
	KMS.11		Liverpool — E C.2 — Gibraltar
	KMF.11		Liverpool — E 2. — Gibraltar
GIBR.→U.K.	XK.2	Gibr. 38.	E — Liverpool
	MKF.10A		Gibraltar — 44. — E — Liverpool
	MKS.9		Gibraltar — C.1 — E — Liverpool
	MKF.108		Gibraltar — C.4 — E — Liverpool
	XK.3		Gibraltar — E — Liv
GIBR.→USA	GUS.4	TF.38	New York
	GUF.5	G TF.36	New York
	TO.2		Gibraltar
	GUS.5		Oran — G TF.65
	GUS.5A		Oran — G TF.67
	GUS.58		Oran — G
USA→GIBR	UGS.5A	TF.37	Gibraltar
	UGS.6		New York — TF.33 — G — Oran
	UGF.6		New York — TF.34 — G — Oran
	UGS.6A		New York — TG.60.1

6th Escort Group (6th Support Group): (Capt. G. E. Short, USN)
Escort carrier: USS *Bogue* (L)
Destroyers: USS *Belknap*, USS *George E. Badger*, USS *Osmond-Ingram*
(In the yards: USS *Greene*, USS *Clemson*, USS *Lea* in Norfolk)
It was lying in Argentina. Its first deployment was on March 5 in support
of convoy HX.228 and from March 20 SC.123.

20th Escort Group (Seven destroyers for Murmansk convoys)

21st Escort Group (Six destroyers for Iceland convoys)

22nd Escort Group (Four corvettes for Murmansk convoys)

23rd Escort Group (Four corvettes for Murmansk convoys)

24th Escort Group (Four corvettes for Murmansk convoys)

37th Escort Group (Cdr. Rodney Thomson, RN)
Sloop: HMS *Black Swan* (L)
Corvettes: HMS *Campion*, HMS *Carnation*, FFS *La Malouine*, HMS *Myosotis*, HMS *Mallow*
(In the yards: sloop HMS *Fowey* in Milford Haven, corvette HMS *Stonecrop* in Manchester)
Black Swan and *La Malouine* were with convoy MKS.8 on the way to the
North Channel, where they arrived on March 5. The other four corvettes
had arrived in Liverpool on February 24. *Campion* and *Mallow* were dispatched to support convoy SC.121.

38th Escort Group (Cdr. A. H. Davies, RNVR)
Corvettes: HMS *Anchusa*, HMS *Columbine*, HMS *Coreopsis* (L), HMS *Jonquil*, HMS *Aubrietia*, HMS *Violet*
(In the yards: sloops HMS *Enchantress*, HMS *Sandwich*, HMS *Leith*)
The first four corvettes were with convoy KX.2 from the North Channel
to Gibraltar. *Aubrietia* lay in Gibraltar, *Violet* had arrived in Londonderry on
February 25. The group was to take over XK.2.

39th Escort Group (Cdr. H. V. King, RN)
Sloops: HMS *Rochester* (L), HMS *Fleetwood*, HMS *Scarborough*
Corvettes: HMS *Balsam*, HMS *Coltsfoot*, HMS *Spirea*, HMS *Mignonette*
(In the yards: corvettes HMS *Azalea*, HMS *Geranium*)

The group had arrived in Londonderry at the end of February and put to sea on March 5 with the convoy OS.44 for Freetown.

40th Escort Group (Cdr. J. S. Dalison, RN)
Sloops: HMS *Aberdeen*, HMS *Hastings*
Ex-Coast Guard cutters: HMS *Landguard*, HMS *Lulworth*
Frigates: HMS *Moyola*, HMS *Waveney*
(In the yards: sloops HMS *Londonderry* in Plymouth, HMS *Bideford* in Avonmouth, frigate HMS *Nith* in Leith)
Attached destroyers HMS *Panther*, HMS *Penn* in the Clyde, HMS *Pathfinder* in Plymouth
The group lay in Londonderry and proceeded at the beginning of March to St John's to escort convoy HX.229A on March 16.

42nd Escort Group (Cdr. L. F. Durnford-Slater, RN)
Sloops: HMS *Weston* (L), HMS *Folkestone*
Ex-Coast Guard cutters: HMS *Gorleston*, HMS *Totland*
Frigates: HMS *Exe*, HMS *Ness*
(In the yards: sloops HMS *Lowestoft* in Falmouth, HMS *Wellington* in Sheerness, cutter HMS *Bradford* in Liverpool)
The group had gone with convoy UC.1 to the Caribbean.
The US destroyers USS *Madison*, USS *Charles F. Hughes*, USS *Hilary P. Jones* and USS *Lansdale* operated as Support Group. The group returned with the convoy CU.1 on March 20. *Gorleston* (L) (Cdr. R. W. Keymer, RN) *Weston, Folkestone, Totland* sailed independently for the Azores on March 18 and joined CU.1 as Support Group on March 29.

44th Escort Group (Cdr. C. S. R. Farquhar, RN)
Destroyer: HMS *Clare*
Sloops: HMS *Egret* (L), HMS *Erne*
Coast Guard cutter: HMS *Fishguard*
Frigate: HMS *Test*
(In the yards: the cutter HMS *Banff* in Immingham, the frigates HMS *Teviot* in Tobermory, HMS *Trent* in Bristol, HMS *Bayntun* in Bermuda)
The group was proceeding with convoy KMF.10A to Gibraltar, where it arrived on March 3 to take over convoy MKF.10A on March 8.

The following US Task Forces received numbers in the 60s instead of in the 30s on March 15, 1943: TF 36 became TF 66.
Task Force 32 (Capt. Burgess Watson, RN, CO *LST 320*)
TF 62 consisted of 10 British LSTs, 6 US LSTs and 24 US LCIs.

Task Group 32.1: Destroyers: USS *Herbert,* USS *Bernadou,* USS *Cole,* USS *Dallas*

Minesweeper: USS *Chickadee*

Oiler: USS *Mattole*

Fleet Tug: USS *Moreno.* It escorted convoy GUS.5B from Gibraltar to USA from March 27 to April 11.

Task Force 33 (63) (Capt. C. Wellborn, JR., USN)

Destroyers: USS *Wainwright* (L), USS *Mayrant,* USS *Rowan,* USS *Rhind,* USS *Trippe,* USS *Champlin,* USS *Hobby,* USS *Du Pont*

Oiler: USS *Chiwawa*

It escorted the convoy UGS.6 from New York to Gibraltar from March 4 to March 21.

Task Force 34 (64) (Capt. S. Umsted, USN)

Battleship: USS *New York* (L)

Cruiser: USS *Brooklyn*

Destroyers: USS *Buck,* USS *Woolsey,* USS *Ludlow,* USS *Edison,* USS *Wilkes,* USS *Swanson,* USS *Roe,* USS *Bristol,* USS *Nicholson*

Oiler: USS *Mattaponi*

It escorted the convoy UGF.6 from New York to Gibraltar from March 5 to March 18.

Task Force 35 (65) (Capt. T. L. Wattles, USN)

Destroyers: USS *Parker* (L), USS *Boyle,* USS *Laub,* USS *MacLeish,* USS *McCormick,* USS *Overton*

Oiler: USS *Merrimack*

It escorted convoy GUS.5 from Oran to New York from March 13 to April 1.

Task Force 36 (66) (Rear-Adm. L. A. Davidson, USN)

Battleship: USS *Arkansas*

Cruiser: USS *Philadelphia* (L)

Destroyers: USS *Mervine,* USS *Quick,* USS *Beatty,* USS *Emmons,* USS *Knight,* USS *Earle,* USS *Macomb*

Oiler: USS *Winooski*

It escorted the convoy GUF.5 from Gibraltar to New York from February 27 to March 11.

Task Force 37 (67) (Cdr. J. B. Rooney, USN)

Destroyers: USS *Gherardi* (L), USS *Jeffers*, USS *Murphy*, USS *Bainbridge*, USS *Broome*, USS *Simpson*

Oiler: USS *Chemung*

It escorted the convoy UGS.5A from New York to Gibraltar from February 18 to March 4.

Task Force 38 (68) (Cdr. G. L. Menocal, USN)

Destroyers: USS *Plunkett* (L), USS *Benson*, USS *Gleaves*, USS *Mayo*

Minesweepers: USS *Raven*, USS *Osprey*

Oilers: USS *Housatonic*, USS *Kaweah*

It escorted the convoy GUS.4 from Gibraltar to New York from February 21 until March 11.

Task Force 39 (69)

consisted of 5 US APAs, 5 US AKAs and 1 US AS.

Destroyers: USS *Carmick* (Cdr. W. S. Whiteside, USN), USS *MacKenzie*, USS *McLanahan*

Western Support Force (Task Group 24.12)

The Support Group Task Units 24.12.1–4 were formed from the following vessels according to need and availability. Their composition varied.

Destroyers: HMS *Witherington*, HMS *Chelsea*, HMS *Leamington*, HMS *Mansfield*, HMS *Montgomery*, HMS *Salisbury*

(In the yards: destroyer HMS *Buxton* in Boston, HMS *Caldwell* in Boston, HMS *Georgetown* in Charleston, HMS *Roxborough* in Charleston, HNo.MS *Lincoln* in Charleston)

Western Escort Force (Task Group 24.18)

The WLN and WLS Escort Groups W 1–W 12 were formed from the following vessels according to need and availability. Their composition varied.

Destroyers: HMCS *Annapolis*, HMCS *Hamilton*, HMCS *Niagara*, HMCS *St Clair*

Corvettes: HMCS *Barrie*, HMCS *Brantford*, HMCS *Buctouche*, HMCS *Chicoutimi*, HMCS *Cobalt*, HMCS *Dundas*, HMCS *Dunvegan*, HMCS *Fennel*, HMCS *Camsack*, HMCS *Matapedia*, HMCS *Moncton*, HMCS *Nanaimo*, HMCS *New Westminster*, HMCS *Quesnel*, HMCS *Rimouski*, HMCS *Saskatoon*, HMCS *The Pas*, HMCS *Trail*, HMCS *Timmins*

Minesweepers: (steam) HMCS *Blairmore*, HMCS *Cowichan*, HMCS *Drummondville*, HMCS *Gananoque*, HMCS *Grandmere*, HMCS *Kenora*, HMCS *Medicine Hat*, HMCS *Nipigon*, HMCS *Red Deer*; (diesel) HMCS *Digby*, HMCS *Granby*, HMCS *Lachine*, HMCS *Truro*, HMCS *Trois Rivieres* (temporarily attached)

(In the yards: destroyers HMCS *Columbia*, HMCS *St Francis*, corvettes: HMCS *Arrowhead*, HMCS *Edmundston*, HMCS *Hepatica*, HMCS *Midland*, HMCS *Shawinigan*; minesweepers (steam) HMCS *Burlington*, HMCS *Chedabucto*, HMCS *Minas*, (diesel) HMCS *Melville*, HMCS *Noranda*)

MARCH 1943: THE GERMAN U-BOAT ARM

In the spring of 1943 the German U-boat arm approximately reached the strength which the Commander U-boats had called for in his memorandum in 1939. On March, 1943, there were, in all, 400 U-boats in service. Another 47 were being fitted out and 245 were on the slipways. Seven completed U-boats were out of service for conversion. Of the 400 available U-boats, 52 (13%) were training boats, 119 (29.8%) were being worked up, seven (1.7%) were experimental boats and 222 (55.5%) were front-line boats.

Of these front-line boats 18 were in the Arctic, 19 in the Mediterranean and three in the Black Sea; 182 were available for the Atlantic operations. Of the Atlantic front-line boats on March 1, 1943, 114 (62.6%) were at sea and 68 (37.4%) were in French harbors. Of the boats at sea 44 were on the way out or the way back (24.2% of the front-line boats). The remaining 70 (38.4%) were in the operational areas: 45 in the North Atlantic, 13 in the Central Atlantic, five in the Western Atlantic and seven in the South Atlantic.

After operations against a number of westbound convoys in the second half of February the following situation existed on March 1:

From February 17 to February 20 12 U-boats, forming the *Haudegen* group, had in turn followed convoy ONS.165, which was escorted by Escort Group B 6. The boats then went to replenish from *U 460* and from the supply area they were drawn into the operations in the Central North Atlantic which began on February 20 and which the *Knappen* and *Ritter* groups conducted against convoy ON.166, escorted by Escort Group A 3. The operation, in which 15 ships totaling 97,382 tons were sunk, lasted until February 25 and ended in the area southeast of Newfoundland. Twenty-one U-boats participated: most of them then began the return journey but some went to replenish from *U 460*. On February 21, east of ON.166, the next convoy, ONS.167 (Escort Group B 3), was located by an outward-bound boat. This convoy was also proceeding on the southern route. The 13 outward-bound boats close enough to reach it were formed into the *Sturmbock* group and pursued the enemy until February 23.

Because of these operations, which were mainly on the southern route, the Allied Command expected strong U-boat concentrations in this area and therefore directed the next convoys along the northern route, close to the Greenland coast. There, on February 27, the most northerly boat of the *Neptun* group, stationed in the area, reported the eastbound convoy HX.227.

Radio interference prevented the seven other boats of the group being deployed in time and *U 759* was driven off by the escort of the 62-ship convoy, Escort Group B 6. *U 376*, *U 377*, *U 608*, *U 448*, *U 359* and *U 135* took up the pursuit, but only *U 405* was able to sink a Liberty ship left behind. Nor did the two boats *U 709* and *U 634*, which joined on February 28, get up to the convoy. On March 1 *U 759* pursued an independent ship between Greenland and Iceland which *U 634* was able to sink in the evening.

While looking for HX.227 and the individual ships reported, *U 376* sighted at midday on March 1 the tanker *Empire Light*, which, with five other ships, had lost its convoy ON.168 (Commodore: Adm. Sir C. G. Ramsay, KCB, RN) in the storm on February 28. At midday on March 1 there were still 41 of the original 52 ships with the convoy. Four of the stragglers closed up again in the afternoon. *U 376*'s report was located by the ships with the convoy equipped with HF/DF, the destroyer leader *Havelock*, the destroyer *Volunteer* and the rescue ship *Dewsbury*. The *Volunteer* at once followed the bearing for 20 miles. She found the *Empire Light* and a group of three more stragglers, but the U-boat was able to turn away in time. At 1321 hrs *U 608* sent a contact signal from the other side of the convoy. The *Havelock* followed the DF bearing at once, but her asdic was out of order because of the heavy seas with the result that she could not find the U-boat which submerged on the destroyer's approach. She hoved to in order to repair the equipment. *U 608* and, soon, *U 376* again approached the convoy in the afternoon. By 1700 hrs the *Havelock* had completed the repairs and closed up at high speed. Shortly after 1900 hrs a boat was again contacted by HF/DF at very close range. Cdr. Boyle turned the *Havelock* on to the beam and called up the *Volunteer*. After five minutes a U-boat was sighted and hunted for 20 minutes until it submerged at a distance of six miles. When the *Volunteer* came up the *Havelock* pursued a second bearing and soon found the other U-boat on it. Both were then forced underwater for several hours and contact was lost. *U 405*, *U 359*, *U 659* and *U 448*, which were in the vicinity and operating against the convoy, were also unable to find it. Nor were the other *Neptun* boats able to find HX.227 by March 3.

In addition to these groups in the North Atlantic, the Commander U-boats had tried in the second half of February to find US–Gibraltar convoys, north and south of the Azores, with the *Robbe* and *Rochen* groups which consisted of eight and 10 boats respectively. But the convoys expected here after calculating the convoy timetable, the UGS.5 and UGF.5, as well as the convoys in the opposite direction, the GUS.4 and GUF.4, could not be found. By chance *U 522*, which was proceeding on its own east of the formations, came across the tanker convoy UC.1 on February 22. This consisted of 33 ships with Escort Group 42 comprising the sloops *Weston* and *Folkestone*, the cutters

Gorleston and *Totland*, the frigates *Exe* and *Ness* and an American Support Group with the destroyers *Madison, Charles F. Hughes, Hilary P. Jones* and *Lansdowne.* The *Rochen* group and the two southern *Robbe* boats, which were deployed, followed the convoy until February 27. They sank three tankers totaling 26,682 tons and torpedoed two more. Some of the boats had to turn back and others replenished from the tanker *U 461* and then formed the *Tummler* group in the area of the Canaries to operate against southbound convoys. The remaining five *Robbe* boats were concentrated west of the Straits of Gibraltar so as to catch MKS and MKF convoys as well as the GUS and GUF.

Despite failures here with the America–Gibraltar convoys, the Commander U-boats wanted to launch a new attempt at the beginning of March since the critical situation for the German-Italian bridgehead in Tunis made it essential to attack the Allied supply line to Africa. Because the number of boats was inadequate in the wide expanses of the Central Atlantic where the U-boats could be avoided, the Commander U-boats proposed to concentrate off the American coast large Type IX-C boats which were originally envisaged for the Cape Town area. There some boats acting as advance patrols were to find the convoys and lead them to the "interceptor" group which waited further back, outside the range of the shore-based air cover.

CHAPTER 5

Convoy Control in March 1943

PREPARATIONS FOR THE DEPARTURE OF CONVOYS SC.122, HX.229 AND HX.229A

At the end of February the staffs of the Trade Plot Room in the Admiralty and the Convoy and Routing Section of COMINCH began to give preliminary thought to the question of routing the convoys in the middle of March. On February 26, when the Admiralty made its first proposals to COMINCH for the routes for SC.122, the operations against convoy ON.166 on the southern route had just ended. Some days before U-boats had lost contact with the following convoy, ONS.167, on the same route. Both operations appeared to have drawn the majority of the German U-boats at sea to the southern part of the North Atlantic route. Accordingly, it was at first proposed that the new convoys should take the northern route. On March 1 and 2 similar proposals were made for the convoys HX.229 and HX.229A. For the first time it was necessary to divide an HX convoy into parts because of the presence of many fast merchantmen on the western side of the Atlantic. After confirmation by COMINCH the appropriate instructions were issued by the New York Port Director and, on the next day, by the Commander Eastern Sea Frontier to the authorities and ships concerned.

The course instructions provided that the three convoys should proceed eastward from New York as far as the longitude of Cape Sable in order to turn then to the northeast and pass relatively close to Halifax, at a distance of about 100–150 miles. SC.122 was to reach HOMP on the evening of March 9, HX.229 at midday on March 11 and HX.229A in the early afternoon of March 12. The convoys would then turn again on a somewhat more easterly course as far as Cape Race, which was to be passed at a distance of 40 to 200 miles. Then they would turn somewhat further southeast on to the NNE course for the northern route. SC.122 was to reach WOMP on March 12, HX.229 on the morning of March 14 and HX.229A on the evening of March 14. The route then led to the latitude of Cape Farewell, the southern part of Greenland, where an easterly course would be taken to the longitude of Iceland. Then the convoys, coming from the NW, would turn toward the

North Channel. The stragglers' routes ran from a point NE of St John's, a little to the south and parallel to the convoy routes (see map, p. 27).

But on March 1 and 2 the radio traffic of the U-boats looking for HX.227 and then, until March 3, for convoy ON.168, was located by D/F; it showed that U-boats were also to be expected on this northern route. In particular many bearings were obtained on March 2. The Commander U-boats wanted to know which boats of the *Neptun* group were near the eastbound HX.227 and which were near the westbound ON. 168 and ordered the boats to report their positions. The boats which were looking for ON.168 south of Cape Farewell were moved south toward Newfoundland to form a new patrol line *Wildfang* with 8–9 boats for March 3: this was to be an extension of the 9–11 boat patrol line *Burggraf* which had arrived in this area. The two patrol lines were to wait there for the convoy SC.121 which was due to arrive on March 5: this was known from course instructions which the "B" Service had deciphered on March 3. The seven boats stationed to the east were ordered to lie in wait behind this formation. The 16 boats coming from Germany were to form a new patrol line SE of Cape Farewell as the *Neuland* group on March 7, following the order issued on March 3. The Allied shore-based D/F stations were also able to establish many positions from among these outward-bound boats because, while en route, they had been asked on March 3 by the Commander U-boats to give a report on the situation in the Iceland passage.

INTERLUDE ON THE BRITAIN–GIBRALTAR ROUTE

On March 4 the attention of both sides was diverted for 3 days to the Britain–Gibraltar route, where two convoys met in the area of Vigo. They were the KMS.10 from the north and the XK.2 which had set out from Gibraltar on February 28. The KMS.10 consisted of 50 merchant ships and was screened by the Canadian Escort Group C 1 (Lt. Cdr. A. H. Dobson, RCNR). It comprised the destroyer *St Croix* (L) and the corvettes *Shediac*, *Battleford*, *Kenogami* and *Napanee*. In the meantime another Canadian group, comprising the corvettes *Baddeck*, *Regina* and *Prescott* and the *Bangor* minesweepers *Fort York*, *Qualicum* and *Wedgeport*, had arrived as a Support Group. The XK.2 consisted of 20 merchantmen and was screened by the 38th Escort Group, whose best fighting vessels were, however, all in the yards. It comprised the corvettes *Coreopsis* (SOE), *Anchusa*, *Columbine* and *Jonquil*, the A/S trawler *Loch Arskaig* and the destroyer *Vanoc* attached for support. The escort of XK.2 had already twice contacted the enemy, although there had been no reports about the convoy. At 2230 hrs on March 1 the *Columbine* had located with her radar a U-boat some 5,000 meters astern of the convoy, SW of Cape St Vincent. The U-boat was forced underwater and was probably *U 445*. At 1430 hrs on March 3 the Catalina flying boat E/202, which was covering the convoy, had sighted a German FW 200 Condor reconnaissance aircraft and driven it off before it was able to report the convoy. Nevertheless, the German Command now knew from radio intelligence that convoys were at sea in the area west of Spain and the Bay of Biscay.

In consequence, the available aircraft of the Air Commander, Atlantic (*Flieger-Führer, Atlantik*), were deployed on armed reconnaissance on the morning of March 4. Two FW 200s of *I/KG 40* approached convoy KMS.10 at 1135 hrs. They reported it in CG 1294 on a southern course, comprising 50 merchant ships and 10 escorts. An attempted attack led to some near-misses on the steamer sailing in position 24 but they produced no serious damage. The Catalina flying boat 0/202 covering the convoy attacked the Condors and drove them off with the help of the AA fire from the escorts and merchant ships. Almost simultaneously another FW 200 found XK.2 a little further to the west and attacked it in conjunction with a Do 217 from *II/KG 40* at 1144 hrs. The steamer *Chateauroux* (4,765 tons) in position 35 was hit by a bomb that failed to explode and sustained slight damage from two near-misses. The bombs from the Do 217 fell 10 minutes later between columns 6 and 7 without doing any damage. The FW 200 reported at 1150 hrs that the convoy was in CG 1453 on a northern course and comprising 20 steamers and six escorts.

As a planned U-boat operation seemed hardly feasible in this area which was provided with strong Allied air cover, only the boats in the vicinity received orders to exploit favorable opportunities to attack. The German "B" Service intercepted the radio message in which KMS.10 and XK.2 reported the air attacks and deciphered their code names, *Leveret* and *Horse*, as well as the texts, in the next two days.

As a result of the German air reconnaissance reports, *U 87*, which was returning from the North Atlantic came into the vicinity of KMS.10 at midday on March 4, but it had to submerge before it could send a contact signal. At 1347 hrs it was located by the asdic of *Shediac* six miles to the stern of the convoy and was straddled with 32 depth charges in five approaches. Rising air bubbles and oil indicated damage at least, but Lt. Cdr. Dobson could not remain behind any longer because of the air threat. In consequence it was not known whether success had been achieved in sinking the U-boat.

Hardly had the two vessels got back to the convoy when three Do 217s of *II/KG 40* tried to attack at 1750 hrs. The Catalina D/120, which was now providing cover, tried to drive off the approaching aircraft, but the AA fire from the merchantmen and escorts was so heavy that it had to turn away with the two attacking German planes whose bombs dropped into the sea without effect. The report of this attack on the convoy *Leveret* was also intercepted and deciphered by the German "B" Service.

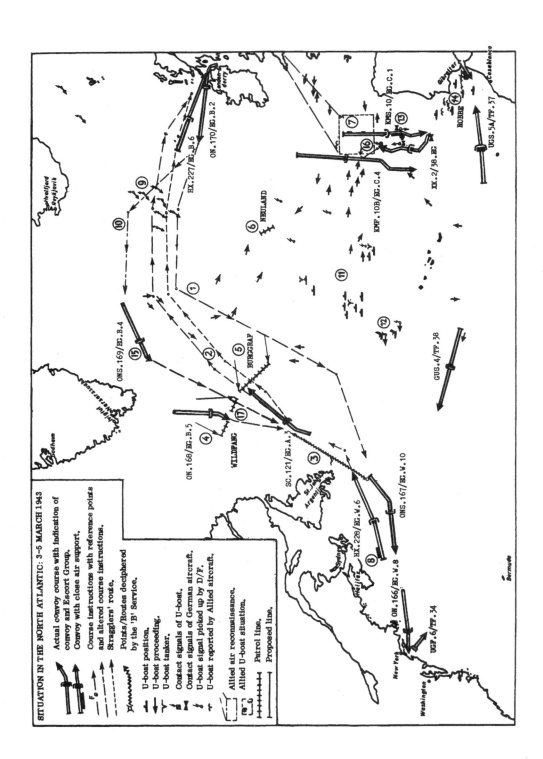

SITUATION IN THE NORTH ATLANTIC: 3-5 MARCH 1943

Actual convoy course with indication of
convoy and Escort Group.

Convoy with close air support.

Course instructions with reference points
and altered course instructions.

Stragglers' route.

Points/Routes deciphered
by the 'B' Service.

U-boat position.

U-boat proceeding.

U-boat tanker.

Contact signals of U-boat.

Contact signals of German aircraft.

U-boat signal picked up by D/F.

U-boat reported by Allied aircraft.

Allied air reconnaissance.

Allied U-boat situation.

Patrol line.

Proposed line.

The situation in the North Atlantic: Mar 3 (1200 hrs GMT) to Mar 5 (1200 hrs GMT), 1943

#	Date/Time	Event
1	Mar 3 midday	Course instructions for ON.170.
2	Mar 3 midday	Course instructions for SC.121 with stragglers' route.
3	Mar 3 midday	German 'B' service deciphers part of course instructions for SC.121.
4	Mar 3 midday	The Cdr U-boats, after the end of unsuccessful operation against ON.168, deploys operational U-boats as *Wildfang* Group and U-boats coming from the East as
5		*Burggraf* group in an angle-formed patrol line against SC.121 expected in the area on Mar 5,
6	Mar 3 afternoon	The Cdr U-boats orders formation of a new patrol line *Neuland* in the Central North Atlantic for Mar 7.
7	Mar 3 afternoon	No 19 Group RAF Coastal Command flies protective sweeps for KMS.10.
8	Mar 3 afternoon	HX.228 passes HOMP, encounters storms on Mar 5.
9	Mar 3 evening	The Cdr U-boats orders 10 boats in Iceland passage to report situation. The Allied shore-based D/F stations take bearings on the radio signals.
10	Mar 3-4 night	CINCWA orders ON.170 to take evasive action to North.
11	Mar 3-5	U-tankers *U 119*, *U 462* and *U 463* replenish combat U-boats for further operation or return journey.
12	Mar 4 morning	*U 172* and *U 515* report sinking of the independents *City of Pretoria* and *California Star*.
13	Mar 4 1030 hrs 1150	German air reconnaissance finds convoys KMS.10 and XK.2. In attacks by individual aircraft there are near-misses and unexploded hits. Outward and homeward bound U-boats in the area are given freedom to operate against the convoys. *U 87* is found by the escort of KMS.10 and sunk. CINCWA orders KMF.10B to take evasive action to the West.
14	Mar 4	Because of numerous sighting and attack reports by Allied aircraft picked up by the 'B' service, the U-boats of the *Robbe* group are permitted to move from the area off Gibraltar to the West and SW. On Mar 5 *U 445* reports GC.3 setting out from Gibraltar and is forced to submerge by the escort.
15	Mar 4 1400 hrs	ONS.169 encounters severe storm. Stragglers remain behind.
16	Mar 5 0930 hrs	*U 130* establishes contact with XK.2.
17	Mar 5 midday	ON.168, which has been delayed by the storm, passes the *Wildfang* group unobserved through a gap formed by the loss of *U 529* (unknown to German Command).

At 0930 hrs on the morning of March 5 the outward-bound *U 130* (Oblt Keller), which was operating on the basis of the air reports, made contact with XK.2 and reported it to be in BE 9764 at 1030 hrs: it was said to consist of 16–20 ships, to have a weak escort and to be proceeding on a course of 020° at 5–7 knots. With a two-hour interval the U-boat repeated its contact signals from BE 9498 and BE 9495. The signals could not be located by D/F because at this time there were only four corvettes with the convoy and they were not equipped with HF/DF. The result was that *U 130* was able, in the absence of air cover, to get forward unimpeded at the extreme limit of visibility and to submerge in the afternoon for a daylight underwater attack. At 1645 hrs Oblt Keller fired a bow salvo of four torpedoes at the starboard columns from a central position in front of the convoy and then turned to fire a stern salvo of two at the port columns. Three of the torpedoes hit the freighters *Trefusis* (5,299 tons) and *Empire Tower* (4,378 tons) in positions 61 and 71. They sank at once. The stern salvo was recognized by the merchant ships in positions 41 and 31 from the bubble tracks but No 31, the steamer *Ger-y-Bryn* (5,108 tons), and the *Fidra* (1,574 tons) were not able to take evasive action in time. The latter also sank at once; the *Ger-y-Bryn* at first remained stationary and on fire. Oblt Keller had seen the first two ships sinking with his periscope before he was compelled to submerge because No 21 had recognized him. After the convoy made an emergency turn of 45° to port, the corvettes carried out an "artichoke" operation. At 1721 hrs the *Coreopsis* contacted the U-boat at 1,500 meters with her asdic and made two depth charge attacks, each with 10 charges. Then she had to break off and close up. *U 130* was able to send its success signal one hour later. It received orders to continue its journey. The *Anchusa, Loch Arkaig* and a steamer were able to rescue the survivors.

About this time the Commander U-boats received a report from *U 445* that it had been found by the air and naval escort of an outward-bound convoy just west of Gibraltar in CG 9577 and had been shadowed for 12 hrs.

Meanwhile, further to the SE, an FW 200 had come into the vicinity of KMS.10 at 1400 hrs but was again prevented from approaching by the Catalina D/202. However, at 1830 hrs there was a sighting report from an FW 200 of *I/KG 40* from CG 4611. Of the five boats of the *Robbe* group, operating west of Gibraltar, *U 107* was the first to get to CG 8134 at 0930 hrs on the morning of March 6, but it was soon found by an aircraft deployed on a D/F beam and forced underwater. At 1400 hrs *U 410* (Oblt Fenski) encountered the convoy in CG 8511; it recognized "25 ships and several destroyers." Although at this time there were several escorts present, the U-boat was able to submerge in a favorable position and to make its daylight attack from the port beam. A torpedo hit the *Fort Paskoyac* (7,134 tons) in position 13, but the effect was so reduced by the use of the torpedo protection net that the steamer could be brought into harbor. A torpedo passed just to the stern of the *Spero* at the end of the second column and another hit the *Fort Battle River* (7,133 tons) in position 55 which sank. While the *St Croix* hunted a dubious asdic contact on the port bow, the *Shediac* with a steamer rescued the survivors of the sunken freighter. At 1520 hrs *U 410* sent its success report and tried to approach the torpedoed freighter. But it was located by the *Shediac*'s asdic at 900 meters and straddled with 10 depth charges in two approaches. Later, the U-boat was also bombed by an aircraft and sustained slight damage.

THE SC.121 AND HX.228 CONVOY BATTLES

The Allied U-boat situation maps from March 1 to 6, based on "special intelligence" and D/F locations, showed a massing of U-boat groups on the northern convoy route, their numbers climbing from 31 to 49. Between Newfoundland and Greenland there lay in wait the two groups *Burggraf* and *Wildfang* with a total of 24 boats in dog-leg patrol line for SC.121. Behind the patrol line seven more boats were lying in wait. But in the prevailing heavy storms not all the boats were apparently in their intended positions with the result that the convoy which was, to some extent, widely scattered and behind which many stragglers were following, passed the patrol line unobserved on March 5. Only at 0956 hrs on the next day did one of the boats waiting behind the patrol line, *U 405* (K.Kpt Hopmann), find the SC.121, which consisted originally of 59 ships and which was escorted by the Escort Group A 3 under Capt. Heineman, USN, with the US Coast Guard cutter *Spencer*, the US destroyer *Greer*, the Canadian corvettes *Rosthern* and *Trillium* and the British corvette *Dianthus*. The Commander U-boats deployed against this convoy the *Westmark* group comprising *U 405*, *U 409*, *U 591*, *U 230*, *U 228*, *U 566*, *U 616*, *U 448*, *U 526*, *U 634*, *U 527*, *U 659*, *U 523*, *U 709*, *U 359*, *U 332* and *U 432*. At the same time he ordered *U 229*, *U 665*, *U 641*, *U 447*, *U 190*, *U 439*, *U 530*, *U 618* and *U 642*, which were within range and which were proceeding to their new patrol line *Neuland* envisaged for March 8, to form another patrol line, *Ostmark*, on the suspected convoy route.

The contact signals from *U 405* were located by the HF/DF equipment on the *Spencer* with the result that *U 405* was driven off. However, *U 566* and *U 230* established contact in the night March 6–7. During the still stormy night and in poor visibility *U 230* (Kptlt Siegmann) was able to sink the freighter *Egyptian* without the escort or most of the ships being aware of her going down. Only the freighter *Empire Impala* stayed behind to pick up survivors. But she was hit and sunk in the morning by *U 591* (Kptlt Zetzsche). Despite wind force 10 and many snow and hail showers, *U 228*, *U 230*, *U 591*,

U 409, *U 526* and *U 634* were able to maintain contact on March 7. But it was impossible to attack in such weather. On the morning of March 8 the storm abated and visibility became variable. An attack by *U 527* (Kptlt Uhlig) failed, but *U 526* (Kptlt Möglich) sank the steamer *Guido* which had become separated from the convoy. On the evening of March 8 *U 527*, *U 591* and *U 190* (Kptlt Wintermeyer), which were pursuing the convoy, and *U 642* (Kptlt Brüning) were each able to sink one of the stragglers behind the convoy: the freighters *Fort Lamy*, *Vojvoda Putnik*, *Empire Lakeland* and *Leadgate*.

In this situation the Allied Command sought to reinforce the escort of the threatened convoy. In addition to the Coast Guard cutter *Ingham* and the US destroyer *Babbitt*, which were to pick up the Iceland part of the convoy, the cutter *Bibb*, which had set out with the British destroyer *Rockingham* to meet the Iceland part of the ONS.171 convoy, was redirected to SC.121. The three ships arrived as a reinforcement with the convoy on March 9. They were to stay with it until the danger from the U-boats subsided. On the same day the Liberators of No 120 RAF Squadron were able for the first time to provide protection for the convoy from Iceland. One of the aircraft drove off the contact-keeper *U 566*. But by nightfall, of the many boats deployed, *U 229*, *U 409*, *U 427*, *U 641*, *U 332*, *U 230*, *U 405* and *U 665* had come up. Two of them were driven off by aircraft bombs and four by depth charge attacks from the escort ships *Spencer*, *Babbitt*, *Rosthern* and *Dauphin*. The *Dauphin* was a British corvette which had joined in the meantime. Only *U 229* (Oblt Schetelig) tried an underwater daylight attack, but this failed. On the evening of March 9 *U 530* (Kptlt Lange) sank the Swedish freighter *Milos*, a straggler. In the night two U-boats, *U 409* (Oblt Massmann) and *U 405* succeeded for the first time in attacking almost simultaneously. They sank the two ships *Malantic* and *Bonneville*, when the convoy Commodore, Birnie, perished, and the tanker *Rosewood*. A good hour later *U 229* succeeded in making a successful surface attack in which the merchant ship *Nailsea Court* was sunk and the *Coulmore* damaged.

On March 10 the storm again increased to wind force 10 with the result that the attacks attempted by *U 229* and *U 616* (Oblt Koitschka) failed. *U 523* and *U 642* once again encountered stragglers but attacks were not possible owing to the weather. The last contact-keeper, *U 634*, was driven off in the afternoon. In these operations the escorts were impeded because the weather made it impossible to use the radio and radar equipment following storm damage. On March 10 welcome reinforcements reached the convoy in the form of the British corvettes *Campion* and *Mallow*. Because the convoy was approaching the North Channel the operation was broken off by the Commander U-boats early on March 11.

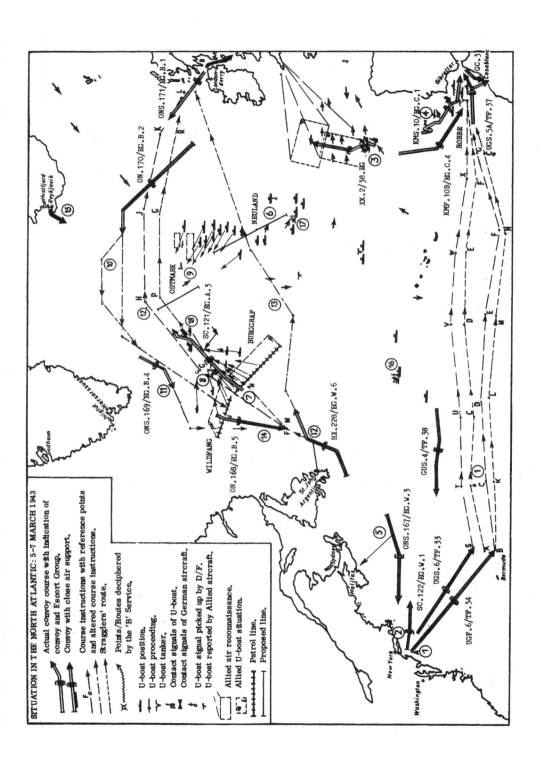

SITUATION IN THE NORTH ATLANTIC: 5-7 MARCH 1943

Actual convoy course with indication of convoy and Escort Group.

Convoy with close air support.

Course instructions with reference points and altered course instructions.

Stragglers' route.

Points/Routes deciphered by the 'B' Service.

U-boat position.

U-boat proceeding.

U-boat tanker.

Contact signals of U-boat.

Contact signals of German aircraft.

U-boat signal picked up by D/F.

U-boat reported by Allied aircraft.

Allied air reconnaissance.

Allied U-boat situation.

Patrol line.

Proposed line.

The situation in the North Atlantic: March 5 (1200 hrs GMT) to March 7 (1200 hrs GMT), 1943

1	Mar 5 midday	Port Director New York sends by radio course instructions for UGF.6 and UGS.6 with stragglers' routes.
2	Mar 5 1330 hrs	SC.122 sets out from New York. It encounters a severe storm in the night Mar 6-7, 11 stragglers, of which 2 return, 6 make for Halifax, 2 rejoin convoy and 1 missing.
3	Mar 5 1645 hrs	U 130 attacks XK.2. 4 ships sunk in one approach. On Mar 6 and 7 19 Group, RAF Coastal Command, flies protective sweeps.
4	Mar 5 1730 hrs	German air reconnaissance again reports KMS.10, but opposite course steered temporarily on orders of CINCWA causes confusion. At 0830 hrs on Mar 6 U 107 reports the convoy, but is driven off. At 1420 hrs U 410 attacks: 2 ships hit and one of them sunk.
5	Mar 5 1900 hrs	ONS.167 passes HOMP.
6	Mar 5 evening	Neuland patrol line ordered for Mar 7 to operate against convoys on Southern route.
7	Mar 5 2200 hrs	SC.121 has passed the Burggraf group unobserved in the storm. The Cdr U-boats orders Burggraf and Wildfang to proceed to NE in the night, so as not to fall behind the convoy.
8	Mar 6 0956 hrs	U 405, one of the U-boats stationed in waiting positions in the rear of Burggraf and Wildfang, reports SC.122. The Cdr U-boats deploys the 17 favourably positioned boats of these groups as the Westmark group and
9	Mar 6	orders the 10 Northern Neuland boats to form a new patrol line for March 7 on the suspected convoy route.
10	Mar 6 afternoon	On the basis of U-boat signals picked up by D/F in the area of SC.121, CINCWA orders ON.170 to take new evasive action further to the North; at the same time
11	Mar 6	COMINCH orders ONS.169, which has been delayed by the storm, to take evasive action further to the West and
12	Mar 6	HX.228 to deviate sharply to the Southern route instead of maintaining Northern course ordered in the earlier course instructions.
13	Mar 6	ON.168, which has been delayed by the storm, does not arrive at WOMP at scheduled time.
14	Mar 6	
15	Mar 6	2 escorts set out from Reykjavik as reinforcements for SC.121's screen.
16	Mar 6 2207 hrs	U 172 reports the sinking of the independent Thorstrand.
17	Mar 7 morning	U 221 reports the sinking of the independent Jamaica.
18	Mar 7 morning	The U-boats deployed against SC.121 secure first successes against stragglers in the heavy storms.

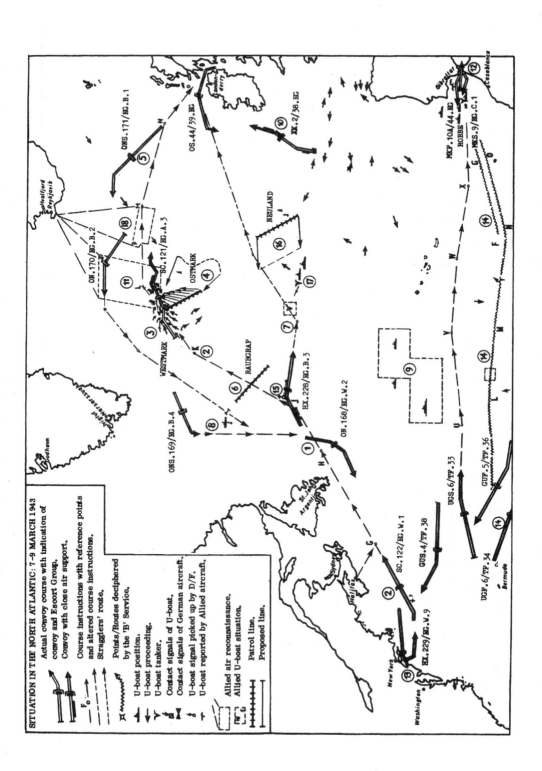

SITUATION IN THE NORTH ATLANTIC: 7-9 MARCH 1943

Actual convoy course with indication of convoy and Escort Group.

Convoy with close air support.

Course instructions with reference points and altered course instructions.

Stragglers' route.

Points/Routes deciphered by the 'B' Service.

U-boat position.

U-boat proceeding.

U-boat tanker.

Contact signals of U-boat.

Contact signals of German aircraft.

U-boat signal picked up by D/F.

U-boat reported by Allied aircraft.

Allied air reconnaissance.

Allied U-boat situation.

Patrol line.

Proposed line.

The situation in the North Atlantic: March 7 (1200 hrs GMT) to March 9 (1200 hrs GMT), 1943

1 Mar 7 — ON.168, having been delayed by the storm, passes WOMP.

2 Mar 7 — SC.122 re-forms after having been disorganised by a heavy storm. Positions G to O course instructions of SC.121.

3 Mar 7-8 — *Westmark* group shadows SC.121 in the storm. A few successes, chiefly against stragglers.

4 Mar 7 — Deployment of the *Ostmark* group against SC.121.

5 Mar 7 — CINCWA diverts ONS.171 to North because U-boats suspected to be near SC.121 and to the south of it.

6 Mar 7 — The remaining boats of the old *Wildfang* and *Burggraf* groups form a new *Raubgraf* patrol line to operate against HX.228 which, according to plotting, is expected on Mar 7

7 Mar 7 — but the convoy has already been diverted to the Southern route.

8 Mar 7 — At the western end of the *Raubgraf* patrol line *U 631* torpedoes the tanker *Empire Light* left behind from ON.168 without observing it in the bad weather. The ONS.169 proceeds further to the West.

9 Mar 7 — Waiting areas laid down for type IX boats which are scheduled to operate off the US East coast.

10 Mar 7-8 — XK.2 receives air cover from 19 Group, RAF Coastal Command.

11 Mar 8 day — No 120 Sq RAF and USN Squadron 84 from Iceland fly protective sweeps for ON.170 and SC.121. In the bad weather they are unable to drive off U-boats from SC.121. Further attacks and sinkings.

12 Mar 8 1630 hrs — German agents near Gibraltar report the departure of convoys MKS.9 and MKF.10A.

13 Mar 8 1851 hrs — Shortly before departure COMINCH orders an alteration in course instructions for HX.229.

14 Mar 9 — German 'B' Service deciphers the stragglers' route reported by radio by PD New York on Mar 5 and part of the convoy route of UGF.6. The type IX boats stationed in the waiting areas receive details of reference points to make for on the stragglers' route (Meanwhile the convoy route is altered).

15 Mar 9 — German 'B' service deciphers reference point of altered course instructions for HX.228.

16 Mar 9 — The Cdr U-boats moves *Neuland* group to North towards HX.228.

17 Mar 9 — U-tanker *U 463* reaches supply point to fuel U-boats coming from convoy operations.

18 Mar 9 — Protective sweeps by aircraft from Iceland and air cover for SC.121 make U-boat operations considerably more difficult. Several U-boats have to break off operations with bomb damage.

In the meantime convoy HX.228 had turned off to the southern route on March 7 because of the operation in the North. On March 9 the German "B" Service deciphered a position envisaged for the convoy on March 8; accordingly, the Commander U-boats moved the patrol lines formed from the remaining boats of the *Neuland* group, *U 659, U 448, U 608, U 757, U 406, U 86, U 373, U 441, U 440, U 221, U 444, U 336* and *U 590*, further to the north in front of the suspected convoy course. At midday on March 10 the most southerly boat of this group, *U 336* (Kptlt Hunger), sighted the expected HX.228. This consisted of 60 ships and was escorted by Escort Group B 3, comprising the destroyers *Harvester, Escapade, Garland* (Polish) and *Burza* (Polish), as well as the corvettes *Narcissus, Orchis, Aconit, Roselys* and *Renoncule* (the last three French). For the first time this convoy had been given a Support Group, TU 24.4.1 (or, according to British nomenclature, the 6th Escort Group). It consisted of the American escort carrier *Bogue* and the two destroyers *Belknap* and *Osmond-Ingram* under Capt. G. E. Short. This group operated with the convoy from March 5 to March 14. When there were air operations, the escort carrier, accompanied by the destroyers proceeded independently of the convoy, but in the vicinity. Once the air operations were over, the carrier slipped into the safest position, a space in the convoy between the two center columns. The two destroyers then reinforced the escort. The Commander U-boats deployed the *Neuland* group against the convoy and, in addition, the outward-bound *U 333, U 432, U 405, U 566* and *U 359*. *U 336* was located by D/F soon after it sent its contact signals and was driven off, but the next boat, *U 444* (Oblt Langfeld), came up so quickly as the second contact-keeper that several boats were able to close up in the night March 10–11. In the evening *U 221* (Oblt Trojer) sank the two freighters *Tucurinca* and *Andrew F. Luckenbach* and hit the *Lawton B. Evans* with a torpedo which failed to explode. Then *U 336, U 86* and *U 406*, and probably *U 444* also, attacked the convoy with several salvoes including FATs (pattern running torpedoes). In these attacks the American freighter *William C. Gorgas* and the British steamer *Jamaica Producer* were torpedoed and were left damaged and stationary. Later in the night *U 757*, in an attack, sank a munitions freighter, the *Brant County*, which was blown to pieces in a violent explosion, when the U-boat also suffered substantial damage. But a good hour later it was able to finish off and sink the wreck of the *William C. Gorgas*, which had remained behind. Attacks by *U 228* against the convoy and by *U 359* against a straggler were unsuccessful on the morning of March 11.

During the night *U 444* had been sighted by the *Harvester* when it tried to attack. The U-boat submerged but then had to surface after being depth

charged by the destroyer and was rammed by the destroyer at high speed. In
the process the destroyer got a propeller shaft caught up with the U-boat for
about 10 minutes. At first the destroyer lay unmaneuverable and *U 444* tried
to pull off slowly, unable to submerge. But it was located an hour later by the
French corvette *Aconit* under Lt. Levasseur, which was summoned to the
scene, and it was sunk by ramming. After repairs to her engine the *Harvester*
followed the convoy slowly but the *Aconit* closed up again quickly to
strengthen the escort. In the morning, however, the second shaft of the *Harvester* broke and the destroyer came to a standstill. Toward midday *U 432*
(Kptlt Eckhardt) approached and finished her off with a torpedo. The SOE
(Cdr. Tait) perished. The *Aconit*, which had in the meantime been called
back for help, was able with some luck, to locate the U-boat, which had withdrawn under water, with asdic and she forced it to surface with depth
charges. This boat was also sunk by gunfire and another ramming. The lost
contact with the convoy was reestablished on March 11 at midday by *U 228*
and *U 406*, but the boats were driven off, as were later also *U 359*, *U 590* and
U 405. Further attacks in the night by *U 440* and *U 590* failed. Toward morning the last contact-keeper, *U 590*, was also driven off. The deployment of
the *Bogue*, which continued until March 14, was not fully effective because
the carrier remained most of the time in the convoy on account of the great
U-boat danger and so had little freedom of movement for the launching
and landing of aircraft.

SC.122 AND HX.229: NEW YORK TO NEWFOUNDLAND
While the operations of the German U-boats continued against the convoys
SC.121 and HX.228 on the north and south route, the following three convoys started to set out.

SC.122. When the captains of the convoy SC.122 met for their conference in New York on the evening of March 4, the Port Director, New York,
announced in a first telegram dated 041800Z (1800 hrs EWT on March 4, or
2300 hrs GMT on March 4) that the convoy would leave on the next day. At
0730Z hrs (1230 hrs GMT) the convoy left New York. On the evening of
March 5 at 2130 hrs the first part of the sailing telegram was sent to the
Admiralty from the radio office of the New York Port Director. Simultaneously, the telegram was sent for information to NSHQ in Ottawa, FONF in St
John's, CTF 24 in Argentina, COMESF in Washington, CTG in Reykjavik,
NOIC (Naval Officer in Charge) in Sydney and COAC in Halifax and the
Convoy and Routing Section of COMINCH. The telegram said that the convoy would proceed in 14 columns with 2, 4, 4, 3, 4, 5, 5, 3, 3, 4, 4, 4, 3, 2
ships. The Convoy Commodore was Capt. S. N. White, RNR on the steamer

Glenapp and the Vice Commodore, F. R. Neil, the master of the freighter *Boston City*. In para 14 details were given about the ciphers which the individual ships were taking. The second part of the sailing telegram, which followed an hour later, contained the complete list of the ships in the convoy, their nationality, name, speed, cargo and destination. In addition, there were details about the guard ships for radio D/F and communication and about oilers. (The full text of the two telegrams is reproduced in Appendix 5). The convoy began its journey in the route order opposite.

For escort the convoy was given Task Unit 24.18.1, comprising the Canadian corvettes, *The Pas*, *Rimouski*, *New Westminster* and the *Bangor* class minesweeper *Blairmore*. On March 6 the convoy proceeded in an easterly direction toward the first reference point 66°30'W. The wind continued to come up in the course of the day and toward evening and in the night developed into a heavy southern storm which particularly affected the ships as they had to proceed across its path. The Greek ship *Georgios P* which was in position 65 was the first ship to fall behind at 1830 Z hrs (2330 GMT) and the next day she returned to her port of departure. At dawn on March 7 the convoy route order was upset and 11 ships were missing. Of these the *Polarland* (position 22) and *McKeesport* (141) returned to New York on March 8. The *Alcedo* (24), *Eastern Guide* (33) and *Gudvor* (34) successively put into Halifax on the same day. The next day the *Livingston* (23), *Empire Summer* (53) and *English Monarch* (123) also arrived there with some heavy damage. The *Clarissa Radcliffe* (83) apparently followed the convoy without finding it again (see p. 103), but the *Vinriver* (91) and *Kedoe* (142) were able to catch up the convoy on March 13.

In the course of March 7 the convoy re-formed in its original route order and proceeded on a course of 61° and at a speed of 6.7 knots toward the meeting point with the Halifax convoy, HSC.122, fixed for March 9. The composition of this convoy was communicated by radio to the relevant authorities by COAC at 2020 Z hrs on March 6 (0020 hrs GMT on March 7). The convoy set out from Halifax with 14 ships at 1200 Z hrs (1600 hrs GMT) on March 8. It was accompanied by the flush-deck destroyer *Leamington*, lent to the Canadian Navy, the Canadian corvette *Dunvegan* and the Canadian *Bangor* type minesweeper *Cowichan*. At 1413 Z hrs and 1415 Z hrs (1813 and 1815 hours GMT) COAC sent the sailing telegram for HSC.122.

At 2000 hrs on March 7 the Commodore of SC.122 reported his evening position at 40°36'N 66°23'W, course 61°, speed 7 knots with 11 stragglers.

At 1500 hrs on March 8 there followed a further report giving the position as 41°29'N 64°37'W with a speed of 6.7 knots. These details helped the convoy HSC.122 to determine correctly the meeting point for March 9.

Route order for convoy SC.122 on leaving New York on March 5, 1943

Tactical number, nationality, type, name, destination.

			12 brit MS *Asbjörn* Halifax	11 pan MT *Permian* Halifax
	24 pan SS *Alcedo* Reykjavik	23 brit SS *Livingston* St. John's	22 norw SS *Polarland* St. John's	21 brit S/Wh *Sevilla* St. John's
	34 norw SS *Gudvor* Reykjavik	33 amer SS *Eastern Guide* Reykjavik	32 amer SS *Cartago* Reykjavik	31 norw SS *Askepot* Reykjavik
		43 brit SS *Carso* Loch Ewe	42 isl SS *Godafoss* Reykjavik	41 pan SS *Granville* Reykjavik
	54 swed SS *Atland* Loch Ewe	53 brit SS *Empire Summer* Loch Ewe	52 brit SS *King Gruffydd* Loch Ewe	51 brit SS *Kingsbury* Loch Ewe
65 greek SS *Georgis P* Clyde	64 brit ST *Beacon Oil* Clyde	63 brit MS *Innesmoor* Loch Ewe	62 brit ST *Empire Galahad* United Kingdom	61 dutch SS *Alderamin* Loch Ewe
75 brit SS *Aymeric* Loch Ewe	74 brit SS *Baron Elgin* Loch Ewe	73 brit SS *Bridgepool* Loch Ewe	72 brit MT *Christian Holm* United Kingdom	71 brit SS *Baron Stranraer* Loch Ewe
		83 brit SS *Clarissa Radcliffe* Loch Ewe	82 brit MT *Benedick* Clyde	81 brit MS *Glenapp* Mersey
		93 brit SS *Orminister* Loch Ewe	92 brit SS *Historian* Mersey	91 brit SS *Vinriver* Clyde
	104 amer LST *LST 365* United Kingdom	103 brit SS *Filleigh* Mersey	102 brit ST *Gloxinia* Mersey	101 brit MS *Losada* Mersey
	114 amer LST *LST 305* United Kingdom	113 brit SS *Boston City* Belfast	112 brit ST *Shirvan* Belfast	111 brit SS *Empire Dunstan* Mersey
	124 brit SS *Fort Cedar Lake* Belfast	123 brit SS *English Monarch* Belfast	122 amer MT *Vistula* Belfast	121 brit SS *Dolius* Belfast
		133 pan SS *Bonita* United Kingdom	132 greek SS *Carras* Belfast	131 brit SS *Baron Semple* Belfast
			142 dutch MS *Kedoe* Belfast	141 amer SS *McKeesport* United Kingdom

Convoy Commodore: 81 *Glenapp*
Vice Commodore: 113 *Boston City*
Escort Oiler: 82 *Benedick*
Standby Oiler: 72 *Christian Holm*

Western Local Escort South
Task Unit (TU) 24.18.1
Corvette HMCS *The Pas*
Corvette HMCS *Rimouski*
Corvette HMCS *New Westminster*
M/Sweeper HMCS *Blairmore*

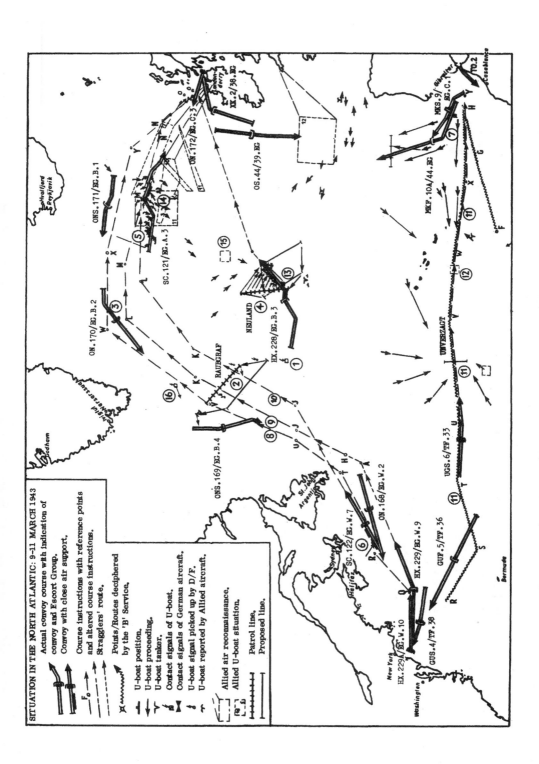

SITUATION IN THE NORTH ATLANTIC: 9-11 MARCH 1943

Actual convoy course with indication of convoy and Escort Group.

Convoy with close air support.

Course instructions with reference points and altered course instructions.

Stragglers' route.

Points/Routes deciphered by the 'B' Service.

U-boat position.

U-boat proceeding.

U-boat tanker.

Contact signals of U-boat.

Contact signals of German aircraft.

U-boat signal picked up by D/F.

U-boat reported by Allied aircraft.

Allied air reconnaissance.

Allied U-boat situation.

Patrol line.

Proposed line.

The situation in the North Atlantic: March 9 (1200 hrs GMT) to March 11 (1200 hrs GMT), 1943

1	Mar 9	The reference point for HX.228's evasive route, deciphered by the German 'B' Service, shows that an operation with the *Raubgraf* group is longer possible.
2	Mar 9	Accordingly the Cdr U-boats orders the patrol to proceed northwards to meet ON.170 expected on March 10.
3	Mar 9	The convoy is, however, delayed by storms.
4	Mar 9	Simultaneously, the Cdr U-boats moves the *Neuland* group to the North on to the direct route from the deciphered reference point to the North Channel.
5	Mar 9-10	The *Westmark* and *Ostmark* groups continue the operation against SC.121 in spite of the reinforcing of the naval escort. After the air cover has left, 3 U-boats attack repeatedly in the night. 4 ships from the convoy and a straggler are sunk.
6	Mar 9 1800 hrs	SC.122 passes HOMP. 2 ships are detached. The feeder convoy HSC.122, comprising 14 ships, is met. The Local Escort Group is relieved.
7	Mar 9 1900 hrs	*U 107* reports MKF.10A, but cannot keep contact owing to its high speed and is driven off. The remaining boats of the *Robbe* group are withdrawn from the area off Gibraltar, which is closely covered from the air, and are stationed in another patrol in front of the expected course of MKS.9 and MKF.10A.
8	Mar 9	Original course instructions for HX.229A.
9	Mar 9	Original course instructions for HX.229.
10	Mar 9	Original course instructions for SC.122.
11	Mar 10	'B' Service deciphers the course instructions for UGS.6 on Mar 4 with the stragglers' route. The boats concentrating on an area earlier deciphered on the stragglers' route of UGF.6 are assembled in a *Unverzagt* patrol line on the slower and so more promising UGS.6 route. It is expected to pass on Mar 12.
12	Mar 10	Simultaneously, the Type IX operational boats further to the East are deployed against an area of the deciphered route of UGS.6, south of the Azores.
13	Mar 10 1235 hrs	*U 336*, stationed at the South end of the *Neuland* group, which has been moved to the North, reports HX.228. The Cdr U-boats deploys the *Neuland* group which closes up in the course of the afternoon. In the night 6 boats attack and sink 4 ships. 2 others attack stragglers in the morning. *U 444* is sunk by Escort Group B.3. *U 432* sinks the damaged leader *Harvester* but is then sunk by the French corvette *Aconit*.
14	Mar 10-11	Reinforced naval and air escort and protective sweeps by 15 Group, RAF Coastal Command increasingly drive off the U-boats from SC.121. The Cdr U-boats orders the operation to be broken off on Mar 11 and the boats proceed westwards.
15	Mar 11	The Cdr U-boats indicates an area for a new formation for the operational boats coming from SC.121 and those which are outward-bound.
16	Mar 11 early	The 'B' Service deciphers a (false) reference point for ONS.169 on Mar 9 which hove to in the storm. On the basis of the course details, the Cdr U-boats orders the *Raubgraf* group westwards. But ONS.169 has already passed to the west of the formation. In the patrol line the U-boats report independent stragglers from ONS.168 and ONS.169.

At 1200 Z hrs (1600 hrs GMT) on March 9 the two ships from SC.122, destined for Halifax, *Permian* (11) and *Asbjörn* (12) were detached with the escorts *The Pas* and *Blairmore*. They arrived at their destination the next day. At 1500 Z hrs (1900 hrs GMT) the convoy HSC.122 with the Western Local North Escort Group (WLN), TU 24.18.7, already mentioned, reached the main convoy. The 14 steamers were distributed in the various positions which had become vacant and, after being re-formed, the SC.122 adopted the route order opposite.

The reported position at 1900 hrs in the evening put the convoy at 43°08'N 60°33'W, course 60°, speed 7 knots. At 60°16'W the course was to be altered to 62°. The position of the part convoy was also given in this report.

THE HX.229 AND HX.229A

In the meantime the convoy HX.229 had also left New York. At 1704 Z hrs (2204 hrs GMT) on March 4 COMESF had issued general course instructions for the convoy. At 2046 Z hrs on March 7 (0146 hrs GMT on March 8) the New York Port Director sent his preparatory signal for the convoy and, after the convoy conference, the first part of the sailing telegram came at 0914 Z hrs on March 8 (1414 hrs GMT) and the second part at 2240 Z hrs (0340 hrs GMT) in similar outward form to that of SC.122. At 2300 Z hrs (0400 hrs GMT) on March 9 the HX.229 left New York with 40 ships. It proceeded in 11 columns of 3, 3, 4, 3, 4, 4, 4, 4, 4, 4, 3, ships. The Convoy Commodore was Commodore M. J. D. Mayall, RNR, on the Norwegian freighter *Abraham Lincoln*, the Vice-Commodore R. J. Parry, Master of the freighter *Clan Matheson*. The convoy's route order was as shown overleaf.

The Western Local South Escort Group (WLS) was formed by TU 14.18.9 with the destroyer *Chelsea*, which was lent to the Canadian Navy, the new American destroyer *Kendrick* and the Canadian corvettes *Fredericton* and *Oakville*.

Before the convoy HX.229 left New York the Convoy and Routing Section of COMINCH had ordered a change of course at 1851 hrs on March 8. From point B at 40°15'N 66°00'W the convoy was to proceed on a course of 70°and, leaving out points F and G, was to make for a point A at 44°15'N 51°30'W, SW of Cape Race. From there it was to proceed on the new course of 28°. With this course it was intended to avoid the oncoming convoy ON.168 and save distance and time. In addition, the interval between it and the following convoy HX.229A was to be somewhat increased. In the meantime the convoy's conference had taken place and this convoy set out at 0830 Z hrs (1330 hrs GMT) on March 9 from New York with 39 ships.

TABLE No. 2

Route order for Convoy SC.122 after meeting the feeder convoy HSC.122 at 1900 hrs GMT on March 9 until March 12

			12 icel SS *Sellfoss* Reykjavik	11 icel SS *Fjallfoss* Reykjavik
				21 brit SWh *Sevilla* St. John's
			32 amer SS *Cartago* Reykjavik	31 norw SS *Askepot* Reykjavik
45 yugo SS *Franka* Loch Ewe	44 brit SS *Carso* Loch Ewe	43 icel SS *Godafoss* Reykjavik	42 brit SS *Ogmore Castle* Loch Ewe	41 pan SS *Granville* Reykjavik
55 dutch SS *Parkhaven* Loch Ewe	54 swed SS *Atland* Loch Ewe	53 brit SS *Baron Semple* Belfast?	52 brit SS *King Gruffydd* Loch Ewe	51 brit SS *Kingsbury* Loch Ewe
65 brit SS *Drakepool* Loch Ewe	64 brit ST *Beaconoil* Clyde	63 brit MS *Innesmoor* Loch Ewe	62 brit ST *Empire Galahad* United Kingdom	61 dutch SS *Alderamin* Loch Ewe
75 brit SS *Aymeric* Loch Ewe	74 brit SS *Baron Elgin* Loch Ewe	73 brit SS *Bridgepool* Loch Ewe	72 brit ST *Christian Holm* United Kingdom	71 brit SS *Baron Stranraer* Loch Ewe
85 brit SS *P.L.M. 13* Loch Ewe	84 brit SS *Zouave* Loch Ewe	83 *straggler*	82 brit MT *Benedick* Clyde	81 brit MS *Glenapp* Mersey
95 brit Resc *Zamalek* Greenock	94 brit SS *Orminister* Loch Ewe	93 brit SS *Historian* Mersey	92 brit SS *Port Auckland* Mersey	91 *straggler*
105 amer LST *LST 365* United Kingdom	104 brit SS *Badjestan* Glasgow	103 brit SS *Filleigh* Mersey	102 brit ST *Gloxinia* Mersey	101 brit MS *Losada* Mersey
115 amer LST *LST 305* United Kingdom	114 swed SS *Porjus* Mersey	113 brit SS *Boston City* Belfast	112 brit ST *Shirvan* Belfast	111 brit SS *Empire Dunstan* Mersey
	124 brit SS *Fort Cedar Lake* Belfast	123 pan SS *Bonita* United Kingdom	122 amer ST *Vistula* Belfast	121 brit SS *Dolius* Belfast
		133 brit SS *Helencrest* Mersey	132 greek SS *Carras* Belfast	131 brit SS *Empire Morn* Belfast
			142 *straggler*	

Convoy Commodore:	81 *Glenapp*
Vice Commodore:	113 *Boston City*
Escort Oiler:	82 *Benedick*
Standby Oiler:	72 *Christian Holm*

Western Local North Escort Group
Task Unit 24.18.7
Destroyer HMS *Leamington*
Corvette HMCS *Dunvegan*
M/Sweeper HMCS *Cowichan*
Corvette HMCS *Rimouski*
Corvette HMCS *New Westminster*

TABLE No. 3

Route order for Convoy HX.229
on leaving New York on March 8, 1943

	13 brit SS *Empire Knight* Clyde	12 amer SS *Robert Howe* Mersey	11 brit SS *Cape Breton* Clyde
	23 amer SS *Stephen C. Foster* Mersey	22 amer SS *William Eustis* Clyde	21 amer SS *Walter Q. Gresham* Clyde
34 amer SS *Mathew Lucken-* *bach* United Kingdom	33 brit MS *Canadian Star* United Kingdom	32 brit MS *Kaipara* Mersey	31 brit SS *Fort Anne* Loch Ewe
	43 brit MS *Antar* Mersey	42 brit MT *Regent Panther* United Kingdom	41 brit SS *Nebraska* Mersey
54 brit SS *Empire Cavalier* Mersey	53 amer ST *Pan Rhode Island* Mersey	52 brit MT *San Veronica* Mersey	51 pan MT *Belgian Gulf* Mersey
64 amer SS *Kofresi* Mersey	63 amer SS *Jean* Mersey	62 amer ST *Gulf Disc* Clyde	61 norw MS *Abraham Lincoln* Belfast
74 amer SS *Margaret Lykes* Mersey	73 pan SS *El Mundo* Mersey	72 brit SWh *Southern Princess* Clyde	71 brit SS *City of Agra* Mersey
84 brit SS *Tekoa* Mersey	83 brit MT *Nicania* Mersey	82 brit SS *Coracero* Mersey	81 amer SS *Irenee du Pont* Mersey
94 amer SS *James Oglethorpe* Mersey	93 dutch MT *Magdala* Belfast	92 brit SS *Nariva* Mersey	91 brit SS *Clan Matheson* Loch Ewe
104 dutch SS *Terkoelei* Belfast	103 dutch SS *Zaanland* Belfast	102 brit MT *Luculus* Belfast	101 norw SS *Elin K.* Belfast
	113 amer SS *Hugh Williamson* Belfast	112 amer SS *Daniel Webster* Belfast	111 amer SS *Harry Luckenbach* United Kingdom

Convoy Commodore: 61 *Abraham Lincoln*
Vice Commodore: 91 *Clan Matheson*
Escort Oiler: 62 *Gulf Disc*
Standby Oiler: 72 *Southern Princess*

Western Local Escort South + North
Task Unit 24.18.9
Destroyer HMS   *Chelsea*
Destroyer USS   *Kendrick*
Corvette   HMCS *Fredericton*
Corvette   HMCS *Oakville*

Planned Route Order:
11 *Empire Knight*; 12 *Cape Breton*; 13 *Robert Howe*; 42 *Iris* (joined HX.229A);
43 *Empire Barrie* (not joined); 44 *Antar*

The WLS Escort Group was formed from the US flushdeck destroyer *Cowie*, the Canadian corvette *Snowberry* and the Canadian *Bangor* type minesweepers *Noranda* and *Digby*.

As the HX.229 had no ships with it destined for Halifax or St John's, it could continue its journey at 9.5 to 10 knots without waiting. On the afternoon of March 10 the steamer *Clan Matheson*, proceeding in position 91, experienced difficulties and could not maintain the convoy's speed. The Captain had to ask the Commodore to release the ship because of her inadequate speed and at 2000 hrs GMT he turned away to Halifax in order to join a slow convoy later. It therefore became necessary to appoint a new Vice-Commodore. The merchant ship *Nariva* moved up to position 91 and took over this role.

THE PROBLEMS OF THE OCEAN ESCORT GROUPS

The Ocean Escort Groups B 5 and B 4, earmarked for convoys SC.122 and HX.229, which were proceeding with ON.168 and ONS.169 on the northerly route, would have normally been relieved at WOMP on about March 4 and March 7. But the orders given to the two convoys by CINCWA on the evening of February 23 after heavy attacks on ON.166, to make wide diversions to the north, almost to Cape Farewell, had lengthened their journeys by two and three days respectively. Severe southwest storms on February 27–28 had held up the two convoys, several ships had remained behind and various escorts had suffered damage, particularly to their asdic equipment. When the weather temporarily abated most of the stragglers were able to close up again in the next few days. On March 1 Escort Group B 5 was able to drive off two U-boats by the skillful use of HF/DF before their contact signals were able to bring up other boats of the *Neuland* group (cf. p. 48). But in the case of ON.168 the weather made it impossible for the escorts to be refueled from the two tankers *Laurelwood* and *Melime*, whose equipment was still inadequate. On March 4 the wind again increased to a SW force 6–7. Several ships, some of which had their ballast badly stowed to cope with the sea, experienced difficulties. Four of them remained behind, including the tanker *Empire Light*, for the second time. In the evening the corvette *Buttercup* remained behind with heavy storm damage. About midday on March 5 the SOE, Cdr. Boyle, had to turn away with the *Havelock*, to look for her. At first, Cdr. Luther on the *Volunteer* took over his role. In the meantime the corvettes *Saxifrage* and *Lavender*, whose fuel states had reached the critical limit, had also to be sent to St John's. A little later the frigate *Swale*, whose asdic was not working, was sent after them as escort.

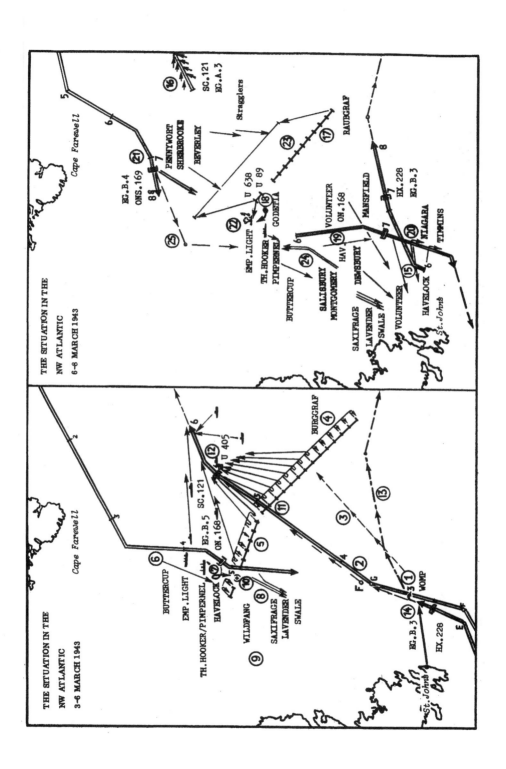

THE SITUATION IN THE
NW ATLANTIC
3-6 MARCH 1943

Cape Farewell

THE SITUATION IN THE
NW ATLANTIC
6-8 MARCH 1943

Cape Farewell

The situation in the NW Atlantic: March 3-6, 1943

1	Mar 3	SC.121 passes WOMP. Escort relieved by Ocean Escort Group A.3.
2	Mar 3	Original course instruction for SC.121 via F — G.
3	Mar 3	'B' Service deciphers former course instructions for SC.121.
4	Mar 3	*Burgraf* group receives orders to wait for SC.121 on Mar 5.
5	Mar 3	*Wildfang* group and U-boats stationed to rear also await SC.121.
6	Mar 4	ON.168 is again held up by freshening SW storms force 6-7. Corvette *Buttercup*, tanker *Empire Light* and freighter *Thomas Hooker* stay behind with storm damage.
7	Mar 4	Leader of Escort Group B.5, *Havelock*, looks for *Buttercup*. Corvette *Pimpernel* dispatched to help *Thomas Hooker*.
8	Mar 4	The corvettes *Saxifrage* and *Lavender* are released because of lack of fuel and proceed to St John's, accompanied by the frigate *Swale*.
9	Mar 5	The storm increases to SW force 9.
10	Mar 5	ON.168 passes *Wildfang* patrol line in gap resulting from loss of *U 529* (unknown to Germans).
11	Mar 5	SC.121 passes *Burggraf* patrol line unobserved in storm.
12	Mar 6	*U 405* reports SC.121. The Cdr U-boats deploys the favourably stationed *Burggraf* and *Wildfang* boats for attack.
13	Mar 6	COMINCH diverts HX.228 to Southern route where radio picture shows operation against SC.121.
14	Mar 6	Ocean Escort Group B 3 takes over HX.228 at WOMP.

The situation in NW Atlantic: Mar 6-8, 1943

15	Mar 6	HX.228 proceeds on evasive course as instructed.
16	Mar 6	*Wildfang* and *Raubgraf* groups continue pursuit of SC.121 as *Westmark* group.
17	Mar 6	The remaining boats of the two groups form the new *Raubgraf* group against HX.228 expected on Mar 7.
18	Mar 6	Corvette *Godetia* is detached from ON.168 to help the *Thomas Hooker* which is breaking up. She encounters *U 89* on the way, but it is soon lost in the bad weather.
19	Mar 6	Destroyer *Volunteer* is now only escort with ON.168. Leader *Havelock* tries to close up. Rescue ship *Dewsbury* is released with heavy storm damage. 10 stragglers to stern of convoy. Western Local Escort Group does not find the convoy. Destroyer *Mansfield*, coming from SC.121, passes.
20	Mar 7	After improvement in weather, there are again 35 ships with the convoy. *Havelock* and *Volunteer* are relieved by destroyer *Niagara* and corvette *Timmins* of Local Escort Group.
21	Mar 6-7	ONS.169, likewise delayed by heavy storm, has 5 stragglers. Destroyer *Beverley*, corvettes *Pennywort* and *Sherbrooke* are detached owing to lack of fuel on Mar 6. Storm SW 11.
22	Mar 7	*U 638* attacks damaged *Empire Light* but does not observe torpedo hit obtained in heavy sea.
23	Mar 8	*Raubgraf* group moved somewhat to N.
24	Mar 8	To expedite relief of Escort Group B 4, required for HX.229 and to reinforce escort for ONS.169, weakened by detachments, a Support Group, comprising the destroyers *Salisbury* and *Montgomery*, are sent to the convoy.
25	Mar 8	ONS.169 is ordered as far West as possible to avoid the *U 89* and *U 638* respectively sighted and located by D/F.

However, ON.168, which then had only three escorts, had luck. It passed the slowly approaching patrol line of the *Wildfang* group where *U 529*, which had been sunk on February 15, and whose loss was still unknown, should have been stationed. About the same time *U 405* reported convoy SC.121 200 miles further east. The Commander U-boats at once deployed against it the 18 boats of the *Wildfang* and *Raubgraf* group which were situated nearest. He ordered the other 13 boats to form a new patrol line for the morning of March 7 in the center of the previous one.

The storm increased to force 9 in the night March 5–6. The American freighter *Thomas Hooker* developed cracks in her side and had to heave to, screened by the corvette *Pimpernel*, which was to take the crew off if necessary. When a report was received on the morning of March 6 that the freighter was in danger of breaking up, the last corvette, *Godetia*, was ordered by Cdr. Boyle to go to the damaged ship. On the way she had a brief encounter with a U-boat which was trying to reach its new position. The *Volunteer* was now on her own with the remaining 28 ships of the convoy, which were trying to keep on course in very extended formation. Ten stragglers followed astern. The rescue ship *Dewsbury* also had to leave the convoy with heavy storm damage. The WLN Group, TU 24.18.2, with the part convoy WON.168 waited in vain at WOMP. At 1615 hrs the convoy proceeded on its own to Halifax with the minesweeper *Medicine Hat*, while the rest of the group, comprising the destroyer *Niagara* and the corvettes *Buctouche*, *Timmins* and *Trail*, continued the search. The *Volunteer*'s efforts to bring up the group and the leader *Havelock* with D/F bearings were not successful. On the morning of March 7 several stragglers found the convoy again when the wind abated. The Commodore, Adm. Sir C. G. Ramsey, could now count 35 ships. In the morning the destroyer *Mansfield* was sighted coming from SC.121, but her fuel was only sufficient to reach St John's. Eventually, at 1230 hrs, Cdr. Boyle and the *Havelock* found the convoy again so that the *Volunteer* which was also very low in oil, could go to St John's. At 2100 hrs the *Niagara* at last arrived and was able to relieve the *Havelock*. Three hours later the corvette *Timmins* joined the escort, but the other two vessels of the WLN Escort Group, the *Trail* and *Buctouche*, only arrived on the morning of March 9 to give the convoy again a complete escort group. The vessels of Escort Group B 5 arrived one after the other in St John's during March 8 and the morning of March 9. The last to arrive were the *Pimpernel* with the survivors of the *Thomas Hooker* and the *Godetia* which had remained with the ship until the evening of March 7 when she seemed to break up. The group had only two to three days to recover from the storm, to repair damage and to prepare its departure for SC.122.

The situation was even more difficult in the case of Escort Group B 4 with ONS.169. The convoy, which had set out with 37 ships under the command of Commodore J. Powell, had encountered a severe SW storm on February 27–28 and had to head into wind at slow speed. When on February 28 the wind suddenly veered to the NW, the ships were in such trouble that the leader of the Escort Group, the destroyer *Highlander* (Cdr. E. C. L. Day, RN), damaged her asdic dome. After a brief pause, when the corvettes *Anemone*, *Abelia* and *Sherbrooke*, were able to replenish their supplies from the tankers *British Lady* and *Acme*, bad weather again set in on March 3 before the corvette *Pennywort* and the destroyers *Beverley* and *Highlander* had time to refuel. In the night March 3–4 the wind reached storm force. Until midday on March 9 a series of storms passed over the convoy. In the heavy seas the ships repeatedly had to heave to. On March 6 five ships lost contact and on March 9 a further one. The average speed of the convoy was only 3.4 knots instead of about 7 knots. On March 6 the destroyer *Beverley* was the first escort to be sent to St John's because of lack of fuel. She was followed by the corvettes *Pennywort* and *Sherbrooke* on March 7 when there was a force 11 wind. On the evening of the same day the tanker *Empire Light*, which had been left behind by ON.168 because she was damaged, reported that she had been torpedoed and needed help. It is very probable that this was the attack on a 5,000-ton freighter reported by *U 638* on the same day (see p. 95).

When the distress signal was received FONF in St John's sent the American tug *Tenacity* to help. But she did not arrive before March 9. As the corvettes *Pimpernel* and *Godetia*, which had at first remained in the vicinity of the damaged freighter *Thomas Hooker*, had meanwhile gone off to the south, the *Pennywort* which had been detached from ON.169, received orders to go to the damaged *Empire Light* to provide support. But she only got to the drifting tanker at 1900 hrs on March 9 and reported her position as 470 miles NNE of St John's. Because of her limited fuel supplies the *Pennywort* could not stay long. In consequence, the corvette *Clematis* from the escort group of the following convoy, ON.170, was detached to bring the tanker into port with the *Tenacity*.

Although ONS.169's position report at 1000 hrs on March 9 showed that the convoy was still further behind than expected and had virtually hoved to with a speed of 2 knots, it was necessary to divert it further to the west round the dangerous U-boat positions after *Godetia* had reported an attack on this course and after the report of the torpedoing of the *Empire Light* and the locating by D/F of *U 638*'s signal. This inevitably reduced the already very limited time which the Escort Group B 4 had before it was to set out for the next convoy. If the group was to set sail from St John's on March

13, as planned, so as to meet HX.229 at WOMP on the following day, the ships had to reach harbor by March 11 at the latest, to have at least two days for the urgently required rest and the repairs which could no longer be put off. But as the Western Local Escort Group, 24.18.5, earmarked for the relief, could not leave St John's before March 10, FONF sent to the convoy the Support Group 24.12.2, comprising the two available destroyers *Salisbury* and *Montgomery*. They were ordered to proceed on the route used by ON.168 in order to drive off any U-boats following the convoy. They reached the convoy on the morning of March 9. This meant that Cdr. Day with his leader *Highlander*, whose asdic dome needed to be repaired before setting out, could hand over his task as SOE to the Commander of the corvette, *Anemone*, Lt. King, and proceed ahead to St John's. There were now four escorts with the convoy, including the two destroyers and the corvette *Abelia*.

In the night March 9–10 the rescue ship *Gothland*, which was in the convoy, located with her HF/DF a number of German U-boat messages on bearings of 060°–123° but they were clearly not on ground wave and so were at some distance. The weather improved on the morning of March 10 and toward midday an American Catalina flying boat came to the convoy as air cover. But the convoy then entered the drifting ice fields NNE of Newfoundland with the occasional dangerous iceberg; in consequence, the Commodore had to order the convoy to head further to the east. Fortunately for the convoy, it had already passed the reconnaissance patrol line of the *Raubgraf* group, which lay further to the east and was proceeding slowly northward. When the *Salisbury*, whose asdic had been put out of order, owing to damage by ice, requested permission to proceed to St John's, the SOE, Lt. King, declined the request, because he had noticed at daybreak that this vessel also had a HF/DF mast and he did not want to forgo this useful aid in detecting U-boats. In fact, the *Gothland* and the *Salisbury* again intercepted U-boat signals on bearings of 047°–070° in the night March 10–11. They probably came from *U 621* at the SE end of the *Raubgraf* line.

The Western Local North Escort Group, 24.18.5, comprising the minesweeper *Granby* (SOE, Lt. Cdr. Davis, RCNR) and the corvettes *Matapedia* and *Chicoutimi*, waited in vain at the meeting point on the morning of March 11, because ONS.169 had changed course. Now the two HF/DF pieces of equipment proved very useful in bringing up the group with D/F bearings. At 2000 hrs the TU 28.18.5 reached the convoy and relieved the *Anemone* which at 2300 hrs proceeded to St John's. The *Abelia* had to stay with the convoy until dawn, as she had to accompany the rescue ship and a ship damaged by ice to St John's. The leader of TU 28.18.5, the destroyer *Hamilton*, after urgent repairs, was only able to leave St John's on March 12 and met ONS.169 on March 13.

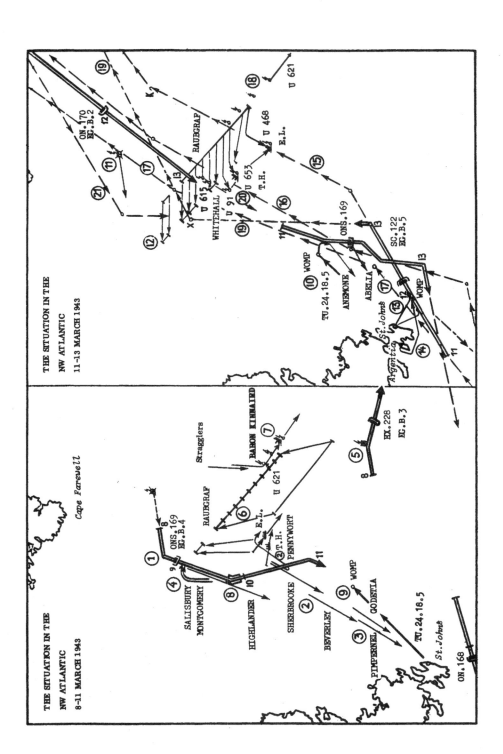

THE SITUATION IN THE
NW ATLANTIC
8-11 MARCH 1943

THE SITUATION IN THE
NW ATLANTIC
11-13 MARCH 1943

The situation in the NW Atlantic: March 8-11, 1943

1	Mar 8-9	ONS.169 has hove to in the storm with reduced Escort Group B 5.
2	Mar 8-9	From the escorts detached from ONS.169 the corvette *Pennywort* is sent to the damaged *Thomas Hooker* whose crew is taken on by the corvette *Pimpernel*.
3	Mar 9	The last escorts of Group B 5 from ONS.168 arrive in St John's.
4	Mar 9	The Support Group, TU 24.12.2, comprising the *Salisbury* and *Montgomery*, reaches ONS.169. The leader of E.G.B 4, destroyer *Havelock*, has damaged asdic, and hands over command to corvette *Anemone* and proceeds ahead to St John's.
5	Mar 9	'B' service deciphers new reference point of evasive route of HX.228, which has been passed on Mar 8.
6	Mar 9	As operation against HX.228 with *Raubgraf* group no longer possible, the group is moved further to the North in order to be deployed against ON.170, expected on Mar 10.
7	Mar 10	*U 621* reports an independent, the straggler *Baron Kinnaird* from ON.168. It shadows her on Mar 11 and sinks her on Mar 12 after several failures. A number of radio signals.
8	Mar 10	Rescue ship *Gothland* with ONS.169 picks up messages from *U 621* but treats them as 'sky-wave'. The convoy has to take SSE course owing to ice-fields. It receives air cover.
9	Mar 11	The Western Local Escort Group, TU 24.18.5, does not find ONS.169 at WOMP which has been moved to the North.

The situation in the NW Atlantic: March 11-13, 1943

10	Mar 11	TU.24.18.5 waits at WOMP and meets ONS.169 late in evening. The corvette *Anemone* is relieved. The last corvette of Group B 4, *Abelia*, stays until the morning of March 12 to escort the rescue ship *Gothland*.
11	Mar 11	'B' Service deciphers a (false) passing point of ONS.169 on Mar 9.
12	Mar 11	The Cdr U-boats moves the *Raubgraf* group to the West to catch ONS.169, but latter is already far to south.
13	Mar 12	SC.122 meets feeder convoy at WOMP; Escort Group B 5 takes over escort.
14	Mar 12	US destroyer *Upshur* is allocated to SC.122 as additional escort.
15	Mar 12	Course instructions for SC.122.
16	Mar 12	Course instructions for HX.229.
17	Mar 12	Course instructions for HX.229A.
18	Mar 12	After sinking of *Baron Kinnaird*, *U 621* proceeds to supply point.
19	Mar 12	COMINCH orders an evasive course to the West for SC.122 at 1416 hrs because *U 621*'s signals have been picked up on its course.
20	Mar 12-13	*U 615* and *U 91* report sighting the corvette *Clematis* which has gone to help the *Thomas Hooker* and the tug *Tenacity* as well as the destroyer *Whitehall*, detached from ON.170. *U 653* sinks the drifting wreck of the *Thomas Hooker*. *U 468* sinks the damaged tanker *Empire Light*.
21	Mar 12	Because of the *Raubgraf* group's radio traffic, COMINCH orders an evasive course for ON.170 further to the West. Also decides to divert the convoys SC.122 and HX.229 south of the detected U-boat formations.

The vessels of Escort Group B 4 came into St John's singly one after the other. The *Beverley* was the first to arrive on the morning of March 11, followed by the *Sherbrooke* at midday and the *Highlander* at 2210 hrs in the evening. The *Pennywort*, the *Anemone* and, finally, the *Abelia* came in the course of March 12. The *Highlander*, whose asdic dome had come apart, and which had a large leak to be sealed under the fuse magazine, had to go into dock before she undertook a new mission. The same applied to the *Sherbrooke* which had put in with storm damage. As the authorities had to make the best use of the limited dock space available, it was decided to put both ships together in dock. This caused delays. The two ships could not enter dock before 1300 hrs GMT on March 13 and they did not leave dock until 2200 hrs on March 15.

CTF 24 realized on March 8 that the Local Escort Group could not hand over HX.229 to the Ocean Escort Group at the prescribed time. Since the destroyer leader of the WLN Group, the *Chelsea*, was a "short-leg" destroyer, her sister ship, the *Annapolis*, received orders on the evening of the same day to set out from Halifax at 2300 hrs on March 10 and to relieve the *Chelsea* at 1700 hrs on March 11. To make up a little time HX.229 received orders for a new change of course at 1416 hrs on March 12. It was to continue to proceed on a course of 070° as far as longitude 50°W and only then to make for the prescribed reference point J on a new course of 019°.

Because HX.229, despite the slight delay thus caused, would pass WOMP at the latest on March 14, because the relieving Ocean Escort Group B 4 had at this time no vessel equipped with HF/DF and because the convoy had no rescue ship so equipped, FONF, Commodore H. E. Reid, RCN, decided to allocate the destroyer *Volunteer* from Escort Group B 5, as a temporary leader of Escort Group B 4 for HX.229 for the crossing of the next convoy pair.

On the evening of March 11 SC.122 approached Cape Race which was passed at a distance of only 30 miles. In the meantime a merchant ship, the *Reaveley*, intended for this convoy, had set out escorted by the corvette *Saxifrage*, from St John's, at 1330 hrs. Half an hour later the Escort Group B 5 followed it, comprising the *Havelock*, *Swale*, *Buttercup*, *Lavender*, *Pimpernel* and *Godetia* and the attached A/S trawler *Campobello*. On the morning of March 12 SC.122 reached WOMP. At 0730 hrs the British whaling depot ship *Sevilla* was sent to St John's with two corvettes of the WLN Escort Group. Two hours later the Escort Group B 5 reached the convoy and relieved the WLN Escort Group, 24.18.7. Another half an hour later the ore-carrier *PLM 13* had to ask to go to St John's because of boiler trouble. Finally, at 1000 hrs the *Reaveley* reached the convoy with the *Saxifrage*. The convoy then proceeded in its final formation. At 1128 hrs the American destroyer *Upshur* joined as additional escort. It was to accompany the convoy as far as ICOMP and then to escort the ships destined for Iceland to Reykjavik.

TABLE No. 4

**Route Order for Convoy HX.229A
after relief of WLN Escort on
March 15, 1943**

14 pan SS *Alcedo* Reykjavik	13 dutch MT *Regina* Loch Ewe	12 dutch SS *Ganymedes* Loch Ewe	11 brit MS *Belgian Airman* Reykjavik
24 brit SS *Manchester Trader* Manchester	23 brit SS *Bothnia* Loch Ewe	22 brit MS *Taybank* Mersey	21 brit SS *Fort Drew* Loch Ewe
34 brit SS *Fresno Star* Belfast	33 amer SS *Michigan* ?	32 brit SS *Tudor Star* Manchester	31 brit SS *Akaroa* Belfast
44 brit SS *Tortuguero* Belfast	43 pan SS *North King* ?	42 brit MT *Daphnella* Belfast	41 amer ST *Pan Florida* Loch Ewe
54 amer SS *Lone Star* Belfast	53 brit SS *Empire Airman* Mersey	52 pan MT *Orville Harden* Clyde	51 brit SS *Esperance Bay* Mersey
64 brit SS *Port Melbourne* Clyde	63 brit MT *Clausina* Belfast	62 amer ST *Esso Baytown* Belfast	61 amer ST *Pan Maine* Mersey
74 brit SS *Arabian Prince* Mersey	73 pan MS *Rosemont* Mersey	72 brit SS *Empire Nugget* Belfast	71 amer ST *Socony Vacuum* Manchester
84 brit MS *Lossie Bank* Mersey	83 amer SS *Henry S. Grove* Mersey	82 brit SS *City of Oran* Clyde	81 brit SWh *Svend Foyn* ?
94 brit SS *Norwegian* Clyde	93 brit SS *Tactician* Clyde	92 brit MS *Tahsinia* Mersey	91 amer SS *John Fiske* Manchester

Convoy Commodore: 51 *Esperance Bay*	*Ocean Escort Group*
Vice Commodore: 81 *Svend Foyn*	40th Escort Group
Escort Oiler: 52 *Orville Harden*	Sloop HMS *Aberdeen*
Standby Oiler: ?	Cutter HMS *Lulworth*
	Cutter HMS *Landguard* (joined later)
	Frigate HMS *Moyola*
	Frigate HMS *Waveney*
	Sloop HMS *Hastings*

New York to Halifax:
11 brit S/S *Fort Amherst*; 12 amer S/T *Esso Baltimore*; 22 brit S/S *Iris*; 23 pan M/T *Esso Belgium*; .. amer S/S *Shickshinny*; .. amer S/S *Pierre Soule*.
New York to St. John's:
32 amer S/S *Fairfax*.
Halifax to St. John's:
22 brit S/S *Lady Rodney*.

On March 12 HX.229 proceeded on its course of 070° without any particular incident. The *Chelsea*, which had at first stayed with the convoy, turned away in the evening for St John's.

On this day convoy ON.168 and HX.229A, which was passing just to the north of it, met on the latitude of St John's. The ships from HX.229A destined for Halifax, the two tankers *Esso Baltimore* and *Esso Belgium*, and the freighters *Fort Amherst* and *Iris* and the ships of ON.169 were released in the company of the Canadian corvettes *Snowberry* and *Barrie* and the minesweepers *Gananoque* and *Digby*. At the same time the Halifax part of HX.229A, consisting of the 14 ships *Bothnia, Manchester Trader, Taybank, Fresno Star, Tudor Star, Lady Rodney, City of Oran, Akaroa, Norwegian, Alcedo, Tarsinia, Lossiebank, Arabian Prince* and *Rosemont* with the WLN Escort Group, the destroyer *St Clair*, the corvettes *The Pas* and *Kamsack* and the minesweeper *Blairmore* met the convoy. In the night of March 12 the convoy encountered fog in the area of Sable Isle when the two merchant ships *Shickshinny* and *Pierre Soule* lost contact with the convoy and had to turn back to Halifax. In the convoy *Lady Rodney* was destined for St John's; the remainder adopted the route order overleaf after March 15.

CHAPTER 6

The Gibraltar Convoy Routes

Apart from the three North Atlantic convoys, another two large convoys left New York on March 4 and March 5 for Casablanca, Gibraltar and Oran. The preparations for these convoys were similar to those already mentioned. At 2240 Z hrs (0340 GMT) on March 3 a radio message from the New York Port Director announced the departure of UGS.6 for the following day at 1800 Z hrs (2300 GMT) and informed the relevant authorities of the course instructions and the stragglers' route. At 1948 Z hrs and 0030 Z hrs the two parts of the sailing telegram came with details of the route order for the 45 ships of the convoy, their names, cargoes and destinations. At 0050 Z hrs and 1538 Z hrs on March 5 and at 0156 Z hrs on March 6 the corresponding radio messages went out for the fast convoy UGF.6, which consisted of 22 ships.

The faster convoy with the troop transports was not only escorted by the usual destroyer screen. It also had heavy naval ships with it, as was usually the case with such troop convoys. Task Force 34 consisted of the old battleship *New York*, the cruiser *Brooklyn* and the destroyers *Buck*, *Woolsey*, *Ludlow*, *Edison*, *Wilkes*, *Swanson*, *Roe*, *Bristol* and *Nicholson*. The slow UGS.6 with its freighters of war material was escorted by Task Force 33, comprising the destroyers *Wainwright*, *Mayrant*, *Rowan*, *Rhind*, *Trippe*, *Champlin* and *Hobby*.

On March 7 there occurred one of those accidents to which ships sometimes fell victim without enemy intervention. Despite good visibility the independent Norwegian freighter *Tamesis*, which had already been located over 18,000 meters away by the new SGR radar on the *Hobby*, crossed the convoy route and could not be prevented from ramming the *Alcoa Guard*, the leading ship in the port column. The result was that the *Tamesis* sank and the *Alcoa Guard* was badly damaged and left stationary. A ship had to remain behind to pick up survivors and a tug, which was summoned, brought the damaged ship to Bermuda on March 14. The UGS.6 continued its journey with two ships less.

At a time when both convoys were still far to the west the German "B" Service had on March 8 deciphered the first two messages about the imminent departure of the convoy UGS.6 on March 4 and UGF.6 on March 5–6.

On March 9 the decoded route instructions for the UGF.6 were available: it was to proceed in eight columns with 3, 3, 3, 3, 3, 3, 3, 2 ships, escorted by Task Force 34, consisting of 12 American warships, at 13.5 knots. Twelve of the reference points were known: (Z) the swept channel off New York (F) 32°20'N 24°40'W, (G) 34°30'N 15°30'W, (H) 35°28'N 09°50'W and (J) 34°01'N 07°59'W and the points on the stragglers' route (K) 32°59'N 53°52'W, (L) 33°18'N 44°20'W, (M) 32°46'N 34°30'W, (N) 31°40'N 24°45'W, (0) 33°54'N 15°25'W, (P) 34°35'N 09°50'W, (Q) 34°01'N 07°50'W. The names of 12 of the ships with some of the numbers of troops embarked on the transports could be decoded.

On March 10 the corresponding details about UGS.6 were also decoded and laid before the Commander U-boats. According to these, this convoy was proceeding in 12 columns with 2, 3, 3, 5, 5, 4, 5, 5, 4, 2, 2 ships. It was due to be at point (Z) at 1900 hrs on March 4, at (R) 37°15'N 67°05'W at 1000 hrs on March 6 and then to proceed via the following points: (S) 34°30'N 61°50'W, (T) 35°45'N 54°30'W, (U) unknown, (V) 35°45'N 35°40'W, (W) 36°15'N 27°01'W. The following points were ascertained for the stragglers' route: (A) 33°40'N 61°59'W, (B) 34°56'N 54°30'W, (C) 34°45'N 46°20'W, (D) 35°50'N 35°45'W, (E) 35°30'N 27°02'W, (F) 34°20'N 18°30'W, (G) 35°10'N 09°55'W and (H) 34°04'N 08°01'W.

On the basis of these precise "B" reports, the Commander U-boats decided to try once more to conduct a group operation in mid-ocean. On March 9 six boats, which were waiting for the signal to proceed to the US coast, were deployed as the *Unverzagt* group against the point which it was calculated that UGF.6 would pass on March 12. When the course instructions for UGS.6 were received on the following day the Commander U-boats decided, instead of operating against the fast convoy, to operate against this slower one with which the U-boats could more easily maintain contact. Accordingly, the *Unverzagt* boats *U 130, U 515, U 172, U 513, U 106* and *U 167* received orders to take up a patrol line from square CD 8381 to DF 2221 with a course of 270° and a speed of five knots by 0800 hrs on March 12. The boats were told not to take up their positions earlier than instructed and to maintain strict radio silence before contacting the enemy in order not to compromise the patrol line. The following U-boats *U 159, U 67, U 109, U 521, U 524* and *U 103*, were ordered to make for a point in CE 86 to form a second patrol line *Wohlgemut* on March 13 on the convoy course SW of the Azores.

In the meantime, however, the Allied shore-based D/F stations had located various German U-boat signals in the area of the Azores. On March 4 *U 515* and *U 172* had sunk two independents, the refrigerator ships *California Star* and *City of Pretoria*, NW of the islands. On the evening before, D/F bearings had appeared to indicate a U-boat in the vicinity of the westbound convoy GUS.4 (escort: Task Force 38) SW of the Azores. This was probably a report from *U 513*. On March 6 *U 172* had reported the sinking of another Norwegian freighter, the *Thorstrand*. On March 8 *U 130*, which was proceeding westward, reported an air attack and a sound bearing of a northbound convoy. Then on March 10 *U 180*, which was taking the Indian freedom-fighter Subhas Chandra Bose to a meeting point with a Japanese submarine in the Indian Ocean, sent a message in answer to a question about how long its passage would last from the area SW of the Azores. These located U-boat positions prompted COMINCH to order UGF.6 to take evasive action to the south. It was hoped to get UGS.6 through on the original course between the U-boats located NW and SW of the Azores.

THE UGS.6 CONVOY BATTLE

On March 12 the Commander U-boats ordered the *Unverzagt* group to turn back with the patrol line at 2100 hrs, if by then it had established no contact, and to proceed on a course of 090° at 8 knots during the night to prevent the expected UGS.6 passing in the dark. The *Wohlgemut* group received orders to take up a patrol line at 0800 hrs on March 14 on the known route south of the Azores from CE 8272 to CE 8878. But shortly before the *Unverzagt* group turned, *U 130* (Oblt Keller) sighted a destroyer with UGS.6 at the north end of the patrol line at about the expected time. At 1741 hrs it sent its first contact signal in CD 8256. At 1900 hrs Oblt Keller reported the convoy itself in CD 8272 on a course of 075° and proceeding at 7–8 knots.

The Commander U-boats at once deployed the *Unverzagt* group and the *Wohlgemut*, which was waiting further eastward, at high speed against the convoy and ordered *U 130* to attack only when another U-boat had established contact. At 2200 hrs *U 130* again reported the convoy in CD 8258 on a course of 080° and proceeding at 8 knots. About the same time the nearest U-boat, *U 515*, asked for D/F bearings from the contact-keeper. Then *U 130* started to send D/F signals and prepared to attack.

The situation in this convoy differed in two respects from that in the north. None of the American destroyers was yet equipped with HF/DF. They therefore could not locate the contact signals of the German U-boats and were dependent on information from shore-based D/F stations. These very quickly identified by cross bearings the U-boat signals as contact signals with convoy UGS.6. The result was that COMINCH ordered the convoy to take evasive action to the north, although the order only arrived at noon on the following day. Although the SOE, Capt. Wellborn, on the *Wainwright*, could not locate the messages from the U-boats with the convoy, his destroyers were equipped with the most modern radar of the type SG, SC and FD and the QC projector, whose range considerably exceeded that of the British 271 M. With this ships could be located in calm seas up to about 20,000 meters and U-boats up to about 10,000 meters.

Thus it was that *U 130* was located by the *Champlin*'s radar at a range of 3,700 meters as it approached at 2350 hrs. Lt. Cdr. Melsom ordered the destroyer to turn on to the radar target at high speed. Eight minutes later the U-boat was sighted at a distance of 1,800 meters from its phosphorescent wake and fire was opened with the two forward 5-inch guns. Oblt Keller, who had at first tried to escape on the surface, decided too late to submerge. The *Champlin* was hardly 150 meters away when the stern of *U 130* disappeared under the water. The destroyer dropped two depth charges where the boat had submerged. By 0358 hrs the stricken U-boat was destroyed by four further depth charges. However, the large oil patch, indicating success, was only seen at 0845 hrs when it became light.

U 172, which had seen the *Champlin*'s star shells and heard the depth charge detonations, reported at 0400 hrs that it had been forced to submerge by a destroyer in CD 8316 and had been straddled with depth charges. Contact was lost for the time being.

The Commander U-boats proposed to establish a patrol line for March 14 with all the boats with a view to catching the convoy. But before his order was issued, *U 513* (Kptlt Guggenberger) again reported contact at 1130 hrs on March 13 in CD 9111. The boat was able to maintain contact until 1826 hrs in CD 6795 and bring up again *U 167* and *U 172*. But all three were again driven off by the destroyers' offensive sorties before dusk. *U 172* (Kptlt Emmermann) encountered at 2232 hrs in the evening, in the course of the pursuit, an independent freighter, the American *Keystone* (5,565 tons), which was proceeding as a straggler 50 miles behind the convoy and was not, as ordered, taking the stragglers' route further to the south. She was sunk. After contact had again been lost, the Commander U-boats ordered a patrol line to be formed for 0800 hrs on March 14 from CD 6385 through CE 4743 to CE 7414. He hoped thus to be able to catch any evasive movements just west of the Azores, either to the north or south of the islands. He also ordered the *Tümmler* group, comprising *U 521*, *U 504*, *U 43*, *U 66*, *U 202* and *U 558*, which was operating in the area of the Canary Islands, to be deployed against what was regarded as the very important UGS.6 convoy.

At 0810 hrs on the morning of March 14 *U 513* first reported several clouds of smoke in CE 4476 and then was able to maintain contact with the convoy through CE 4464 and CE 4274 as far as CE 4273 at 1849 hrs. *U 167* and *U 106* were the first to approach the convoy. The U-boats received instructions to try to get ahead and only keep loose contact with the convoy so as to be able to make an attack, as simultaneously as possible, when darkness approached. Apart from the three boats mentioned, *U 515*, *U 524* and *U 172* also approached the vicinity.

The Commodore, who was on board the freighter *Chiwawa* at the head of the seventh column, tried to shake off the U-boats by various changes of course. But contact was only lost when Capt. Wellborn ordered the destroyers shortly before dark to make quick sweeps on both sides from bow to stern. *U 513* was driven off to the south and *U 167* to the west. The Commander U-boats at once ordered the boats to try to close up. At 0140 hrs *U 515* (Kptlt Henke) found the convoy, but when it first tried to attack it was again located by the destroyers' radar and had, according to its last report, at 0315 hrs, to submerge. It was damaged by depth charges, but in the morning Kptlt Henke was able to continue the operation despite the damage. It was apparent from the U-boats' report that they had all been prematurely detected in their attempts to attack and had been driven off by the offensive action of the escorts. In order not to withdraw any of the boats which might still be in a favorable position, no new patrol line was ordered for March 15. But the boats were informed that the convoy apparently intended to go round north of the Azores and proceed to Gibraltar.

When it became light, at 0829 hrs, on March 15, *U 524* (Kptlt von Steinaecker) sighted smoke clouds from the convoy in CE 5132 and maintained contact, through CE 5223 at 1348 hrs and CE 5236 at 1507 hrs, as far as CE 5326 at 2000 hrs. It reported the convoy to consist of over 40 passenger-freighters and tankers and to be provided with a strong close and distant escort. On the basis of its reports, *U 172*, *U 521*, *U 167*, *U 159*, *U 67* and *U 109* approached the convoy, but again they were generally located by the escorts' radar before they were in a position to attack and were driven off by the distant escort. *U 159* (Kptlt Witte) tried to make a daylight underwater attack but was unable to fire because of a sudden sharp change of course on the part of the convoy. In the afternoon COMINCH had informed the SOE that at least four U-boats were in contact with the convoy. Capt. Wellborn ordered the destroyers *Hobby* and *Mayrant* to make quick sorties up to 10 miles to the sides of the convoy before dusk.

Before the approach of dusk *U 524* had reached a favorable forward position and managed to infiltrate into the convoy submerged. It was detected by the *Wainwright* with sonar at 2030 hrs but Capt. Wellborn, who was in front of the convoy, could not long keep up with the quickly lost contact and went back to his position. In this way Kptlt von Steinaecker was able to fire at a distance of only 600 meters and hit the freighter *Wyoming* (8,062 tons) with two torpedoes with the result that she sank at once. The *Champlin* was diverted to rescue the survivors, while the *Hobby* screened her. At 0140 hrs the *Hobby* established radar contact at 8,300 meters but this time the boat escaped on the surface from the destroyer whose star shells apparently impeded her own vision.

On March 16 *U 106* (Kptlt Rasch) found the convoy again in CF 6269. Shortly after, there were contact signals from *U 103* and *U 558*. Contact was maintained until the following morning at 0738 hrs in CF 4694. In the course of the day and following night *U 202, U 521, U 167, U 66, U 504* and *U 524* also came up. Once again most of the boats were prematurely detected by radar when they tried to attack and were forced to withdraw. However, the attempt that evening to make a simultaneous attack with several boats shortly after dusk was more successful. At 1940 hrs in CF 4515 *U 524* and *U 172* approached in quick succession under water and delivered their salvoes with only an 8-minute interval. The torpedoes from *U 524* just missed their targets, but *U 172*, which had aimed at two passenger freighters and two ordinary freighters totaling 30,000 tons, thought it had heard six of its own torpedo detonations and four from the other boats and the sound of four ships sinking, as a result of its own torpedoes, and three other ships. In fact, however, only the American freighter *Benjamin Harrison* (7,171 tons) received a hit and sank. In the case of the other detonations, it was probably depth charges which the destroyer *Rhind* dropped at this time against *U 524*. It had been located by sonar after the destroyer had only just avoided the boat's torpedoes. The attack was also observed by *U 103* which reported torpedo detonations and star shells. Toward morning at 0637 hrs *U 558* (Kptlt Krech) fired a salvo of two against the convoy in CF 4694 and thought it heard detonations, but this attack evidently went unnoticed.

On March 17 the U-boats kept loose contact with the clouds of smoke which had been reported in CF 5496 at 1200 hrs and tried again to approach. Some of the commanders tried to maintain contact by using their search receivers with which they could intercept the radar impulses of the escort. *U 558, U 167, U 524, U 202, U 521, U 504, U 106* and *U 103* reported in turn that they were with the convoy. Again the boats were to try to make joint attacks at dusk. But on that afternoon the first Catalina flying boats from Morocco reached the convoy in CF 59 at 1600 hrs. As a result of the deployment of the air escort most of the boats dropped to the stern. Only *U 167* (K.Kpt Sturm) was able to make its dusk underwater attack at 1934 hrs. From the salvo of four torpedoes fired at great distance from the port quarter, one hit the American freighter *Molly Pitcher* (7,200 tons) in the bows. *U 167* escaped undetected by the *Rowan's* search. The damaged freighter was finished off the next morning at 0500 hrs by *U 521* (Kptlt Bargsten). Another unsuccessful attack on the convoy by *U 558* at 0538 hrs in CF 6719 was again undetected.

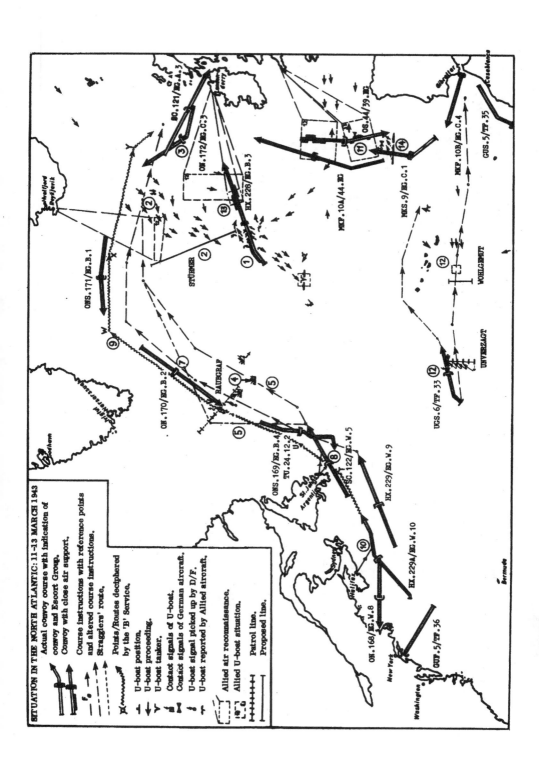

SITUATION IN THE NORTH ATLANTIC: 11–13 MARCH 1943

Actual convoy course with indication of convoy and Escort Group.

Convoy with close air support.

Course instructions with reference points and altered course instructions.

Stragglers' route.

Points/Routes deciphered by the 'B' Service.

U-boat position.

U-boat proceeding.

U-boat tanker.

Contact signals of U-boat.

Contact signals of German aircraft.

U-boat signal picked up by D/F.

U-boat reported by Allied aircraft.

Allied air reconnaissance.

Allied U-boat situation.

Patrol line.

Proposed line.

The situation in the North Atlantic: March 11 (1200 hrs GMT) to March 13 (1200 hrs GMT), 1943

No.	Date	Event
1	Mar 11 afternoon	The air cover provided by 15 Group, RAF Coastal Command to the limit of its range prevents the *Neuland* group from manoeuvring into a forward position. Only 3 U-boats make unsuccessful attacks against stragglers. U-boats that are damaged and short of fuel go to the U-tankers *U 463* and *U 119*.
2	Mar 11 afternoon	After breaking off the operation against SC.121, the U-boats with adequate fuel supplies together with the outward-bound boats are ordered, on the basis of their situation and success reports, to form a new *Stürmer* patrol line for Mar 15 to intercept HX.229 expected then.
3	Mar 11	Because the U-boats with SC.121, whose signals are picked up by D/F, move to the West and SW, CINCWA orders ON.172 to take an evasive course to the north of the suspected U-boats.
4	Mar 11-12	5 boats of the *Raubgraf* group report the sinking of 3 independents and the sighting of more escort ships (stragglers from ON.168 and 169).
5	Mar 12 1416 hrs	As the messages picked up by D/F are on the course allocated to SC.121, this convoy is ordered by COMINCH to take evasive action to the west of the U-boats.
7	Mar 12	ON.170 is not able to avoid the U-boat formation because of the escort's shortage of fuel.
8	Mar 12	SC.122 passes WOMP according to plan. Escort Group B 5 takes over the screening. ONS. 169 is delayed in reaching WOMP: the result is that EG B 4, earmarked for HX.229, has very little time in port.
9	Mar 12	German 'B' Service deciphers the course instructions for HX.229A of Mar 4 but attributes them to HX.229 (this was the first A convoy to appear in the HX series for some time). The Cdr U-boats proposes to operate against this convoy expected on Mar 16 with the *Raubgraf* group.
10	Mar 12	HX.229A passes HOMP.
11	Mar 12	German air reconnaissance finds OS.44 which gets close cover and protective sweeps from 19 Group, RAF Coastal Command on Mar 12 and 13. The Cdr U-boats deploys the 3 remaining boats of the *Robbe* group against OS.44.
12	Mar 12	The expected UGS.6 is found by the northern boat of the *Unverzagt* group. The evasive action north of the Azores ordered when U-boats were detected south of the Azores was not enough. The Cdr U-boats deploys the *Unverzagt* group. The *Wohlgemut* group forms a patrol line further east on the deciphered (but no longer valid) course. *U 130* is found and sunk by the Escort Group.
13	Mar 12-13	Air cover and protective sweeps provided by 15 Group, RAF Coastal Command and the aircraft of the US escort carrier *Bogue* which accompanies the convoy with the 6th Support Group make a further advance with HX.228 impossible. The Cdr U-boats breaks off the operation at dawn on Mar 13.
14	Mar 13 0930 hrs	German air reconnaissance finds MKS.9. Favourably stationed homeward and outward bound U-boats are given freedom to operate against it.

On the morning of March 18 the air escort was soon deployed again. Nevertheless, *U 524*, which had reestablished contact at 0700 hrs, followed the convoy at a distance of about 25 miles and continually sent signals. It also kept in contact with the easily recognizable flying boats of the air escort, whose frequent sorties it was able to avoid, in the good visibility, by submerging. In these circumstances it was no longer possible to get near the convoy. After *U 524* had reported the last sound bearing at 2200 hrs in CF 9345, the Commander U-boats decided to break off the operation on the morning of March 19 because the boats were exhausted after the uninterrupted six-day pursuit of the convoy and they were running an additional risk with the air escort without any corresponding chance of success. At 1030 hrs on March 19 the last signal from the convoy came from CG 7286.

The seven destroyers of Task Force 33, which were equipped with efficient radar, had been able to prevent all surface night attacks in the calm sea which favored radar location. Captain Wellborn had also largely frustrated the attempts to make joint underwater attacks at dusk by sorties in the afternoon and substantial changes of course by the convoy. The sonar equipment was not, however, efficient enough wholly to prevent the underwater infiltration of the U-boats into the convoy or to find U-boats after underwater attacks. The loss of *U 130* was largely the result of the faulty tactical procedure of the Commander who would have had a good chance of escaping had he submerged in time.

THE OPERATIONS ON THE BRITISH–GIBRALTAR ROUTE

While these planned operations were going on on the USA–Gibraltar route, there were individual encounters between U-boats and convoys on the British–Gibraltar route, where radio intelligence and air reconnaissance also played some part.

At 1630 hrs on March 8 the German agents opposite Gibraltar observed the departure of a convoy, comprising 23 steamers, 11 transports and nine escorts. Soon after, the "B" Service was able to decode the departure report and identify the convoy as the MKS.9. This convoy consisted of 56 ships in all and was escorted by the Escort Group C 1 (Lt. Cdr. Dobson RCNR). This comprised the Canadian destroyer *St Croix* and the Canadian corvettes *Shediac*, *Battleford*, *Kenogami* and *Napanee*. In addition, it had a Support Group comprising the Canadian corvettes *Baddeck*, *Regina* and *Prescott* and the minesweepers *Qualicum*, *Wedgeport* and *Fort York*. In accordance with previous experience the Germans calculated that this convoy would proceed at 7.5 knots via CG 8550 and CG 8150.

The next day the German "B" Service established that a second convoy, MKF.10A, had followed MKS.9 after a one-hour interval. It consisted of six ships and was escorted by Escort Group 44 (Cdr. Farquhar, RN). The latter comprised the sloops *Egret, Erne* and *Fishguard* and the new frigate *Test.* The three Hunt destroyers *Wheatland, Calpe* and *Holcombe* were deployed as a Support Group.

The remaining boats of the *Robbe* group had been in the area west of Gibraltar for 10 days. Generally these four boats had so little fuel that no major operations could be undertaken with them. They therefore received orders to leave the strongly air-patrolled area off Gibraltar and to form an extended patrol line with *U 445, U 103, U 410* and *U 107* further north from CF 35 to CG 15, so as possibly to catch the Gibraltar traffic. At 1700 hrs on March 9 *U 107* reported a convoy in CG 8185 proceeding westward at 12 knots: it was evidently the MKF.10A. But despite a search of northern and northwestern courses, the boat lost contact with the result that it had to break off further pursuit at midnight. Decoded sighting reports from Gibraltar-based aircraft indicated that the other boats also could not reach the convoys.

On March 12 the two northbound convoys had to come within the range of German air reconnaissance west of the Bay of Biscay. In addition, the German "B" Service reported on that day that the convoy OS.44 would be in CG 1521 at 1026 hrs on a course of 145° and proceeding at eight knots. This convoy had set out with 48 ships on March 5. It was escorted by Escort Group 39 (Cdr. H. V. King, RN), which comprised the sloops *Rochester, Scarborough* and *Fleetwood* and the corvettes *Balsam, Coltsfoot, Spirea* and *Mignonette.* In view of this, the Air Commander Atlantic was requested to provide air reconnaissance. At 0830 hrs the first aircraft reported a northbound convoy of 32 ships and nine escorts in BE 9728. The same convoy was located at 1431 hrs by the "B" Service at 41°30'N 15°05'W on a course of 022° and proceeding at eight knots, when it reported German aircraft. It was the convoy MKS.9. In addition, the German "B" Service picked up a similar report on the same day from the convoy OS.44 using the code name "Mangle." It reported at 1115 hrs from 45°06'N 14°03'W that it was on a course of 169° and proceeding at eight knots. At 1350 hrs, at 44°45'N 13°38'W, it reported seeing German aircraft. The convoy was reported by the German aircraft to be in BE 9284 on a course of 160° and to consist of 47 steamers and six escorts. This convoy seemed to be the most worthwhile target and so the remaining *Robbe* boats, *U 445, U 410* and *U 107*, were deployed against it in the afternoon.

In the night March 12–13 *U 107* (Kptlt Gelhaus) was the first to make contact. But at first it sent no signal. The convoy, which was proceeding in eleven columns, had no screen ahead. The corvettes *Mignonette* and *Coltsfoot* were 2 miles ahead to port and starboard respectively. Between them was a gap of 7.5 miles. In the force 4 sea Kptlt Gelhaus could get into a good firing position on the surface on the starboard side between the convoy and the sloop *Fleetwood* some 2.5 miles on the starboard beam. He could not be picked up by the radar equipment which was blinded by the wave echoes nor could he be seen by the human eye despite visibility of 5 miles. *U 107* at first fired off a salvo of four torpedoes from the bow tubes at 0438 hrs, then turned and fired a stern salvo of two. All six torpedoes hit. At first, the freighters *Clan Alpine* (5,442 tons), *Oporto* (2,352 tons) and *Marcella* (4,592 tons) in positions 84, 74 and 64 were hit successively, then the *Sembilangan* (4,990 tons) in position 92. As he submerged, Kptlt Gelhaus could see three of the ships sinking: the fourth followed shortly after. The SOE on the sloop *Rochester* to the stern of the convoy at once ordered the "half-raspberry" operation. The escorts already mentioned, the *Spirea* on the starboard quarter, the *Scarborough* on the port quarter and the *Balsam* on the port beam closed up on the convoy and began to fire star shells at 0452 hrs. As she approached, the *Rochester* obtained asdic contact and attacked it with 10 depth charges. But it was probably the sinking wreck of the *Oporto*. Ten minutes later the *Spirea* also obtained asdic contact, but she was not ready to attack. *U 107* let the apparent pursuit pass over it. After nearly an hour the noises faded and most of the escorts had closed up again to the convoy. The *Scarborough* and *Spirea* had stopped in the area of the wreckages to rescue survivors. In the morning the U-boat could surface and report its success.

Meanwhile, on the morning of March 13 German air reconnaissance had again been launched against both convoys. The "B" Service was able at 0910 hrs to put MKS.9 in 43°52'N 14°57'W and at 1020 hrs to put OS.44 in 41°58'N 13°28'W, when they gave their reports about the sighting of the German reconnaissance aircraft. At 2300 hrs in the evening, on the basis of these reports, *U 410* also came into the area of the convoy in CG 1943, but it was located and bombed by the night air escort of the convoy before it could make an attack. As a result of the explosions, the attack periscope was put out of order and the boat could no longer proceed at top speed. It had to break off the operation. *U 445* failed to reach the convoy.

U 107 continued the pursuit of the convoy and again established contact in CG 4639 at about 1100 hrs. But shortly after reporting it was located by an aircraft and forced to submerge. All efforts to surface again quickly and to get forward were frustrated by the air escorts. The boat reported that on the day before it had found in the area of the attack lifeboats and wreckage from what were probably three sunken merchant ships. After *U 107* had been driven off and there was no more contact, the three U-boats received orders to return to their previous attack areas and to operate there until their fuel was exhausted.

On March 14 the German "B" Service again intercepted a report from MKS.9 about an aircraft contact from BE 6498. But there were now no U-boats within range to be deployed against the convoys. As a result the following convoys, which set out in the period March 12–15, were not molested. They included the MKF.10 with four ships which set out from Gibraltar at 1900 hrs on March 12. This was escorted by Escort Group C 4 (Cdr. G. N. Brewer, RN), comprising the British destroyer *Churchill*, the Canadian destroyer *Restigouche*, the Canadian corvettes *Amherst*, *Brandon* and *Collingwood*, and the British corvette *Celandine*.

Although it was not possible to organize any major operations on this route, a single U-boat had succeeded in firing with all its tubes and obtaining an unusually high percentage of hits.

CHAPTER 7

The Search and Evasive Actions up to March 16

THE MOVEMENTS OF THE GERMAN U-BOATS MARCH 7–12

In the Central North Atlantic the convoy battles against SC.121 were fought with the *Westmark* and *Ostmark* groups and HX.228 with the *Neuland* group. Northeast of Newfoundland the *Raubgraf* group operated. It had been formed on the orders of the Commander U-boats on March 6 (p. 73) from the boats of the old *Burggraf* and *Wildfang* groups which had not operated against SC.121. On March 7 *U 638*, *U 89*, *U 529* (whose loss on February 15 was not yet known), *U 758*, *U 664*, *U 84*, *U 615*, *U 435*, *U 603*, *U 91*, *U 653*, *U 621*, *U 600* and *U 468* were to form a patrol line from AJ 5982 to AJ 7775 against HX.228 which was expected on that day on the northern route behind SC.121 after plotting the convoy timetable.

But, in fact, HX.228 had been diverted by COMINCH to a southern route, when the authorities learned of the start of the U-boat attack on SC.121. ON.168, coming from the north, at the same time passed the *Wildfang* patrol line, which was still intact, just where there was a gap caused by the loss of *U 529* and the deployment of the next boat, *U 432*, against SC.121.

On March 7 *U 638*, which was at the NW end of the new *Raubgraf* line in AJ 5897, sighted an independent freighter of 5,000–6,000 tons proceeding on a WSW course. The ship appeared to be altering speed sharply. Shortly after *U 638* fired a salvo of three torpedoes at 1820 hrs, the ship seemed to stop. Kptlt Bernbeck then fired another single torpedo. It, too, failed to hit but in the boat the crew heard three loud and several lesser detonations which were thought to be deterrent bombs or gunfire. Shortly after, the steamer appeared to turn away and picked up speed. The U-boat reported the attack with the addition "regard U-boat trap as possible," Actually, it must have been the *Empire Light* which was possibly proceeding at irregular speed because of the damage she had sustained (see p. 76). She reported a torpedo hit at 1839 hrs. In the severe storm and heavy seas the U-boat was apparently unable to establish the identity of the ship or whether she was hit.

On March 9 the German "B" Service was able to decode a position report from convoy HX.228 for 1900 hrs on March 8: 49°37'N 39°41'W and a speed of nine knots. Although the course could not be decoded, the position was already too far to the SE for an operation with the *Raubgraf* group, if, as was now assumed, the convoy was on a more southerly route. Accordingly, the *Neuland* group, which was stationed further east, was moved and it located the convoy on March 10 (see p. 63). The *Raubgraf* group received orders to set off in a patrol line at 1900 hrs on March 9 on a course of 345° and at a speed of six knots: it was meant to catch the ON.170 which was expected in this area on March 10, after calculating the convoy timetable and decoding the meeting points for the Iceland section and the main convoy.

On March 10 the Commander U-boats ordered the group to remain in a patrol line from AJ 5268 to AJ 9383, as it was not expected that the convoy would proceed further to the west, particularly since the heavy west and northwest storms were likely to delay the convoy. Another reason was the report from *U 621* (Oblt Kruschka), in AJ 9319, in the southern part of the patrol line, that an independent freighter was proceeding southward. The freighter, which was estimated to be of 6,000 tons, was high out of the water and seemed to be making slow progress at about four knots in a northwest swell, wind force 5 and rising. At 2214 hrs *U 621* fired a single torpedo which, however, missed. The boat submerged to reload. The next morning the boat found the freighter after some searching. But the ship now appeared to be abandoned and drifting. At 1751 hrs the U-boat tried to finish her off with a torpedo which clearly went under the keel. A second at 1812 hrs also went under the ship's bows. The third torpedo, five minutes later, after traveling for 44 seconds, hit in the area of the stern hold. A great hole was torn in both sides and the ship settled by the stern but remained afloat for the time being. At 1848 hrs Oblt Kruschka fired a further torpedo which again went under the ship as did a sixth which missed the rear of the drifting ship by five meters. Her stern was awash. *U 621* remained near the ship which eventually sank at about 1100 hrs on March 12 in AK 7174. It is probable that this ship was the freighter *Baron Kinnaird* (3,355 tons) which, in the heavy storm, had, with four other ships, lost its convoy ONS.169 on March 6 and was regarded as missing from March 7. Her course would bring her approximately to the position where *U 621* first sighted her (see p. 76).

Meanwhile, on March 11, the German "B" Service had succeeded in deciphering ONS.169's position report at 1000 hrs on March 9. This said that the convoy had hoved to at 57°N 42°30'W on a course of 260° and a speed of two knots. The decoding showed that the convoys ONS.169 and ON.170 had apparently been much more delayed by the severe storms than expected and were proceeding further westward. The Commander U-boats therefore moved the *Raubgraf* group for March 12 on a course of 270° and at a speed of six knots. But, in fact, ONS.169 had gone round to the west of the *Raubgraf* patrol line on March 10 and various radio signals from U-boats of the group were picked up by its rescue ship *Gothland* and also by the destroyer leader *Highlander* proceeding ahead in the NE.

Apart from *U 621*, *U 615* (Kptlt Kapitzky) also sent three signals on this day from the patrol line which were picked by the HF/DF ships with ONS.169. First, *U 615* sighted a stationary guard ship for several hours in AJ 6715 in the middle of the patrol line: this was probably the tug *Tenacity* looking for the *Empire Light* or the corvette *Clematis* searching for the tug. Later, Kptlt Kapitzky reported from AJ 6741 a destroyer proceeding at high speed on a southern course, somewhat further to the SW. It was probably the *Whitehall* detached from ON.170. The U-boat searched in vain for several hours for the suspected convoy, then reported its lack of success and returned to its position in the patrol line.

On March 12 the German "B" Service succeeded in decoding the course instructions for convoy HX.229A sent by radio from COMINCH on March 4. According to these the convoy was to be at point (P) at 40°10'N 73°01'W at 2000 hrs on March 9. The subsequent convoy route was to be: (Q) 40°20'N 60°31'W, (R) 43°15'N 62°03'W, the Halifax meeting point 43°22'N 60°47'W at 1500 hrs on March 12, (S) 43°30'N 59°20'W, (T) 45°55'N 52°27'W, the meeting point off St John's (NF) 47°29'N 50°59'W at 1900 hrs on March 14, (U) 49°00'N 49°00'W, (V) 55°00'N 45°00'W, (W) 61°00'N 36°00'W, (X) 61°00'N 27°00'W, (Y) 60°10'N 15°00'W, (Z) 56°20'N 08°30'W. The following points were designated for the stragglers' route: (A) 49°00'N 49°00'W, (B) 54°32'N 43°36'W, (C) 60°13'N 35°11'W, (D) 60°15'N 27°22'W, (E) 58°19'N 14°21'W, (F) 56°20'N 08°30'W.

This decoding was very precise. The only thing lacking, which was to cause some confusion, was the still unknown fact that the convoy was divided into HX.229 and HX.229A, with the result that this was thought to be the valid route for HX.229.

The Commander U-boats decided, on the basis of this early decoding, to operate against HX.229. The *Raubgraf* group was left in the patrol line it had reached, since the expected ONS.169 must have by then passed. In fact, it had already gone round the line on the night March 9–10 as a subsequent decoding of the position at 1100 hrs on March 10 showed.

In order to catch the convoy, should the HX.229 take evasive action to the south, the new formations in the Central North Atlantic were extended. On March 10 *U 305*, which was outward-bound in the Iceland Passage and *U*

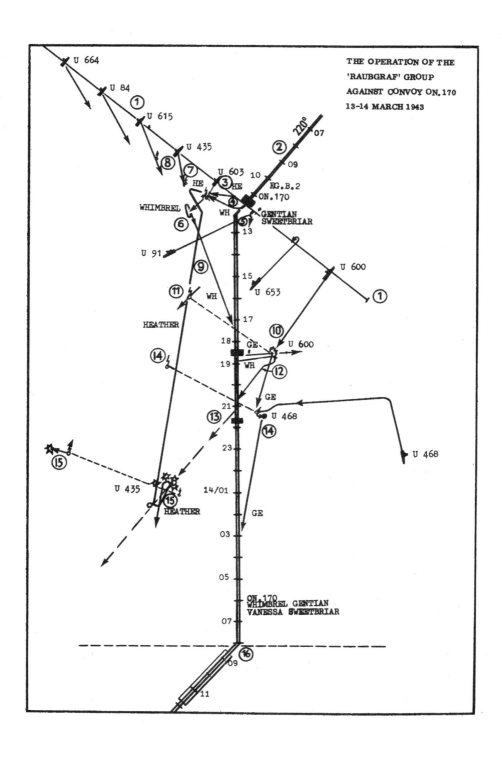

THE OPERATION OF THE
'RAUBGRAF' GROUP
AGAINST CONVOY ON.170
13-14 MARCH 1943

#	Date/Time	Event
1	Mar 13 early	Raubgraf group patrol line. U 91, U 653 and U 468 are not back in position after pursuing independents.
2	Mar 13 1100 hrs	Despite COMINCH's orders for an evasive movement to the West, following D/F bearings on U-boat signals, ON.170 has maintained the existing course of 220° because the escort's fuel reserves were insufficient for evasive action and the storms made it impossible to refuel from the escort tanker. The destroyer Vanessa is only able to begin refuelling in the morning when the wind subsides (SE force 5, sea 3-2, visibility 3-5 miles).
3	Mar 13 1128 hrs	U 603 sights ON.170 which passes the patrol line in the gap not yet closed up by U 91 and sends a contact signal. The Cdr U-boats deploys the Raubgraf group at full speed.
4	Mar 13 1130 hrs	The signal is picked up by the HF/DF of the sloop Whimbrel, the leader of E.G. B 2. The SOE, in addition to Whimbrel, deploys the corvette Heather on the bearing of 284°. At 1141 hrs Whimbrel sights the U-boat at 295°. At 1147 hrs the U-boat sees the approaching 'destroyer' and submerges. Whimbrel and Heather carry out an asdic 'box search' and force the U-boat under water until 1315 hrs.
5	Mar 13 1208 hrs	SOE requests the Commodore to make an emergency turn of 40° to port to 180°.
6	Mar 13 1315 hrs	Whimbrel sets off on a feigned SW course and after 30 minutes proceeds towards convoy.
7	Mar 13 1320 hrs	U 435 sights two escorts where U 603 submerged and reports them. The signal is picked up by D/F on Whimbrel which deploys the Heather against it. Heather forces U 435 under water.
8	Mar 13 1350 hrs	U 615 asks for bearings from contact-keeper. This is picked up by D/F on Whimbrel which quickly turns round. U 615 submerges before approaching 'destroyers'.
9	Mar 13 1430 hrs	Whimbrel follows the convoy. Heather is ordered to continue to keep U-boats under water and then to set off for SW to mislead the U-boats, which try to shadow, about the convoy course. She is to be back with the convoy by dark.
10	Mar 13 1843 hrs	U 600 sights and reports convoy in bad visibility on incorrect course of 220°. U-boat makes a plotting error of about 40 miles and so confirms the Cdr U-boats' assumption that convoy is on SW course.
11	Mar 13	Whimbrel picks up signal from U 600 and proceeds with corvette Gentian on the bearing. U 600 submerges before approaching 'destroyers'. Escorts continue search until 1915 hrs.
12	Mar 13	Commodore proposes not to change to old general course at 2100 hrs, as planned, but to maintain the 180° course through the night. SOE agrees and orders Heather on reaching the proposed course to fire star-shells to draw the U-boats on to the SW course.
13	Mar 13 2100 hrs	U 468 sights the oncoming corvette Gentian in poor visibility. Gentian shortly afterwards locates U 468 with radar and approaches. U 468 submerges before approaching 'destroyer' and, after being located with asdic, is attacked with depth charges. Gentian continues search until 2244 hrs.
14	Mar 13 2130 hrs	Heather fires star-shells. They are observed by U 435 at 286°. Like the report from U 468, this is some 40 miles too far to the West owing to faulty plotting. It again seems to confirm the SW course. U-boats search in the wrong direction.
15	Mar 14 0000 hrs	Convoy goes back to 220° course. Air escort arrives and drives off shadowing U-boats.
16	Mar 14 0800 hrs	

631, U 384, U 598, U 134, U 600 and *U 260,* coming from the French bases, had been ordered to make for AK 69 as an assembly point for a new patrol line. On March 11 the operation against SC.121 NW of the North Channel had ended. The two participating groups, *Ostmark* and *Westmark* were dissolved. *U 332,* which had been at sea a long time but still had plenty of fuel, after taking on more, received orders to search the SC 121's course in a westerly direction for damaged ships and stragglers. *U 634, U 409, U 591, U 228, U 616* and *U 230* were to proceed at an economic speed to the supply boat *U 463* in BD 2455 in order to fill up for the return journey. The *U 305,* which had already arrived, was to form the *Stürmer* group with the boats that still had adequate fuel supplies in the order: *U 305, U 527, U 666, U 523, U 229, U 526, U 642, U 439, U 338, U 641, U 665, U 618, U 190* and *U 530.* It was to form a line from AK 0371 to AL 7278 and set off as a reconnaissance patrol at five knots. In order to prevent the premature discovery of the line by the Allied radar-equipped air reconnaissance, the boats were not to arrive at their position before they were instructed to do so and were to maintain radio silence.

On March 12 the *Stürmer* group was reinforced by the new arrivals, *U 631, U 598, U 384* and *U 134,* and was then to form a patrol line at 1900 hrs on March 14 from AK 3563 to AL 7215 and to proceed toward the next convoy on a course of 260° and at a speed of five knots.

After contact with HX.228 appeared to be lost on March 12 the *Neuland* group boats, which were still operating against the convoy, received orders to continue the search until the morning of March 13 and then to break off. When by morning no further reports were received, the group got orders to take up a patrol line as the *Dränger* group, south of the *Stürmer* group, from AL 4887 to BE 1255 at 0700 hrs on March 15 and to move off on a course of 260° and at a speed of five knots. The order was: *U 373, U 86, U 336, U 440, U 590, U 441, U 406, U 608, U 333, U 221* and *U 610.* The group was to comb the southern route. It was felt that with three groups, amounting in all to 33 boats, all North Atlantic routes were sufficiently covered.

THE *RAUBGRAF* GROUP OPERATIONS AGAINST ON.170

Convoy ON.170 had set out with 52 ships from Liverpool on March 3. On March 4 the Ocean Escort Group B 2 met the convoy (Commodore Charles Turle, RNR). Its leader, the destroyer *Hesperus,* was in the yards. Her captain, Commander Donald Macintyre, DSO, RN, had rammed and sunk the *U 357* which had been located by D/F when it sent its first contact signal in the vicinity of HX.219 on December 26, 1942. In consequence, Cdr. Macintyre was not present at the beginning of February when his group screened SC.118 which was heavily attacked by U-boats and lost nine steamers and three stragglers. Macintyre did not want to risk spoiling the excellent record of his group to date and therefore asked for a temporary replacement for the *Hesperus* equipped with HF/DF. As there were no destroyers available, his group was allocated the new sloop *Whimbrel* (Lt. Cdr. J. W. Moore, RN) from the 2nd Escort Group which was in process of formation. Macintyre was aboard the sloop. Among the other escorts of B 2 were the destroyers *Vanessa* and *Whitehall* (both still without HF/DF) and the corvettes *Gentian*, *Heather* and *Sweet Briar*. The corvette *Clematis*, which also belonged to the group, did not join it and was then detailed to screen the damaged tanker *Empire Light* and the tug *Tenacity*.

On March 5–6 two ships had to return because of technical trouble. After March 7 ON.170 encountered bad weather and had to cope with the same severe storms which had held up ONS.169. On March 8 another ship, the *Empire Puma*, stayed behind and on March 9 the freighter *Steel Traveller* lost her top masts with the rolling and pitching and on the *Karamea* the deck cargoes of aircraft crates were smashed. During March 9–11 the daily average speed was 4.3 knots, 4.4 knots and 3.6 knots. In the heavy seas it was not possible to replenish the escorts from the convoy tankers. Commodore Turle was therefore compelled to diverge from the course last prescribed by CINCWA. ON.170, which was originally to proceed on a course similar to that of SC.121, had already been diverted to the north on March 5 in order to avoid the U-boats following SC.121. On March 7 a new change of course was ordered so as to pass to the north and west of the U-boats suspected to be between Newfoundland and Greenland. Then the escorts' fuel situation compelled Commodore Turle on March 11 to propose to the Escort Commander a more direct course to Newfoundland. The convoy altered course from 240° to 220° and so steered straight toward the *Raubgraf* patrol line which had been moved somewhat westward.

The route order for convoy ON.170 on March 11 was as opposite.

Because the weather continued to be bad on March 11 the destroyer *Whitehall*, which had the lowest fuel supplies, had to proceed on her own to St John's. Nor did the wind moderate sufficiently on March 12 for the tankers to begin to replenish the escorts. There was no alternative but to maintain the 220° course in spite of the fact that on March 10 and 11 U-boats were located by D/F ahead. Nor was there any change when on March 12 more radio signals were located ahead.

At first *U 621* reported the sinking of the independent freighter which it had shadowed since March 10 (see p. 96). Another series of signals came from *U 468* (Oblt Schamong), stationed at the SE end of the *Raubgraf* patrol line. It first reported that it was hunting a large *Cadillac* type tanker on southern courses. At 2112 hrs the boat attacked in the dusk. The single torpedo hit

TABLE No. 5

Route order for convoy ON.170 on March 11

111	112 brit MS *Empire Faith* Halifax	113 dutch SS *Ulysses* Halifax	114 brit MS *Eastgate* Halifax	115 brit MS *Bradford City* Halifax	
101	102 brit SS *Corner Brook* Halifax	103 norw MS *John Bakke* Halifax	104 greek SS *Ameriki* Halifax	105 brit SS *Pachesham* Halifax	106 brit MS *Daghestan* Halifax
91	92 brit SS *Settler* Curaçao	93 amer SS *Alcoa Cutter* New York	94 norw MS *Glarona* New York	95 norw MS *Noreg* New York	
81	82 norw MS *Ivaran* New York	83 brit MT *British Character* New York	84 belg SS *Ville D'Anvers* New York	85 norw MS *Villanger* New York	86 brit SS *Pandorian* New York
71	72 brit ST *Empire Cobbett* New York	73 brit SS *Empire Pakeha* New York	74 brit MT *British Valour* New York	75 brit MS *Empire Fletcher* New York	
61 brit SS *Port Adelaide* New York	62 brit MT *Abbeydale* New York	63 amer ST *O.M. Bernuth* Houston	64 brit MT *Robert F. Hand* New York	65 brit MS *Devis* New York	66 brit SS *Sovac* Philadelphia
51	52 norw MT *Norvinn* New York	53 brit MT *British Vigour* New York	54 brit SS *City of Khios* New York	55 brit SS *Canara* New York	56 amer SS *Atenas* New York
41	42 brit MS *Port Huon* New York/ Panama	43 norw ST *Norheim* New York	44 swed MP *Axel Johnson* New York	45 norw MS *Fernwood* New York	46 brit MS *Kaituna* New York
31	32 brit MS *Karamea* Panama	33 norw MT *Katy* New York	34 brit MT *Henry Dundas* New York	35 brit MS *Fernmoor* New York	
21	22 amer SS *Carillo* New York	23 brit SS *Port Darwin* New York	24 hond SS *Maya* New York	25 amer SS *William Wirt* New York	
11	12 norw MS *Samuel Bakke* New York	13 amer SS *Steel Traveler* New York	14 norw SS *Skiensfjord* New York		

Convoy Commodore:	61	*Port Adelaide*	
Vice Commodore:	55	*Canara*	
Rear Commodore:	101	*Corner Brook*	
Escort Oiler:	52	*Norvinn*	
Standby Oiler:	74	*British Valour*	

Ocean Escort Group B.2

Sloop	HMS *Whimbrel* (2nd EG)
Destroyer	HMS *Vanessa*
Destroyer	HMS *Whitehall*
Corvette	HMS *Gentian*
Corvette	HMS *Heather*
Corvette	HMS *Sweetbriar*

under the bridge and caused the usual column, of smoke. The tanker reduced speed. A second torpedo at 2125 hrs hit the engine room. Several small darting flames were seen bursting out of the ship's side. The tanker acquired a slight list. At 2138 hrs and 2139 hrs *U 468* fired two successive torpedoes to finish her off. But with the heavy swell from the NW, and wind force 4–5, they broke surface, diverged from their course and missed the ship. Another torpedo was fired at 2230 hrs after the tanker had stopped completely. This hit amidships. The tanker broke in two and sank in 10 minutes. It can only have been the *Empire Light* (6,537 tons), which had been torpedoed and damaged by *U 638* on March 7 and which, as a result of the western and northwest storm over several days, had been driven far to the SE.

In addition, *U 91* (Kptlt Walkerling) encountered on the same afternoon, somewhat further to the NW, in AJ 8335 a "suspicious-looking 1,500-ton steamship." Despite imprecise data, it fired a salvo of three torpedoes at it which missed. The U-boat was then depth charged and it again expressed the suspicion that it might be a U-boat trap. This encounter cannot be substantiated in Allied documents. It could have been the *Tenacity* with the corvette *Clematis* which was still looking for the *Empire Light*.

On the morning of March 13 *U 653* (Kptlt Feiler), which was stationed SE of *U 91* in the *Burggraf* patrol line, reported that on the previous day it had sunk a freighter of 4,000 tons proceeding on a SW course in AJ 9154. This reported sinking also cannot be clarified with certainty. The most probable hypothesis is that it was the *Thomas Hooker* (7,176 tons), damaged on March 6. It was not seen after the crew was taken off by the *Pimpernel* and the *Godetia* left her on March 9. In this case she would have been driven to the SE like the *Empire Light*. The old theory that it was a ship sunk by *U 621*, *U 468* and *U 653*, in addition to the *Baron Kinnaird* and the *Empire Light*, and was in fact the *Clarissa Radcliffe* missing from convoy SC.122 from March 7 cannot be upheld. With her speed of 7.5 knots she could not have reached the reported sinking positions from the point of her last sighting on the stragglers' route prescribed for SC.122. Nor could she have been on the south and SW course reported by the U-boats. Perhaps she sank so quickly in the storm off New York (March 6–7) that she was not able to send a distress signal; or perhaps the report of *The Pas*, of which Middlebrook speaks (*op. cit.*, 282–3), is true and she was lost later. (see p. 175).

The radio messages sent on March 11 and 12 and the morning of March 13 by *U 621*, *U 615*, *U 468*, *U 91* and *U 653* from the area of the *Raubgraf* group were again located by the Allied shore-based D/F stations and clearly indicated both the dangers for ON.170 and the threat to the courses prescribed for the convoys SC.122, HX.229 and HX.229A. Accordingly at 1000 hrs on March 13 the Admiralty suggested to COMINCH a diversion to the east for SC.122 and HX.229. The suggestion was accepted by COMINCH and, in fact, even more drastic changes of course were ordered. At 1602 hrs on March 13 SC.122 received orders when at 48°52'N 46°40'W at 1900 hrs to proceed on a course of 073° instead of 067°. HX.229 was to proceed on a course of 089° instead of 028° from the position J. A little later orders followed that SC.122 should proceed from a position C at 50°20'N 39°10'W on a course of 031°, while HX.229 was to make for the old position M from the position V at 49°20'N 38°00'W. It was hoped that with these instructions it would be possible to avoid the U-boats NE of Newfoundland (the *Raubgraf* group) and the new outward-bound boats west of Ireland coming from convoys SC.121 and HX.228. The latter had been sighted there by air reconnaissance or had been located by D/F when they reported their positions and successes.

Meanwhile ON.170 had continued its journey on a course of 220° with slowly improving wind and sea conditions. The wind had veered round to SE force 5, the sea had moderated to state 3–2 and visibility, except in frequent snow showers, extended to 3–5 miles. Cdr. Macintyre wanted to take advantage of the improved weather to replenish at once and had accordingly ordered the *Vanessa* to go first to the tanker *British Valour*. But there were difficulties because of the incomplete equipment on the tanker and the destroyer captain's lack of experience of such operations. In consequence, only 85 tons of oil were taken on board after a whole day's efforts. The *Norvinn*'s equipment had proved to be quite inadequate in an exercise at the beginning of the trip.

So Cdr. Macintyre with his sloop *Whimbrel* proceeded on the morning of March 13 in position A ahead of the convoy; the corvette *Heather* (Lt. Cdr. N. Turner, RNR) covered the starboard side in position F, while the position C on the starboard bow, vacated by *Vanessa*, remained unfilled. The corvettes *Sweetbriar* (Lt. Cdr. J. W. Cooper, RNR) and *Gentian* (Lt. Cdr. H. N. Russell, RNR) proceeded in positions M and O on the port bow and beam.

Not all the U-boats of the *Raubgraf* group had yet resumed their stations after the various actions on March 11 and 12. As a result, the convoy passed the prescribed line at the NW end of the gap, which had not yet been closed again by *U 91* and *U 653*. However, *U 603* (Oblt Bertelsmann), the nearest boat in the north, sighted the convoy about 1100 hrs, kept with it for some time in order to plot the course and speed and then sent its first contact report "AJ 6747 convoy on SW course." The Commander U-boats correctly calculated, when he received the report, that it must be the ON.170 which had been delayed 2–3 days. He at once deployed the *Raubgraf* group against the convoy at high speed.

Although only the *Whimbrel* was fitted with HF/DF among the convoy, the very experienced D/F expert, Lt. H. Walker, RNVR, was able to locate the first signal clearly at 284° from the *Whimbrel.* Cdr. Macintyre turned the *Whimbrel* at once on to the bearing and called up the *Heather* which was stationed in the vicinity. At 1141 hrs the conning tower of the U-boat was recognized from the crow's nest of the *Whimbrel* at 295° and a range of 12 miles. At 1147 hrs the U-boat submerged as the two escorts approached. Then Macintyre requested the Commodore to change the course of the convoy by 40° to port to 180°. At 1208 hrs the convoy had carried out its emergency turn without the contact-keeper being aware of it. Until 1315 hrs the two escorts hunted the U-boat in a "box sweep" with their asdics without being able to locate it. Macintyre felt he dare not stay away longer from the convoy which was now screened only by two slow corvettes. At first he went off on a feigned course for 30 minutes before he turned back to the convoy. At 1329 hrs, in a first radio message, he reported to his superiors on shore that a U-boat signal had been intercepted and then at 1404 hrs that the U-boat had been driven off and the course changed. At the same time he gave precise instructions to the *Heather* over the radio telephone. She was to keep the U-boat underwater and, in particular, to prevent it getting ahead again. The corvette was to stay in the area and only return to the convoy before dark. She was to proceed on a feigned course for at least one hour when she turned away. In the event of poor visibility or continuous snowfall she was to follow the convoy at once.

Meanwhile *U 435* (Kptlt Strelow) had sighted from the NW the two escorts searching for *U 603* and at 1320 hrs it sent a signal which was also picked up by the *Whimbrel.* At 1356 hrs the *Heather* got sight of this U-boat at 300° and proceeded toward it. At the same time, the *Whimbrel* again located a signal from this boat at 351° and immediately turned. When the *Heather* reported at 1412 hrs that this U-boat had also submerged, the *Whimbrel* went back to the convoy which she reached at 1730 hrs. On the way Lt. Walker also located *U 615* astern when this boat asked the contact-keeper for bearings by radio.

The signals from the *Whimbrel* and the D/F locations from the shore-based stations indicated to the Allies that U-boats were still in contact with ON.170. Accordingly at 1530 hrs CTF.24 ordered Task Unit 24.12.4, comprising the destroyers *Chelsea* and *Salisbury*, which had just put into St John's after their operations with HX.229 and ONS.169, to prepare to go to sea again and to proceed to ON.170. At 1655 hrs the US destroyer *Upshur*, which had reached SC.122, was ordered to go at high speed to TU 24.1.16 with ON.170 which at 1430 hrs had been at 54°17'N 44°34'W. At 2030 hrs in the evening the WLN escort, TU 24.18.6, consisting of the Canadian destroyer *Niagara*, the corvettes *Brantford* and *Dundas* and the minesweepers *Grandmere* and *Minas*, also set out from St John's for ON.170.

However all these ships could not arrive before March 14 or 15. So only the aircraft, based in Newfoundland, could provide a prompt and additional escort. In Argentia there were two US Navy Squadrons each with an establishment of 12 aircraft and comprising Catalina or Mariner flying boats and Ventura patrol bombers respectively. These were used by CTF 24 primarily to protect the stretch between Halifax and Newfoundland. In the area east and NE of Newfoundland the RCAF forces stationed on the island were the main element. The Air Officer, Commanding Eastern Air Command in Halifax, was in overall control of the Canadian aircraft. The tactical command was in the hands of the Air Officer, Commanding No 1 Group in St John's, who worked closely with FONF. He also cooperated closely with the American Navy and Army authorities, since the latter had a squadron of B 17 Fortress bombers on the airfield at Gander. These could occasionally be co-opted to protect the convoys.

At this time the AOC No 1 Group had under him some 12 Canso A flying boats (the Canadian version of the Catalina), of which eight belonged to No 5 Squadron (bomber reconnaissance) and two each to No 10 Squadron (BR) and No 162 Squadron (BR) in Gander and 11 Lockheed Hudsons (corresponding to the Ventura bombers of the USN and USAAF) of No 145 Squadron (BR) in Torbay.

Of these aircraft the American Venturas and the Canadian Hudsons were used for the convoys close to Newfoundland and the Catalinas or Canso flying boats and the B 17s for greater distances.

The air operations for the convoys were very often impeded in the middle of March by the storms, the poor visibility and fog. Thus on March 13 there were no flights and on March 14 most were canceled on account of the weather. Only ON.170 and SC.122 received limited air support on that day.

Of the U-boats coming up on the east side of the convoy, *U 600* (Kptlt Zurmühlen) had first sighted the convoy shortly after 1800 hrs. At 1843 hrs it reported the convoy in AJ 8328, on a course of 225° and with some 16–20 steamers. In the driving snow visibility was soon reduced to 1–2 miles and the boat lost contact before Cdr. Macintyre could come up with the *Whimbrel*, which had located the signal, and the *Gentian*. The two escorts searched in vain until 1945 hrs and then proceeded behind the convoy. The *Whimbrel* with her 18.5 knots regained her position shortly before dark at 2045 hrs. Cdr. Macintyre had intended to make for the old reference point DD after sunset. But Commodore Turle proposed to him in a signal at 2033 hrs that the course of 180° should be maintained until dawn so as to get further away from the old SW course on which the U-boats would probably look for the convoy. Cdr. Macintyre accepted the idea and the convoy maintained its southern course.

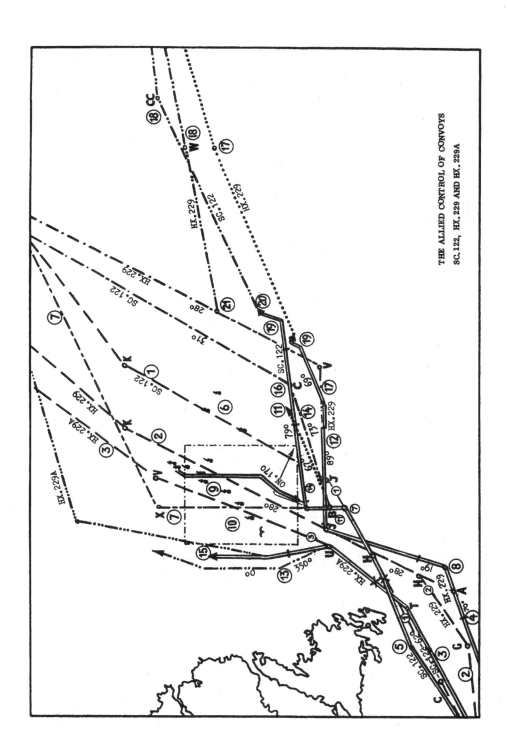

THE ALLIED CONTROL OF CONVOYS
SC.122, HX.229 AND HX.229A

The Allied control of convoys SC.122, HX.229 and HX.229A

1	Feb 28	Course instructions for SC.122.
2	Mar 4	Course instructions for HX.229.
3	Mar 4	Course instructions for HX.229A.
4	Mar 8 1851 hrs	First course alterations for HX.229: route shortened by leaving out points F and G. Course 070° to point A and from there 028° to old point H.
5	Mar 11	SC.122 proceeds closer to Newfoundland.
6	Mar 11-12	Radio messages (U 621) picked up by D/F on SC.122's route.
7	Mar 12 1416 hrs	SC.122 diverted from position reached to course 000° as far as new point X, from there to old point L to avoid U-boat positions established by D/F.
8	Mar 12 1416 hrs	Second course alteration for HX.229: continuation on course 070° to a point from which old point J is reached on course of 019°
9	Mar 13 1128 hrs	After various reports of U-boats on routes prescribed for HX.229 and HX.229A on Mar 12-13 (U 615, U 91, U 653, U 468), a contact signal (U 603) is located near ON.170, followed by others.
10	Mar 13 afternoon	U-boat formation with some 12 boats suspected in area 50°-54' N 43°-49' W.
11	Mar 13 1602 hrs	Second diversion for SC.122: from new point B on a course of 067° to point C, from there on 031° to old point L to avoid suspected U-boat area.
12	Mar 13 1602 hrs	Third diversion for HX.229: from old point J on 089° to new point V, from there on 028° to old point M to avoid suspected U-boat area.
13	Mar 13 evening	First diversion for HX.229A: from old point U on 350° to latitude 51°05' N, then course 000° to avoid suspected U-boat area.
14	Mar 13 evening	SC.122 has passed point B: accordingly prescribed course of 067° altered to 073°. But in fact course to point C was 079°.
15	Mar 14 evening	Second diversion for HX.229A on to a course closer to the suspected U-boat area because of ice difficulties on more westerly course.
16	Mar 15 1100 hrs	Because of severe NW storm, SC.122 has to maintain course of 079° beyond point C.
17	Mar 15 1500 hrs	SOE with HX.229 suggests that, instead of proceeding on Northern course from point V, convoy should make for point 53°N 25°W on course of 069° and then proceed direct to North Channel so that ships do not have to proceed through heavy sea (NW 11) and shorten route, as refuelling of the escorts is impossible.
18	Mar 15 1758 hrs	Admiralty recommends to COMINCH to direct SC.122 via point 55°N 22°W and HX.229 via point 54°N 25°W and from there straight to North Channel.
19	Mar 16 1000 hrs	After storm subsides and because no radio order received from COMINCH, SC.122 and HX.229 continue on prescribed courses of 031° and 028° respectively.
20	Mar 16 1330 hrs	Diversion order from COMINCH for both convoys issued (only received in the evening). SC.122 is to make for point CC and HX.229 from new point on course of 028° to make for new point W from Mar 17.
21	Mar 16	

From the east *U 468* (Oblt Schamong), which, after the sinking of the wreck of the *Empire Light*, was south of its prescribed position in the patrol line, tried to make contact with the convoy. In deteriorating visibility of hardly more than 1–2 miles it first sighted a "destroyer" and reported, apparently without being located by D/F. But the contact was soon lost in a snow squall. At 2130 hrs the boat was about nine miles on the port beam of the convoy which could not be seen but which could be heard with the listening equipment. At this time the corvette *Gentian* was proceeding on the port quarter on a course of 210° at 15 knots in order to resume her position O and was still about 5,500 meters from the last ship in the port column and 3,000 meters from her own position when she located a target with her radar at 130° and at a distance of 53,000 meters. She turned at once at high speed toward the contact. At 2,750 meters the contact began to disappear: the U-boat had recognized the approaching corvette and had submerged. But the asdic found the U-boat at 2,600 meters and Lt. Cdr. Russell was able to make a depth charge approach. At 2147 hrs the depth charges were dropped, set to 15 and 45 meters. One of the port throwers failed due to heavy storm damage with the result that only nine charges detonated. Shortly after the U-boat was briefly seen astern as it emerged from the detonation whirlpools but it immediately fell away. The *Gentian* at once turned to ram the U-boat but in the meantime the boat had disappeared. Asdic contact was not reestablished before 2207 hrs. The second approach had to be broken off because contact was lost at about 550 meters as a result of the U-boat's skillful evasive movements. The same thing happened with the third approach, but Lt. Cdr. Russell ordered the depth charges to be dropped. This time there were only eight which detonated after being set to 100 and 150 meters. In the fourth approach it was proposed to use the hedgehog thrower, but contact was lost at 900 meters. Since he had now been more than an hour absent and there were still only two escorts with the convoy, Russell decided at 2244 hrs to return to the convoy which he reached at 0230 hrs.

The radio signals from *U 600* and from *U 468*, after surfacing, giving their positions, were some 40 miles NW of the actual ones. In consequence, the Commander U-boats, imagined, as a result of the course of 225° given by *U 600*, that the convoy was on a more southwesterly route. This was just the impression that Commodore Turle and Cdr. Macintyre wanted to create with their tactics. The corvette *Heather*, which had so altered her course that she should have met the convoy at 0100 hrs had it gone back to its old general course after dark, as anticipated, could not find the convoy and asked for bearings. She received orders not to approach the convoy, so as not to bring up the U-boats which were obviously shadowing her. Lt. Cdr. Turner therefore turned away for a while, went back to his old course and fired star shells.

They were observed by *U 435* from AJ 8583 in the direction of 286°, but a sortie in this area produced no results. In fact, *U 435* must have been between the convoy and the *Heather* and was thus diverted from its real target, as were the other boats of the *Raubgraf* group which were searching in a SW direction as a result of this last report from one of the boats of the group. As in the prevailing weather conditions—rain, driving snow and occasional fog—it could not be excluded that U-boats might encounter the convoy, parts of it or stragglers, the operation was continued for the time being.

However, the U-boats were unable to regain contact because they were searching on the wrong track. When on March 14 air cover was reported, the Commander U-boats broke off the operation. On the same day the destroyer *Chelsea* reached the ON.170 to reinforce the escort. On the morning of March 15 TU 24.18.6 relieved the Ocean Escort Group B 2 as convoy screen.

The operations involving the ON.170 are a good example of how, in not all too unfavorable conditions, even a very weak escort group, under an experienced escort commander, could succeed in avoiding a U-boat group by the skillful use of the limited technical equipment available. Cdr. Macintyre's group had, almost exactly two years earlier, when with HX.112, sunk two of the most successful U-boat commanders—Kretschmer on *U 99* and Schepke on *U 100*. Here and in many other operations which were not properly part of the "convoy battles" prompt and effective tactical reaction, once an able HF/DF operator picked up the contact signals, was of decisive importance.

MARCH 14, 1943

This is the situation which confronted the Allied Commands on the morning of March 14. Convoy ON.170 was proceeding southward some 200 miles NE of Newfoundland, screened by the Escort Group B 2. The RCAF provided air support. As a result of this defense, those U-boats which were still searching for the convoy could not close up. In the course of the day the HF/DF bearings of the *Whimbrel* indicated that the U-boats had fallen back to the north. At 1247 hrs the *Whimbrel* sent a radio message to this effect. Then COMINCH ordered the destroyer *Upshur*, which had not reached ON.170, to return at 1408 hrs to SC.122 which COMINCH's D/F stations now regarded at greater risk, two bearings seeming to be in the vicinity of the convoys.

The SC.122 was proceeding at about seven knots on its course of 073° to which it had been keeping since 1900 hrs on March 13. It was hoped that the approximately 12 U-boats which had been located by radio intelligence in the area of the convoys ONS.169 and ONS.170 and whose position was reported during the day in the U-boat situation report as being between 50° and 54°N and 43° and 49°W could be avoided by the evasive action ordered in the south.

The HX.229 caused greater concern because of its inadequate escort. Escort Group B 4 had only been able to set out from St John's at 2100 hrs on March 13 with two of its own units, the *Beverley* and *Anemone*. The destroyer *Volunteer* belonging to Escort Group B 5 had been assigned as leader. But the three ships were not able to be at WOMP on time—1000 hrs was the time fixed—since the convoys had proceeded more quickly than expected as the result of a stern wind. In the morning the new Liberty ship *Stephen Foster* developed cracks in her welding joints. At 1330 hrs she had to be detached to St John's with the corvette *Oakville* because of heavy flooding. At 1800 hrs the Ocean Escort Group met the convoy which from 1500 hrs, after passing reference point J, had been proceeding on a new course of 089°. The WLN Escort Group, comprising the Canadian destroyer *Annapolis*, the American destroyer *Kendrick* and the Canadian corvette *Fredericton*, turned away and Support Group TU 24.12.3 with the two British destroyers *Witherington* and *Mansfield* received orders from CTF 24 to remain with the convoy until further notice. These two destroyers functioned as a distant escort ahead of the convoy to the port and starboard. The *Volunteer* took the position A (see the diagram with the escort positions), the *Beverley* position G and the *Anemone* position Q. The two other corvettes in the group, *Pennywort* and *Abelia*, put to sea from St John's as soon as they were ready, at 0500 hrs and 2100 hrs respectively, to meet the convoy. The leader *Highlander* was still in dock.

Convoy HX.229A passed very close to Cape Race on March 14. It received orders from COMINCH to avoid the U-boat danger area on its course by proceeding to the west of it.

The Commander U-boats in the Hotel Steinstrasse in Berlin received in the course of the day a number of radio messages about increasing air support in the afternoon from the U-boats *U 615, U 600, U 603, U 91, U 435* and *U 468* which were trying to reestablish contact lost with convoy ON.170 in AJ 88 and BE 21 as they proceeded on southern courses. In the prevailing weather and poor visibility and because of the proximity to Newfoundland the future prospects of the operation did not appear to be very good.

But once again in this situation the "B" Service was to provide two very promising sources of assistance. First, it succeeded in deciphering the New York Port Director's sailing telegram for SC.122 of 21.36 Z hrs on March 5, after the convoy left in 14 columns composed as follows: 2, 4, 4, 3, 3, 5, 5, 3, 3, 4, 4, 4, 3, 2 (i.e., 49 ships in all). The Commodore was on board the steamer *Glenapp* (9,053 tons). From the details of the cipher material on board the ships the tankers *Beaconoil* (6,893 tons), *Vistula* (8,537 tons), *Permian* (8,890 tons), *Shirvan* (6,017 tons), *Gloxinia* (3,336 tons), *Christian Holm* (9,119 tons) and the steamer *Cartago* (4,772 tons) were among those identified. From the Commodore's report at 2000 hrs on March 7 the position, course and speed

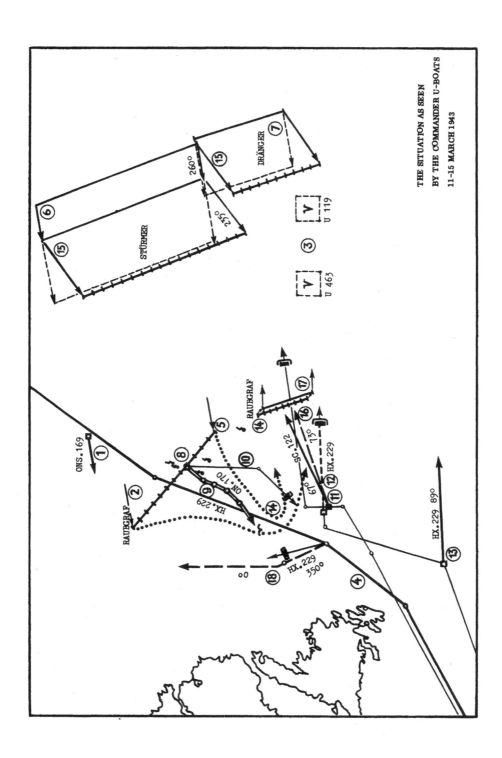

THE STUATION AS SEEN
BY THE COMMANDER U-BOATS
11–15 MARCH 1943

The situation as seen by the Cdr U-boats: March 11-15, 1943

1	Mar 11	The 'B' Service deciphers an (inaccurate) passing point for ON.169 on Mar 9. (It actually passed on Mar 7).
2	Mar 11	The Cdr U-boats orders the *Raubgraf* group to proceed westwards to catch ONS.169.
3	Mar 11	Positions of U-tankers *U 463* and *U 119*.
4	Mar 12	The 'B' Service deciphers the course instructions for HX.229A on March 4 but takes them for those of HX.229.
5	Mar 12	The Cdr U-boats halts the *Raubgraf* group to catch HX.229.
6	Mar 12	The Cdr U-boats orders the *Stürmer* group to proceed westwards from 1900 hrs on Mar 14 on a course of 260° and at a speed of 5 knots to meet HX.229.
7	Mar 13	The Cdr U-boats orders the *Dränger* group to proceed westwards from 0700 hrs on Mar 15 on a course of 260° and at a speed of 5 knots to cover any possible evasive movements to the south.
8	Mar 13 1128 hrs	*U 603* reports ON.170 in the *Raubgraf* line. The Cdr U-boats deploys the group at top speed against the convoy.
9	Mar 13-14	The *Raubgraf* group sends many reports on the shadowing of ON.170 but has no success because of the bad weather and poor visibility.
10	Mar 13	(In fact the convoy has taken evasive action to the south while the U-boats search on the original general SW course, thanks to the feigned movements of the escorts and their own faulty calculations).
11	Mar 14	The 'B' Service deciphers the course instructions for SC.122 of Mar 13 according to which the convoy is to adopt a course of 067° from point B from 1900 hrs on Mar 13.
12	Mar 14	The 'B' Service deciphers the course instructions for HX.229 of Mar 13 according to which the convoy is to
13	Mar 14	proceed on a course of 069° from a point (in fact, the altered WOMP). But according to the Cdr U-boats plotting the convoy cannot be so far north. As a result the reference point for the change to 089° is made the deciphered point of the last change of course ordered to the north.
14	Mar 14 afternoon	The Cdr U-boats breaks off the unsuccessful operation against ON.170 and concentrates the *Raubgraf* group in a narrow patrol line on course of SC.122 for 1500 hrs on Mar 15.
15	Mar 14	The *Stürmer* and *Dränger* groups receive orders to proceed on a course of 235° instead of 260° from 0700 hrs on Mar 15 in order to catch both convoys.
16	Mar 15	The 'B' Service deciphers the altered course instructions of 073° for SC.122.
17	Mar 15	The Cdr U-boats accordingly moves the *Raubgraf* patrol line 15 miles further south and orders it to proceed eastwards during the night so as not to fall behind the expected SC.122 (in fact it is already to the east).
18	Mar 16	The 'B' Service deciphers the altered course instructions for HX.229A of Mar 13 but does not connect them with HX.229.

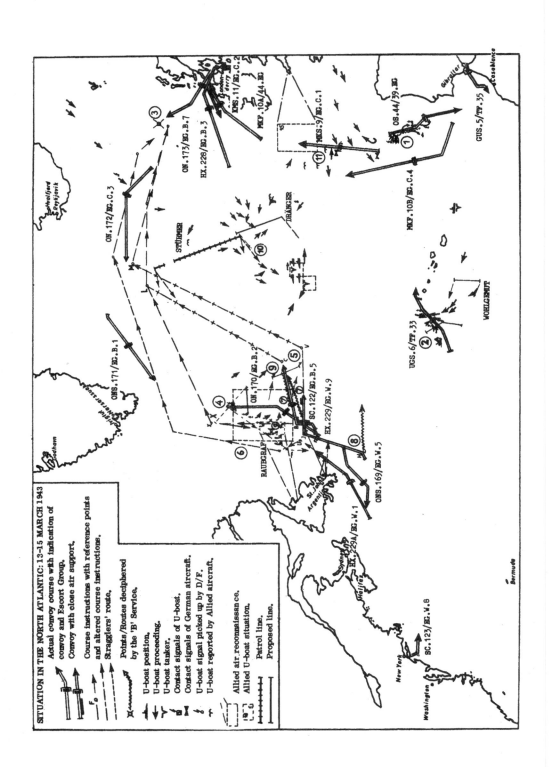

SITUATION IN THE NORTH ATLANTIC: 13-15 MARCH 1943

Actual convoy course with indication of
convoy and Escort Group.

Convoy with close air support.

Course instructions with reference points
and altered course instructions.

Stragglers' route.

Points/Routes deciphered
by the 'B' Service.

U-boat position.

U-boat proceeding.

U-boat tanker.

Contact signals of U-boat.

Contact signals of German aircraft.

U-boat signal picked up by D/F.

U-boat reported by Allied aircraft.

Allied air reconnaissance.

Allied U-boat situation.

Patrol line.

Proposed line.

The situation in the North Atlantic: March 13 (1200 hrs GMT) to March 15 (1200 hrs GMT), 1943

1	Mar 13 0439 hrs	*U 107* attacks OS.44 and sinks 4 ships in one approach. For further operation with 3 boats of the *Robbe* group, the 'B' Service provides the decoding of the prescribed convoy course, but the U-boats are not able to attack.
2	Mar 13 1100 hrs	The new evasive course closer to the Azores prescribed for UGS.6 after intercepting the first contact signals is no more successful than the sinking of the first contact-keeper, *U 130*. The remaining 11 boats of the *Unverzagt* and *Wohlgemut* groups are concentrated into an angled patrol line on the possible northern and southern courses round the Azores and find the UGS.6 again. In clear visibility the Escort Group (with radar on the mast-top) drives off the U-boats and only 1 straggler is sunk. Contact is, however, maintained with the convoy.
3	Mar 13 1214 hrs	German air force listening post locates a passing point for ON.172. Details seem too vague for an operation.
4	Mar 13 1138 hrs	ON.170 runs into the middle of the *Raubgraf* patrol line and is reported by *U 603*. The Cdr U-boats deploys the group against the convoy's reported SW course. Escort Group B.2 forces the contact-keeper, detected by HF/DF, under water, successfully tricks the closing U-boats into thinking that the SW course is being maintained, while ON.170 in fact proceeds on southern course until the morning of Mar 14. U-boats proceed on SW course and on Nov 14 are forced under water by USAAF aircraft from Newfoundland.
5	Mar 13 1900 hrs	As a result of many radio signals from U-boats in the area of ON.170 and therefore on the present courses of SC.122 and HX.229, COMINCH orders SC.122 to proceed on a course of 067° from the new reference point B to point C and from there on a course of 031° to the old point L. HX.229 receives orders to proceed on a course of 089° from the old reference point J to the new point V and from there on a course of 028° to the old point M. In this way it is hoped also to avoid the suspected new formations of U-boats in the Eastern part of the North Atlantic after the operations against SC.121 and HX.228. As SC.122 had already passed point B on receipt of the new instructions, the course had to be altered to point C on 073°.
6	Mar 14	HX.229A receives orders from COMINCH to proceed west of the suspected U-boat area between 50 -54 N and 43 -49 W.
7	Mar 14	50°-54' N and 43°-49' W. 067° course instruction for SC.122 and the 089° for HX.229 with the relevant reference points. As the reference point for 1900 hrs Mar 13, according to the Cdr U-boats' plotting of HX.229, cannot be right, the 089° course is applied to point H which seems more appropriate to the Cdr U-boats' staff.
8	Mar 14	The Cdr U-boats breaks off the unsuccessful operation against ON.170 and concentrates the *Raubgraf* boats in a narrow patrol line on the course of SC.122 for Mar 15. When the change of course to 073° is deciphered by the 'B' Service, he moves the patrol line accordingly.
9	Mar 14	The *Stürmer* group and the new *Dränger* group to be formed from the HX.228 boats receive new orders to proceed SW to catch both convoys.
10	Mar 14	
11	Mar 14-15	MKS.9, which is found by German air reconnaissance on Mar 13 and 14, gets protective sweeps from 19 Group, RAF Coastal Command on Mar 15.

were deciphered as well as the fact that 11 ships were stragglers, including *Polarland, Eastern Guide, Gudvor, Clarissa Radcliffe, McKeesport, Kedoe, —Summer* (garbled), *Vinriver, —Alce—*(garbled) and *English* (or *Imperial*) *Monarch.* More important still was the speedy deciphering of COMINCH's course instructions of 1602 hrs on March 12, according to which SC.122, when at 48°52'N 46°40'W (BC 2752) at 1900 hrs on March 13, was to proceed on a course of 067°. HX.229 was to change its course to 089°. But there was a mistake here in connection with the reference point. The "B" Service correctly assumed that it was reference point J but the time of reaching it was not clear. It was therefore assumed that this would also be on the evening of March 13. The Commander U-boats, in calculating the course in accordance with the earlier instructions for March 13, thought a point lying so far to the north impossible and therefore fixed the new course at the previous reference point A in BC 7518.

It was at first decided to use all boats that could be reached and were operational to catch the SC.122. The hopeless operation against ON.170 was broken off at 1800 hrs. Of the boats called on to report, nine—*U 468, U 435, U 603, U 615, U 600, U 758, U 664, U 84* and *U 91*—were to assemble in front of the convoy as the *Raubgraf* group for 1500 on March 15 in a narrowed patrol line from AJ 9945 to BC 3566. *U 89* and *U 653* had to return to base because of reported engine trouble and *U 529*, which had not reported after sending a weather message south of Iceland on February 12, could no longer be counted on. The reconnaissance patrols formed further to the east, *Stürmer* with 18 boats and *Dränger* with 11 boats, which were proceeding westward on a course of 260° and at five knots, were instructed to proceed somewhat further to the SW on a course of 235° from 0700 hrs on March 15, so that the two expected convoys could be caught with these two extended patrols. The *U 228, U 616, U 409* and *U 591*, which had reached the supply boat *U 463* in BD 24, were to be quickly replenished for a further operation and *U 634* and *U 230* were to be replenished for the return journey. The eight boats on the way out, *U 572, U 415, U 260, U 592, U 306, U 564, U 663* and *U 188*, received orders to make for AK 83 so as to be able to form a new patrol-line after the expected operation.

MARCH 15, 1943

On March 15 the German "B" Service was able to decipher the modified course instructions of 073° for the SC.122 on March 13. Accordingly the *Raubgraf* group patrol line was moved 15 miles to the south to bring it back again in front of the convoy. During the night the boats were to proceed eastward, so as not to fall behind the convoy. Then by day they were to approach it at slow speed. But, in fact, because of the gathering western storm some of the boats failed to reach their 1500 hrs position on time. The convoy had advanced more quickly and had already passed the line of the proposed patrol in the morning. At 1200 hrs it reached Point C when, in accordance with the diversionary orders of the afternoon of March 13, the course was to be changed to 031°. But the weather did not permit this change of course because the ships were unable to make headway across the path of the storm. The Commodore, therefore, kept temporarily to the original course.

In view of the weakness of HX.229's escort, CTF 24 decided to leave Support Group TU 24.12.3 with the convoy and at 1345 hrs the two destroyers were ordered to continue on the way to the North Channel, after refueling from the escort oiler with Escort Group B 4. At 1300 hrs the corvette *Pennywort* reached the convoy and took up position S. But it was not possible to carry out the refueling as ordered, because of the force 9–10 west wind and the sea which was increasing to state 7–8. At 1500 hrs *Volunteer* suggested to COMINCH and CINCWA by radio that the route from reference point V north to point M should not be taken but that, in view of the progress of the convoy at an average speed of 10.5 knots and the weather, it should proceed via point 53°N 25°W and from there take the great circle route to the North Channel. At 1738 hrs the Admiralty recommended to COMINCH, in the light of the latest U-boat situation and so as to profit from the air escort from Iceland and Northern Ireland, that the SC.122 should be directed to the North Channel via 55°N 22°W and the HX.229 via 54°N 25°W. However, it was not until 1330 hrs on the following day that the order went out from COMINCH. The weather compelled the destroyer *Witherington*, whose supplies were already badly run down, to heave to at 1604 hrs. At 2000 hrs the SOE had to request the Commodore to change course to 069°. He hoped that it would be possible on this course to prevent the cargoes on the sorely pressed ships from moving about, without having to proceed on the new course to position M, as ordered. The freighter *Hugh Williamson* (position 113) fell back astern and soon got out of sight.

Before HX.229 passed, on the new course, some 20–25 miles to the south of the *Raubgraf* patrol line between 2000 hrs and 2200 hrs, the most southerly boat, *U 91*, came across the *Witherington* shortly before 1900 hrs which had hoved to on a NE course. But it lost her at once, again because visibility was restricted to 500–1000 meters. On receiving its report at 1900 hrs the Commander U-boats deployed *U 84*, *U 664* and *U 758* in the search and the other *Raubgraf* boats were told to proceed eastward at seven knots so as not to fall behind the convoy. But the search was unsuccessful. Only *U 91* heard a broad noise band in the sector between 350° and 140°: probably HX.229 from which more ships were left behind in the night with the result that, in the morning, the formation was very loose. After the *Witherington* stayed behind

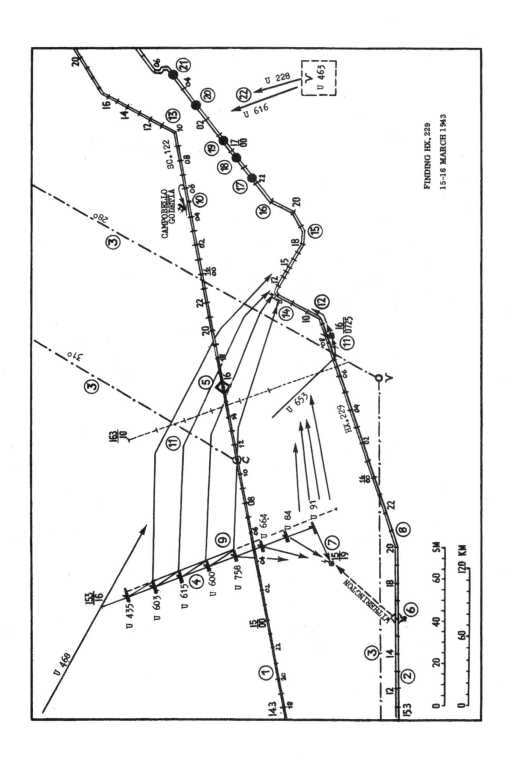

FINDING HX. 229
15-16 MARCH 1943

Finding HX.229: March 15-16, 1943

1		Actual course of SC.122 with times (GMT).
2		Actual course of HX.229 with times (GMT).
3	Mar 13 1602 hrs	The prescribed convoy courses after the altered instructions on Mar 13, 1602 hrs.
4	Mar 15 1600 hrs	Patrol line which the *Raubgraf* group is ordered to adopt.
5	Mar 15 1600 hrs	Position of SC.122.
6	Mar 15 1600 hrs	Position of HX.229. Destroyer *Witherington* has to heave to because of sea, and fuel shortage.
7	Mar 15 1900 hrs	*U 91*, the most southerly *Raubgraf* boat, briefly sights the *Witherington*, hove to in severe storm; in spite of nearest 3 boats being deployed, neither the convoy nor the destroyer are found.
8	Mar 15 2000 hrs	SOE orders HX.229 to proceed on 069° because of the severe storm in order to shorten the route.
9	Mar 15	After receiving the deciphered new course instruction of 073° for SC.122 the patrol line of the *Raubgraf* group is moved 15 miles south and receives orders to advance so as not to fall behind the convoy.
10	Mar 16 0600 hrs	The trawler *Campobello* stays behind with a leak. The corvette *Godetia* is detached for help. Later the trawler has to be abandoned after rescuing the crew.
11	Mar 16 0725 hrs	The homeward-bound *U 653* sights and reports HX.229, which has already passed the *Raubgraf* patrol line envisaged for Mar 16 1000 hrs. At first the Cdr U-boats thinks the reported convoy is SC.122. The *Raubgraf* group and the 11 southern *Stürmer* boats are deployed at high speed.
12	Mar 16 0930 hrs	HX.229 goes on prescribed course of 028° after abatement of the storm.
13	Mar 16 1000 hrs	SC.122 goes on prescribed course of 031° after abatement of the storm.
14	Mar 16 1200 hrs	U-boats of the *Raubgraf* group establish contact with HX.229 and send signals which are picked up by the HF/DF of the leader of Escort Group B 4, *Volunteer*. The convoy makes two emergency turns, while the destroyer *Mansfield* forces the U-boats under water. The convoy slows down to permit the stragglers left behind in the storm to close up.
15	Mar 16 1800 hrs	HX.229 goes back to the general course of 028° in two turns.
16	Mar 16 2100 hrs	After receiving the order to change course (COMINCH Mar 16, 1330 hrs) HX.229 goes on to new course of 053°.
17	Mar 16 2200 hrs	First attack by *U 603*.
18	Mar 16 2300 hrs	Second attack by *U 758*.
19	Mar 17 0020 hrs	Third attack by *U 435*.
20	Mar 17 0230 hrs	Fourth attack by *U 435* and *U 91*.
21	Mar 17 0450 hrs	Fifth attack by *U 600*.
22	Mar 17	U-boats come up from supply boat.

the destroyer *Mansfield* asked to close up more because of the poor visibility and she was put in position M to the port side ahead of the convoy. The *Beverley* proceeded in position C, the corvettes *Anemone* and *Pennywort* in positions Q and G respectively and the leader in position S to the stern.

On the evening of March 15 the repairs to the *Highlander* were completed and the destroyer was able to leave dock at 2300 hrs. She put to sea at 0223 hrs on March 16. On the morning of March 15 FONF had ordered the Canadian corvette *Sherbrooke* of Escort Group B 4 also to follow the convoy after leaving dock.

HX.229A, which was passing by close to Newfoundland, was to proceed on a course of 350° at 1900 hrs on March 15 in order to avoid, by a westward diversion, the area where the day before some 12 U-boats were suspected to be. The Ocean Escort Group, Escort Group 40, which normally operated on the Freetown–Gibraltar–UK route, had set out late in the evening of March 14 from St John's, with the sloops *Aberdeen* (Cdr. Dalison), *Lulworth* and *Hastings* and the new frigates *Moyola* and *Waveney*. The sloop *Landguard* was delayed and could not follow before the afternoon of March 15. The group was held up for about five hours on the way to WOMP by ice fields with the result that Cdr. Dalison had to increase speed. The *Aberdeen*, in crossing a thick ice layer, broke off her asdic dome. At 1500 hrs on March 15 they met the convoy and were able to relieve the WLN Escort Group, TU 24.18.1, comprising the destroyer *St Clair*, the corvettes *The Pas* and *Kamsack* and the minesweeper *Blairmore*, which arrived back in St John's on March 17.

During the storm in the night March 15–16 a leak developed in the boiler room of the trawler *Campobello* which belonged to the escort of SC.122. The flooding could not be stopped and the boiler fires had to be put out. At 0600 hrs the ship, which had fallen 10 miles behind, sent out a distress signal. The corvette *Godetia* was detailed from the convoy to give help. When the situation became serious, she took on the crew and at 1700 hrs the *Campobello* sank. In addition, the Icelandic steamer *Selfoss* was left behind.

MARCH 16, 1943: THE SIGHTING OF HX.229

On the morning of March 16 the weather became somewhat calmer, but there was still a strong swell from the NW. HX.229 was pretty dislocated and between 0600 hrs and 0700 hrs passed the southern end of the reconnaissance patrol line which the *Raubgraf* group was meant to have reached at 1000 hrs. But the southern four boats, which had searched the evening before for the destroyer sighted by *U 91*, had not yet closed up. The most northerly boat, *U 468*, which on March 14 had tried longest to reestablish contact with ON.170, was still far from the position it had been ordered to take up. The result was that only four boats were moving at seven knots on the course ordered for the reconnaissance line. The HX.229 would, therefore, have passed the *Raubgraf* group unnoticed—despite all the "B" Service reports—if *U 653* (Kptlt Feiler), which was returning because of engine trouble, had not crossed the convoy course. At 0725 hrs, after briefly observing the course of the convoy and its speed, it sent its first contact signal: "BD 1491 convoy, course 070°. *U 653.*"

The Commander U-boats assumed that it was the anticipated SC.122. At once the eight *Raubgraf* boats in the area—*U 91*, *U 84*, *U 664*, *U 758*, *U 600*, *U 615*, *U 603*, and *U 435*—and the two which had already replenished from *U 463*, *U 228* and *U 616*, were deployed against the convoy at high speed. From the *Stürmer* group, the 11 southern boats—*U 134*, *U 384*, *U 598*, *U 631*, *U 530*, *U 190*, *U 618*, *U 665*, *U 641* (this boat, however, had not yet reached its position), *U 338* and *U 439*—received orders to operate so that they could reach the convoy on the morning of March 17. The remaining boats—*U 642*, *U 526*, *U 523*, *U 666*, *U 527*, and *U 305*—were first to proceed on a course of 160° and at 11 knots, so as to be in front of the convoy, if contact was lost, and to form a new patrol-line. The *Dränger* group—*U 373*, *U 86*, *U 440*, *U 590*, *U 441*, *U 406*, *U 608*, *U 333*, *U 221*, and *U 610*—received orders to continue on its existing course in order to catch the second convoy, HX.229, which was expected further south. *U 229* was sent to the region east of Cape Farewell to act as a weather boat: its function was to send regular weather reports from there for the returning blockade-runner *Regensburg*.

The first contact signal from *U 653* and the further signals which followed at approximately two-hour intervals were evidently not picked up by the only destroyer with HX.229 that was equipped with HF/DF, the *Volunteer*. At 1000 hrs the convoy turned to 028° in the direction of the reference point M as laid down on March 13; the request to change course had not yet received an affirmative answer from COMINCH. Simultaneously, speed was reduced to eight knots to enable stragglers to close up. This change of course was to prove fateful. Had the U-boats operated on the assumption that the supposed SC convoy was proceeding at the expected seven knots on the old course, they would certainly have passed by to the stern. Now the convoy cut across the U-boats' course of pursuit. From 1600 hrs *U 600* and *U 615* came up in quick succession, plotted the course and sent their contact signals at 1342 hrs and 1355 hrs.

These signals were located by the *Volunteer* at 318° and 353°. The D/F operator estimated the distances to be 20 miles and "very near." At the same time radio messages came from COMINCH at 1205 hrs and from the Admiralty at 1352 hrs indicating that the shore-based D/F stations had bearings on "B bar signals"* in the vicinity of the convoy. The SOE, Lt. Cdr. Luther,

---

*The German U-Boat contact signals from convoys were preceeded by the Greek letter "beta" given twice. This corresponded to the British B-bar morse symbol, so these contact signals got the name "B-bar signals."

ordered the *Mansfield* to follow the D/F beams to a distance of 15 miles and to force the U-boats under water until 1700 hrs. He also requested the Commodore to make a sharp evasive turn of 90° to starboard. At 1400 hrs the convoy turned, in two successive moves, to 118°. This course was maintained until 1800 hrs, then HX.229 went back to 090° and by 2000 hrs the old course of 028° was again reached with two more turns.

U 600 and *U 615* had to submerge before the *Mansfield*. But of the remaining *Raubgraf* boats some at first established contact with six stragglers, one of which *U 91* tried to attack at 1625 hrs. But it had to break off its approach on account of the heavy sea. Because the convoy reverted to its old course of 028°, some of the boats, coming up from the stern, at first went past, then came up on the starboard side of the convoy. In the course of the afternoon *U 664*, *U 758*, *U 84*, *U 91* and after dark the returning *U 89* and *U 603* approached the convoy which had now closed up again.

The numerous radio signals located by the *Volunteer* and the shore-based D/F stations made it clear that the convoy was threatened. Lt. Cdr. Luther felt he could not detach more escort vessels to make sorties because he had now only four escorts with the convoy. The *Mansfield* tried to join up again from the port quarter. Her radar equipment was not working when she pursued the two U-boats in the heavy seas.

The Allied Commands felt it was necessary to reinforce the escort. In the meantime the corvettes of Escort Group B 4, the *Abelia* and the *Sherbrooke*, and the real destroyer leader *Highlander* had put to sea. At 1435 hrs the destroyer *Vimy*, which belonged to Escort Group B 4 and was lying in Reykjavik, received orders to go to HX.229. But she was only able to put to sea at 0318 hrs on March 18. However, at 1845 hrs on March 16 the US Coast Guard cutter *Ingham* and the US destroyer *Babbitt* had put to sea, as Task Unit 24.6.4, from Reykjavik in order to meet the Iceland section of SC.122 at ICOMP and to bring it to Iceland together with the US destroyer *Upshur*, which was with the convoy.

Before dark, at 1800 hrs, the *Volunteer* tried to refuel by canvas hose from the escort oiler *Gulf Disc* but, because of the swell and the stiff breeze, the two ships had so much difficulty that, after an hour, the unsuccessful attempt had to be abandoned. The HF/DF reports indicated that the U-boats were still in contact with the convoy. At 2000 hrs the convoy passed the Change of Operational Control (CHOP) line and control was transferred from COMINCH to CINCWA. The *Volunteer* sent several reports to CINCWA in the evening.

SC.122 had continued its journey on March 16. The formation, which had become rather loose because of the storm, was restored despite the swell. Like HX.229, SC.122 had at 1000 hrs turned first on to the 031°

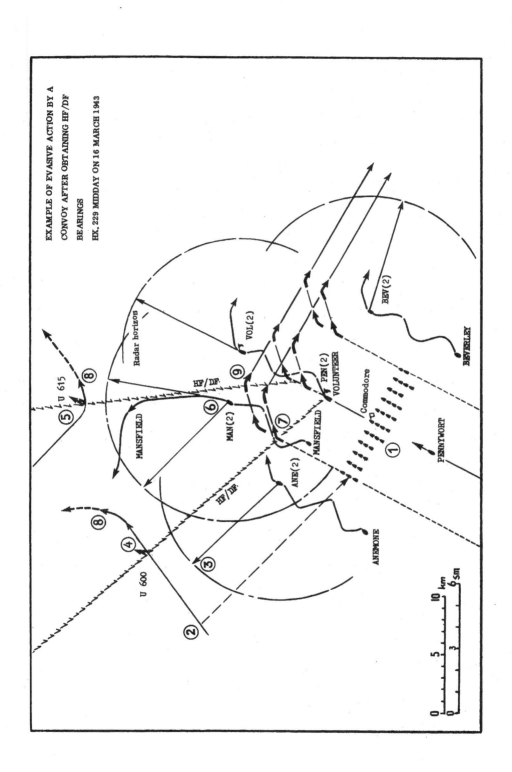

EXAMPLE OF EVASIVE ACTION BY A
CONVOY AFTER OBTAINING HF/DF
BEARINGS

HX. 229 MIDDAY ON 16 MARCH 1943

Example of evasive action by a convoy after obtaining HF/DF bearings: HX.229 midday March 16

1 Mar 16 1300 hrs Route order of Convoy HX.229 (Depicted here is the planned order with 11 columns of 3, 3, 3, 3, 4, 4, 4, 3, 4, 2 ships with a front of some 6 miles and a depth of about 2 miles. The escorts are about 5000 m away from the nearest convoy ships. In fact, owing to the severe storm on Mar 15 and the night of Mar 15-16, the convoy was at this time in considerable disarray and there were 10 stragglers in the morning.

2 Mar 16 1300 hrs *U 600* proceeds with the convoy at the limit of visibility (about 9 miles), plots the course and speed of the convoy.

3 Mar 16 1340 hrs In the prevailing sea, the escort's radar range against the U-boats is a maximum of 5-6 miles. *U 600* and *U 615* can see further than the escorts can use their radar to detect the U-boats.

4 Mar 16 1342 hrs *U 600* sends its contact signal which is picked up by the HF/DF of *Volunteer*.

5 Mar 16 1355 hrs *U 615* sends its contact signal which is picked up by the HF/DF of *Volunteer*.

6 Mar 16 1400 hrs The SOE on *Volunteer* orders the destroyer *Mansfield* which is on the port bow to follow the last bearing. She has orders to follow the two bearings in turn to a distance of 15 miles and keep the U-boats submerged until 1700 hrs.

7 Mar 16 1402 hrs At the request of the SOE the Commodore orders a first emergency turn of 45° to starboard.

8 Mar 16 1415 hrs The U-boats sight the approaching destroyer *Mansfield* before she can locate them and they submerge. The *Mansfield* cannot find the submerged U-boats with her asdic.

9 Mar 16 1417 hrs Second emergency turn by the convoy which now proceeds with a narrower silhouette at right angles to the previous course.

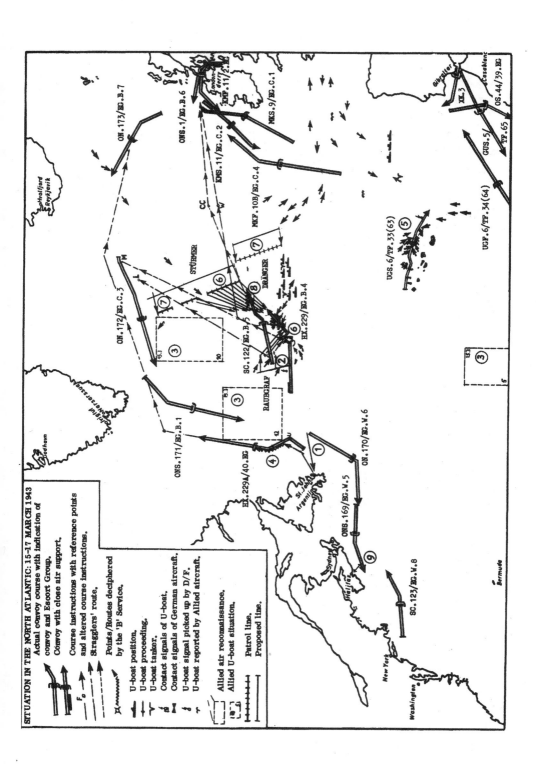

SITUATION IN THE NORTH ATLANTIC: 15-17 MARCH 1943

Actual convoy course with indication of
convoy and Escort Group.

Convoy with close air support.

Course instructions with reference points
and altered course instructions.

Stragglers' route.

Points/Routes deciphered
by the 'B' Service.

U-boat position.

U-boat proceeding.

U-boat tanker.

Contact signals of U-boat.

Contact signals of German aircraft.

U-boat signal picked up by D/F.

U-boat reported by Allied aircraft.

Allied air reconnaissance.

Allied U-boat situation.

Patrol line.

Proposed line.

The situation in the North Atlantic: March 15 (1200 hrs GMT) to March 17 (1200 hrs GMT), 1943

1 Mar 15 early

ON.170 passes WOMP. Relief of Ocean Escort Group B 2. Escort Group 40, setting out from St John's, reaches its convoy HX.229A late because of trouble with ice.

2 Mar 15 1500 hrs

SC.122 has already passed the *Raubgraf* group before the boats, which are delayed by the storm and fog, have reached their patrol line.

HX.229 passes the line just to the south in stormy weather and poor visibility. In the evening the destroyer *Witherington* which has hove to because of fuel shortage is sighted by *U 91*, the most southerly boat of the *Raubgraf* group. But the deployment of the 4 southern boats is without result.

3 Mar 15 afternoon

German 'B' Service deciphers Allied U-boat situation reports of the same day.

4 Mar 15 1900 hrs

COMINCH orders HX.229A to take an evasive course of 350° from the old reference point U as far as latitude 51°50′ N, then 000°. This course instruction is deciphered by the 'B' Service on Mar 16, but is initially connected with HX.229.

5 Mar 15-16

The *Unverzagt* and *Wohlgemut* groups continue their operation against UGS.6. It is very difficult to get ahead because of good radar range and visibility. The Cdr U-boats orders boats to head towards ships' smoke. Attempts at daylight underwater attacks. 2 ships sunk in single attacks.

6 Mar 16 0725 hrs

U 653, while on the way to the supply boat, sights HX.229. The reported convoy is thought by the Cdr U-boats to be SC.122 (see para 4). The Cdr U-boats deploys the *Raubgraf* group, 2 newly refuelled boats and the 11 southern boats of the *Stürmer* group. The remaining *Stürmer* boats are to take a southern course. At 1100 hrs HX.229 goes on to 028° at point V, as ordered. At 1205 hrs contact signals are picked up by HF/DF for first time by leader of EG B 4. At 1414 hrs the convoy turns away to SE as part of an evasive movement which lasts several hours. But contact is maintained: in the night the U-boats attack and sink 8 ships.

7 Mar 16 afternoon

After receiving the deciphered course instructions for HX.229A (see para 4), the Cdr U-boats at first does not expect HX.229, so the remaining *Stürmer* and *Dränger* boats are deployed against the convoy reported by *U 653* which is still thought to be SC.122.

8 Mar 17 0200 hrs

The *Stürmer* boat, *U 338*, coming from the NE, sights SC.122 and attacks. 4 ships are sunk in one approach. As a result of the position report, it is clear to the Cdr U-boats in the morning that there are two convoys. SC.122 and HX.229 are now correctly identified and HX.229A is seen to be a special convoy.

9 Mar 17

ONS.169 passes HOMP.

course which had been laid down on March 13; this was before the new evasive action orders were received in the late afternoon from COMINCH. The new course to point D at 55°N 22°W was 068°. So far, it seemed that no U-boats had had contact with the convoy. SC.122 was also meant to pass CHOP at 2000 hrs.

HX.229A had had some difficulties on its evasive course. Ice fields close to the pack ice boundary had to be repeatedly passed. There was a danger of icebergs. For this reason, one of the escorts went ahead and illuminated icebergs in the area of the convoy with its searchlight. But in the ice fields the freighter *North King* sustained damage from ice. The ship was taking water in No 1 hold. The Commodore sent her back to St John's because there were some 400 troops for Iceland on board. In the evening the freighter *Michigan* also stayed behind because she could only do 6.5 knots with her poor quality coal. She, too, was sent to St John's on the morning of March 17. As a result of the journey through the ice in the night the convoy's formation became somewhat disorganized and in the morning there were some stragglers.

In the course of the afternoon the Commander U-boats received further deciphered information from the "B" Service which, initially, caused some confusion. According to this, HX.229 was at 1900 hrs on March 15 to take a course of 350° from BC 1240 and at 51°05'N to turn to a course of 000°(N). It was impossible to explain this major diversion from the existing course instructions and it was attributed to the known Allied U-boat situation report on March 14 which had likewise been deciphered shortly before. Since it was believed that HX.229 was no longer expected, the remaining *Stürmer* boats—*U 642, U 526, U 523, U 666, U 527* and *U 305*—and all the *Dränger*—*U 373, U 86, U 336, U 440, U 590, U 441, U 406, U 608, U 333, U 221* and *U 610*—were deployed against the convoy found in the morning. This was at first thought to be SC.122. It only became clear on March 19 that this deciphered course instructions referred to the "part convoy," HX.229A. HX.229 was proceeding on the course laid down on March 13 and had been located first by the U-boats.

CHAPTER 8

The First Night

HX.229: THE ATTACK BY *U 603*

By dusk on March 16 the stragglers from convoy HX.229 had closed up again except for the *Hugh Williamson*. The convoy proceeded on a course of 028° in the route order overleaf (see p.131).

The Convoy Commodore, Commodore M. J. D. Mayall, RNR, was on the *Abraham Lincoln* in position 61 in the middle of the convoy. The SOE, Lt. Cdr. Luther, had stationed his four ships with the convoy in the formation NE 5: the *Volunteer* herself in position M on the port bow, the *Beverley* (Lt. Cdr. Rodney Price, RN) in position C on the starboard bow, the *Pennywort* (Lt. O. G. Stuart, RCNVR) in position G on the starboard beam and the *Anemone* (Lt. Cdr. P. G. A. King, RNR) in position Q on the port beam. The *Mansfield* (Lt. Cdr. L. C. Hill, RN), after closing up, was to go into position S astern of the convoy.

At 2105 hrs the *Volunteer* received the 1330 hrs signal from COMINCH, in which the change of course to a more southerly direction, suggested by the SOE and the Admiralty the day before, was confirmed. But the new point W was fixed at 55°N 25°W. The SOE suggested to the Commodore a change of course to 053°. With this he also hoped to evade the U-boats, located by D/F to the north and west of the convoy. A signal about the bearings went also to CINCWA. At 2125 hrs the Commodore ordered a change of course in two turns of 20° and 5° by means of colored lights. On the right wing of the convoy there was some confusion because the Norwegian freighter *Elin K.* let her lights burn too long, so that the course instruction had then to be given with the blue signal lamp.

At this point *U 603* (Kptlt Bertelsmann) was preparing to come up on the starboard side to make a surface night attack. Owing to the convoy's turn it got into a forward position sooner than anticipated. The weather was favorable for an attack. There was a full moon but a cloud density of 9–10. The scene was only intermittently illuminated: generally twilight conditions prevailed. Visibility was excellent and the ships could be recognized by the

U-boat at a distance of almost 9,000 meters. A north wind of force 2 was blowing; the sea was comparatively calm but there was a slight southwest swell of state 1. With a distance of about 10,000 meters between the *Beverley* on the starboard bow and the *Pennywort* on the starboard quarter, which could be plainly picked out by the U-boat, it was not difficult for Kptlt Bertelsmann to get up into the gap on the starboard side of the convoy. At 2200 hrs *U 603* at first fired a salvo of three FAT torpedoes. These pattern-running torpedoes had a pre-set steering. The U-boat could fire the torpedoes at any desired angle up to 90°. The torpedoes ran a course, fixed by the distance to the convoy, at a speed of 30 knots. They could then make short or large loops at right angles to the course and in this way cut across the convoy's route several times. Shortly after the salvo, *U 603* fired another single G 7e torpedo (electrically-driven with no bubble track) from tube 3 at a 6,000-ton steamer which was proceeding outside on the right. The distance from the target was at this stage about 3,000 meters. After a period of more than four minutes, corresponding to a distance of a good 4,000 meters, a detonation was heard in the boat and also a possible second one.

At 2205 hrs the freighter *Elin K.*, already mentioned, which was proceeding in position 101, received a torpedo hit on the starboard side. The ship was able to fire off two white rockets and then sank within four minutes. The white rockets were sighted by the escorts and the SOE at once gave orders for a "half-raspberry" operation. The escorts steamed a triangular course in their sector of the convoy, a usual procedure at the time, by which it was hoped to locate the surfaced attacking submarines and engage them so as to deter them from further attacks. *U 603* sighted the two escorts, *Beverley* and *Pennywort*, proceeding on the starboard side. They seemed to turn directly toward the U-boat with the result that Kptlt Bertelsmann decided to submerge. In fact, both escorts neither saw the U-boat nor contacted it with their radar or asdic. At first, the escorts did not know what had happened since they had seen no damaged ship fall back in the stern. Only when the *Pennywort*, in the last part of her "raspberry" course, was trying to get back to her position, did she sight two lifeboats to the rear of the convoy. The *Pennywort* informed the *Volunteer* by radio telephone of her intention to go back and rescue survivors, after completing the "raspberry" operation. Having taken up the survivors, including the captain, the *Pennywort* again proceeded toward the convoy at 2315 hrs.

TABLE No. 6

Route order for Convoy HX.229 before the beginning of the attack on the evening of March 16

	13 brit SS *Empire Knight* Clyde	12 amer SS *Robert Howe* Mersey	11 brit SS *Cape Breton* Clyde
	23 amer SS *Mathew Luckenbach* United Kingdom	22 amer SS *William Eustis* Clyde	21 amer SS *Walter Q. Gresham* Clyde
	33 brit MS *Canadian Star* United Kingdom	32 brit MS *Kaipara* Mersey	31 brit SS *Fort Anne* Loch Ewe
	43 brit MS *Antar* Mersey	42 mrit MT *Regent Panther* United Kingdom	41 brit SS *Nebraska* Mersey
54 brit SS *Empire Cavalier* Mersey	53 amer ST *Pan Rhode Island* Mersey	52 brit MT *San Veronica* Mersey	51 pan MT *Belgian Gulf* Mersey
64 amer SS *Kofresi* Mersey	63 amer SS *Jean* Mersey	62 amer ST *Gulf Disc* Clyde	61 norw MS *Abraham Lincoln* Belfast
74 amer SS *Margaret Lykes* Mersey	73 pan SS *El Mundo* Mersey	72 brit SWh *Southern Princess* Clyde	71 brit SS *City of Agra* Mersey
84 brit SS *Tekoa* Mersey	83 brit MT *Nicania* Mersey	82 brit SS *Coracero* Mersey	81 amer SS *Irenee Du Pont* Mersey
	93 amer SS *James Oglethorpe* Mersey	92 dutch MT *Magdala* Belfast	91 brit SS *Nariva* Mersey
104 dutch SS *Terkoelei* Belfast	103 dutch SS *Zaanland* Belfast	102 brit MT *Luculus* Belfast	101 norw SS *Elin K.* Belfast
	113 straggler	112 amer SS *Daniel Webster* Belfast	111 amer SS *Harry Luckenbach* United Kingdom

Convoy Commodore:	61	*Abraham Lincoln*
Vice Commodore:	91	*Nariva*
Escort Oiler:	62	*Gulf Disc*
Standby Oiler:	72	*Southern Princess*

Ocean Escort Group B.4
Destroyer HMS *Volunteer* (from B.5)
Destroyer HMS *Beverley*
Corvette   HMS *Anemone*
Corvette   HMS *Pennywort*
Task Unit 24.12.3
Destroyer HMS *Mansfield* (straggler)

THE ATTACK BY *U 758*

Contrary to usual practice, Commodore Mayall did not order an emergency turn in the direction from which the U-boat had turned away but maintained his course. In this way the other U-boats shadowing the convoy were able to continue their intended operation without difficulty. Shortly after 2300 hrs *U 758* (Kptlt Manseck) had reached a position on the starboard bow and turned to attack the convoy. Meanwhile the *Beverley* had resumed her position C on the starboard bow ahead of the convoy. The *Pennywort* closed in from the stern and was still about 11,000 meters behind the convoy. This meant that the starboard side of the convoy was virtually uncovered and in the good visibility *U 758* was able to pick out its targets at leisure. The wind had turned N to E and had freshened up to force 3. The swell was also now given as state 3.

At 2323 hrs Kptlt Manseck fired a FAT torpedo at a freighter of 6,000 tons in the starboard column, one minute later a G 7e at a freighter of 7,000 tons, at 2325 hrs a FAT torpedo at a tanker of 8,000 tons behind her and at 2332 hrs a G 7e at a freighter of 4,000 tons. Shortly after 2330 hrs the Dutch freighter *Zaanland* at position 103 and the American *James Oglethorpe* at 93 received almost simultaneously torpedo hits on the starboard side. *U 758* observed the hits and thought it had sunk the first two named ships and torpedoed the other two: she then had to break off to refuel.

In fact, the *Zaanland*, which had a cargo of frozen wheat, textiles and zinc on board, was hit amidships, remained stationary and slowly settled down. A distress signal was sent off and white distress rockets were fired, as ordered. The survivors began to leave the ship in boats and rafts.

The Liberty ship *James Oglethorpe*, which had a cargo of steel, cotton and food and, on deck, aircraft, tractors and trucks for the US Army, was hit in No 1 hold, where a fire broke out. But it was put out within 15 minutes. The rudder was turned hard to port, the engines still ran and the ship turned in a wide circle to port at about eight knots.

Lt. Cdr. Luther at once ordered another "half-raspberry" operation. During this the *Beverley* came across the two torpedoed ships at 2359 hrs and then carried out the operation "observant" in order to locate U-boats in the area and, if necessary, to engage them. She reported that it was the two ships *Zaanland* and *James Oglethorpe*. Then she stopped to take on survivors. The *Pennywort*, coming up from the stern, reached the damaged ships shortly after midnight and also carried out the operation "observant" before she, too, stopped to take on survivors. Meanwhile the *Beverley* received orders from the SOE to rejoin the convoy and the *Pennywort* continued the rescue work on her own. The *Beverley* had taken on board nine survivors from the

THE ROUTE ORDER OF CONVOY HX. 229

16 MARCH 1943 /afternoon

N

O

P

Q▲
ANEMONE

R

S

M
VOLUNTEER

L

A

B
BEVERLEY

C

D

E

F

▲G
PENNYWORT

H

J

K

S
U

T

S

11   21   31   41   51   61   71   81   91   101   111

12   22   32   42   52   62   72   82   92   102   112

13   23   33   43   53   63   73   83   93   103

54   64   74   84   104

Zaanland. Forty-three men were rescued by the Pennywort: one man was missing. From the *James Oglethorpe* 25 men were put off in a boat while the ship was still moving slowly. They were also picked up by the *Pennywort* which now had more than 100 survivors on board from the three ships. The rest of the crew of the *James Oglethorpe,* the captain and some 30 men, remained at first on board and tried to get up steam again and to get the freighter, which was only damaged in the bows, under way so as to reach St John's. Lt. Stuart decided to remain with the ship for the time being and reported over radio telephone to the *Volunteer* that he intended to hand over the survivors from the ships to the *James Oglethorpe.*

The *Anemone* was still doing the second part of her "raspberry" triangle when, at about 2355 hrs, she sighted slightly to the port bow a surfaced U-boat at an approximate range of 3,000 meters. The U-boat was apparently trying to get to the port side of the convoy. Lt. Cdr. King at once turned toward the U-boat which withdrew and tried to escape on the surface. When the corvette was within 2,000 meters the asdic equipment registered noises from the U-boat. The *Anemone* came up slowly. When she was still 300 meters away, the U-boat submerged. The *Anemone* dropped five shallow-set depth charges where the U-boat had dived at 0009 hrs. The detonations put the radar and radio equipment temporarily out of action. At first contact with the U-boat was lost in the swirling waters. At 0025 hrs the *Anemone* again made asdic contact with the U-boat. While she prepared to approach, the U-boat surfaced at a range of about 1,400 meters. The boat was again pursued on the surface for 12 minutes before it submerged. The *Anemone* made immediate asdic contact and prepared to attack. But when about 200 meters from the target there was a short circuit and the depth charge throwers on both sides fired their charges prematurely at 0048 hrs. For four minutes the asdic equipment was out of action. Then the search was resumed. At 1,730 meters there was again contact. Ten depth charges set to 45 and 90 meters were dropped. Some 30 seconds after the last depth charge detonation there was another muffled detonation. To the stern a 30-meter high column of water arose. At 0118 hrs asdic contact was again established at a range of about 1700 meters and hardly seemed to change. At 0126 hrs the *Anemone* fired a salvo ahead with her "hedgehog" thrower at a range of 300 meters but 20 of the projectiles failed and only four hit the water without an explosion following. Contact was then lost and the *Anemone* set course for the convoy. At 0143 hrs there was again asdic contact at 1,800 meters. The *Anemone* turned in the direction of the bearing. Again a carpet of ten depth charges, set to 45 and 120 meters, was dropped at 0147 hrs. After that contact was finally lost and the *Anemone* again made for the convoy.

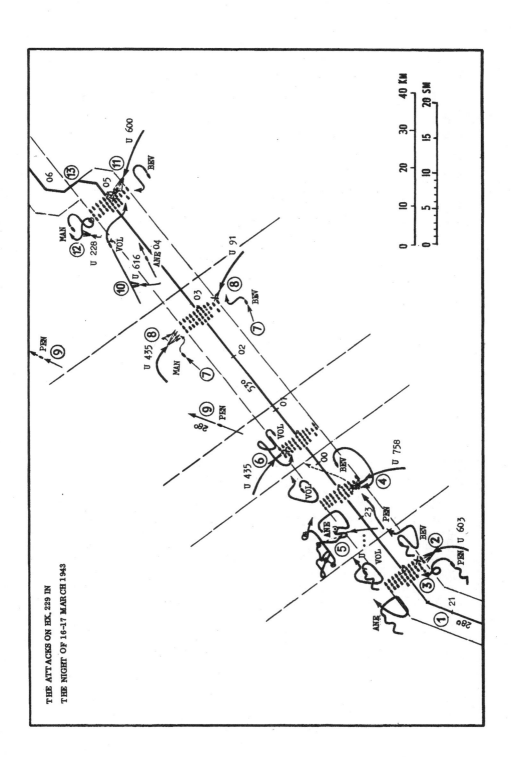

THE ATTACKS ON HX. 229 IN
THE NIGHT OF 16-17 MARCH 1943

The attacks on HX.229 in the night March 16-17, 1943

1 Mar 16 2105 hrs   New course instructions received from COMINCH. Commodore orders the convoy to proceed on new course of 053°. Weather: full moon, good visibility (about 9 miles from U-boat to merchantman), wind North force 2, swell NNW 1-2.

2 Mar 16 2200 hrs   First attack: *U 603* fires 4 torpedoes. Hit on No 101 *Elin K* which sinks in 4 minutes. SOE orders 'half raspberry' (without illumination).

3 Mar 16   Corvette *Pennywort* engaged until 2315 hrs rescuing survivors.

4 Mar 16 2320 hrs   Second attack: *U 758* fires 4 torpedoes. Hits on No 103 *Zaanland* and No 92 *James Oglethorpe*. Both at first remain stationary. SOE orders 'half raspberry'. *Beverley* rescues survivors.

5 Mar 17 2355 hrs   In carrying out 'half raspberry' *Anemone* sights a U-boat which submerges and after asdic contact is attacked with depth charges in several approaches up to 0147 hrs.

6 Mar 17 0020 hrs   Weather: full moon, partly covered by cloud. Visibility about 5 miles. Wind freshening to force 5 and turning to NE. Increasing 2-3 sea.
Third attack: *U 435* fires 2 FAT torpedoes, hit on No 22 *William Eustis*. The only escort at the time, *Volunteer*, notices the damaged ships only when she patrols to the stern. Survivors rescued. Orders to the escorts to close up as soon as possible. *Volunteer* follows at 0250 hrs.

7 Mar 17 0230 hrs   *Mansfield* and *Beverley* are again with the convoy.

8 Mar 17 0230 hrs   Fourth attack: Simultaneous approach by *U 435* from port (4 torpedoes at excessive range, no hits) and by *U 91* from starboard (4 torpedoes, 2 hits on No 111 *Harry Luckenbach* which sinks at once). Destroyers search in vain for U-boats.

9 Mar 17 0230 hrs   Corvette *Pennywort* follows the convoy on the wrong course because she did not receive the change to 53°.

10 Mar 17 0418 hrs *U 616* attacks destroyer *Volunteer* unsuccessfully.

11 Mar 17 0450 hrs Fifth attack: *U 600* fires 4 bow and 1 stern torpedo. 1 hit on No 91 *Nariva*, 2 hits on No 81 *Irenee du Pont*, 1 hit on No 72 *Southern Princess*. No 72 sinks, the other two remain stationary. Destroyers' search for U-boats at first unsuccessful, then *Mansfield* establishes asdic contact and attacks with depth charges.

12 Mar 17 0534 hrs *U 228* misses the destroyer *Mansfield* with a salvo of three.

13 Mar 17 0500 hrs At request of SOE, Commodore orders a double emergency turn of 45° to port and then a return to the general course.

Abbreviations: VOL destroyer leader *Volunteer*
BEV destroyer *Beverley*
MAN destroyer *Mansfield*
ANE corvette *Anemone*
PEN corvette *Pennywort*

THE ATTACK BY *U 435*

During these actions the next German U-boat, *U 435*, under Kptlt Strelow, had reached a favorable attacking position on the port side. The *Anemone* was still hunting her U-boats on the port quarter. The *Volunteer*, after the first two stages of her "raspberry" operation, again proceeded to position M. The *U 435* came up behind the *Volunteer* and at 0022 hrs fired a salvo of two FAT torpedoes at a tanker of 7,000 tons at a great range. At 0030 hrs the torpedo hit the freighter *William Eustis* in position 22 on the port side. The ship had no opportunity to send a distress signal or to fire distress rockets. She immediately acquired a list and settled in the stern without it at first being noticed in the convoy. At this moment Lt. Cdr. Luther, who had just got back to his position M, decided at 0031 hrs to make a sweep with the *Volunteer* to the stern of the convoy. This seemed necessary because the two corvettes stationed in the rear, *Anemone* and *Pennywort*, had stayed behind to pursue the U-boat and to recover the survivors from the *James Oglethorpe* and the *Beverley* had not yet got back to her position. In this sweep the *Volunteer* came across the wreck of the *William Eustis*, which was pouring out smoke while the crew got into the boats. After an "observant" operation the *Volunteer* began to recover the survivors at 0120 hrs. This proved to be particularly difficult as many of the crew were swimming in the water and were already widely dispersed.

Lt. Cdr. Luther now had to make a difficult decision. He did not know whether the *Beverley* had yet reached the convoy and her position again and whether the *Pennywort* was still engaged in her rescue work. It was clear from the sound of depth charges astern that the *Anemone* had not yet closed up, but Luther also did not know whether the *Mansfield* was back in the vicinity again. He could not, therefore, act on the suggestion of the chief engineer who had just been rescued and the captain of the *William Eustis* that he should wait until the morning and try to salvage the damaged ship. Because there was doubt about the fate of ship's papers, he had to decide to sink the steamer. Accordingly he approached close to the ship and fired a salvo of four shallow-set depth charges under the hull. The air whistled as it escaped from the after hold and the noise of breaking bulkheads inside the ship could be heard. When the *Volunteer* left the ship it looked as if she were settling by the stern and a fire had broken out under the bridge. It was 0250 hrs when the *Volunteer* came up behind the convoy at 20 knots.

THE ATTACKS BY *U 435* **AND** *U 91*

For a good hour the *Beverley* was the only escort with the convoy. Then at 0230 hrs the *Mansfield* arrived and at first took the position S behind the convoy as instructed. Shortly after, however, she received orders from Lt.

Cdr. Rodney Price, now the senior officer and commander of the *Beverley*, to cover the port side, while the *Beverley* took over the starboard.

But meanwhile from the port and starboard bows two U-boats had made their attacks. *U 435*, which had escaped from the *Volunteer* after its first attack, without being observed, had come up with great speed and reloaded its torpedo tubes. At 0230 hrs Kptlt Strelow fired first a salvo of two FATs at a freighter of 7,000 tons, at 0231 hrs a G 7e at a freighter of 6,000 tons and, one minute later, another at a freighter of 4,500 tons. After periods of 3 minutes 38 seconds to 3 minutes 40 seconds *U 435* heard several detonations and assumed that it had sunk the last two ships and torpedoed the first one. In fact, at this point, however, *U 91* (Kptlt Walkerling), from the starboard bow, had reached a firing position some 1,800 meters from the starboard wing ship of the convoy. First, at 0237 hrs, it fired a salvo of two torpedoes at a steamer of 8,000 tons and heard, after 120 seconds, two muffled detonations. At 0241 hrs it fired another salvo of two at a freighter with double masts of the *Beaverbrook* type (10,000 tons). After 83 seconds two huge detonations were again heard and astern two clear columns of smoke could be seen. According to the U-boat's observation, the ship went down in four minutes stern first. Actually, at this time, only one ship, the American *Harry Luckenbach* in position 111, received several hits on the starboard side and quickly sank. The detonations heard by *U 435* must have been those of *U 91*'s torpedoes. A G 7e fired from the stern tube by *U 435* at 0255 hrs went unnoticed, although Kptlt Strelow thought he had hit and sunk a 7,000 ton tanker. But it is remarkable that, with good visibility and at a distance of only 1,280 meters from the target, *U 91* reported that it had definitely torpedoed two ships with the last hits and that the first radio message from the *Beverley* at 0259 hrs also referred to two torpedoed ships.

Neither the *Mansfield* nor the *Beverley* were able to make contact with the U-boats in their search. At 0320 hrs the *Beverley* sighted several lifeboats with survivors three miles astern of the convoy. But the *Beverley* left them behind on the assumption that the *Volunteer* and *Anemone* which were coming up from astern, would find and rescue them. Lt. Cdr. Rodney Price ordered the *Mansfield* by radio telephone to take up position P on the port beam, while he himself went to the corresponding position F on the starboard beam.

To the stern of the convoy the *Anemone* first received two radar echoes at a distance of seven miles at 0225 hrs. When she came up she recognized the echoes to be those of a torpedoed ship with the *Pennywort* lying near for assistance. As help was not required, the *Anemone* continued on her way. At 0250 hrs she passed the empty rafts and lifeboats of the *William Eustis* and was informed by the *Volunteer*, which was still standing by, that the survivors had already been picked up. Consequently, the *Anemone* followed the *Volunteer* at 0310 hrs in the direction of the convoy. At 0402 hrs the *Volunteer* passed three boats of survivors from the *Harry Luckenbach*, reported by the *Beverley* 40 minutes earlier. As Lt. Cdr. Luther wanted to rejoin the convoy as soon as possible, he ordered the *Anemone* to rescue the survivors and continued on his way to the convoy. At 0418 hrs the destroyer was seen by *U 616* (Oblt Koitschka). The boat was able to fire a salvo of four torpedoes from a favorable position and at a range of 1,500 meters. But it clearly underestimated the speed of the destroyer and the torpedoes passed to the stern of the ship. The destroyer neither noticed the attack with her radar nor sighted a surface-breaking torpedo of the salvo.

Lt. Stuart on the *Pennywort* had decided, after receiving the *Beverley*'s report about the attack at 0250 hrs, to return to the convoy at high speed, when the *James Oglethorpe* was still afloat. About five miles to the north the *Pennywort* sighted the *William Eustis* lying high out of the water and apparently in a condition to be salvaged. Because of the heavy radio and telephone traffic *Pennywort* could only get her question through at 0500 hrs as to whether she should remain with the two ships which were still afloat and the lifeboats which had been sighted. She then received orders from the *Volunteer* to close up as soon as possible because there had just been a new attack.

THE ATTACK BY *U 600*

At 0456 hrs, just when the *Volunteer* had reached her position behind the convoy, *U 600* (Kptlt Zurmühlen) fired from the starboard bow, and unnoticed, a salvo of four FATs at the convoy. It then turned away and fired a stern torpedo after that. In quick succession the *Nariva* in position 91 was hit by one torpedo, the *Irenée Du Pont* in position 81 by two torpedoes and the whaling depot ship *Southern Princess* in position 72 by one torpedo on the starboard side. All three ships were brought to a halt. Lt. Cdr. Luther ordered the *Mansfield* and *Beverley* to make sweeps down their sides of the convoy and he himself went to the port side behind the convoy. At 0517 hrs the *Mansfield* had an asdic contact and dropped some depth charges. It may have been *U 89* which reported a depth charge attack at 0615 hrs. When by 0535 hrs the search produced no further results, Lt. Cdr. Luther ordered the *Mansfield* to carry out the "observant" operation round the three wrecks and then to rescue the survivors. He himself went with the *Volunteer* to position P on the port side and the *Beverley* proceeded once more in position F on the starboard side. The *Anemone* and *Pennywort* received orders to help the rescue operation to the stern of the convoy.

At this point the Convoy Commodore had received no information or suggestions from the escorts and could not himself follow their movements. All he knew was that some of them were looking for survivors in the rear. He himself assumed that the U-boats were stationed on the convoy's line of advance and that he must do something to shake them off. He waited a while until he could assume that the destroyers which were proceeding in all directions had forced the U-boats to submerge and then he gave orders at 0515 hrs for an emergency turn of 45° to port. This order was only given with sound signals. At 0530 hrs there was another emergency turn to port. But at 0545 hrs he had to revert, in two turns, to the general course of 053° to avoid collisions, because it was apparent that some ships had not heard or understood the signals. While the *Mansfield* was trying to approach the three damaged ships, *U 228* (Oblt Christophersen) seems to have attacked the destroyer with a salvo of three torpedoes, which missed. Although the range was reduced to 1,240 meters, the destroyer did not even then observe the U-boat. With 9–10 cloud density, visibility at this time was six miles. There was a NNE wind of force 4 and a medium swell of state 3.

The appreciation of the situation by the escorts is seen most clearly in the paragraph of Lt. Cdr. Luther's report:

"The outlook at this time was not encouraging with the possibility of more attacks to come and so few escorts available to deal with them. I ordered escorts to act offensively by making frequent dashes outwards at high speed dropping occasional single depth charges in the hope that it might deter an intending attacker. No more attacks did, however, take place and dawn broke on a somewhat decimated convoy and a scattered and rather embittered escort who felt that they had been beaten by facts outside their control and by pure weight of numbers."

At 0635 hrs the *Beverley,* which was proceeding 4,000 meters on the starboard beam of the convoy, located for the first time, with her radar, a U-boat at about 3,000 meters on the starboard quarter. She turned in the direction of the U-boat and increased speed to 15 knots, but then reduced it again to 12 knots so as to reveal no bow wave when she was 2,400 meters from the U-boat. Radar contact was lost after about 1,200 meters, but the U-boat, which had in the meantime submerged, was picked up by asdic. The U-boat tried to break out to port away from the approaching destroyer's course. When the destroyer turned toward it, the U-boat made a sharp change of course to the starboard and so came inside the destroyer's arc. When she was in the vicinity of the suspected U-boat position, the *Beverley* dropped her carpet of depth charges. The depth charges from the two throwers on the starboard and port side were set to 15 and 45 meters and the three heavy depth charges from each of the two chutes in the stern to 15 meters. The port chute had, however, been blocked by the heavy seas a few days earlier with the result that only seven depth charges could be dropped. Later attempts to reestablish asdic contact with the U-boat failed and at 0721 hrs the *Beverley* turned back to the convoy. At 0880 hrs *U 228* reported this attack and "contact lost."

THE SINKING OF THE DAMAGED SHIPS BY *U 91*

The *Pennywort* had left the two damaged ships astern shortly after 0500 hrs as instructed. The *James Oglethorpe*, which had been started up again by her captain and the 30 remaining members of the crew, came up to the burning *William Eustis*. At 0700 hrs *U 91* had caught sight of a burning wreck and a freighter coming up on the starboard side of the ship. At 0739 hrs *U 91* fired, at a range of about 3,200 meters, a salvo of three torpedoes at the almost overlapping ships. The *James Oglethorpe* was hit after three minutes 30 seconds by two torpedoes astern and amidships. The ship stopped and poured out white smoke. Soon she acquired a heavy list and slowly settled down in the water. The third torpedo hit the *William Eustis*, lying about 150 meters further away, after three minutes 40 seconds. A loud detonation, followed by an explosion, leaping flames and heavy smoke were observed, but this ship, too, only settled down in the water slowly. She finally sank at 1013 hrs and the *James Oglethorpe* went down at 1400 hrs.

When, after the last U-boat attack, the three ships *Nariva*, *Irenée Du Pont* and *Southern Princess* were left stationary and badly hit, the captain of the *Tekoa* (Capt. Hocken) in position 84 decided to stay behind to rescue survivors with his ship so as to relieve the convoy's weak escort of this task. The *Tekoa* was able to rescue 138 survivors from the *Irenée Du Pont* and the *Southern Princess* by dawn. At 0515 hrs the corvette *Anemone*, coming up from astern, obtained a radar contact eight miles ahead. At first she recognized a burning ship. When she got nearer she established that it was four ships and that many boats and rafts were drifting in the water. The corvette then carried out an "observant" operation at 0545 hrs and, after, stopped to rescue survivors. Four boatloads of survivors from the *Nariva* were taken on board. But many other boats in the area were empty. Lt. Cdr. King decided to wait until it was light as all four ships were still afloat. The *Southern Princess* was burning fiercely forward up to the bridge. Only with daylight did the *Anemone* realize that one of the ships, the *Tekoa*, had not been torpedoed but had stayed behind to rescue survivors. She received orders from the *Mansfield*, which had now also arrived on the scene, to close up to the convoy.

In the meantime, the *Anemone* tried to investigate the state of the still floating *Nariva*. The Captain and Chief Engineer went on board to examine the prospects of salvaging her. When they returned they reported that the boiler was empty and the water pipes were broken in places. In addition, the forward deck was partly awash and the ship on fire in the bows. They appeared to think that it would not be possible to get up steam. As all the boats had been lost, the crew were not eager to go back on board. Apart from that, no further escort with the convoy could be spared. The *Anemone* reported the situation to the *Mansfield* and Lt. Cdr. Hill gave orders to sink the ships. At 0930 hrs the *Southern Princess* capsized and remained afloat for half an hour with her bottom upward before she completely sank. The two escorts fired some 4-inch shells into the water line of the *Nariva* and *Irenée Du Pont* and also, in passing, dropped a depth charge under each ship. Both seemed to sink slowly, with the result that at 1115 hrs the escorts set out on a course of 053° and at 14 knots behind the convoy which was now 60 miles ahead. The *Anemone* had 94 survivors, the whole crew of the *Nariva*, on board and the *Mansfield* others.

In the afternoon *U 91* encountered the two wrecks and finished them off, reporting this to Commander U-boats by radio at 1508 hrs. *U 603* and *U 615* had sighted them earlier but could not attack.

THE FIRST ATTACK BY *U 338* ON SC.122

Until dark on the evening of March 16 the SC.122 had escaped detection by the U-boats. Most of the boats of the *Stürmer* group, which had been deployed in the morning against HX.229, were proceeding south of the convoy's course and the remainder of the *Stürmer* group which were only deployed in the afternoon of March 16 and the *Dränger* boats were still further off. The convoy was steaming on a course of 066° at a speed of seven knots in a once more compact formation of 50 ships in 11 columns. The Commodore, Capt. S. N. White, RNR, was on the freighter *Glenapp* in position 81 in the center of the convoy. The table opposite shows the route order of the convoy.

The escorts of Escort Group B 5 had assumed the night screen formation NE 6. The destroyer leader *Havelock* (Cdr. R. C. Boyle, RN) proceeded in position H, the four corvettes *Pimpernel* (Lt. H. D. Hayes, RNR) in C, *Buttercup* (Lt. Cdr. J. C. Dawson, RNR) in F, *Saxifrage* (Lt. M. L. Knight, RNR) in R and *Lavender* (Lt. L. G. Pilcher, RNR) in M. The American destroyer *Upshur* (Cdr. G. McCabe, USN), attached to the group, had occupied position P. These units maintained a distance of about 4,500 meters from the nearest ships of the convoy and proceeded on slightly zigzag courses. The frigate *Swale* (Lt. Cdr. J. Jackson, RNR) was pushed out about 7,500 meters to the starboard to position DD. The corvette *Godetia* (Lt. M. A. F. Larose, RNR) was still coming up from the stern, after rescuing the crew of the *Campobello*.

TABLE No. 7

Route order for Convoy SC.122 before the beginning of the attack on the evening of March 16

35 brit SS *Vinriver* Clyde	34 icel SS *Fjallfoss* Reykjavik	33 straggler	32 amer SS *Cartago* Reykjavik	31 norw SS *Askepot* Reykjavik
45 yugo SS *Franka* Loch Ewe	44 brit SS *Carso* Loch Ewe	43 icel SS *Godafoss* Reykjavik	42 brit SS *Ogmore Castle* Loch Ewe	41 norw SS *Granville* Reykjavik
55 dutch SS *Parkhaven* Loch Ewe	54 swed SS *Atland* Loch Ewe	53 brit SS *Baron Semple* Belfast (?)	52 brit SS *King Gruffydd* Loch Ewe	51 brit SS *Kingsbury* Loch Ewe
65 brit SS *Drakepool* Loch Ewe	64 brit ST *Beacon Oil* Clyde	63 brit MS *Innesmoor* Loch Ewe	62 brit ST *Empire Galahad* United Kingdom	61 dutch SS *Alderamin* Loch Ewe
75 brit SS *Aymeric* Loch Ewe	74 brit SS *Baron Elgin* Loch Ewe	73 brit SS *Bridgepool* Loch Ewe	72 brit ST *Christian Holm* United Kingdom	71 brit SS *Baron Stranrear* Loch Ewe
	84 brit SS *Zouave* Loch Ewe	83 brit SS *Reaveley* Mersey	82 brit MT *Benedick* Clyde	81 brit MS *Glenapp* Mersey
95 brit Resc *Zamalek* Greenock	94 brit SS *Orminister* Loch Ewe	93	92 brit SS *Port Auckland* Mersey	91 brit SS *Historian* Mersey
105 amer LST *LST 365* United Kingdom	104 brit SS *Badjestan* Glasgow	103 brit SS *Filleigh* Mersey	102 brit ST *Gloxinia* Mersey	101 brit MS *Losada* Mersey
115 amer LST *LST 305* United Kingdom	114 swed SS *Porjus* Mersey	113 brit SS *Boston City* Belfast	112 brit ST *Shirvan* Belfast	111 brit SS *Empire Dunstan* Mersey
	124 brit SS *Fort Cedar Lake* Belfast	123 pan SS *Bonita* United Kingdom	122 amer ST *Vistula* Belfast	121 brit SS *Dolius* Belfast
	134 dutch MS *Kedoe* Belfast	133 brit SS *Helencrest* Mersey	132 greek SS *Carras* Belfast	131 brit SS *Empire Morn* Belfast

Convoy Commodore: 81 *Glenapp*
Vice Commodore: 113 *Boston City*
Escort Oiler: 82 *Benedick*
Standby Oiler: 72 *Christian Holm*

Ocean Escort Group B.5
Task Unit 24.1.19
Destroyer HMS *Havelock*
Frigate HMS *Swale*
Corvette HMS *Lavender*
Corvette HMS *Pimpernel*
Corvette HMS *Buttercup*
Corvette HMS *Saxifrage*
(Corvette HMS *Godetia* — straggler)
Task Unit 24.12.
Destroyer USS *Upshur*

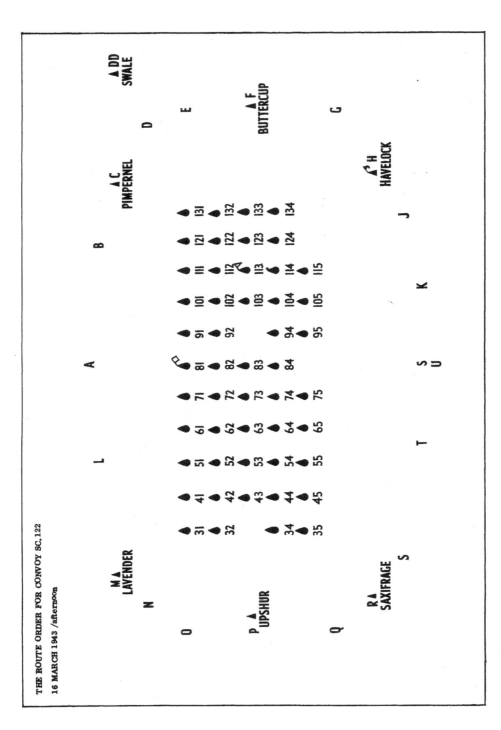

THE ROUTE ORDER FOR CONVOY SC.122

16 MARCH 1943 /afternoon

In contrast to convoy HX.229, the SC.122 had a specially equipped rescue ship, the *Zamalek*, which proceeded at the rear and in the center of the convoy at position 95. The *Havelock* and *Zamalek* were equipped with HF/DF.

Shortly before 0200 hrs *U 338* (Kptlt Kinzel), which was trying to reach the plotted meeting point with HX.229 on a southerly course, saw shadows on the starboard bow at a great distance. The cloud density was 7–10, but it was very bright because of the high moon and visibility was 12 miles. There was a slight force 2–3 wind from the NNW and a mild swell of state 1–2 from the west. Soon after, Kptlt Kinzel recognized a convoy advancing with a broad front directly toward the U-boat. He reduced speed in order to slip through unobserved between two clearly recognizable escorts steaming ahead of the convoy. He sent off a contact signal at 0202 hrs only just before his attack. This signal was located by the HF/DF stations on the *Havelock* and *Zamalek* as a contact signal just in front of the convoy, but the warning to the escorts was only being prepared when *U 338* attacked.

At 0205 hrs the distance to the ships was still about 1,500 meters and Kptlt Kinzel gave the first officer of the watch, Lt. Zeissler, who, as usual in a surface attack, was in charge of the torpedoes, permission to fire. The first salvo of two was directed toward the freighter, estimated to be of 5,000 tons, which was at the head of the third column. It was the British *Kingsbury* (4,898 tons) in position 51. After traveling for 110 seconds, equivalent to a distance of 1,584 meters, a torpedo hit. Shortly after, a second detonation was heard. On the ship which was the target of the torpedo a 100-meter high column of smoke was seen. The ship quickly acquired a list to starboard and caught fire. In the U-boat it was assumed that both torpedoes had hit the same ship. But, in fact, the second torpedo had hit the British freighter *King Gruffydd* (5,072 tons) in position 52, which had closed up somewhat too much. She was obscured from the U-boat's view by the freighter in position 61. This four-masted freighter of the *Empire Endurance* type was estimated to be of 8,500 tons and it was the target for the next salvo of two torpedoes. At a range of about 800 meters both torpedoes hit their target after traveling 60 seconds. The ship broke up in a huge explosion: bow and stern reared briefly out of the water and then sank in about two minutes. It was the four-masted Dutch *Alderamin* (7,886 tons). In turning away, *U 338* fired her stern torpedo at a freighter of 4,000 tons: this was probably the *Baron Stranraer* in position 71, but she was not hit. Only the *Kingsbury* was able to send a radio distress signal and apparently also fired two white distress rockets. These rockets prompted many of the merchantmen in the convoy to fire off their "snowflake" rockets with the result that the convoy was brightly illuminated. The U-boat, which was still on the surface but just about to dive, was sighted by the *Baron Stranraer* a short distance ahead and the *Baron Stranraer*, the *Glenapp* and the *Historian* opened fire on the U-boat with their machine guns. The signal rockets

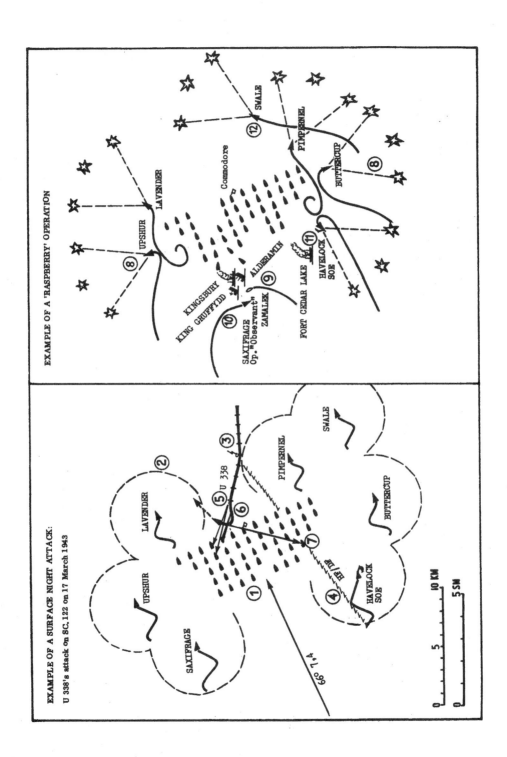

EXAMPLE OF A SURFACE NIGHT ATTACK:

U 338's attack on SC. 122 on 17 March 1943

EXAMPLE OF A 'RASPBERRY' OPERATION

Example of a surface night attack: U 338's attack on SC.122 in the night March 16-17, 1943

1. Route formation for convoy SC.122: 13 columns 1, 2, 5, 5, 5, 5, 4, 5, 5, 4, 3, 2. Front of convoy 7 miles, depth about 2.5 miles. Escorts about 4 000 m from the nearest ship. Weather: full moon, very good visibility (about 12 miles from U-boat to merchantman), wind west force 2-3, freshening up, sea 2 increasing.

2. Mar 17 0201 hrs — Radar range of 271 M equipment up to about 4 000 m against U-boats.

3. Mar 17 0201 hrs — *U 338* approaches the convoy from ahead towards gap between the two forward escorts (*Lavender* and *Pimpernel* about 12 000 metres apart). Contact signal sent at 0201 hrs on approach shortly before firing.

4. Mar 17 0202 hrs — Contact signal is picked up by HF/DF of leader of Escort Group, destroyer *Havelock*. Preparing to evaluate and issue warning when

5. Mar 17 0205 hrs — *U 338* fires the first salvo of two from bow tubes at the ship in position 51 (no column 1). After 110 seconds (1 584 metres), U-boat observes one, and, shortly after, a second detonation. Sinking of a ship observed. In fact, 1 hit on No 51 *Kingsbury* and 1 hit on No 52 *King Gruffyd*.

6. Mar 17 0206 hrs — *U 338* fires second salvo of two at ship in position 61. After 60 seconds (= 864 metres) two hits observed on No 61 *Alderamin* which sinks.

7. Mar 17 0207 hrs — *U 338* turns away and fires stern torpedo at ship in position 71 or 81. Misses target. Torpedo runs through convoy and hits No 124 *Fort Cedar Lake*. *U 338* does not observe this because it submerges in the meantime when fired on by Nos 71, 81 and 91.

8. Mar 17 0207 hrs — After first hits, white distress signals are fired. SOE orders 'half raspberry'. Escorts close up to convoy, turn near the outside ships and fire star-shells. Merchant ships fire 'snowflakes'. The area of the convoy is clearly illuminated but no U-boat can be seen, *U 338* having submerged in the meantime.

9. Mar 17 0215 hrs — *King Gruffyd* and *Alderamin* sink, *Kingsbury* on fire. Rescue ship *Zamalek* goes to wrecks to recover survivors.

10. Mar 17 0232 hrs — At the end of the 'half raspberry' operation, corvette *Saxifrage* closes up and begins 'observant' operation to cover the *Zamalek's* rescue action.

11. Mar 17 0240 hrs — *Havelock* discovers wreck of *Fort Cedar Lake*.

12. Mar 17 0242 hrs — SOE orders frigate *Swale* to position in front of the convoy.

and the tracer fire were observed by the escorts ahead which turned at once in their direction. A few seconds later Cdr. Boyle ordered the escorts over the radio telephone to carry out a "half-raspberry" operation. All the escorts performed their triangular movements according to plan and, after about an hour, again reached their prescribed positions with the convoy. The *Swale* received instructions to proceed some 4,000–8,000 meters in front of the convoy to prevent another infiltration by a U-boat from this direction.

The rescue ship *Zamalek* (Capt. O. C. Morris) had fallen astern when the white rockets and torpedo detonations were observed and proceeded to the spot where the wrecks could be seen. Cdr. Boyle detached the corvette *Saxifrage*, which was nearest, to screen and support the *Zamalek*. When the *Zamalek* and *Saxifrage* came up, the *King Gruffydd* and the *Alderamin* had already gone down and the *Kingsbury* was burning fiercely. When hit, the ships had had no time to get their boats into the water in orderly fashion. Many survivors were swimming in the sea with their life jackets on and could be recognized by the flashing red lights. The *Zamalek* lowered her motor lifeboat and tried herself to pick up survivors by putting out rescue nets and taking them on board from rafts.

At 0300 hrs the *Saxifrage* sighted another drifting merchantman. It was the *Fort Cedar Lake*, which had received a torpedo hit on the port side at 0214 hrs but which, for the time being, remained afloat. For a long time people were puzzled from where this torpedo could have come, because there appeared to be no attack report by a U-boat to fit the case. A detailed investigation of *U 338*'s attack has now shown that it was clearly the stern torpedo of the boat which first missed its intended target but then ran through the entire convoy and, after traveling for about six minutes, hit the *Fort Cedar Lake*, the ship in position 124.

In the rescue operation which lasted until about 0900 hrs in the morning the *Zamalek* took on board, in all, 44 survivors from the *Kingsbury*, 25 from the *King Gruffydd*, 12 from the *Alderamin* and, finally, 50 from the now abandoned *Fort Cedar Lake*. The *Saxifrage* rescued another 37 men from the *Alderamin* from several rafts about 0745 hrs. The wreck of the *Kingsbury* broke up about 0515 hrs and sank. The eventual fate of the *Fort Cedar Lake* is not known. She probably went down at 0830 hrs shortly after the *Zamalek* and *Saxifrage* left. But, conceivably, it was this ship which fell victim to the attacks reported by *U 228* at 0958 hrs and *U 665* (Oblt Haupt) at 1057 hrs. In these attacks it was claimed that hits were obtained on a steamer of 6,000 and 5,000 tons respectively.

The two rescue ships decided to go off on an apparently northern course so as not to lead any U-boat, which might be in the area, straight to the convoy. They only turned toward the convoy after four hours.

CHAPTER 9

March 17, 1943

THE SITUATION ON THE MORNING OF MARCH 17

When day broke on March 17 Commodore Mayall and Lt. Cdr. Luther had first to reorganize the convoy which had been considerably dislocated by the heavy losses in the night and the evasive action taken during the last attack. There were still 28 merchantmen in sight. As the losses had been largely on the starboard side of the convoy and had created considerable gaps in the columns there, Commodore Mayall decided to reduce the number of columns to nine and to reorganize the ships on the starboard side in columns seven, eight and nine, as the table overleaf on p. 151 shows.

The Captain of the British ship *Nebraska* proceeding in position 41 was appointed Vice Commodore in place of the Captain of the sunken *Nariva*.

Lt. Cdr. Luther with his escort group found himself in a very desperate situation. He only had with the convoy his leader, the Volunteer, which was in position P on the port side and the *Beverley* which was in position E on the starboard side. Shortly after the last attack Lt. Cdr. Luther had, at 0530 hrs, ordered the escorts, which remained behind to rescue survivors, to close up as soon as possible. The *Mansfield* was able to get back to her position about midday. The corvette *Anemone* was still involved with the freighter *Tekoa* in taking on the survivors of the three last ships torpedoed. At 1115 hrs the *Anemone* proceeded at 14 knots on a course of 053° so as to catch up the convoy which was estimated to be about 60 miles ahead.

A few minutes later, at 1127 hrs, the *Anemone* sighted a U-boat proceeding in the opposite direction on the port beam at a distance of about six miles: she turned at once toward it. The U-boat submerged, while the corvette proceeded at high speed to reach the spot where the boat had dived. When she got near the position, her speed was again reduced to help her locate the U-boat with asdic. At 1150 hrs the asdic located it at 030° and a range of 1,800 meters. Lt. Cdr. King at once increased speed and, at 1154 hrs, dropped a carpet of depth charges set to 45 and 120 meters. The detonations put the asdic out of action. The *Anemone* remained about half an hour in the area, but the asdic could not be repaired in time. Lt. Cdr. King therefore decided to return to the convoy which was only reached at 2215 hrs.

The second corvette *Pennywort* had abandoned the wreck of the *James Oglethorpe* and proceeded toward the convoy after the *Volunteer* gave the alarm during the attack at about 0300 hrs. It was hoped to reach the convoy toward morning. But the *Pennywort*, after she had passed the wreck of the *William Eustis*, which was in the vicinity, proceeded on a course of 028°, because in the evening, when Commodore Mayall ordered the change of course from 028° to 053° with light signals, she was going across the direction of the convoy in a sweep and did not receive the signal. When, shortly after 0600 hrs, the convoy did not come into sight, as expected, the *Pennywort* asked the *Volunteer* by radio whether the convoy had changed course. At first she received no reply and maintained her existing course. The *Volunteer*'s signal of 0530 hrs to the Pennywort, telling her to close up, had not been received. It was only at 1800 hrs that the *Pennywort* received details of the position, course and speed from the *Volunteer* and could then take the proper course, helped by HF/DF bearing signals from the *Volunteer*. She reached the convoy at 2330 hrs.

The situation looked better with SC.122. Although four ships had been lost in the night, Commodore White could look on a much better organized convoy and Commander Day disposed of seven escorts as the *Godetia* had closed up in place of the *Saxifrage* which had remained behind with the rescue ship *Zamalek*.

The Allied Commands on shore and, in particular, CINCWA, Adm. Sir Max Horton in Liverpool, were not yet able to form a very clear picture of the situation with HX.229 and SC.122 in the night from the fragmentary radio messages so far received. At 2350 hrs the *Volunteer* had reported that the convoy had been attacked in the position 50°27'N 35°09'W and that one or two ships were torpedoed. The "or" was at first read as "and" with the result that it was believed that three ships had been torpedoed. As more stragglers from the convoy were expected, CINCWA gave the convoy an improved and supplementary stragglers' route at 0125 hrs. It was to run via point CD at 53°55'N 35°00'W and CF at 55°50'N 25°01'W to point U without touching the old point BB. In the morning the further report from the *Volunteer* at 0502 hrs reached CINCWA that three more attacks had taken place and that eight ships, in all, were torpedoed. It was clear from the radio traffic that SC.122 had also been attacked. Among other things, the SSS report was received from the *Kingsbury* using the code sign "TQ 51" (TQ was the radio call sign for convoy SC.122 and 51 the tactical number of the steamer in the convoy). Toward midday the *Havelock* with the SC.122 gave her answer,

TABLE No. 8

Route order for Convoy HX.229 after re-forming on the morning of March 17

		13 brit SS *Empire Knight* Clyde	12 amer SS *Robert Howe* Mersey	11 brit SS *Cape Breton* Clyde
		23 amer SS *Mathew Luckenbach* United Kingdom		21 amer SS *Walter Q. Gresham* Clyde
		33 brit MS *Canadian Star* United Kingdom	32 brit MS *Kaipara* Mersey	31 brit SS *Fort Anne* Loch Ewe
		43 brit MS *Antar* Mersey	42 brit MT *Regent Panther* United Kingdom	41 brit SS *Nebraska* Mersey
	54 brit SS *Empire Cavalier* Mersey	53 amer ST *Pan Rhode Island* Mersey	52 brit MT *San Veronica* Mersey	51 pan MT *Belgian Gulf* Mersey
	64 amer SS *Kofresi* Mersey	63 amer SS *Jean* Mersey	62 amer ST *Gulf Disc* Clyde	61 norw MS *Abraham Lincoln* Belfast
		73 pan SS *El Mundo* Mersey	72 dutch MT *Magdala* Belfast	71 brit SS *City of Agra* Mersey
	84 straggler	83 brit MT *Nicania* Mersey	82 brit MT *Luculus* Belfast	81 brit SS *Coracero* Mersey
		93 amer SS *Margaret Lykes* Mersey	92 amer SS *Daniel Webster* Belfast	91 dutch SS *Terkoelei* Belfast
		113 straggler		

Convoy Commodore: 61 *Abraham Lincoln*
Vice Commodore: 41 *Nebraska*
Escort Oiler: 62 *Gulf Disc*

Ocean Escort Group B.4
Task Unit 24.1.18
Destroyer HMS *Volunteer*
Destroyer HMS *Beverley*
Corvette   HMS *Anemone* (rejoining)
Corvette   HMS *Pennywort* (rejoining)
Task Unit 24.12.3
Destroyer HMS *Manfield* (rejoining)

divided according to the system "AC 1 Article 39 para 5." This contained the
following points:

(a) Number and time of the attacks and their position.

(b) Number of attacking U-boats.

(c) Side from which the attack came.

(d) Details of losses and rescued survivors.

(e) Details of ships that could be salvaged.

(f) Details of intentions of the rescue ships.

(g) Other observations.

(h) Weather situation.

The German signals interception service was able to pick up the SSS
report "TQ 51" and the cryptographers were able to decode a substantial
part of the *Havelock*'s report. Among other things, it appeared from the
decoding that in the U-boat attack four ships had been sunk, including No.
51, *Kings . . . . y* (garbled) and No 52, *King Gruffydd.*

The *Volunteer* was not able to send her report before 1545 hrs. Her radio
personnel were not adequate to cope with the duties falling to an escort
leader. Many switches had to be manned for reception and there was also
her own radio and telephone traffic with the escort group and the convoy.
In addition, the HF/DF station and the MF/DF frequencies to provide aircraft and escort ships with bearings had to be serviced. The vital radio traffic
could only be dealt with by using the HF/DF personnel from time to time.
This meant, however, that at these times the convoy could not take bearings
on the U-boat signals, because no other ship with the convoy was equipped
for this purpose. The message from the *Volunteer* had the following text:

To: AIG.303

From: ETU 24.1.18

ACI, Art.39 Para (5)

2 (a) Four attacks 2215Z/16 to 0508Z/17 in position 5038N
3446W.

(b) Four, details unknown.

(c) To starboard.

(d) *William Eustis, Southern Princess, Irenée Du Pont, James
Oglethorpe, Elin K, H. Luckenbach, Zaaland, Nariva.* Survivors *Pennywort* 9, *Volunteer* 66, *Mansfield* 20, *Beverley* 30,
Tekoa 200, *Anemone* considerable number, details
unknown.

(e) *Nariva* being investigated.

(f) All rejoining.

(g) Nil.

(h) 3581, 0485

1545Z/17.

This message was also partly garbled when it reached Command Head-quarters. But it was already clear to CINCWA from the little information that he had toward morning on March 17 and from the reports from the British D/F stations about the bearings of U-boat signals in the region of the convoys that both convoys were in great danger and that something had to be done quickly to help them. The only possibility was to request the AOC No 15 Group, RAF Coastal Command, Air Vice-Marshal Slatter, who had a joint situation center and command post with CINCWA in Derby House, Liverpool, to provide air escort as soon as possible for the convoys and to the limit of its range.

At this time No 15 Group contained the following units. Most important of all were the Very Long Range (VLR) aircraft of the Liberator IIIA type. Of the combined established strength of 32 aircraft of 120 and 86 squadrons only 13, or about 40% were operational on March 15. The squadrons had each an establishment strength of 16 aircraft. 120 Squadron was stationed at Aldergrove near Londonderry in Northern Ireland and 86 Squadron at Thorney Island, near Portsmouth, and was under the command there of No 16 Group. In the case of 120 Squadron, some aircraft were, from time to time, detached to Reykjavik in Iceland and 86 Squadron transferred some aircraft to Aldergrove as a replacement. As the convoy positions on March 17 could only be reached from Aldergrove when use was made of the Liberators' extreme range, only the aircraft available there were suitable for deployment. It was decided to use them in relays in the morning and afternoon.

The other aircraft of No 15 Group, because of their reduced range (about 600 miles on average) could not reach the convoys before March 18. They included 220 Squadron in Aldergrove and No 206 in Benbecula in the Hebrides. They each had an establishment of nine Flying Fortresses. But, in fact, of the 27 aircraft in the three squadrons with Coastal Command on March 15, only 10 were ready for immediate operations. No 15 Group also had five squadrons, each of which should have had six Sunderland flying boats: of these, 201 and 228 Squadrons and 423 (RCAF) Squadron were stationed in Castle Archdale in Northern Ireland, 246 Squadron in Bowmore at the entrance to the North Channel and 422 (RCAF) Squadron in Oban. Of a total of 48 Sunderland flying boats with Coastal Command 22 were operational on March 15. Thus it was that on March 15 there should have been six to seven Fortress bombers and 13–14 Sunderland flying boats with No 15 Group available for deployment over medium ranges up to about 600 miles. In Iceland there was also the US Navy Patrol 84 Squadron with an establishment of 12 Catalina flying boats: they were stationed in Reykjavik and could cover a range of about 600 miles.

The German Commander U-boats had looked forward to the operation on the evening of March 16 with high hopes since the *Raubgraf* group
was in a very favorable position and a large number of contact reports had
already come in. By the morning of March 17 reports of success were
received from five boats and clearly several boats had made repeated
attacks. *U 603, U 435, U 91, U 758, U 435* again and *U 600* had reported the
sinking of 12 ships in all totaling 77,500 tons and the torpedoing of six
more. According to the reports received, the escort screen did not appear
to be very strong. On the other hand, the arrival of the 11 southern *Stürmer*
boats was expected on March 17 and, later, the remaining boats of the
Stürmer and *Dränger* groups. Even if some of the *Raubgraf* boats had to break
off the operation because of fuel shortage and some of the other boats did
not arrive, there were good prospects of operating against the convoy with
up to 20 boats in the coming night.

Toward morning it became clear from a report from *U 338* that it was
evidently not a case of one convoy, as had been thought hitherto, but of two.
It was realized in the course of the morning that the convoy, which was first
reported and attacked and which was sailing on a general course of 045° at
about eight knots, was the HX convoy and that the one which was some 120
miles further ahead and was proceeding on a general course of 070° at 6.5
knots must be the SC convoy. The Commander U-boats gave this new information to the U-boats deployed against the convoy. He ordered the northern *Stürmer* boats which were favorably placed in relation to the new convoy
and the *Dränger* boats which were not far away to operate on the forward
convoy with which there was uninterrupted contact from 0900 hrs in the
morning until 2300 hrs in the evening. The other boats operated against
HX.229 from which regular contact signals were received from 0900 hrs. It
looked as if there were good prospects for great success on the second night.

THE DAYLIGHT ATTACKS BY *U 384* AND *U 631* ON HX.229

The HX.229 had adopted its new route formation of nine columns about
midday on March 17. Its port side was screened by the *Volunteer* and its starboard side by the *Beverley*. About 1300 hrs the *Mansfield* had closed up from
the rear to about three miles from her prescribed position S behind the convoy when the next attack began.

The weather was cloudy, but clear. Visibility was about eight miles. The
wind had freshened up to a NNE force 5 and the sea was estimated to be
state 3–5. The convoy had maintained its course of 053° since the previous
night. The two escorts had to remain near the convoy and could make no
more sorties to drive off U-boats in the vicinity. In addition, the use of the
Volunteer's HF/DF was restricted because the destroyer had to provide bear-

ings for the expected aircraft and also tried to pick up their signals in order to give the first aircraft the right approach course. Because the personnel were not yet familiar with this equipment, the bearings were incorrect by 180° and were transmitted as such to the aircraft. This mistake prevented the arrival of the first Liberator in the morning but was corrected later.

In the circumstances it was relatively easy for *U 384* (Oblt von Rosenberg-Gruszczinski) and *U 631* (Oblt Krüger) to come up on the starboard side of the convoy by overtaking it in a great arc at the limit of visibility, in order then to submerge and to wait for the convoy's approach. With the prevailing visibility the U-boats could usually pick out the ships and masts at greater distances than, for instance, the *Beverley* could detect a U-boat with her radar in the rough sea. Consequently, both boats were undetected. It happened by chance that they were almost simultaneously in a position to fire and they discharged their torpedo salvoes in an underwater attack at 1305 hrs and 1306 hrs. *U 384* aimed at a freighter of 6,000 tons, a freighter of 4,000 tons and a freighter of 2,500 tons, probably the ships of the starboard column. *U 631* fired its torpedoes at a tanker of 7,000 tons, probably one in the second row.

In quick succession the Dutch ship *Terkoelei* in position 91 and the British *Coracero* behind her in position 81 were hit on the starboard side. The *Terkoelei* was apparently ripped open by several torpedoes and sank almost at once. The *Coracero* settled markedly by the stern but remained afloat for the time being. The *Volunteer* at once gave the alarm and proceeded at high speed across the front of the convoy to the starboard.

The *Beverley* steamed along the starboard side of the convoy, turned round behind the convoy and rushed through the columns of the convoy to position A near the Commodore's ship. The *Mansfield*, which came up in the stern, also turned to the starboard side and met the *Volunteer*, without, however, one of the ships locating a U-boat with asdic. At 1312 hrs the Convoy Commodore ordered an emergency turn to port. In two 45° turns the convoy veered away from the suspected area of the U-boats' attack. At 1333 hrs Lt. Cdr. Luther gave orders to the *Mansfield* to rescue survivors while he himself with the *Volunteer* carried out an "observant" operation round the *Mansfield* at 1345 hrs.

When the torpedoes detonated, Lt. Cdr. Luther thought the time had come to ask for help. With attacks by day and night and with the escorts having the dual role of screening and recovering survivors, there seemed only little chance of saving more than a fraction of the convoy. In addition, in the prevailing weather and with the constant attacks, it was impossible to replenish the escorts with fuel. The destroyer *Mansfield*'s supplies were already very low. Consequently the *Volunteer* sent the message at 1310 hrs: "HX.229

attacked, two ships torpedoed. Request early reinforcements for the convoy 51°45'N 32°26'W." At 1437 hrs Lt. Cdr. Luther sent a second message to CINCWA and to the leader, *Highlander*, which was coming up behind the convoy: "Have *Beverley* and *Mansfield* in company. *Pennywort* and *Anemone* overtaking astern. Persistent attacks will not permit refueling and situation is becoming critical. D/F sightings indicate many U-boats in contact." Before the *Volunteer* left the *Mansfield*, after completing the operation "observant," Lt. Cdr. Luther gave instructions to the *Beverley*, the only escort with the convoy, to request the Commodore to resume the general course.

Hardly had the convoy reverted to its old course of 053° and the *Beverley* almost reached her position A ahead of the convoy when, at 1352 hrs, a U-boat was sighted almost immediately ahead of the convoy at a distance of eight miles. The U-boat was on a course of 310°. Having maneuvered forward, it had reached an almost ideal position for a daylight underwater attack. The *Beverley* at once increased speed to 22 knots and tried to keep the boat always somewhat to the starboard bow in order to drive it off in this direction away from the convoy. At the same time Lt. Cdr. Rodney Price asked the Convoy Commodore to make another emergency turn to port. While the *Beverley* approached the U-boat at 22 knots, the lookout man in the crow's nest sighted a second U-boat behind the first on a similar bearing further ahead. When the *Beverley* had got within five miles, the first U-boat began to turn away to the starboard and when the distance between them had been reduced to three miles, the boat submerged at 1440 hrs. At 1450 hrs the *Beverley* slowed down to asdic search speed and two minutes later found the U-boat at a distance of 1,500 meters. But when the distance was about 1,000 meters, contact was again momentarily lost.

The *Beverley* began a "box search." At 1459 hrs a single depth charge with a very deep setting of 120 meters was dropped to keep the U-boat in the square. Asdic contact was again established at a range of 1,200 meters, but the *Beverley* had first to move off a little in order to turn. Her speed was reduced to 10 knots to enable her to make a "hedgehog" attack. But again only a brief echo was received which was not sufficient to provide target data. In consequence, the attack was broken off and only a depth charge set to 120 meters was dropped. At 1515 hrs contact was again established at 900 meters, more to the stern than to the beam, and again the *Beverley* had to move away before she could make another "hedgehog" attack at 1518 hrs. At 1521 hrs the "hedgehog" salvo was fired, but the U-boat was obviously inside the arc and no detonation followed. Contact was again lost and a new "box search" had to be made in which a single depth charge was again dropped at 1538 hrs. At 1543 hrs an asdic echo was obtained at a range of 1,400 meters. The *Beverley* at once approached and at 1548 hrs dropped a carpet of 10 depth charges set to depths of 45 and 90 meters. After this attack there was trouble with the asdic equipment. As a result of a technical fault in the indicator section, some wrong information reached the bridge. In consequence, the U-boat, which tried to sneak away, was undetected for an hour. Then at 1632 hrs a new contact was obtained at a range of 1,200 meters and the *Beverley* again rushed to attack with 10 depth charges which were dropped at 1635 hrs. As the U-boat did not appear to move much, the *Beverley* hove to and at 1657 dropped one of the new heavy Mark X depth charges which, however, failed to detonate. A final five-charge carpet also brought no result at 1718 hrs. It was then time for Lt. Cdr. Rodney Price to return to the convoy, so as to resume his position in time before dark for the expected night attacks.

The *Volunteer*, which at first stayed with the *Mansfield*, came up at high speed behind the convoy when the *Beverley* embarked on her U-boat hunt. For several hours the *Volunteer* was the only escort with the convoy. Consequently, Lt. Cdr. Luther gave the *Mansfield* orders to finish the rescue work as soon as possible and to close up with the convoy. The *Mansfield* took on board 52 men from the *Coracero* and 55 from the *Terkoelei*. On her return to the convoy, the *Mansfield* also sighted a U-boat to the stern of the convoy. It submerged and was attacked with a carpet of depth charges. But Lt. Cdr. Hill did not stay longer with this U-boat which lay to the stern and was therefore not immediately dangerous. He followed behind the convoy at high speed and reached it again at about 1800 hrs. A little later the *Beverley* also turned up. The *Volunteer* and the *Beverley* took up the positions O and E to the port and starboard and the *Mansfield* the position S astern.

The convoy's situation would certainly have become very critical after dark, as Lt. Cdr. Luther had predicted in his radio messages, if at 1630 hrs the Liberator J/120, led to the scene by now correctly calculated bearings from the *Volunteer*, had not found the convoy. But as the radio personnel on the *Volunteer* were at first busy with the aircraft signal bearings and, from 1800 hrs, in providing bearings to bring up the *Pennywort*, it was not possible to pick up the contact signals of the U-boat and to use them for the deployment of the aircraft. In consequence, the bomber had to rely on visual observation. At 1908 hrs it sighted two U-boats about 25 miles on the starboard beam of the convoy. The first submerged in time, the second just got under water when the bomber came up and dropped its five depth charges. But they apparently went beyond the target and the U-boat escaped. At 1947 hrs the aircraft sighted three U-boats in succession 25 miles away on the starboard quarter. Again the first submerged very quickly. The second was attacked, while submerging, with the last remaining depth charge and with the aircraft's guns. And in the case of the third boat the aircraft flew over the area where the U-boat had dived, using its guns. At 1956 hrs the aircraft

sighted a sixth U-boat, not far from the others, and again fired at it as it
dived as there were no more depth charges on board. Immediately after
sighting the first two U-boats the aircraft tried to establish radio contact with
the convoy, but this was not successful. The aircraft then approached the
convoy at 2005 hrs after its last attack and signaled to the *Volunteer* with its
searchlight: "Six hearses bearing 130°, 25 miles—I go." This somewhat care-
lessly formulated signal was not properly understood on the *Volunteer*; in
addition, the figures were wrongly read as 180° and 5 miles. The aircraft also
asked whether the *Volunteer* wanted to start a U-boat search. But Lt. Cdr.
Luther felt he could not detach one of his few escorts and asked the aircraft
whether it could help. The aircraft then flew off to the rear, but it evidently
did not find the U-boats which were still under water and it had to turn away
to base at 2045 hrs. In all, the aircraft remained 18 hrs in the air, two hours
longer than was normally possible. Although there had been no direct cooperation between escorts and the aircraft, the latter was, without doubt,
chiefly responsible for the fact that the following night proved, contrary to
all expectations, to be a quiet one for the HX.229.

THE SECOND ATTACK BY *U 338* ON SC.122

Cooperation between the escort groups and the aircraft was much better in
the case of SC.122. The main reason for this was that the leader *Havelock* was
more suitably equipped for its task both technically and in respect of personnel. This meant that there was proper radio and technical traffic and
that the various D/F devices could be manned. Up to the morning of March
17 HF/DF bearings had shown that at least six U-boats were within 20 miles
of the convoy. The *Upshur* and the *Swale* were used for sweeps against two
bearings, but they produced no result.

The first Liberator, M/86, had left Aldergrove at midnight. At 0755 hrs
the aircraft began to send bearing signals which were received by the *Havelock* with the result that the aircraft could be given its approach course. At
0822 hrs, while it was flying toward the convoy, a surfaced U-boat was sighted
some 20 miles on the port beam. It submerged as the aircraft approached.
Four depth charges were dropped where it dived. At 0850 hrs the aircraft
reached the convoy and reported the incident. Cdr. Day then requested the
Commodore to make an emergency turn to starboard. At 0910 hrs the aircraft began its patrol, as instructed, and at 1035 hrs it again sighted a U-boat
about 10 miles on the port bow. It was attacked with the two remaining
depth charges before it could submerge, but the depth charges were not sufficiently accurate. The convoy also went round this position with a new evasive move.

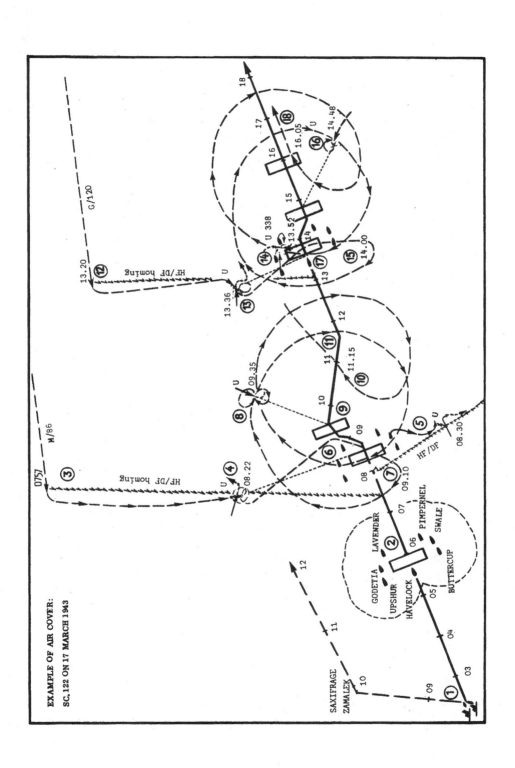

EXAMPLE OF AIR COVER:
SC.122 ON 17 MARCH 1943

Example of air cover for a convoy: SC.122 on March 17, 1943

1	Mar 17 0205 hrs	Position of *U 338*'s attack. At 0830 hrs the rescue ship *Zamalek* has completed the rescue work with the wrecks of the *Kingsbury* and *Fort Cedar Lake* and sets off on a feigned course with the screening corvette *Saxifrage*.
2	Mar 17 0600 hrs	Day-time route order and disposition of the escorts with approximate radar horizon.
3	Mar 17 0757 hrs	The M/86 Liberator which set off from Aldergrove at midnight is guided to the convoy with HF/DF bearings.
4	Mar 17 0822 hrs	M/86, in approaching the convoy, sights about 20 miles on the port beam of the convoy a surfaced U-boat trying to get in front of the convoy. It attacks it with 4 depth charges as it submerges.
5	Mar 17 0830 hrs	The leader *Havelock* picks up with HF/DF the contact signal of a U-boat on the starboard beam and details the frigate *Swale* to make a sortie on the bearing. The U-boat is forced under water. The convoy makes an emergency turn.
6	Mar 17 0850 hrs	The M/86 Liberator reports to the SOE and receives orders to carry out a 'Cobra' patrol 10 miles round the convoy.
7	Mar 17 0910 hrs	M/86 begins its 'Cobra' patrol.
8	Mar 17 0935 hrs	M/86 sights an approaching U-boat, attacks it with 2 depth charges as it submerges and then, after making some circling movements, continues the 'Cobra' patrol.
9	Mar 17 0940 hrs	Convoy makes another emergency turn of 45° to starboard.
10	Mar 17 1115 hrs	M/86 ends 'Cobra' patrol and reports to SOE that it proposes to return to base.
11	Mar 17 1140 hrs	Convoy goes back to its general course. The G/120 Liberator which set out from Aldergrove at 0706 hrs is guided to the convoy by HF/DF bearings.
12	Mar 17 1320 hrs	
13	Mar 17 1336 hrs	G/120, in approaching the convoy, sights a surfaced U-boat 10 miles on the convoy's port beam. It attacks it with 4 depth charges as it submerges and then, after making some circling movements, continues its flight to the convoy.
14	Mar 17 1352 hrs	*U 338* has got into a forward position, unobserved, to make an underwater attack and during a pause in the air cover between 1115 and 1400 hrs has reached its attacking position by a determined effort to close in. Shortly after the firing, the corvette *Godetia* notices a surface-breaker, but her warning does not prevent a hit on No 41 (2nd column) *Granville*.
15	Mar 17 1400 hrs	G/120 observes the depth charge pursuit of the attacking U-boat and, on the instructions of the SOE, begins its 'Cobra' patrol 10 miles round the convoy.
16	Mar 17 1448 hrs	G/120 sights submerging U-boat and attacks in a sharp dive. But 2 depth charges hang up. After circling movements G/120 continues 'Cobra' patrol.
17	Mar 17 1515 hrs	G/120 sights the wreck of the *Granville* with the *Godetia*.
18	Mar 17 1605 hrs	G/120 ends 'Cobra' patrol and reports to SOE that it is to fly back to base. In the 'Manta' or 'Viper' procedure the aircraft are deployed on HF/DF bearings against U-boats located by the escorts' radio or against U-boats located in sectors from the convoy centre according to the hrs of the clock (0 or 12 ahead). In the 'Frog' procedure the aircraft fly probing sorties in the most probable attacking directions of the U-boats.

Toward midday the convoy was again on its old course of 66° and the escorts had taken up the daytime screening formation DE 7—with the corvettes *Lavender* (Lt. Pilcher) and *Godetia* (Lt. Larose) and the destroyer *Upshur* (Cdr. McCabe) on the port side in positions L, N and P and the corvette *Pimpernel* (Lt. Hayes), the frigate *Swale* (Lt. Cdr. Jackson) and the corvette *Buttercup* (Lt. Cdr. Dawson) on the starboard side in the positions B, D and F and the leader *Havelock* in the position S behind the convoy. However, both the asdic and radar equipment on the *Havelock* were out of action for the time being.

The corvette *Saxifrage* had been on the way to the convoy since 1000 hrs with the rescue ship *Zamalek*. On the *Saxifrage* they had heard part of the order to take evasive action, but had wrongly interpreted the beam on which the action was taken. The result was that, initially, both ships proceeded on the wrong course and it was only when they failed to find the convoy at the expected position at 1700 hrs that they asked the *Havelock* for position, course and speed. The two ships reached the convoy after dark.

SC.122 had better weather than HX.229. The cloud density was 8–10 and visibility was excellent, extending to about 14 miles. There was a light NW force 2 wind and a NW swell of state 2–3.

Because of the aircraft circling round the convoy, most of the six U-boats in the area had fallen astern. Only *U 338* had got forward enough by observing the aircraft and, seeing its departure at 1215 hrs, moved up. When the escorts appeared over the horizon, Kptlt Kinzel dived, hoping to get between two escorts in order to make an underwater attack on the port side of the convoy. He wanted to repeat his success of the previous night with deliberate and coordinated single firings. His first target was a ship thought to be a passenger freighter of the *Antenor* type (10,000 tons). In fact, it was the American refrigerator ship *Cartago* (4,732 tons) in position 32, whose silhouette bore a certain resemblance to the *Antenor*. At 1352 hrs Kptlt Kinzel fired his first torpedo at a range of about 1,200 meters. The second target was a modern, normal type freighter, estimated at 5,000 tons, and probably the Norwegian *Askepot* (1,312 tons), built in 1937. But owing to an operational error in the bow, not just the intended torpedo was dispatched, but all three torpedoes in the bow tubes were fired off successively as an unintended salvo. Kptlt Kinzel could not see the torpedoes proceed to their destination because one of them broke surface and the port escort turned toward the U-boat.

At the time of the firing by *U 338* the *Godetia* was not at its prescribed position N but had fallen back somewhat to the level of position P and the *Upshur* was a little further back. At 1352 hrs the *Godetia* sighted, at about 2,700 meters on the starboard bow, spray in the choppy sea which was

apparently moving toward the convoy. Before it was realized that it was a surface-breaking torpedo, the first ship of the second column, the *Granville*,
received a torpedo hit on the port side. The *Granville* was a Panamanian
freighter of 4,103 tons which had been chartered as a transport by the US
Army. According to the report of Capt. F. Matzen, the torpedo hit the port
side in the area of the second hold at 1356 hrs. A hole of about 25 square
meters was torn in the water line. The detonation blew out the second hold
and, in addition, the bulkheads between the second and third holds were
smashed in. In the third hold there was bunkering coal and as the coal was
being trimmed for the boiler rooms the watertight bulkheads between the
boiler room and the third hold were not closed. The result was that the
boiler and engine rooms began at once to flood and had to be abandoned.
In consequence, the "stop" signal given by the captain over the machine
telegraph was not carried out. At 1401 hrs the captain gave the order to
abandon ship. The hull of the port lifeboat was damaged as it was being lowered and was thrown against the side of the ship. The captain then turned to
port and lowered the starboard lifeboat but this boat, too, soon filled with
water, after it had been freed from the still turning propeller and then capsized. The crew held on to the bottom and tried to climb up. All rafts were
thrown out and some of the crew and gun personnel left the ship on three
of them. The LCT which was lashed down on the forward deck was also
released. The captain, who had first hoped that the ship would be kept
afloat, soon realized she could not be saved after the gasoline cargo in No. 1
hold had also burst into flame and thick smoke poured out of it. The ship
now began to break up in the area of No. 2 hold. The captain, with the chief
engineer and three other members of the crew, got onto the lifeboat which
was drifting upside down and which had been made fast near No. 5 hold.
Shortly after the ship broke in two and quickly sank.

In the meantime the *Godetia* had proceeded toward the spray she had
sighted and at 1402 hrs obtained asdic contact at a distance of 1,000 meters.
But the results of the contacts were very poor. It later transpired in dock that
the asdic dome had apparently been damaged during the journey through
the ice off Newfoundland with ON.168 and this caused it to reproduce its
own sounds. Despite the inaccurate target data, Lt. Larose, at 1407 hrs,
ordered a carpet of depth charges, set to 30 and 70 meters, to be dropped at
the approximate position of the U-boat. Immediately after, the destroyer
Upshur came up from the stern and in each of two approaches dropped four
depth charges on the *U 338*, which had been located. Both ships continued
the hunt until 1505 hrs and then resumed course for the convoy. Meanwhile, Commodore White had ordered an emergency turn of 45° to starboard at 1405 hrs. At 1420 hrs the convoy reverted to its old course.

Commander Boyle ordered the escorts remaining with the convoy at 1410 hrs to adopt the screening formation DE 4. The *Pimpernel* went to the port bow, the *Swale* to the starboard bow, the *Havelock* to the port quarter and the *Buttercup* to the starboard quarter. At 1422 hrs the *Lavender* received orders to proceed to the damaged ship and to rescue survivors. Twenty-three men were taken on board from the three rafts and the capsized boat and 10 more from the small boat put out from the *Lavender*. When the *Lavender* was about to turn away, another crew member was suddenly sighted in the water, apparently alive. As it was difficult to maneuver the corvette close to him, the first officer of the watch, Lt. W. F. Weller, RNVR, jumped overboard and brought the now unconscious man to the ship. In spite of three hours' efforts to revive him, the attempts were not successful and at 1800 hrs the dead man had to be put back into the sea. At 1605 hrs the *Lavender* had hauled her boat on board again and left the empty rafts, the capsized lifeboats and the capsized landing craft behind. She reached the convoy again at 1940 hrs.

The second Liberator G/120 had left Aldergrove at 0706 hrs and had begun to transmit bearings at 1320 hrs. Shortly after the convoy had resumed its old general course following the attack, the aircraft sighted it and noticed a U-boat at 1436 hrs which was submerging some 10 miles on the port beam. A few minutes later the aircraft dropped four depth charges just near the place where it had dived. After the attack traces of oil could be seen. At 1445 hrs the aircraft arrived over the convoy and at 1500 hrs it began to patrol an area 10 miles round the convoy. At 1548 hrs a periscope was sighted 900 meters away on the starboard beam. The aircraft at once went into a steep dive to attack, but the two remaining depth charges could not be released. The convoy was informed by radio. At 1615 hrs the Liberator flew over the *Lavender* while she was carrying out her rescue operation and began the return flight at 1705 hrs. At 0030 hrs on March 18 the aircraft arrived back in Benbecula in Scotland. This aircraft, too, was 17 hours in the air.

In order to close the gaps caused by the attacks on the port side of the convoy and to tighten up the formation, Commodore White scrapped column 3 and had the ships on the port side of the convoy form columns 4, 5 and 6, each with five ships. In consequence, the convoy now had 10 columns in all.

THE NIGHT ATTACK BY *U 338* ON SC.122

In the course of the afternoon of March 17 the six northern *Stürmer* boats, which had operated on *U 338*'s contact report, came into the vicinity of SC.122. But some of them had been attacked by the two aircraft and impeded in their efforts to get in a forward position. Three contact-keepers had been located from their short signals by the *Havelock* and had been forced under water by the sorties of this ship and those of the *Swale* and the American destroyer *Upshur*.

So as to put as much distance to the east as possible from the U-boats, which had been driven off to the stern, Commodore White maintained the general course of 067°. Commander Boyle gave orders for the night-screening position NE 6 to be adopted when it became dark. On the port side at about 3,700 meters from the ships, and in zigzag courses, the corvette *Lavender* proceeded in position M, the destroyer *Upshur* in P and the corvette *Buttercup* in R; on the starboard side the corvette *Pimpernel* in position C, the frigate *Swale* in F and the corvette *Godetia* in H. The leader, *Havelock*, which had her radar operating again but not the asdic, zigzagged in broad sweeps some 5,500 meters ahead of the convoy.

Toward 2200 hrs the wind had freshened up to NW force 5; there was a 3–4 sea state and a mild swell from the NW. There was moonlight between the gaps in the clouds. Visibility extended to about six miles.

U 305 (Kptlt Bahr) which had sighted the convoy shortly before dark, had got forward at the limit of visibility on the starboard side. About 2130 hrs it approached to attack. Kptlt Bahr wanted to penetrate between the two escorts on the starboard bow of the convoy in order to get into a firing position. As the two ships frequently zigzagged, it was difficult to judge whether the U-boat had been seen or not, when one of the ships suddenly changed course. At 2300 hrs *U 305* was about 3,000 meters from the *Pimpernel* (Lt. Hayes) which was some 70° on the starboard bow. The *Swale* (Lt. Cdr. Jackson) looked more dangerous: she was approaching the U-boat at an acute angle about 2,500 meters away. But the U-boat was undetected. Kptlt Bahr kept to his course of 310° in the direction of the starboard leading ship of the convoy, the *Empire Morn*. The distance between the U-boat and the *Pimpernel* slowly increased, but at 2204 hrs the distance to the *Swale* was reduced to only a little more than 1,000 meters, before the frigate turned away again. In the meantime the first officer of the watch, Lt. Sander, sent his firing data down to the torpedo track calculator in the conning tower, while Kptlt Bahr and the lookouts searched for any sign of activity on the part of the two escorts. But they seemed to be asleep on the *Swale*.

Then, at 2206 hrs, the radar screen on the *Pimpernel* suddenly indicated a contact at 3,700 meters. The duty officer of the watch recognized a U-boat between the *Swale*, which was proceeding on the starboard quarter, and the convoy which could be seen immediately astern. With rudder hard over, he turned at once toward the U-boat, proceeding at high speed. The search-light signal "U-boat in sight on the starboard" was sent to the *Swale* and the radio signal "S for Sugar between pos. C and E" to the *Havelock*.

But, at the same moment, at 2208 hrs, Kptlt Bahr had seen the *Pimpernel* turn and gave his officer of the watch the order to fire quickly. Lt. Sander at first fired a salvo of two G 7es from tubes 1 and 3 at the second ship in the starboard column about 1,500 meters away. A minute later the second salvo was to be fired at the leader of the column. As a result of an operational mistake, the torpedo in tube 4 was not released and only the torpedo from tube 2 headed for the target. Immediately after the firing, Kptlt Bahr gave the alarm and *U 305* submerged. Aboard the *Pimpernel,* which had in the meantime come up at high speed, the scanning spot disappeared from the radar screen. At 2210 hrs she came within asdic range of the area where the U-boat was thought to have dived. But no echo was obtained. The *Swale* failed to locate the U-boat either with her radar or asdic. In that direction she could only hear the approaching *Pimpernel.* She turned to a course of 110° at 2209 hrs and proceeded at 16 knots, but in this way she moved away from the area where the U-boat had submerged.

As the enemy's speed was somewhat overestimated at eight knots, the torpedoes missed the intended target and also passed through the next columns until the first torpedo, after a run of nearly 5,000 meters, hit the *Port Auckland* (8,789 tons) in position 92 on the starboard side at 2214 hrs. The second torpedo continued on its way and, one minute 20 seconds later, hit the *Zouave* (4,256 tons) in position 84. The U-boat thought it heard the third torpedo detonate three minutes 58 seconds after firing, but it was probably the depth charge that *Pimpernel* dropped in what was thought to be the area where the boat submerged.

The *Zouave* was hit in No. 4 hold by the engine room bulkhead. Both compartments were at once flooded and the ship sank in a few minutes. But she was able to send a radio distress report which was deciphered two days later by the "B" Service. The *Port Auckland* was hit in the engine room and was brought to a standstill. She fired two white distress rockets: these were seen by the corvette *Saxifrage* which was with the rescue ship *Zamalek* about 40 miles NW of the convoy.

At 2216 hrs Cdr. Boyle ordered the escort to carry out a "half raspberry." The *Lavender, Upshur* and *Buttercup* proceeded on their courses, as instructed, on the port side and were back in position between 2225 hrs and 2248 hrs. The *Swale* also resumed her position at 2245 hrs, having neither seen nor located a U-boat. The *Pimpernel* searched unsuccessfully until 2306 hrs and the *Havelock* continued her broad sweeps in front of the convoy. The *Godetia* (Lt. Larose), stationed on the starboard quarter, had seen a sinking ship on the first stage of her "raspberry" course behind the convoy and at 2225 hrs came to the area where the boats of the *Zouave* and the wreck of the *Port Auckland* were drifting. At first she searched for U-boats behind the convoy but at 2233 hrs she received orders from the SOE to rescue survivors. Two men from the *Zouave* were seen drifting in the water between the bits of wreckage and calling out. One was brought on board; the other was unable to hold on to the line thrown out to him and was not found again when a second approach was made. Then 28 men from a boat of the *Zouave* and one man from a raft were taken on board. Finally, 32 men were taken aboard from a boat of the *Port Auckland* which was still drifting in the area. Suddenly a new echo appeared on the radar screen at a range of 2,700 meters. The rest of the survivors were brought on board in great haste. But before it was possible to start up, a new torpedo crashed into the starboard side of the *Port Auckland*.

U 305 had surfaced after the convoy had passed and had soon recognized the damaged freighter in the vicinity and the "destroyer" rescuing the survivors. The freighter had apparently received a hit in the engine room and lay stationary, burning and drifting broadside. Kptlt Bahr approached at once to finish her off and at 2341 hrs fired a G 7e from the stern tube. It hit amidships causing a 200-meter-high black cloud of smoke, although it did not seem to have any immediate effect on the ship.

Meanwhile the *Godetia* had made visual contact with the U-boat and turned toward it at 14 knots. The radar and lookouts kept a sharp eye on the U-boat which apparently tried to get away on the surface. Lt. Larose ordered full speed in order to close up and to be able to open fire with the 4 inch gun on the forecastle. Then *U 305* dived at 0005 hrs after sending off a report of its success. The *Godetia* approached nearer and then went over to asdic search. The corvette dropped a depth charge set to 30 meters where the U-boat had submerged. After 2,000 meters the *Godetia* turned and searched again in the opposite direction but without success because the asdic, as already explained, was damaged.

At 0030 hrs the *Godetia* again reached the wreck of the *Port Auckland*. At first an empty raft was found, then 68 men from two more lifeboats were rescued. When, despite much searching of the wreckage area, no more survivors could be found, the *Godetia* returned to the convoy at 0105 hrs. Thirteen men from the *Zouave* and eight from the *Port Auckland* were still missing, chiefly stokers and coal trimmers on the watch in the engine room of both ships.

The attack by *U 305* had been observed by *U 338* which was assiduously trying to reestablish contact. It reached a position forward on the port side of the convoy and at 2400 hrs sent off a contact signal. But this was picked up by HF/DF on the *Havelock* which was scurrying to and fro in front of the convoy. Cdr. Boyle turned at once on to the D/F beam since the U-boat was apparently close to the convoy on the port side. The wind had freshened up to force 7 and the sea had increased to state 6. In such weather it was small wonder that *U 338* had sighted the approaching destroyer long before the latter's radar, obscured by wave clatter, could find the U-boat which hardly appeared above the surface of the sea. Kptlt Kinzel had to dive. As the *Havelock*'s asdic was not yet in order again, the submerged U-boat could not be found. However, its attack on the convoy was frustrated.

When *U 338* was able to surface again, the convoy had passed. But, shortly after, a damaged freighter was sighted lying gravely stricken in the heavy swell. It was the wreck of the *Port Auckland*. Kptlt Kinzel made a stern approach and fired a torpedo at 0155 hrs to finish her off. There was no detonation. Apparently, in the heavy swell, the torpedo had gone under the ship. Nevertheless, shortly after, the ship suddenly settled by the stern. The bow stuck out of the water for a brief moment, floating on an air lock; then the ship disappeared. The sound of shattered bulkheads and a muffled explosion—probably the torpedo detonation at the end of its run—were heard by the *U 305*, lying submerged in the vicinity.

In the night the weather quickly deteriorated. The wind freshened up to gale force, heavy snow squalls swept over the tempestuous seas and sometimes reduced visibility to zero. Consequently, none of the U-boats found the convoy again until morning and the convoy's route order became increasingly loose. But, in spite of the weather and visibility, which was restricted to about 1.5 miles in the morning, the *Havelock* succeeded with the help of bearings in bringing up, first, the *Godetia* and then, in the morning, the *Saxifrage*, with the rescue ship *Zamalek*, which had vainly looked for a dubious radar contact before midnight. At 0700 hrs on the morning of March 18 the Commodore changed course to 048° to help the ships in the heavy sea and to counteract the strong drift.

CHAPTER 10

March 18, 1943

THE SITUATION ON THE MORNING OF MARCH 18 AS SEEN BY THE COMMANDER U-BOATS

In the numerous U-boat reports up to the morning of March 18 the Commander U-boats saw confirmation of his assumption on the previous day that the first convoy was the SC.122 and that the "main convoy" engaged first was the HX.229. At 0700 hrs on March 17 there was contact with HX.229 in square BD 2112. In the course of the day six U-boats reported that they were with the convoy. The last report came at 1630 hrs from *U 600* in AK 8943. Contact was then lost, except for three uncertain sound-bearings in the night. The northern *Stürmer* boats and the *Dränger* boats, which were favorably placed from the point of view of distance, operated against SC.122. From 0800 hrs in AK 8655 until 2200 hrs in AK 9529 there was almost constant contact.

The Commander U-boats attributed the loss of contact, despite the many boats operating against the two convoys, mainly to the "very strong air escort" reported by the U-boats in day time. Several boats had reported bomb attacks. The boats had clearly "been impeded by constant air attacks and fallen increasingly astern." The strong air deployment was also confirmed by the "B" Service. In fact, from March 17 to March 18 almost all the radio messages about U-boat sightings and attacks sent by the aircraft with HX.229 and SC.122 were intercepted and made available after being quickly deciphered (see Appendix 8). On the other hand, according to the radio reports from the U-boats, *U 91, U 631, U 384, U 228, U 338* and *U 665* had made underwater attacks and had together reported eight ships of 41,500 tons sunk and four more torpedoed.

By the morning of March 18 twelve U-boats reported that they had broken off the operation: the three homeward-bound boats *U 653, U 89* and *U 638*, which had for a short time tried to make contact; *U 468, U 435, U 603, U 758, U 664* and *U 616* because of lack of fuel; and, further, *U 91, U 600* and *U 665* because of mechanical trouble.

Those still operating against HX.229 were *U 615* and *U 84* from the old *Raubgraf* group as well as *U 228* and *U 230* which came from the supply boat; *U 618*, *U 190*, *U 530*, *U 631*, *U 598*, *U 384* and *U 134* from the southern *Stürmer* boats; and *U 441*, *U 406*, *U 333*, *U 608*, *U 221* and *U 610* from the *Dränger group*—18 boats in all. Those still shadowing SC.122 were the *Stürmer* boats *U 305*, *U 527*, *U 666*, *U 523*, *U 526*, *U 642*, *U 338* and *U 641* and the *Dränger* boats *U 373*, *U 86*, *U 336*, *U 440* and *U 590*—13 boats in all. Some of these had now fallen far to the stern, but with the deteriorating weather there was a possibility that the shadowing boats would find stragglers or damaged ships. Accordingly, the operation was continued and the boats were allowed to operate against whatever turned out to be the most favorable target. Further reinforcements for the U-boats did not appear necessary. As a result, the boats which were approaching and had already reached the area of the convoy operation, *U 564*, *U 572* and *U 663* and which were to constitute a new formation as the *Seeteufel* group for March 21, received new orders. Because of the excessive number of boats already deployed, they were not to operate against the convoys but merely to take advantage of any opportunities presented and then continue their journey to the prescribed patrol line.

THE SITUATION AS SEEN BY THE ADMIRALTY AND CINCWA

The situation on March 18 looked very serious to the Allied Commands. According to the U-boat situation report, transmitted by radio on March 18, account was taken of some U-boats "not located by radio" proceeding westward approximately in the area 41°N 47°W SE of Newfoundland. Radar had located five U-boats south of Iceland on a south to southeast course. According to bearings, at least six U-boats were within 150 miles of point 52°N 30°W in the vicinity of SC.122. Some ten boats were located by bearings between 48° and 50°N and 32° and 39°W, some of them homeward-bound but most of them shadowing HX.229. Another 15 new boats were reckoned, from radio location and aircraft sightings, to be on patrol between 55° and 60°N and 24° and 32°W. It was calculated that there were some ten more boats on patrol SE of Cape Farewell. Two U-boats were within a range of 150 miles of 41°N 38°W and some more boats were still shadowing the eastbound convoy UGS.6 between the Azores and Gibraltar. Finally, there was the possibility of boats returning, or setting out, W of the Bay of Biscay. The chances of being able to reroute all the convoys at sea round these formations looked very unlikely.

This U-boat situation report, which was deciphered some days later by the German "B" Service, contained, however, some clearly faulty estimates which plainly contradicted the suspicion, which always arose on the German side after successful Allied evasive actions, that the enemy had broken the

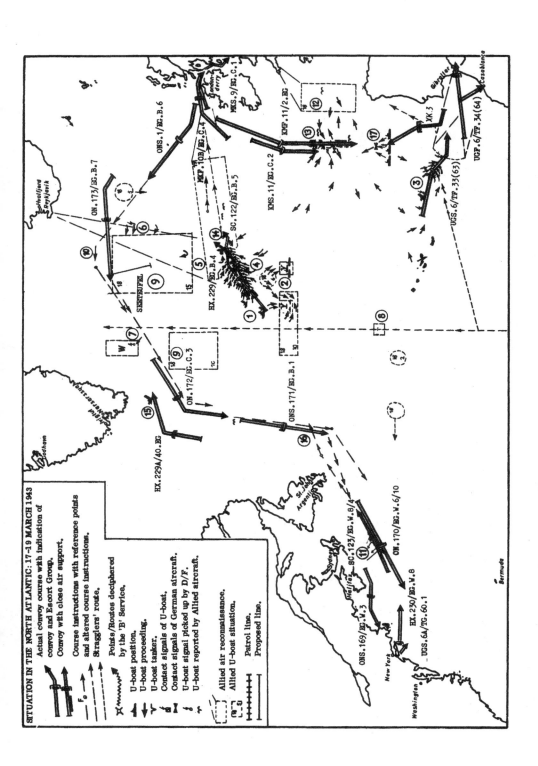

SITUATION IN THE NORTH ATLANTIC: 17–19 MARCH 1943

Actual convoy course with indication of convoy and Escort Group.

Convoy with close air support.

Course instructions with reference points & altered course instructions.

Stragglers' route.

Points/Routes deciphered by the 'B' Service.

✗ U-boat position.

U-boat proceeding.

U-boat tanker.

Contact signals of U-boat.

Contact signals of German aircraft.

U-boat signal picked up by D/F.

U-boat reported by Allied aircraft.

Allied air reconnaissance.

Allied U-boat situation.

Patrol line.

Proposed line.

The situation in the North Atlantic: March 17 (1200 hrs GMT) to March 19 (1200 hrs GMT), 1943

No.	Date	Event
1	Mar 17 day	U-boats of the *Raubgraf, Stürmer* and *Dränger* groups maintain contact with convoys HX.229 and SC.122. 4 Liberators are deployed from N. Ireland by 15 Group, RAF Coastal Command over maximum ranges for air cover. They drive off many U-boats but during a pause at midday 3 U-boats are able to attack and sink 2 ships from HX.229 and 1 from SC.122.
2	Mar 17-18	U-boats turn away from the convoys and proceed to U-tankers *U 463* and *U 119*.
3	Mar 17-18	U-boats maintain contact with convoy UGS.6 but in the good weather they cannot succeed against the escorts which are equipped with long-range radar, especially since air cover is available on the afternoon of Mar 17. 1 ship is sunk in the evening.
4	Mar 18 night	In the case of SC.122 only one U-boat attacks in the night Mar 17-18. 2 ships are sunk.
5	Mar 18 day	15 Group sends 3 Liberators from N. Ireland and 4 from Iceland to HX.229 and SC.122. Together with the naval escort they drive off all attacks. However, *U 221* sinks 2 ships from HX.229 in an underwater attack.
6	Mar 18	Iceland aircraft sight U-boats as they fly to HX.229.
7	Mar 18	The radio signals from *U 229* sent out to transmit ice and weather reports for the expected blockade-runner *Regensburg* (course instructions: meeting point with *U 161* to hand over search receiver = T) lead Allies mistakenly to think there are new U-boat groups on the Northern route.
10	Mar 18	Because of the situation picture on Mar 18 CINCWA diverts ONS.1 further to North.
11	Mar 18 day	SC.123 and ON.170 pass HOMP. Relief of local Escort Groups.
12	Mar 18 day	Heavy air deployment by 19 Group, RAF Coastal Command over the western part of the Bay of Biscay.
13	Mar 18 2000 hrs	*U 621* sights KMF.11 shortly after departure of air cover. Further operations by this boat and other outward and homeward-bound boats operating against the convoy are made impossible on Mar 19 by the air cover and high speed of the convoy.
14	Mar 18-19	In the night individual U-boats maintain contact with HX.229 and SC.122. 1 ship is sunk from SC.122 and in the morning a 'romper' of HX.229 between both convoys. In the morning 15 Group provides strong air cover with 5 Liberators, 2 Catalinas and 6 Sunderlands from Iceland and N. Ireland. U-boats fall back.
15	Mar 19 early	The whaling ship *Svend Foyn* with HX.229A is badly damaged in passing through an iceberg area and has to be abandoned on Mar 20.
16	Mar 19 morning	ONS.171 passes WOMP.
17	Mar 19 morning	German air reconnaissance finds convoy XK.3 twice but the U-boats cannot come up.

cipher in use for the U-boats. At this time there were no U-boat groups operating either north of the present convoy battles nor SE of Cape Farewell. On
the other hand, the strength of the groups deployed against the two convoys
was apparently still underestimated.

The most threatening situation seemed to face the two convoys HX.229
and SC.122 which had been under attack for days and from which the U-
boats sent constant contact reports, as the shore-based D/F stations
reported. But it was not possible to provide the threatened convoys with any
further reinforcements beyond those ships already at sea. And of these only
the destroyer leader of Escort Group B 4, the *Highlander,* was able to reach
her convoy in the course of March 18. The corvettes *Abelia* and *Sherbrooke,*
which had earlier set out from St John's, made only slow progress. The
American ships *Ingham* and *Babbitt,* which had set out from Reykjavik and
which, in good weather and at high speed, could have reached the SC.122 in
the evening, were compelled by the storm during the night March 17–18 to
reduce speed considerably. Despite this they suffered considerable storm
damage on their upper decks as a result of the cross seas. At 1831 hrs when
a new report of an attack on HX.229 was received CINCWA ordered *Babbitt*
to make her way to HX.229, instead of to SC.122. The destroyer *Vimy* was not
able to put to sea from Reykjavik before 0318 hrs on March 18, so she could
not be expected to reach it before the night of March 19–20 at the earliest.

Nor was it possible to take reinforcements from another convoy. The
ON.172 was south of Cape Farewell: it consisted of 17 steamers and the
Escort Group C 3 under Commander R. C. Medley, RN, comprising the
destroyer leader HMS *Burnham,* the Canadian corvettes *Bittersweet, Eyebright,*
Mayflower and *La Malbaie,* with the new frigate HMS *Jed* seconded from the
1st Escort Group. It was both too far away and in an area where a U-boat
group was expected.

The following ON.173 with 39 ships and the Escort Group B 7 under
Cdr. P. W. Gretton, RN, comprising the frigate *Tay* as leader, the destroyer
Vidette and the corvettes *Alisma, Loosestrife, Snowflake* and *Pink,* was to go
round to the north of the suspected German U-boat formation between 55°
and 60°N on March 18–19. The Escort Group was too weak to risk detaching
any units.

The two southbound Gibraltar convoys KMS.11 and KMF.11 SW of Ireland had on March 18–19 to pass the outward and homeward route area of
the German U-boats west of the Bay of Biscay, where, apart from U-boats,
there was the possibility of German long-range bombers and reconnaissance
aircraft. Here, too, sacrifices could not be made. The KMS.11 consisted of 62
merchant men and was screened by Escort Group C 2 under Lt. Cdr. E. H.
Chavasse, RN, comprising the destroyers HMS *Broadway* and HMS *Sherwood,*

the frigate HMS *Lagan,* the corvettes HMS *Primrose,* HMS *Snowdrop,* HMCS *Morden,* HMCS *Drumheller* and HMCS *Chambly,* as well as the Free French Aviso *Savorgnan da Brazza.* The KMF.11 consisted of nine transports screened by an ad hoc group under the command of the 2nd Escort Group, at the time still in the process of formation, but later to win great fame under Capt. Walker. But at the moment it only had the two sloops *Wren* and *Woodpecker* under the command of Lt. Cdr. Proudfoot, to which were allocated from various flotillas the destroyers *Douglas, Eggesford, Badsworth, Whaddon, Goathland* and ORP *Krakowiak,* the last five belonging to the *Hunt* class.

There was therefore no alternative on March 18 except to employ all available VLR Liberators from Reykjavik and Aldergrove to protect the two convoys. In all, there were five Liberators in Aldergrove and four in Reykjavik from No 120 Squadron available for operations. At 0146 hrs the aircraft O/120 set off first from Aldergrove for SC.122. At 0637 hrs and 0643 hrs P/120 and L/120 set out from Reykjavik for SC.122 and HX.229. At 0744 hrs and 0939 hrs the aircraft E/120 and N/120 followed from Aldergrove for SC.122 and HX.229. To relieve these aircraft, B/120 set out at 1031 hrs and M/120 at 1114 hrs from Aldergrove for SC.122 and HX.229 respectively. And from Reykjavik X/120 set out at 1106 hrs for SC.122 and the S/120 at 1114 hrs for HX.229.

But some difficulties were experienced in getting the aircraft to the convoys, particularly in the morning of March 18. First, both convoys were in an area that was very cloudy and subject to frequent snow showers when visibility was sometimes restricted to half a mile. There were additional problems because the same frequency was used by both convoys to give bearings and for the radio traffic between the SOEs and the aircraft with the barely separated convoys. The O/120 began to send bearings at 0620 hrs but it did not get near convoy SC.122 before 1038 hrs. However, in the bad visibility, it was impossible to recognize the convoy and its composition. With a wind strength of 35 knots and constant snow showers, the aircraft began the return flight at 1139 hrs and landed back in Aldergrove at 1756 hrs. So on the morning of March 18 both convoys were without air escort.

THE ATTACK BY *U 221* ON HX.229

Lt. Cdr. Luther had looked forward to the night March 17–18 with considerable anxiety, but the expected attacks had not materialized. All that had happened was that at 0330 hrs the *Volunteer* picked up with her HF/DF a U-boat contact signal close to the convoy. She proceeded at once along the beam at high speed but did not establish contact. Probably the U-boat had submerged in time. The *Volunteer* dropped a depth charge where it was thought the U-boat had dived, then went back to her position. It must have been *U384.*

The varying efficiency of the 271 M radar against U-boats and surface ships in the stormy weather was very apparent from the fact that the *Volunteer* was unable to locate a U-boat in the area whose direction had been correctly ascertained, while the *Anemone*, coming up from astern with no clear position, recognized at 0020 hrs on her radar screen, at a distance of eight miles, the echoes of the merchantmen which stood much higher out of the water.

The SOE was very relieved when at 0200 hrs and 0220 hrs the two corvettes *Pennywort* and *Anemone* reached the convoy and took up positions Q and G. But at 0700 hrs he had to detach the destroyer *Mansfield*; her supplies of oil and water were just sufficient to reach Londonderry on one engine, the refueling from the escort oiler having been made impossible by the enemy and the weather.

After light on March 18 *U60* (Kptlt v Freyberg) had again established contact and sent off a signal at 0800 hrs. The *Volunteer* was not able to intercept this because her HF/DF personnel were again busy receiving bearings from the approaching Liberators, L/120 and N/120, and transmitting D/F beams to the aircraft. Following the signal from *U60*, *U134* (Kptlt Brosin), *U333* (Oblt Schwaft) and *U221* (Oblt Trojer) had established contact about midday in a N/W wind of force 6 and a heavy NW swell. As the convoy had maintained its general course of 053° since March 16, they tried to get forward unobserved in the frequent snow showers, but they sighted escorts and lost contact. *U663* (Kplt Schmidt), southeast of the convoy, sighted a lone freighter and tried to make its underwater attack from the starboard. At 1435 hrs he fired a salvo of three torpedoes at this 6,000 ton merchant ship, but missed. In another single firing five minutes later, he believed he heard a hit. If the report of *The Pas* of March 9 is true, it may well have been the missing *Clarissa Radcliffe*, as Middlebrook assumes.

U 221 came up on the port side and submerged at 1500 hrs in front of the convoy. Propeller noises from approaching ships were increasingly heard in the underwater listening equipment and then suddenly in the SW the pitching and rolling steamers came into periscope sight. They were heading directly toward the boat.

At 1543 hrs Oblt Trojer at first fired the stern torpedo at a ship of the *Salacia* type (5,495 tons), then he turned to make a bow firing on a *Clan MacDougal* type steamer (6,843 tons) in the next column which had, in the meantime, approached very close. Two minutes 51 seconds after the stern firing, the first torpedo hit was heard. Then at 1649 hrs came the salvo of four with a FAT, two G 7es and another FAT torpedo.

After 30 and 32 seconds there were two loud detonations followed at first by subdued, and then loud, sinking noises. After 12 minutes another detonation was heard. It was assumed that one of the FAT torpedoes had also found its target.

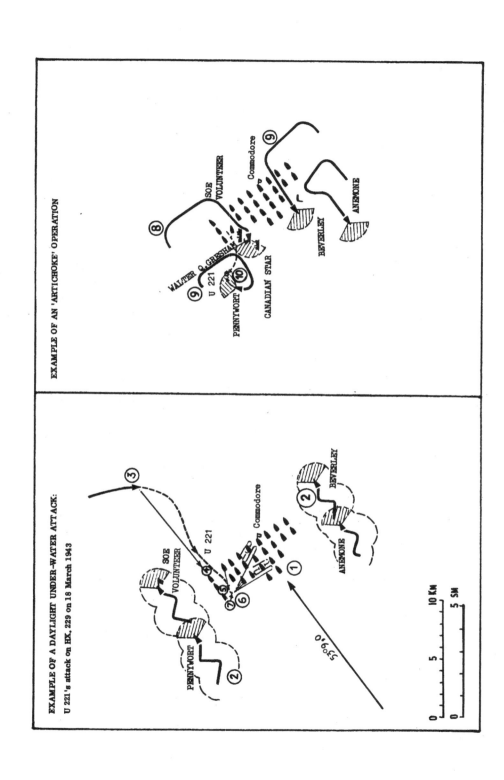

EXAMPLE OF A DAYLIGHT UNDER-WATER ATTACK:
U 221's attack on HX, 229 on 18 March 1943

EXAMPLE OF AN 'ARTICHOKE' OPERATION

Example of daylight underwater attack: U 221's attack on HX.229 on March 18, 1943

1. Route formation of convoy HX.229: in 6 attacks the convoy has already lost 10 ships. The formation is reduced to 9 columns with 3, 2, 3, 3, 4, 4, 3, 2, 2 ships. Width about 4.5 miles, depth about 1.5 to 2 miles. Weather: visibility about 2 miles reducing to 0.5 miles in the frequent snow showers. Cloud density 5/10. NNW wind force 7, sea 5 to 6. Radar range against U-boats very limited because of wave echoes. Bad asdic conditions.

2. An approximate area covered by the escorts' asdic search sectors.

3. Mar 18 1600 hrs — *U 221*, after manoeuvring forward, approaches to attack and submerges before the oncoming convoy.

4. Mar 18 1640 hrs — *U 221* penetrates into the somewhat widened gap between Columns 1 and 2.

5. Mar 18 1643 hrs — *U 221* fires stern torpedo at freighter steaming at head of column 2. After 2 minutes 51 seconds (= 2639 m) there is a hit on No 21 *Walter Q. Gresham*, which remains stationary.

6. Mar 18 1649 hrs — *U 221*, after turning, fires a salvo of four from the bow tubes. 2 G 7e torpedoes hit after 30 and 32 seconds respectively No 33 *Canadian Star*, which begins to sink. 2 FAT torpedoes run inside the convoy but do not hit.

7. Mar 18 — Merchant ships 13 and 23 sight a periscope between the columns and fire at it with machine guns and 4-in gun.

8. Mar 18 1650 hrs — SOE proposes 'artichoke' operation. Here the outer escorts close up to the convoy and the forward escorts pass through the columns in the opposite direction. Escorts form behind the convoy a search line in order to find the attacking, submerged U-boat with overlapping asdic search sectors.

9. Mar 18 1655 hrs — Owing to a mistake in transmitting the order, a 'half raspberry' is ordered instead of 'artichoke'. But the escorts realise the mistake and prepare for an 'artichoke'. *Pennywort* sees Nos 13 and 23 firing at the periscope and tries to find the U-boat in a 'box search'.

10. Mar 18 1737 hrs — On the third and last search patrol the U-boat is located by asdic at 1000 metres and attacked with 6 depth charges. Because of the whirling waters which are stirred up, the U-boat cannot be found again in the poor locating weather. It escapes without serious damage. After an hour *Pennywort* starts to rescue survivors.

The first sign of the attacks for the convoy was the torpedo which detonated at 1547 hrs on the brand-new American Liberty freighter *Walter Q. Gresham* (7,191 tons) proceeding in position 21. It hit the port side near No. 5 hold, tore a hole of 10 meters diameter and ripped open 15 meters of the deck. The stern gun crew's quarters in the deckhouse were destroyed. Evidently the screw was torn off by the detonation. The engines were stopped at once and a distress signal was sent by radio. The captain gave orders to abandon ship and, in accordance with instructions, had secret material thrown overboard. Two of the boats capsized when they were lowered into the rough sea and this caused considerable loss.

At 1552 hrs the British motor ship *Canadian Star* (8,293 tons) in position 33 received two torpedo hits on the port side in quick succession. She began to settle quickly and the crew left her.

At 1555 hrs Lt. Cdr. Luther mistakenly gave orders for a "half raspberry." His intention was to order an "artichoke" operation, as is provided in such cases. This is an A/S maneuver in which the escorts steam through the columns of the convoy and continue the search in the opposite direction behind the convoy. While the *Volunteer*, which had been on the port bow, was turning in to proceed between the second and third columns, the merchant ships *Empire Knight* and *Matthew Luckenbach* in positions 13 and 33 sighted between the columns a periscope quickly disappearing astern and opened fire on it first with machine guns and then with the 4-inch gun. Possibly it was one of the detonating shells which misled Oblt Trojer into assuming it was a FAT torpedo detonation.

On receipt of the "raspberry" signal from the *Volunteer*, the *Pennywort* and *Anemone* turned at once inward. But their commanders, Lt. Stuart and Lt. Cdr. King, soon realized that the SOE intended an "artichoke" operation. When Lt. Stuart saw the fire from the two steamers, he first kept his course as the target clearly lay in the "raspberry" triangle. On the last leg of the search the *Pennywort* obtained a moving asdic location at 1,050 meters—i.e., a U-boat. At 650 meters contact was lost. But Lt. Stuart continued on his course and dropped a carpet of six depth charges where the U-boat was thought to be. Despite an hour's search, contact could not be reestablished.

Shortly after 1600 hrs Lt. Cdr. Luther ordered the *Anemone* to go to the two wrecks and recover survivors while he himself briefly carried out operation "observant." At 1625 hrs the *Anemone* stopped to pick up the survivors drifting on rafts and in boats. The *Canadian Star* sank at 1645 hrs. In the heavy sea it was very difficult to haul up the survivors from the heaving boats and tossing rafts on to the rolling *Anemone*. Lt. Stuart maneuvered the *Anemone* so that she drifted with the wind toward the boats and rafts. In the heavy seas the survivors were unable in many cases to clutch the meshes of the safety net which had been let down until the crew of the corvette seized them and hauled them over the side. Some fell between the corvette and the boats and were only rescued with difficulty and with injuries. One woman died on the next day as a result of her injuries. Many of the survivors were frozen and were scarcely able to help themselves. A woman had to be held by her hair until a sailor could climb into the net, support her and pull her in.

At 1720 hrs the *Pennywort* also came up and took part in the rescue operation. In all, the *Anemone* picked up 51 survivors from the *Canadian Star* and 16 from the *Walter Q. Gresham.* She now had 163 survivors on board, including six women and two children. The *Pennywort* rescued 26 men from the *Walter Q. Gresham* and a number from the *Canadian Star*; 27 men from the *Walter Q. Gresham* were missing.

At 1930 hrs, after a last search, the two corvettes left the *Walter Q. Gresham* which was lying deep in the water. At 1935 hrs she disappeared from sight in a snow squall. She must have sunk shortly after. The corvettes proceeded toward the convoy which they reached again shortly after 0100 hrs on March 19.

AIR ESCORT ON THE AFTERNOON OF MARCH 18

HX.229 continued its journey in bad weather. But, shortly after midday, SC.122 gradually encountered better weather. In particular, the cloud dispersed with the result that the aircraft of No 120 Squadron which set out from Ireland and Iceland were able to find the convoy. The first aircraft to arrive in the area of the convoy was the Liberator P/120 from Reykjavik at 1109 hrs: in the still very changeable weather it could only make out 30 ships and three escorts. The aircraft then made a search some 20 miles to the stern of the convoy. At 1251 hrs the E/120 arrived from Aldergrove and made patrols round the convoy to a distance of 8–10 miles. At 1328 hrs the aircraft sighted a submerging U-boat 10 miles to the starboard quarter of the convoy. It attacked it from a height of 500 feet with four depth charges which fell just near the still visible conning tower. Precise observation was impossible in the rough sea and heavy rain squalls. The aircraft reported the attack to the convoy and a corvette was sent to keep watch on the area. When the Liberator P/120 heard the report of the attack, it approached and requested the SOE to give it instructions. But there were no more signs of U-boats and so the aircraft flew round the convoy in 10-mile sweeps until 1422 hrs when it had to return to its base. The E/120 stayed with the convoy until 2000 hrs but only sighted a straggler 14 miles behind the convoy at 1827 hrs. The aircraft returned to Benbecula at 0140 hrs.

At 1543 hrs and 1629 hrs the next two aircraft, B/120 and X/120 reached SC.122. In addition, L/120 came for a time to the area of SC.122, not being able to find its convoy, HX.229. It tried to ascertain, by signaling to the SOE, the position of HX.229. The aircraft were employed on "Cobra" patrols, partly with the help of HF/DF bearings and partly by visual observation. The flights were rendered more difficult by the still very strong wind and the various showers of rain when visibility was reduced to 1,000 meters. At 1712 hrs B/120 sighted a submerging U-boat. The pilot forced the aircraft down from 2,500 feet to 150 feet and dropped two depth charges, one of which fell a good 100 meters from the area where the submarine had submerged. At 1745 hrs a line of foam was sighted but this disappeared after 7–8 seconds. Five minutes later the aircraft, from the starboard beam, attacked a second U-boat only eight miles on the port quarter of the convoy. Four depth charges were dropped from a height of 150 feet; the first fell just off the port bow, the others further away. The convoy was again informed and after that the search was continued to the stern of the convoy. At 2038 hrs the aircraft again sighted a fully surfaced U-boat, but it was unable to attack it because all the depth charges had been expended. The aircraft had to turn away at 2109 hrs and it landed in Benbecula at 0224 hrs.

At the same time X/120 had, at 1722 hrs, sighted from a height of 1,800 feet a U-boat three miles away (35 miles to the starboard quarter of the convoy). The boat submerged before an effective attack could be made. At 1811 hrs a second U-boat was sighted and four depth charges were dropped from a height of 200 feet which fell on the boat's course about 200 meters from the place where it submerged. The aircraft remained about an hour and a half in the area, but in the heavy swell and frequent rain it could see no further sign of the U-boat. At 1945 hrs the aircraft started the homeward flight and landed at Benbecula at 0124 hrs.

Of the aircraft which set out in the morning for HX.229, L/120 had exchanged bearing signals with the convoy at 0952 hrs, but at 1226 hrs the signals were so weak that they could no longer be evaluated. At 1320 hrs the aircraft had to report by radio that it could not find the convoy. Twenty minutes later it came across SC.122. The second aircraft, N/120, likewise, did not find the convoy until 1630 hrs but was in the area astern of it. At 1640 hrs it sighted a U-boat about 60 miles to the rear of the convoy but, in the heavy swell, could not find the place where the U-boat had dived when it tried to approach. At 1716 hrs the aircraft sighted a corvette approaching the convoy from astern—probably the *Abelia*. The aircraft obtained a radar contact at 1758 hrs about 50 miles to the stern of the convoy and shortly after observed the conning tower of the U-boat. But in this case, too, the aircraft could not turn quickly enough in the poor visibility to reach the place where the submarine had submerged. At 1849 hrs the aircraft encountered M/120, which had set out from Aldergrove, and at 1927 hrs it began the return flight to Benbecula which was reached at 0220 hrs.

The only aircraft to come into the area of HX.229 was M/120 in the evening. At 2005 hrs it sighted a U-boat 40 miles on the starboard quarter and attacked it, in two approaches, with six depth charges. But, again in this case, the U-boat had submerged before the depth charges detonated. M/120 returned to Benbecula at 0158 hrs. The ninth aircraft to set off, S/120, found neither HX.229 nor SC.122 and returned to Reykjavik at 1815 hrs.

All the aircrafts' reports of attacks were again deciphered by the German "B" Service (see Appendix 8).

SC.122 ON THE AFTERNOON OF MARCH 18

As a result of the improved weather and the slackening storm, the Commodore was able to concentrate convoy SC.122 closer together and to restore the prescribed route order. Only the freighter *Empire Morn* in position 131 fell back about 1500 hrs because of boiler trouble and continued her journey alone since, with the threat of U-boat attacks during the night, the SOE could not dispense with an escort.

Cdr. Boyle decided to try to shake off the U-boats which were maintaining contact by an evasive move after dark and a ruse. He asked the Commodore to change course to 095° between 2100 hrs and 0030 hrs and, thereafter, to proceed on the general course of 060°. The aircraft B/120, which was still in the vicinity of the convoy, was requested to fly a "frog" patrol before the change of course and the onset of darkness, so as to force all the U-boats in the area to submerge. In addition, the US Coast Guard cutter *Ingham*, which was approaching the convoy, was asked by radio to attempt a diversion some 40 miles from the convoy by firing star shells and dropping depth charges. But the *Ingham* could not meet this request because she was further away from the meeting point than had been expected.

Since, with the onset of darkness, there was excellent visibility because of the clear moonlight, the order was given to use no snowflake rockets or star shells except when illuminating clearly recognized targets.

Cdr. Boyle ordered the escorts to adopt the screening formation NE 8 for the night. With his leader *Havelock*, whose asdic was still out of order, he went in position S behind the convoy. The corvette *Godetia* also had a defective asdic and was therefore stationed in position H on the starboard quarter. In front of the convoy the corvette *Lavender* proceeded in position M, *Saxifrage* in position A and *Pimpernel* in position C. On the starboard side the frigate *Swale* was in position F, on the port side the destroyer *Upshur* in position P and on the port quarter the corvette *Buttercup* in position R.

Shortly before dark and the carrying out of the signal order to change course the HF/DF of the *Havelock* again picked up a bearing of a U-boat's contact signal. The *Upshur* was ordered to follow up the beam in order to force the U-boat under water. For the period of her absence, the *Saxifrage* received orders to take up the position on the port side.

But evidently the U-boat, or a second U-boat, was able to avoid the *Upshur*'s sortie because at 2157 hrs a U-boat to the port of the convoy and at a relatively short distance again sent a contact signal which was picked up by the *Havelock*'s HF/DF. Cdr. Boyle then ordered his escorts to carry out a "half raspberry" but, meanwhile, the corvette *Lavender* on the port bow had secured a radar contact at 060° some 3,000 meters ahead with her 271 M radar. At first there was some uncertainty whether the contact was possibly the destroyer *Upshur*, which was returning from her sortie, or the expected *Ingham*, which was meant to reach the convoy about this time. At 2152 hrs the noise of propellers was also heard by the asdic. Immediately after, the Commander, Lt. Pilcher, and some men on the bridge watch, were able to see clearly ahead the bow foam and stern wake of a U-boat. At 2154 hrs the *Lavender* fired a star shell to see the target better, but this was not successful. The star shell was also sighted by some of the other escorts. The *Buttercup*, stationed on the port quarter, at first assumed that a ship had been torpedoed and had fired a distress rocket, particularly since, at the same time, an order had been received to carry out a "half raspberry." At 2158 hrs the *Lavender*'s radar showed that the U-boat was slowly gaining ground and Lt. Pilcher gave the order "emergency full speed." To force the U-boat to dive, he ordered two shells to be fired with the 4 inch gun. The U-boat did, in fact, submerge. At 2200 hrs the radar contact was lost but the asdic continued to report the noise of propellers at somewhat more than 3,000 meters away. At 2202 hrs the asdic contact was lost, evidently because the U-boat had in the meantime slipped away. The *Lavender* proceeded to the last-known position without, however, maintaining contact. After 500 meters Lt. Pilcher turned and started to make another asdic search. The *Havelock* and other escorts did not receive the *Lavender*'s report about the radar location and sighting of a U-boat until 2203 hrs. At 2209 hrs Cdr. Boyle, with the signal "negative raspberry," ordered the escorts to resume their positions. Evidently this order was misunderstood on some ships because the *Buttercup* began to carry out a "half raspberry" on receipt of this signal.

At 2215 hrs the *Lavender* again obtained a good asdic contact, at a range of 1,550 meters, with something moving slowly to starboard. At 2220 hrs she dropped a carpet of 10 depth charges set to 30 meters for the normal and 70 meters for the heavy charges. As the asdic contact had been lost, the *Lavender* withdrew for 1,700 meters and then proceeded in the opposite direction. At 2228 hrs the U-boat was again located with asdic at an approximate range of 1,100 meters. In the new approach the depth charges were meant to detonate at 45 and 90 meters, but the cartridge was defective in the case of depth charge thrower No 2 and the depth charges got stuck in the stern chutes with the result that only one normal and two heavy charges could be fired from the remaining three throwers. At 2232 hrs there was an underwater explosion one minute after the charge was dropped. This was followed by a rumbling noise which would be clearly heard for several seconds. Contact could not be reestablished. During the asdic search approach the radar again found a target at 2244 hrs. But, shortly after, it transpired that it was the corvette *Saxifrage* which had closed up and which had herself obtained a not very clear asdic contact at 080° and a range of 2,300 meters. Lt. Cdr. Knight, nevertheless, decided to attack despite the possibly dangerous position of the target and at 2240 hrs dropped seven depth charges with medium settings. Then both corvettes made a "box sweep" search in the area without result and without being able to locate the U-boat again. At 2250 hrs the *Saxifrage* went back to her position and the *Lavender* continued the vain search until 2325 hrs and then came up behind the convoy. At 0015 hrs on March 19 the two corvettes and the *Upshur*, which had in the meantime got back, had resumed their positions in formation NE 8. At 0030 hrs the convoy reverted to its general course of 060°.

This attack was directed against *U338* which reported some damage by depth charges.

HX.229 ON THE AFTERNOON OF MARCH 18

The Commander of the Escort Group B 4, Cdr. Day, hoped to reach HX.229 with his leader, *Highlander*, in the early afternoon. Cdr. Day knew from the intercepted radio traffic, the distress signals picked up from ships 22, 81 and 102 and the signals from *Volunteer* at 0540 hrs and 1437 hrs on March 17 that the convoy had been attacked several times and was in a critical situation. Unfortunately he was not able to follow the situation closely in the afternoon of March 18. At 1210 hrs, a member of the cipher staff, a clerk named Griffin, was on the upper deck bringing the new cipher documents from the radio office to the cabin of the cipher officer, when he was knocked over by a wave in the still considerable swell. He fell and in trying to get a firm grip he dropped the code books which were washed overboard. Cdr. Day reported the loss by radio to CINCWA at 1215 hrs, but it was some time before this message was decoded and made available to the recipients. The result was that in the afternoon the *Highlander* had no clear picture of the way the situation was developing.

On the morning of March 18 a number of HF/DF bearings in a SE direction had shown that the enemy was approaching HX.229. Accordingly Cdr. Day had asked the *Volunteer* by radio in the morning to give a position report. At 1055 hrs the *Volunteer* sent a signal to *Highlander* and the second corvette following, *Abelia*: "My position, course and speed at 1200Z/18th 053°33'N 028°14'W, 053°, 9½ knots." This position was the midday position expected by the Commodore. It was a considerable distance from the position the *Highlander* had plotted and seemed to make clear that the HF/DF bearings were on position behind the convoy. So Commander Day decided to change course by 25° to starboard to 095° in order to force the contact-keepers behind the convoy under water and to catch up the convoy from the stern, since there was still enough daylight time. As a result of this change of course the *Highlander* left the good weather behind and came into the area of bad visibility and frequent snow showers where the convoy was. When it was thought that the convoy course had been reached at 1435 hrs, the *Highlander* proceeded on 053°. A factor here was that an HF/DF bearing received approximately from this direction appeared to indicate that they were on the correct course. Consequently, Cdr. Day did not ask the *Volunteer* for bearings, particularly since he knew that at this time bearings were being observed by the *Volunteer* for aircraft and that the radio personnel on this ship were overworked.

It later transpired that the midday position sent to Cdr. Day was inaccurate by some 40 miles. This meant that the *Highlander* was still some two hours away from the convoy just when *U 221*'s attack was taking place. The situation was only cleared up at 1630 hrs when the *Beverley* reported an "observed position": "Your 1155 to *Highlander*. My observed position at 1300Z/ 053°09'N 028°44'W. *Anemone*'s observed position agreed." This position was some 30 miles SW of the previous position. The *Highlander* turned at once onto the new interception course.

At 1715 hrs the *Volunteer* passed on the Commodore's question to the *Highlander*: "Commodore wishes to alter course now to position O to make better speed. Do you concur?" At 1739 hrs the *Highlander* replied: "Your 1715. Suggest alter to 080° at 1900Z and back to 040° at 2300Z." At 1828 hrs the *Volunteer* also gave an observed position to the *Highlander*: "Observations now put my 1200Z as 53°05'N, 28°95'W, speed 7 knots."

So about 1900 hrs the *Highlander* found the convoy about a mile from the correctly plotted position. Cdr. Day was able to relieve Lt. Cdr. Luther of his heavy task as SOE. At this moment, when the convoy, as instructed in the *Highlander*'s signal, changed its course to 080°, the two corvettes, *Anemone* and *Pennywort*, were still astern of the convoy after rescuing the survivors of the last attack. Cdr. Day ordered the *Highlander* to take up position in front of the convoy, the *Beverley* was stationed on the starboard and the *Volunteer* on the port beam.

About 2200 hrs, approximately one hour before the convoy turned again to a course of 040°, the new SOE observed that the American freighter

Mathew Luckenbach, at the end of the second column, was leaving the convoy and going ahead of it at full speed, nearly 13 knots. The *Highlander* approached the ship and tried to communicate in Morse with her signal searchlight. There was an answer, but it was unintelligible and the captain of the freighter did not obey the order to resume his position. Attempts to give the order by loudspeaker also failed to produce any result. It was clear that the ship had deliberately left the convoy and was refusing to resume her position. This behavior was to have fateful consequences. As it later turned out, the crew and the captain, as a result of the many torpedoings in the convoy, had held a meeting and decided to abandon the convoy.

THE ATTEMPTS TO ATTACK HX.229 IN THE NIGHT OF MARCH 18–19

During March 18–19 nine U-boats had reported contact with convoy HX.229: *U 610*, *U 134*, *U 333*, *U 221*, *U 336*, *U 439*, *U 441*, *U 526*, and *U 406*; seven had reported contact with SC.122: *U 305*, *U 530*, *U 598*, *U 527*, *U 230*, *U 338* and *U 642*. Some of these boats, particularly those with SC.122, had been forced underwater by the air escort and had fallen behind, but closed up again at night at top speed. Following the signals of *U 134* (Oblt. Brosin) which had reestablished contact at 0951 hrs, *U 406*, *U 441*, *U 526*, *U 439*, *U 336*, *U 615*, *U 440*, *U 608*, *U 618* and *U 384* came up to the vicinity of HX.229. At 0404 hrs the corvette *Anemone*, in position S to the stern of the convoy, sighted, in the moonlight reflected on the water, a U-boat some 3,600 meters to the stern on a course of 315°. There was a reduced cloud density of 8–10, clear visibility for about seven miles, the wind was NNW force 4 and the sea was down to state 3–4. The U-boat apparently tried to get to the windward side and down moon in order to be able to attack the ships against the illuminated background, as it was proceeding athwart the convoy. The *Anemone* at once gave the signal: "One sub. 6 o'clock—3 miles—0405." The *Anemone* turned toward the U-boat, proceeding at full speed. The U-boat recognized the "destroyer," as she turned and submerged at 0408 hrs. The *Anemone* obtained asdic contact at 2,300 meters and approached at once at high speed to make her first depth charge attack. At 0410 hrs 10 depth charges were thrown from the four throwers and the stern chutes set to a depth of 45 and 120 meters. The detonations put the asdic temporarily out of action. A flare was dropped where the U-boat was thought to have submerged.

At 0413 hrs Cdr. Day had ordered the *Volunteer*, which was in position Q on the port quarter of the convoy, to close up to support the *Anemone*. Lt. Cdr. Luther turned at once toward the clearly recognized flare and increased his speed. At 0425 hrs he got near the given position and the asdic indicated a target at a distance of 2,200 meters. The *Volunteer* passed over the position of the U-boat at 14 knots and simultaneously dropped 10 depth charges. Contact was at first lost and the *Volunteer* began the operation "observant." Meanwhile, the *Anemone*'s asdic was repaired and at 0429 hrs she obtained a new contact at a range of 1,650 meters. Because he had only a few depth charges left, Lt. Cdr. King decided on a "hedgehog" attack. At 0438 hrs he had maneuvered the *Anemone* into what he thought was a favorable position but, of the 24 bombs from the thrower, 18 failed and the remaining six sank without detonating. As the asdic still had contact, the *Anemone* turned and approached to make a new ten-depth-charge attack at 0452 hrs. Again one of the heavy charges got stuck in the thrower with the result that only nine could be dropped. After the detonations the asdic picked up the U-boat very quickly again and the *Anemone* made her fourth approach. Meanwhile, the *Volunteer* had turned away, on orders from the *Highlander*, to resume positions at 0502 hrs. As the *Anemone* now had no more depth charges ready for use, Lt. Cdr. King decided, despite its uncertain functioning, to make another "hedgehog" attack at 0514 hrs. This time only four bombs were launched and there were no detonations. Twenty failed. Just as this attack ended, the radar located an echo 1,800 meters on the port bow and one at 1,200 meters on the starboard beam. At that moment, a heavy rain squall covered the area with the result that nothing could be seen with the human eye. Lt. Cdr. King turned toward the nearest echo on the starboard side. As the *Anemone* came out of the rain squall, a U-boat was observed on the surface 500 meters ahead. It also saw the corvette at that moment and submerged. The asdic located the U-boat at once and at 0532 hrs Lt. Cdr. King dropped four charges, set to depths of 15 and 40 meters, from the stern chutes which were now operating again. After dropping them, the *Anemone* turned at once and prepared for a new approach. At 0541 hrs another four charges set to 45 and 100 meters were dropped. Following this attack, no further asdic contact could be made. The second radar contact was also soon lost and as the corvette had now only two depth charges on board, she proceeded back to the convoy at 0720 hrs.

While the *Anemone* and *Volunteer* were pursuing the first U-boat located to the stern, the *Highlander* at 0447 hrs sighted another U-boat on the port bow at 340° and a range of 3,650 meters. It was only located by radar at 3,500 meters. All that could be seen was a white bow wave. When the *Highlander* turned toward the U-boat, the latter at once went off on a 290° course. The *Highlander* increased speed to 22 knots and, when the distance was reduced to 1,800 meters, the U-boat submerged. It was *U 608* (Kptlt Struckmeier) which, immediately before diving, fired a salvo of three torpedoes at the destroyer, all of which missed. It was believed on the U-boat that two hits were heard after 5 minutes 34 seconds. The mass detonation of depth charges which followed misled the commander into assuming that a destroyer of the

"D" class had been sunk. But, in fact, the *Highlander* had dropped her first carpet of depth charges $3^1/2$ minutes after the U-boat disappeared. Then she had turned and at 0505 hrs approached to make a second attack with 14 depth charges. After the second approach the asdic obtained a new contact on *U 439*, but Cdr. Day could not carry out his proposed third attack with "hedgehog." He was careful not to lose the U-boat. The distance was increased again to 1,300 meters and the locating became clearer. At 0521 hrs another "hedgehog" attack was carried out at eight knots. But, in turning, the contact again became obscured until the distance was reduced to about 900 meters at 0524 hrs. When Cdr. Day gave the order to fire only two bombs were released from the throwers. Contact was lost and Cdr. Day turned away again to resume the search from a greater distance. At 0536 hrs contact was reestablished and Cdr. Day made a new depth charge attack on the U-boat which promptly maneuvered. At 0542 hrs another depth charge carpet was dropped. Ten minutes later there was a violent explosion just behind the stern of the destroyer as though a depth charge pattern was exploding. Subsequent investigation showed that no other escort had dropped depth charges at this time nor could it have been a charge from the *Highlander* herself. Possibly the U-boat fired another torpedo which exploded in the wake. After that, contact with the U-boat was briefly reestablished several times, but it was too imprecise to make an attack. The *Highlander* continued the search until 0700 hrs. At this stage she was about 20 miles astern of the convoy and Cdr. Day decided to close up so as to be with the convoy in the event of a dawn attack. It also appeared necessary for him to reorganize the screen after the pursuits and attacks.

At this time the *Pennywort* also established contact with a U-boat. At 0520 hrs her asdic got a location 900 meters on the port beam while she was zigzagging in position G about 4,000 meters from the convoy. The U-boat was *U 441* (Kptlt Klaus Hartmann). While the actions were going on on the port side and starboard quarter, Hartmann tried to infiltrate at the head of the convoy. He had reached a firing position at 0450 hrs, undetected by the *Beverley*, and fired, successively, from the bow tubes a FAT torpedo, two G 7es and another FAT. After turning away, he ordered another G 7e torpedo to be fired from the stern tube at 0600 hrs. After immediately submerging, the boat heard three detonations and assumed it had secured hits on a passenger freighter of 7,000 tons and two other freighters of about 5,000 tons. In fact, the U-boat probably mistook depth charge explosions for torpedo hits. The *Pennywort* at once turned hard to port and at 0528 hrs dropped six depth charges where it was thought the U-boat had submerged. However, she was unable to reestablish contact. When at 0528 hrs the *Highlander* ordered the escorts to return to their positions, she broke off the search and resumed her position at 0610 hrs. At 0556 hrs the *Volunteer* had arrived back in her position on the port side so that there were once more three escorts with the convoy.

Ten miles NNW of the convoy the American *Babbitt* (Cdr. Quarles), coming from Iceland, obtained a radar contact at 2,000 meters dead ahead in the direction of the convoy. This disappeared a few minutes later, but, at the same time, the sonar reported a location in the same direction. In quick succession the destroyer made three depth charge attacks with full carpets. After the third attack, the radar again indicated a target suggesting that the U-boat had either been forced to surface by the attack or that it was trying to escape on the surface. The *Babbitt* at once fired star shells but, because of the low clouds, nothing could be seen. The radar contact was affected by the exploding star shells and the U-boat was able to escape. After about 10 minutes a U-boat was again located with sonar. Another full depth charge carpet was dropped and, with a total of seven more attacks, the *Babbitt* continued her pursuit until 1051 hrs. But the number of depth charges thrown had to be reduced by the steadily declining supply. In several attacks large air bubbles and the smell of oil were noticed. After the last attack a large diesel oil patch was seen on the surface and in the oil patch some pieces of cork were recognized, and the destroyer took some samples of oil from the water. When a further search proved fruitless, the *Babbitt* headed for the convoy at 20 knots at 1200 hrs. In all, she had dropped 53 depth charges in 11 attacks.

THE ATTACKS BY *U 666* ON SC.122

Shortly after midnight *U 666* (Oblt Engel), which had moved up unnoticed on the port side of the convoy, began to get into position to attack. The situation was favorable for the boat for, at that moment, a regrouping of the escorts was taking place on the port side of the convoy. The corvette *Lavender* and the destroyer *Upshur* were making for their prescribed positions M and P again, after their U-boat search, and the corvette *Saxifrage*, which had meanwhile screened the port side, was leaving her station to go to her old position A ahead of the convoy. In consequence, the attention of the escorts was divided by this relief operation and the *U 666*, coming from the dark horizon in the north with a light breeze and swell behind it, was able to maneuver into a firing position between the *Saxifrage* which was withdrawing and the *Lavender* which was coming up. The convoy could be clearly seen in the bright moonlight through a gap in the clouds. At 0017 hrs the first officer of the watch, Lt. Fahizius, fired a salvo of four torpedoes at two overlapping freighters, estimated to be of 4,000 and 5,000 tons, on the port side of the convoy. The first torpedo broke surface. The other three functioned normally but there were no detonations. The U-boat had estimated the course of the convoy to be 070° instead of 095°; in addition, the range was obviously greater than the assumed 3,000 meters. The attack was not observed by either the convoy or the escorts.

Oblt Engel turned the boat to port with the convoy so as to be able to fire the stern torpedo. For a quarter of an hour, the boat moved on a course parallel with the convoy in order to reach a position a little further forward. At 0030 hrs Oblt Engel turned away and four minutes later Lt. Fahizius fired his stern torpedo at the leading ship of the port column. In the meantime the clouds had come up again and, shortly after the torpedo was fired, a driving rain squall blocked the view of the convoy. In the U-boat they thought they heard a torpedo detonation but were unable to see any visual effect. This time, too, the U-boat's attack was not observed by the escorts. Although the distances between the U-boat and the *Lavender* and the *Upshur* at this time must have been generally between 2,500 and 3,000 meters the radars of the two ships failed to locate anything. The last torpedo miss was possibly due to the fact that at 0030 hrs the convoy reverted to its old general course of 060°.

U 666 withdrew on the surface and, while reloading the torpedoes, tried to maintain contact so as to be able to attack a second time. As a result of the rain, which began at 0200 hrs, *U 666* probably did not notice the convoy's change of course and so came on to its starboard side. When, at the time of the first attack, it received *U 666*'s contact report, a second U-boat had also established contact on the port quarter shortly before 0400 hrs and sent another contact signal. This was picked up by the *Havelock*'s HF/DF and Cdr. Boyle ordered his destroyer to follow the bearing at once, but she was seen by the U-boat, probably the *U 527*, before her radar could find it. *Havelock*'s asdic was still defective with the result that it was impossible to locate anything under water. She therefore turned away and at 0550 hrs resumed her position S in rear of the convoy.

While the *Havelock* was coming up again from the stern, *U 666* had once more got ahead on the starboard side. Its maneuver was facilitated by the fact that the frigate *Swale* (Lt. Cdr. Jackson), stationed at position F, had fallen behind in her zigzag course and was not, as should have been the case, about 3,600 meters on the starboard beam, but some 3,000 meters on the starboard quarter, close to the corvette *Godetia*. There was thus a wide gap between the corvette *Pimpernel* which was on the starboard bow and the *Swale*. Through this Oblt Engel could make his approach. In a wind freshening up to a NW force 3 and sea state 5, the escorts could not locate the approaching U-boat at a distance of more than 4,000 meters. With visibility of about 6 miles *U 666* could clearly see the ships of the convoy in the light of the waning three-quarter moon. At a distance of 3,000 meters Lt. Fahizius fired his bow torpedoes as coordinated single aims at the ships which could be recognized on the starboard of the convoy: a freighter of 3,000 tons, a freighter of 4,000 tons, a freighter of 7,000 tons and another of 4,000 tons. The first torpedo broke surface, but evidently no one in the convoy noticed it. The second torpedo, after traveling 3 minutes 15 seconds (3,009 meters), hit the Greek ship *Carras* (5,234 tons), which had come up on the starboard side into position 131 vacated by the *Empire Morn*. The U-boat observed a 60–80 meter high and very broad cloud of dark smoke near the target. It hovered for a time over the target and then subsided. A very loud detonation was then heard in the U-boat.

Shortly before the *Carras* was hit, the frigate *Swale* obtained, on her radar, contact at a range of 3,650 meters and she turned toward it. When the torpedo detonated, she was still 3,300 meters from the target. At that very moment Oblt Engel saw, from the bridge of the U-boat, the "destroyer" turning toward the boat and gave orders to submerge. He thought, as he went below from the bridge, that he observed a hit on a further target near the after edge of the funnel in the engine room which caused a 100-meter-high cloud of white smoke. A further detonation followed soon after and the U-boat assumed that it had scored three hits.

Two minutes after the U-boat dived, the *Swale* obtained contact with her asdic at a range of 1,550 meters and approached the U-boat at 15 knots with a view to making a depth charge attack. Contact was lost at about 200 meters from the target, but Lt. Cdr. Jackson maintained course although he was only about 200 meters from the ships of the convoy and dropped his carpet of 14 depth charges set to 15, 40 and 70 meters.

Meanwhile, the convoy escorts had seen the distress rockets fired by the *Carras*. The *Swale*'s signal about her sighting of a U-boat was also picked up by most of the escorts. At 0557 hrs Cdr. Boyle ordered a "half raspberry" and a few minutes later he instructed the rescue ship *Zamalek* to recover survivors and the corvette *Buttercup* to screen the rescue ship. The other escorts made no contact in their searches. In the heavy rain showers which returned the *Zamalek* (Capt. Morris) had some difficulty finding the stricken ship which had clearly begun to sink fairly quickly. But after some time the lifeboats were found from which 34 survivors were recovered. The *Zamalek* had now 165 survivors on board.

On her return to the convoy the *Zamalek* reported that the *Carras* was still afloat and appeared capable of being salvaged and that the Captain had omitted to destroy secret material. The SOE then gave orders for the *Zamalek* to rejoin the convoy at full speed and for the *Buttercup* to turn round and recover the secret material. A boarding party carried out this order. But the *Carras* was still floating when the corvette headed back for the convoy.

CHAPTER 11

The End of the Operation

APPRECIATIONS OF THE SITUATION ON THE MORNING OF MARCH 19

The Commander U-boats had got the impression from the U-boat reports that the operations by day on March 18 against HX.229 had been particularly hindered by the bad weather—a NNW wind of force 6 and snow showers with visibility varying between 500 and 5,000 meters. This had generally rendered contact only possible by sound bearings. Only *U 221* had been able to carry out a successful underwater attack.

In the night March 18–19 nine U-boats reported contact with the convoys, but no satisfactory results were achieved. *U 666* radioed reports about two attacks on SC.122. But the other boats seemed to have been recognized in their approaches in the bright moonlight and to have been driven off by destroyers.

With SC.122, particularly, the escort appeared to have been considerably reinforced, since many boats reported depth charge pursuits by destroyers and also very strong air cover which made it difficult for them to get up to the convoy. The air cover was also apparent from the deciphering of the "B" Service (see Appendix 8).

Nevertheless, there were in the morning contact signals from *U 666* with SC.122 at 0545 hrs and from *U 134* with HX.229 at 0410 hrs. Only three other boats—*U 230*, *U 86* and *U 228*—had reported breaking off their operations against the convoy. The majority of the *Stürmer* and *Dränger* boats were still trying to establish contact. At least 10 boats were very near the convoys. So the Commander U-boats decided to continue the operation until the morning of March 20 despite the fact that strong air cover was expected on March 19 because the convoys were getting nearer land.

On March 19 the "B" Service was able to clear up the uncertainty about the route of HX.229. It realized that the route deciphered on March 12 and the change of course deciphered on March 16 referred to a part-convoy, HX.229A, which had taken the northern route, while the main convoy,

191

HX.229, had proceeded on the southern course decoded on March 15 and had then been located by the U-boats on March 16.

In fact, HX.229A had continued its journey passing just SE of Cape Farewell and, in the night March 18–19, again entered an area with many icebergs. Visibility deteriorated so much as a result of a snow storm that Cdr. Dalison's tactic of sending an escort ahead to illuminate the icebergs with a searchlight was no longer adequate. At 0720 hrs on March 19 the large whaling depot ship *Svend Foyn* (14,795 tons) hit an iceberg and lay stationary, severely damaged. As the ship had many passengers on board, everything had to be tried to save her. Cdr. Dalison, who had remained with her in his leader, the sloop *Aberdeen*, realized that he could not protect the unmaneuverable ship against U-boats, as *Aberdeen*'s asdic was completely out of action. Accordingly, he ordered the sloop *Hastings* to screen the damaged ship and he himself proceeded at high speed after the convoy. At 0923 hrs he sent the Flag Officer Iceland (FOIC) a distress call for the *Svend Foyn* and at 1645 hrs CTF 24 gave instructions to Task Unit 24.8.2, which was being employed to protect convoys on the Greenland route, to send the Coast Guard cutter *Modoc* to the damaged vessel at 58°05'N 43°50'W and, if necessary, to rescue the 195 passengers and the crew.

At 2350 hrs on the evening of March 19 the Coast Guard cutter *Bibb* met HX.229A, which in the meantime had moved further east, to take over the two steamers destined for Iceland the next morning. During the night there was brief excitement when the freighter *Fresno Star* fired two snowflake rockets as the result of an operational mistake and the escorts at first assumed there was a U-boat attack and carried out a "raspberry" operation.

In the course of the day the two freighters *Belgian Airman* and *Lone Star* also reported damage from ice; in consequence the *Aberdeen* sent a report to CINCWA at 1300 hrs on March 20 and then received permission to let the two ships proceed to the nearest harbor. All the radio messages sent by the convoy HX.229A were deciphered by the German "B" Service with three days' delay; but no U-boats could be deployed on the basis of these reports, the distance being too great. But after her crew and passengers had been rescued the *Svend Foyn*, because of the considerable damage she received, was lost without the intervention of any U-boat.

The bearings coming in since the evening of March 18 from the Y stations indicated to CINCWA not only further dangers for the two convoys, HX.229 and SC.122, which had been under attack, but also now for KMS.11 on the Gibraltar route. This consisted of 62 ships and the Canadian escort group C 2 (see p. 173) which was proceeding southward west of the Bay of Biscay. At 2000 hrs *U 621* (Oblt Kruschka) had established contact in square BE 6134 with this convoy which was proceeding on a course of 190° at eight

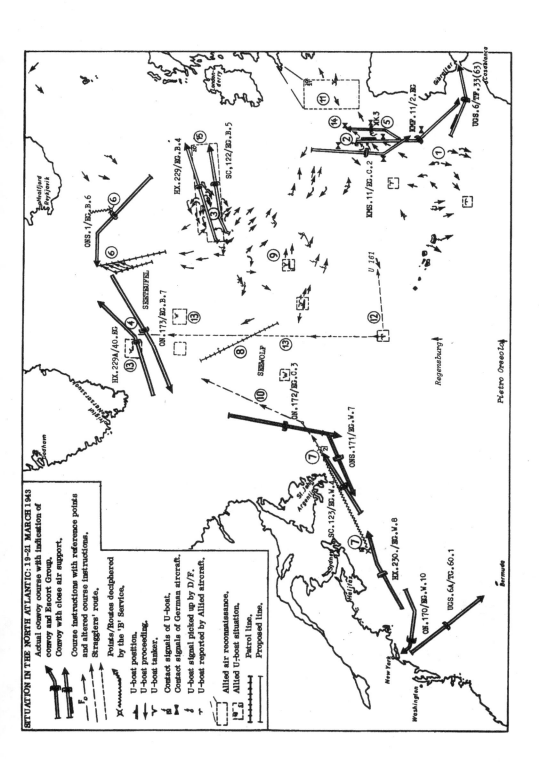

SITUATION IN THE NORTH ATLANTIC: 19–21 MARCH 1943

Actual convoy course with indication of convoy and Escort Group.

Convoy with close air support.

Course instructions with reference points and altered course instructions, Stragglers' route.

Points/Routes deciphered by the 'B' Service.

U-boat position.

U-boat proceeding.

U-boat tanker.

Contact signals of U-boat.

Contact signals of German aircraft.

U-boat signal picked up by D/F.

U-boat reported by Allied aircraft.

Allied air reconnaissance.

Allied U-boat situation.

Patrol line.

Proposed line.

The situation in the North Atlantic: March 19 (1200 hrs GMT) to March 21 (1200 hrs GMT), 1943

#	Date	Event
1	Mar 19 1130 hrs	Since, in view of the strong air cover with UGS.6, the U-boats, which were exhausted after six days of pursuit, had no further hope of success, the Cdr U-boats breaks off the operation. The boats proceed southwards for further operations, to refuel and to establish contact with KMF.11.
2	Mar 19 afternoon	The air cover from 19 Group, RAF Coastal Command drives off *U 621*, which tries tenaciously to maintain contact with KMF.11, and other outward and homeward bound boats. 3 homeward bound boats, coming from UGS.6, are sent to meet the convoy but they do not make contact.
3	Mar 19–20	The remaining boats in contact with HX.229 and SC.122 try once again to get ahead to make night attacks but they are unable to make headway against the naval cover which is reinforced by the arrival of additional escorts and the air cover provided by 15 Group from N. Ireland. Only one damaged ship left behind is sunk. The Cdr U-boats breaks off the operation at dawn on Mar 20. In setting off westward *U 384* is sunk by an aircraft.
4	Mar 20 0700 hrs	USCGC *Bibb* takes over the Iceland section from HX.229A (2 steamers). The convoy again runs into iceberg fields; several ships are damaged by ice.
5	Mar 20 1342 hrs	German air reconnaissance finds the convoys KMS.11 and KMF.11 as well as the north-bound XK.3. There is no planned deployment of U-boats.
6	Mar 20	German 'B' Service deciphers meeting point of Iceland section of ONS.1 with main convoy for Mar 21. The Cdr U-boats stations the *Seeteufel* group to catch the convoy on the morning of Mar 22.
7	Mar 20	German 'B' Service deciphers passing points for SC.123 on Mar 18 and Mar 21. The Cdr U-boats orders formation of new patrol line *Seewolf* which is to catch the convoy on the morning of Mar 25.
8	Mar 20	
9	Mar 20–21	U-boats report the sighting and pursuit of allied and neutral independents. Because their messages are picked up by D/F and in view of the situation reports of the boats leaving HX.229 and SC.122, COMINCH orders SC.123 to take an evasive course of 23° at 2000 hrs on Mar 22, so as to go round to the north of the U-boat area (deciphered by the 'B' Service on Mar 25).
10	Mar 20–21	
11	Mar 20–21	As a result of agents' reports, observations, radio bearings and prisoners' statements, the Allied Command expects the German blockade-runners from Eastern Asia. Accordingly 19 Group, Coastal Command, is strongly deployed in reconnaissance over the Bay of Biscay. *U 161* is to provide the blockade runners from Eastern Asia.
12	Mar 20–26	*Regensburg* and *Pietro Orseolo* with search receiver equipment at the meeting point T (carried out on Mar 23 and Mar 26). The *Regensburg* is then to proceed north through the Denmark Strait to Norway. Weather reporting U-boats which are to recover the crew in an emergency are to be stationed on the route. *P. Orseolo* is to get to the Bay of Biscay.
13	Mar 20–26	*Regensburg* is found by HMS *Glasgow* in the Denmark Strait on Mar 30. *P. Orseolo* is met off Cabo Villano on Mar 30 by 4 German destroyers and brought in.
14	Mar 21	German air reconnaissance again finds XK.3.
15	Mar 21	Additional escorts and units with many survivors are detached from HX.229 and SC.122.

knots. The Commander U-boats ordered the boats in the area to operate against the convoy at high speed, if they could reach it in the night. *U 634* reported its position in the vicinity of the convoy. *U 632* also tried to come up but was forced underwater by an aircraft and then continued on its way. *U 621* sent several contact signals during the night from squares BE 6156, BE 6455 and, finally, from BE 6482 at 0430 hrs, indicating a course of 180° and, now, greater speed. From the material provided by the "B" Service, the Commander U-boats concluded that it was the KMS.11. On the same day, German aircraft west of the Iberian peninsula had attacked an American freighter in square BE 9783 and, later, in CG 1112 and the Commander U-boats deployed the three boats still operating west of Spain—*U 107*, *U 445* and *U 410*—in the area of the position ascertained from the ship's deciphered report.

At 0730 hrs on the morning of March 19 *U 621* again established contact with convoy KMS.11 in BE 6737. Although, in the course of the day, the boat was driven off several times by the escorting aircraft, it constantly returned to the area and was able to maintain contact until 1813 hrs in the evening in square BE 9431. *U 332*, which, with only limited fuel, had operated briefly against the convoy, did not come up. But the Commander U-boats then deployed against the convoy the boats *U 504*, *U 521*, and *U 103* on their return from the operation against UGS.6, taking into account each's fuel supply, and gave similar orders to *U 107*, *U 445* and *U 410*. However, none of these boats reached the convoy. After dark, *U 621* had also to break off the operation and return to base. The many radio reports from the U-boats in the area of this convoy and further sighting reports of returning U-boats west of the Bay of Biscay from independent merchant ships and neutral ships convinced CINCWA of the dangers to KMS.11 and he therefore dispatched to it another support group which was formed from the *Bangor* minesweepers HMCS *Shippigan* and HMCS *Tadoussac*, and the M/S trawlers HMS *Dornoch* and HMS *Ilfracombe*.

But he was more concerned about the convoys HX.229 and SC.122. It was clear from the intercepted radio traffic of the escort groups that the U-boats had tried to attack both convoys. It then became clear in the morning that, in the case of HX.229, they had all been frustrated by the escort group. But at 0607 hrs the Commander of Escort Group B 5 with SC.122 had reported an attack with the loss of one ship and at 0919 hrs the name of the ship was given over radio as the *Carras*.

Nevertheless, in spite of this new loss, the situation appeared more favorable for the coming day than it had on previous days. At daylight both convoys were approaching the 600-mile range limit from the air bases in

Northern Ireland and Iceland. This made possible not only the deployment of the VLR Liberators of No 120 and 86 Squadrons in support but also of the Fortress bombers of No 220 Squadron from Aldergrove and No 206 from Benbecula, as well as the Sunderland flying boats from No 201 and 228 Squadrons and the Canadian No 423 Squadron from Castle Archdale. The Allies could only reckon on the availability of slightly more than one-third of the 18 Fortresses and just half of the Sunderlands, and they also had to take into account that convoy ONS.1 needed to be covered. However, it meant that there was substantial reinforcement for the Liberator squadrons which had been very hard-pressed by their two-day operations to the absolute limit of their range. For the first time it became possible to carry out so-called protective sweeps in the area on both sides of the convoys, in addition to flights for their immediate cover. Four Liberators from Aldergrove, two from Reykjavik, seven Fortresses from Benbecula and three Sunderlands from Castle Archdale were earmarked. In addition, the US Navy squadron, VP 84, in Reykjavik made two Catalina flying boats available for HX.229. The air protection for ONS.1, which was now approaching ICOMP south of Iceland, was organized from Benbecula and Iceland. This did not require to be so strong because there, according to the U-boat situation, only new outward-bound U-boats were expected and no regular formation.

The situation of the naval escort for the two convoys would inevitably improve in the course of March 19. The escorts which had taken part in the convoy battles since March 16–17 were now short of depth charges and were very low in fuel, but, so far, the escort oilers had escaped attack and could provide some replenishment in the improving weather if the aircraft succeeded by day in giving the convoys breathing space. In particular, the leader of Escort Group B 4, the *Highlander*, and the American *Babbitt* had now reached HX.229 so that there were four destroyers and two corvettes. In the afternoon the destroyer *Vimy*, coming from Iceland, and the corvette *Abelia*, which had been following the convoy, were also due to arrive. As for SC.122, it had a stronger group comprising two destroyers, a frigate and four corvettes and this was now to be joined by the very seaworthy and powerful US Coast Guard cutter, *Ingham*. So, for the night, each convoy would have eight escorts. However, to maintain this escort strength with the SC.122, it was necessary not to release the steamers destined for Iceland with *Ingham* and the US destroyer *Upshur* at ICOMP, as had been originally envisaged. So at 1207 CINCWA gave orders to the Commodore that the *Askepot*, *Godafoss* and *Fjallfoss* should remain with the convoy. The *Selfoss*, which had been proceeding as a straggler since March 16, had already taken an independent course for Iceland, where she arrived on March 23.

THE SINKING OF THE *MATHEW LUCKENBACH*

The *Ingham* had not been able to carry out the order in the evening to undertake a diversionary maneuver. In the night she had come so close to SC.122 that she could see the distress rockets when the *Carras* was torpedoed. At 0745 hrs she established visual signal contact with the convoy for the first time. Coming from the north, she reached the convoy at 0829 hrs and proceeded from the head through the columns to a position at the stern, allocated to her by the *Havelock*. She reduced her speed to 12 knots and adopted a zigzag course. The wind and the sea had further abated and in clear visibility and light cloud the sun, which shone for lengthy periods, produced some warmth for the first time.

Meanwhile, the first aircraft had reached the convoys shortly after daybreak. In the case of HX.229, the *Highlander*, which was better equipped as a leader and had a better-trained crew than the *Volunteer*, had no difficulty in guiding Fortress B/206 to the scene with bearings. As the *Highlander* was still 20 miles behind the convoy, the *Anemone* was still closing up and the *Babbitt* was engaged in the pursuit of her U-boat, Cdr. Boyle asked the aircraft first to carry out a reconnaissance round the convoy and then, in particular, to force contact-keeping U-boats underwater in the thinly protected areas. At 0824 hrs B/206 sighted a U-boat some 30 miles on the port quarter, but the approaching aircraft was seen in time by the U-boat. It submerged so promptly that the four depth charges did no damage. The aircraft then flew to the *Babbitt*, which was searching for her U-boat some six miles away, in order to lead her to the boat which had already been attacked. But Cdr. Quarles preferred to hunt his own quarry instead of the more distant target. *U 615* reported at 0815 hrs that it had been forced down by aircraft. Middlebrook has concluded that this attack finished *U 384* (*op. cit.*, 270).

In the case of SC.122 the *Havelock* also had no difficulty in leading to the scene Fortresses N/220 and M/220, which had set out from Benbecula. *U 527* (Kptlt Uhlig) which, in the morning after *U 642* had been driven off, tried to take over the role of contact-keeper, had to dive at once. But Flt. Lt. Knowles in M/220 had not seen this boat but a second one, 16 miles on the starboard quarter. He attacked it at 0914 hrs as it submerged. The four depth charges detonated round the boat, *U 338*, which was thrown up to the surface again by the detonations, before Kptlt Kinzel, himself a former naval pilot, was able to get the boat down before the Fortress's second approach. Flt. Lt. Knowles dropped two more depth charges into the traces of rising oil. After some time and having sustained considerable damage, Kptlt Kinzel was able to surface and return to base.

U 527 had first heard the depth charge detonations. A little later the listening room reported the noise of screws. In his periscope Kptlt Uhlig saw two masts and then a merchant ship which seemed to be proceeding behind the convoy on a straight course at about 10 knots. Kptlt Uhlig had to close up at high underwater speed so as to get into a position to fire on what was thought to be a transport, or because of its armament, an auxiliary cruiser of 8,000 tons.

In fact, it was the American *Mathew Luckenbach* (8,848 tons) which the evening before had on her own initiative left the HX.229 behind.

At 0947 hrs Kptlt Uhlig fired his salvo of three torpedoes at an estimated range of 1,200 meters. He already thought he had missed when, after four minutes 16 seconds, one of the torpedoes exploded near the after mast and produced a mighty column of water. The distance was, in fact, 3,950 meters. The screw sounds stopped at once. It could be seen that the steamer was giving off smoke and was settling by the stern.

The officer of the watch on the bridge of the *Ingham* happened to see, with his binoculars, the column of water caused by the hit on the horizon, as he was scanning the scene before making a zigzag turn. At first he thought it was an aircraft that had dropped bombs. But he could see no aircraft in the sky. Then he noticed a white distress rocket. He ordered the *Ingham* to turn and proceeded at 18 knots toward it. Soon a torpedoed ship was recognized and at 1030 hrs it was identified as the *Mathew Luckenbach*. Three boats and two rafts with survivors were drifting in the area and no attempt was being made to pick up a survivor swimming in the water. As a U-boat must have been in the vicinity Capt. A. Martinson could not stop at once and had to wait until, as a result of his report, the *Upshur*, which was sent by the SOE, arrived.

U 527 had seen, in the meantime, that the steamer was not settling further and wanted to approach to finish her off when screw sounds were again reported from the listening room. An approaching destroyer could be seen in the periscope. Soon after, Kptlt Uhlig saw in his air target periscope not only the approaching destroyer with her thick bow wave but also an aircraft. He submerged and began to escape underwater.

As soon as the *Upshur* began her operation "observant" the *Ingham* stopped by the first boat. Within 30 minutes all 67 survivors were on board, although the *Ingham* had herself to maneuver up to each boat and raft because the survivors did nothing to help themselves. The ship looked as if it could be salvaged. But none of the crew of the *Mathew Luckenbach* was prepared to go back on board. So Capt. Martinson called for a deep-sea tug and proceeded with the *Upshur* back to the convoy.

However, the tug did not find the wreck. *U 527* had waited in the vicinity for the destroyer to leave. At 1525 hrs *U 523* (Kptlt Pietzsch), which was again seeking contact, had sighted the masts of the still-floating *Mathew Luckenbach* and began an underwater attack. More or less simultaneously, toward 1900 hrs, each of the two boats, without knowing about the other, began its torpedo attack on the damaged ship. *U 523* got in only a few moments before *U 527* and fired its torpedo at 1908 hrs. Although it broke surface once, it hit, after 2 minutes 19 seconds, with a loud detonation. Kptlt Uhlig saw a 30–40 meter high column of smoke shoot up from the target and broke off his approach. Both commanders then watched as, some seven minutes after the explosion, the freighter quickly sank.

LOSS OF CONTACT

In the course of the morning the Sunderland and Catalina flying boats also reached the convoys. After dawn the Fortress M/220 had compelled the U-boats in the vicinity of SC.122 to submerge with the result that, after *U 642*'s last report, there were no further contact signals. Then the Canadian Sunderland E/423 and the British Sunderland V/228 prevented any U-boat approaching the convoy. At 1045 hrs, E/423 sighted a periscope 26 miles on the starboard bow. At 1232 hrs the same flying boat attacked a submerging U-boat in a more dangerous position, some five miles on the port beam of the convoy, with two depth charges. The other Sunderland had attacked with four depth charges a third U-boat at 1216 hrs 48 miles to the stern of SC.122.

The strong air cover which forced the U-boats underwater prompted the Convoy Commodore to change course and so to make it more difficult for the contact-keepers to close up. At 1100 hrs the SC.122 went on to 075° and at 1400 hrs to 083°. The HX.229, which had for a time been on a course of 040° in order to get away from the wake of SC.122 and the U-boats that shadowed it, went on to 076° and then proceeded NW of SC.122. As a result of this move, all contact was in fact lost with HX.229 by 1145 hrs.

This situation soon became apparent to the escorts from the lack of further HF/DF bearings. But the U-boats did not yet give up. Some of them tried tenaciously, despite the air cover, to get eastward on the surface so as to be able to come up again when it got dark. At 1830 hrs *U 642* (Kptlt Brünning) sighted the SC.122's clouds of smoke in square AL 5746. Its contact signal was picked up by the *Havelock*'s HF/DF. When, shortly after, Liberator J/120, which was deployed on a protective sweep, asked the SOE for instructions and announced that it would remain with the convoy until 0200 hrs, it was asked to fly on a D/F bearing of 287° for 10 miles and then do a "frog" patrol. At 1925 hrs the aircraft sighted a U-boat at 280°, 45 miles from the convoy. It attacked the boat, which had dived, with two depth charges. At 2148 hrs the *Havelock* located a new signal at 224° and asked the Liberator to fly on that bearing for a range of 5–10 miles. At 2236 hrs the aircraft returned and reported that it had approached two contacts which had then disappeared and that, in addition, it had found a straggler at 215°, 45 miles away. Clearly one of the U-boats soon reappeared because at 2336 hrs the *Havelock* intercepted a new contact signal and asked the aircraft to fly along the same bearing again, concentrating on a range of 3–10 miles. Shortly after, J/120 sighted the U-boat at 240°, nine miles away, and attacked it as it submerged. But this time the depth charge equipment failed and the Liberator had to attack with its guns. This was clearly observed on the *Havelock* from the tracer flashes. At 0142 hrs the aircraft again asked for instructions as it would soon have to fly off. It was asked to sweep the stern sector. At 0155 hrs it reported the straggler at 225°, 14 miles away, and another contact in the same direction at a range of 20 miles. It then flew off. *U 642* had to submerge many times but was able to maintain contact with sound bearings and reported for the last time at 0300 hrs in the morning the sounds of a convoy from square AL 5852 at 040°. The German "B" Service also completely deciphered these aircraft reports (see Appendix 8).

In the afternoon the corvette *Abelia* reached HX.229. The *Highlander*, with her bearings, was able to direct her, as well as other aircraft. These prevented a U-boat, following the convoy in the afternoon, from coming within visual range. At 2050 hrs in the evening *U 631* (Oblt Krüger) sighted an individual destroyer. It was either the *Babbitt* closing up after pursuing a U-boat—she resumed her station at 2130 hrs—or the *Vimy*, which reached the convoy shortly after midnight at 0049 hrs. Coming up very quickly, the *U 631* could hear a noise band at about 0500 hrs in the morning in square AL 5528 and at 060°, but it was not able to get there before daylight.

With that, contact with the two convoys was finally lost. The Commander U-boats had ordered the boats on the evening of March 19 to break off the operation before first light on March 20, since they would then be too far within the range of British air cover. Only boats which happened to find themselves in a favorable position were still to exploit chances to make daylight underwater attacks after daybreak. All boats were then to move off on the convoy course to the SW to intercept any stragglers or damaged ships.

In fact, *U 333* (Oblt Schwaff) had found the abandoned and drifting *Carras* on the evening of March 19. The steamer seemed to Oblt Schwaff to have engine trouble because no movement could be seen although the ship was floating normally and no damage from a torpedo hit could be observed. Oblt Schwaff wanted to fire a salvo of two torpedoes to be sure. But only the torpedo in No 3 tube fired properly: that in No 1 tube failed. *U 333* then had to submerge 20 meters below periscope depth in order to eject the torpedo without it appearing on the surface. The result was that it was impossible to see the effect of the first torpedo which detonated after 138 seconds. Eight minutes after the hit, a muffled explosion was heard and then the noise of sinking. When the submarine surfaced, it saw an oil patch and wreckage at the position.

On the morning of March 20 Air Vice Marshal Slatter, AOC No 15 Group, RAF Coastal Command, ordered his Fortress bombers in Nos 220 and 206 Squadrons and the Sunderland flying boats of Nos 201, 228 and 423 Squadrons to set off before daylight. The Fortress bombers were to provide continuous close cover round the convoys that day and the Sunderland flying boats were earmarked for the wide protective sweeps.

The constant rain that had begun in the night at 0200 hrs in the vicinity of SC.122 slackened off toward 0700 hrs in the morning of March 20 and with a SE wind developed into intermittent squalls. Shortly after 0700 hrs the first Sunderland flying boat, Z/201, arrived in the area of the convoy, just when the *Havelock*, after a rather lengthy pause, had again picked up a U-boat signal with HF/DF. Cdr. Boyle ordered the aircraft to fly along the bearing. At 0750 hrs the aircraft sighted a submerging U-boat about 18 miles on the starboard quarter of the convoy. It attacked it with two depth charges.

Soon after, the two Sunderland flying boats, H/423 and F/423, also arrived in the area of convoy SC.122 and began their flights on the flanks and astern. At 0835 hrs H/423 sighted a submerging U-boat about 35 miles astern of the convoy, but did not arrive in time to make a depth charge attack. Twenty minutes later F/423 attacked a submerging U-boat 110 miles on the starboard quarter of the convoy with five depth charges.

At 0930 hrs Cdr. Boyle, after another not very clear HF/DF bearing, asked the convoy Commodore to make an emergency turn of 045° to port in order to avoid a suspected U-boat on the starboard bow. At 1050 hrs the convoy reverted to 085°. Meanwhile, the Sunderland flying boat F/423 had flown more patrols in the area of the convoy and at 1327 hrs made a low level attack with its last depth charge on a U-boat 60 miles on the starboard quarter. It was clear that, in the meantime, the U-boats had fallen further astern. Thus, in the afternoon at 1613 hrs the Sunderland flying boat T/201 was at first able to force underwater a U-boat 250 miles to the stern of SC.122 and at 1744 hrs it attacked, in a surprise approach, a U-boat 210 miles on the port quarter of the convoy with six depth charges. The U-boat—it was *U 384* (Kptlt von Rosenberg-Gruszczinski)—could not submerge in time and was sunk by two depth charges which detonated directly alongside the boat. This reported success was also deciphered by the German "B" Service (see Appendix 8).

TABLE No. 9

Route order for Convoy HX.229 after the attacks on the morning of March 20

Column 4	Column 3	Column 2	Column 1
	13 brit SS *Empire Knight* Clyde	12 amer SS *Robert Howe* Mersey	11 brit SS *Cape Breton* Clyde
		32 brit MS *Kaipara* Mersey	31 brit SS *Fort Anne* Loch Ewe
44 brit MS *Antar* Mersey	43 brit SS *Tekoa* Mersey	42 brit MT *Regent Panther* United Kingdom	41 brit SS *Nebraska* Mersey
54 brit SS *Empire Cavalier* Mersey	53 amer ST *Pan Rhode Island* Mersey	52 brit MT *San Veronica* Mersey	51 norw MS *Abraham Lincoln* Belfast
64 amer SS *Kofresi* Mersey	63 amer SS *Jean* Mersey	62 amer ST *Gulf Disc* Clyde	61 pan MT *Belgian Gulf* Mersey
	73 pan SS *El Mundo* Mersey	72 dutch MT *Magdala* Belfast	71 brit SS *City of Agra* Mersey
		82 brit MT *Luculus* Belfast	81 brit MT *Nicania* Mersey
		92 amer SS *Margaret Lykes* Mersey	91 amer SS *Daniel Webster* Belfast

Convoy Commodore: 51 *Abraham Lincoln*
Vice Commodore: 41 *Nebraska*
Escort Oiler: 62 *Gulf Disc*

Ocean Escort Group B.4
Task Unit 24.1.18

Destroyer	HMS	*Highlander*
Destroyer	HMS	*Volunteer* (from B.5)
Destroyer	HMS	*Beverley*
Corvette	HMS	*Anemone*
Corvette	HMS	*Pennywort*
Corvette	HMS	*Abelia*
Corvette	HMCS	*Sherbrooke* (straggler)

Supporting ships:

Destroyer	USS	*Babbitt*
Destroyer	HMS	*Vimy*

Route order for Convoy SC.122 after the attacks on March 20

45 brit SS *Vinriver* Clyde	44 icel SS *Fjallfoss* Reykjavik	43 icel SS *Godafoss* Reykjavik	42 amer SS *Cartago* Reykjavik	41 norw SS *Askepot* Reykjavik
55 brit SS *Ogmore Castle* Loch Ewe	54 yugo SS *Franka* Loch Ewe	53 brit SS *Carso* Loch Ewe	52 dutch SS *Parkhaven* Loch Ewe	51 swed SS *Atland* Loch Ewe
65 brit SS *Drakepool* Loch Ewe	64	63 brit MS *Innesmoor* Loch Ewe	62 brit SS *Baron Semple* Belfast ?	61 brit SS *Baron Stranraer* Loch Ewe
75 brit SS *Aymeric* Loch Ewe	74 brit SS *Baron Elgin* Loch Ewe	73 brit SS *Bridgepool* Loch Ewe	72	71 brit MT *Benedick* Clyde
	84 amer LST *LST 365* United Kingdom	83 brit SS *Reaveley* Mersey	82	81 brit MS *Glenapp* Mersey
95 brit ST *Beaconoil* Clyde	94 brit SS *Orminister* Loch Ewe	93 brit ST *Empire Galahad* United Kingdom	92	91 brit SS *Historian* Mersey
105 amer LST *LST 305* United Kingdom	104 brit SS *Badjestan* Glasgow	103 brit SS *Filleigh* Mersey	102 brit ST *Gloxinia* Mersey	101 brit MS *Losada* Mersey
	114 swed SS *Porjus* Mersey	113	112 brit ST *Shirvan* Belfast	111 brit SS *Empire Dunstan* Mersey
		123 dutch MS *Kedoe* Belfast	122 amer ST *Vistula* Belfast	121 brit SS *Dolius* Belfast
	134 pan SS *Bonita* United Kingdom	133 brit SS *Helencrest* Mersey	132 brit ST *Christian Holm* United Kingdom	131 brit SS *Boston City* Belfast

Convoy Commodore: 81 *Glenapp*
Vice Commodore: 131 *Boston City*
Escort Oiler: 71 *Benedick*
Standby Oiler: 132 *Christian Holm*

Ocean Escort Group B.4
Task Unit 24.1.19
Destroyer   HMS *Havelock*
Frigate   HMS *Swale*
Corvette   HMS *Lavender*
Corvette   HMS *Pimpernel*
Corvette   HMS *Buttercup*
Corvette   HMS *Saxifrage*
Corvette   HMS *Godetia*
Task Unit 24.6.
Destroyer   USS *Upshur*
Cutter   USCGC *Ingham*

THE ARRIVAL OF THE CONVOYS

Toward midday on March 20 it became clear to Cdr. Day on the *Highlander* that the U-boats had lost contact with HX.229. He therefore announced his intention by radio at 1316 hrs of detaching the escorts, which were then overloaded with survivors, on the following morning. At 1405 hrs CINCWA confirmed this and also ordered the American destroyer *Babbitt* to proceed to Londonderry early on March 21. In later radio messages at 1530 hrs and 1753 hrs Cdr. Day of the Escort Group announced his further intentions. Meanwhile, Commodore Mayall had reorganized the 24 ships remaining in his convoy into eight columns. The *Tekoa* with her 138 survivors, which had by then closed up, was put in the center, as the table overleaf on the previous page shows.

Tension also slackened off in the SC.122 after the last bearings in the morning. Commodore White was able to reorganize the 40 remaining ships of his convoy, as the table opposite shows.

At 0815 hrs on the morning of March 21 the two American escorts with SC.122, the Coast Guard cutter *Ingham* and the destroyer *Upshur*, were detached. At 0700 hrs the destroyer *Babbitt* left HX.229 just when the Canadian corvette *Sherbrooke*, which had been closing up from the stern, reached the convoy. At 0730 hrs the two corvettes, *Anemone* with 158 and *Pennywort* with 127 survivors, together with the freighter *Tekoa*, were detached in order that their survivors could be landed as soon as possible. At 0800 hrs the *Volunteer* asked to be released because a member of the crew had an acute appendicitis and had to be got to hospital. The *Beverley* had 31 and the *Volunteer* 68 survivors.

Early on March 22 SC.122 arrived in the River Foyle. In the case of HX.229 the ships intended for northern ports were detached at 0930 hrs with the destroyer *Vimy*. At 1400 hrs the Eastern Local Escort Group with the trawler *Aquamarine* relieved the remaining ships of Escort Group B 4, the *Highlander*, *Beverley*, *Sherbrooke* and *Abelia* together with the escort oiler *Gulf Disc*.

Three days later Commodore Casey also brought his convoy HX.229A into the North Channel. It had made a wide sweep to the north and so avoided U-boat formations.

The convoys had reached their destination.

CHAPTER 12

Conclusions Drawn from the Convoy Battle

Immediately after the operations were ended, the command staffs on both sides reviewed the situation and drew up their conclusions.

The final report of the Commander U-boats on March 20 (see Appendix 9) makes clear that the German U-boat Command regarded the operation as having been the greatest success achieved until then in a convoy battle. It was thought particularly satisfactory that in this convoy battle not only had old U-boat hands had successes but that nearly 50% of the participating boats had reported positive results: 32 ships totaling 187,560 tons and a destroyer had been sunk and nine hits had been obtained on other ships. Against these successes it appeared that, during the actual convoy operation, no U-boat loss had been sustained and only one boat—*U 384*—had fallen a victim to enemy air cover after the operation had been broken off.

As in previous operations, it had once again been shown that the best chances of success for the U-boats occurred during the first night, particularly if attacks could be made whilst the convoy was still outside the range of shore-based air cover. The longer the operation lasted, the stronger the defense became. Additional surface forces were brought up and, above all, air support was increased rapidly from both sides of the ever-narrowing "air gap" in the North Atlantic.

Generally, the operation seemed to be an outstanding confirmation of the way the battle against the convoys in the North Atlantic was being conducted and, in this phase, the brilliant successes of the German "B" Service had made a substantial contribution. It also appeared that the basic training in battle tactics which the new U-boats had undergone for many months in the Baltic had proved itself again.

For the future it seemed important that the U-boat formations should be stationed, if possible with the help of radio intelligence, in such a way that they could find an anticipated convoy as early as possible in the day so that the contact-keeping U-boat could bring up the maximum number of boats into an attacking position before the onset of the first night. To be

205

able to exploit this first surprise, it was essential to deny the enemy the possibility of locating the U-boat formations prematurely. As they had been in the past few weeks, the U-boats were to be instructed constantly of the importance of taking up their prescribed patrol or reconnaissance lines shortly before the appointed time to avoid detection by enemy shore-based aircraft which were equipped with radar. To prevent enemy radio intelligence from taking bearings from the many shore-based stations, the U-boats were urged to maintain radio silence until the first contact with the enemy. Once a convoy battle had begun it did not seem that the U-boats' radio traffic would constitute a serious danger, since their presence near the convoy was then already known as a result of the attacks. The threat to the U-boats lay rather in the radar installed in the enemy ships and aircraft as the simultaneous operation against convoy UGS.6 in the Central Atlantic had demonstrated. A promising way of countering enemy radar was for the U-boats to use their own search receivers and station themselves forward close to enemy radar contacts, or to remain out at the limits of the radar range of the air escort during the daylight hours ready to close up before dusk to join in simultaneous underwater attacks with other boats.

It was now vital to follow up promptly the successes against the last two convoys with further ones. Accordingly, on the basis of new decodings received in the meantime from the "B" Service, two new groups, *Seeteufel* and *Seewolf,* were formed in the Central Atlantic. These new groups were then to be used to attack the convoys ONS.1, SC.123 and HX.230 which had been identified in radio intelligence.

For the Allies the picture presented after the first 20 days of March 1943 was bleak. During the Casablanca Conference of Allied Government chiefs and their military advisers in January it had been laid down that victory over the U-boats must be the basic precondition of any future major operation against Europe and, with it, of an Allied victory. On March 1 the Atlantic Convoy Conference, summoned at the insistence of Admiral King, had met in Washington to reorganize responsibilities for fighting the battle against the U-boats and improving convoy protection in the North Atlantic. But, before this conference could take any decisions, developments appeared to cast doubt on the whole convoy system. In the first 10 days of March 41 ships, totaling 229,949 tons, had been sunk. In the second 10 days the U-boats had sunk 44 ships, totaling 282,000. Over half a million tons had been lost and what made these losses so serious was the fact that 68% of the ships had been torpedoed in convoy. On the other hand, escorts with the convoys had sunk only four U-boats and aircraft, in providing distant convoy escort, only another two.

The convoy battles and, above all, the stormy weather during the first months of 1943, had led to an unusually large number of escorts being in the yards for repairs. Moreover, storms had in many cases so delayed the convoy timetable that the whole group organization of the convoy escorts was threatening to collapse.

On the other hand, the number of U-boats was increasing at such a pace that it seemed ever more pointless to base the routing of convoys on radio intelligence and evasive tactics. A convoy which had avoided the concentration of one U-boat pack was likely, shortly after, to fall into the jaws of the next. Losses on the scale of that of the last convoy battles in which convoy after convoy lost four, six, eight or even twelve ships, could not be sustained much longer. The morale and determination of the seamen was being undermined. There was a possibility that the convoy system as an effective form of protection for merchantmen would have to be abandoned. The system which in three and a half years of the Battle of the Atlantic had become the lynchpin of Allied maritime strategy was threatened. On the other hand, the Admiralty and COMINCH in Washington could see no feasible alternative to it.

In December 1943, when the convoy crisis was over, the whole extent of the "crisis of crises" became clear in retrospect. If no one had at the time openly admitted it, the possibility of defeat had seemed for many in March 1943 to be imminent.

However, there were also signs of hope. The Atlantic Convoy Conference did not succeed in appointing an Allied "Super Commander-in-Chief Atlantic" to deal with the centrally directed German U-boat arm, as a number of people had demanded. But it was possible to eliminate the many command and control overlaps that existed in the North Atlantic. The CHOP (Change of Operational Control) line which had until then lain between 35° and 25° W was advanced to 47° W with effect from April 1. A newly formed Canadian North West Atlantic Command took over the control and defense of convoys between the USA and this line, while movements east of it continued to be controlled by CINCWA. The American escort groups were withdrawn from the North Atlantic and the newly formed Tenth Fleet, directly under Admiral King, which was to provide a unified command for all A/S measures in the American area, assumed responsibility for the routes between America and Gibraltar/Morocco and from the Caribbean to Britain. It was also possible to decide on new, coordinated convoy cycles and to make arrangements about the allocation of long-range aircraft and escort carriers as well as about the vitally important development of a D/F network.

CINCWA, Admiral Sir Max Horton, was very anxious to secure his two most important requirements. First, the "air gap" in the North Atlantic had to be closed by the allocation of escort carriers and, second, the Ocean Escort Groups had to be complemented by the long-sought Support Groups which would be independent of the convoys. He pressed the Admiralty to make the escort carriers delivered from American yards in 1942, then being fitted out to British standards, available as soon as possible. Each of these carriers also needed a screen of two to three destroyers with a great radius of action. But these vessels could not be provided from the already strained resources of the Western Approaches Command. Even if he insisted that the time spent by his ships in the yards was reduced, their number was just not sufficient. The other commands felt that, in view of their own commitment, they could not hand over their destroyers, the most prized units in the whole Fleet. Nor could the ships come from the Mediterranean because of the imminent invasion of Sicily. Only when it was decided to stop the Murmansk convoys during the summer of 1943 was the Home Fleet able to make available 12–15 destroyers, from which Adm. Horton formed the 3rd, 4th and 5th Support Groups. These Support Groups were to be provided with the first British escort carriers, *Biter*, *Dasher* and *Archer*, after their completion. In addition, Horton was able to arrange for a number of Liberator bombers intended for Bomber Command and the US Army Air Force to be reequipped for anti-submarine purposes.

All these measures, together with the improved command organization, the extension of the D/F network round the North Atlantic and, above all, the equipping of more escorts with HF/DF, the new 9cm radar and improved A/S weapons, were to herald a turning point in the following weeks. By the middle of May 1943 they brought about an unexpectedly rapid tilt in the scales of battle in the Allies' favor. On May 24 Dönitz had to withdraw his U-boats from the North Atlantic. The Battle of the Atlantic had been decided.

## CHAPTER 13

Tactical and Technical Analysis
of the Operations on Both Sides

In what follows we shall try to make a somewhat different analysis of the causes of success and failure in the tactical and technical field. It will be based on the reports of the Escort Commanders and the A/S tactical reports of the commanders of the escort ships on the one hand and the war diaries and torpedo firing reports of the U-boat commanders on the other. In order to take into account the different situations of the two convoys and the changing effects of the weather, the analysis treats the individual convoys and the phases of the attack during each night and day separately and it is only summarized at the end.

HX.229'S FIRST NIGHT
Throughout the day from early morning there had been contact with the convoy. As a result of the convoy's change of course, ordered earlier, the 11 boats deployed found themselves in a tactically favorable position to begin with. Despite regular radio contact signals, HF/DF played little role. Only 19 signals in "series 8," the frequency used by the U-boats, were intercepted. The only escort equipped with HF/DF—*Volunteer*—was unexpectedly seconded as a leader of an unfamiliar group. There were personnel difficulties in the operation of the equipment. As far as is known, the first bearings were only obtained after five hours. After that, two U-boats were driven off in the early afternoon. Later HF/DF does not seem to have been used as a countermeasure, although the U-boats sent numerous radio signals and messages in the afternoon and, particularly, after the attacks began in the night. Possibly the inadequate number of escorts available—five—played a part. This may have prompted the SOE not to detail more than one ship to follow up HF/DF bearings.

Although all escorts were equipped with the 271 M radar, it was a great disappointment. Despite the fact that all the U-boats made their attacks on the surface and sometimes passed one or two escorts at ranges from 3,000 to 1,200 meters few detections were made and even fewer attacks. It was only toward morning that a surfaced U-boat, which was trying to get ahead, was located by the *Beverley* with radar at a range of just 2,750 meters. After submerging and being located by asdic, it was attacked with seven depth charges. The failure of the radar equipment was partly due to the fact that with visibility between 5 and 9 miles the U-boats could clearly recognize the escorts before they themselves could be located by radar in a state 3–4 sea.

Visual observation from the conning tower of a surfaced U-boat proved, in the prevailing weather conditions, to be superior to radar location and the visual observation from the higher lookouts of the escorts and merchant ships. Only in one case did the corvette *Anemone* recognize visually a U-boat coming up from the stern at a range of 2,700 meters. The boat then dived and, after being located by asdic, was attacked in five approaches with 35 depth charges and a hedgehog salvo. Both pursuers who located U-boats had weapon failures. In *Beverley*'s case the depth charges jammed because of sea damage and in *Anemone*'s case 20 of the 24 hedgehog bombs failed to detonate. All attacking U-boats were undetected before and after the firing. However, a factor here was that because escorts were detailed for rescue operations there was sometimes only one escort, in a tactically unfavorable position (e.g., with the U-boat astern), on the side which was attacked.

Five U-boats in six approaches fired a total of 16 FAT and eight G 7e torpedoes against 18 targets in the convoy. Ten of them hit eight different ships. It is not really possible to make a distinction between the FAT and G 7e hits because several U-boats fired torpedoes of both kinds in one approach. In addition, two U-boats fired seven G 7e torpedoes in two salvoes against two destroyers but they missed.

SC.122'S FIRST NIGHT

The convoy was not found by day. Twenty-five bearings of U-boat signals in "series 8" in the vicinity of the following convoy, HX.229, were picked up by the two ships equipped with HF/DF: in consequence, U-boat attacks on SC.122 had to be anticipated.

During the night, the convoy happened to be found by *U 338* which was operating against HX.229. With the very good visibility of 12 miles and the screening position A not being occupied, the U-boat was able to infiltrate into the convoy from the front through the 10,000 to 11,000 meter gap between the corvettes *Lavender* and *Pimpernel*; nor were these ships able to find the U-boat with their 271 M radar in a state 2 sea.

U 338 sent its first contact signals immediately before firing. It was located with HF/DF by the leader and the rescue ship, but it was too late to take countermeasures. After attacking, the boat was sighted by the forward ships of the convoy and fired on, but it had already delivered its torpedoes and was submerging. After it had fired, the searching escorts were unable to locate the boat with asdic.

U 338 fired two G 7e salvoes of two and one stern G 7e at three ships ranges of 1,560 and 860 meters respectively. According to its observations, the two salvo torpedoes seemed to hit their ships and the stern torpedo missed. In fact, a torpedo of the first salvo hit a third ship. The stern torpedo missed its intended target but hit another ship after 6,000 meters. All four ships sank, the last, possibly, after being finished off by another U-boat.

THE SINKING OF THE DAMAGED SHIPS
The impact of the torpedoes was not entirely satisfactory. Only two ships had sunk at once with HX.229 and another two with SC.122. Two of them had received one hit each and two of them two hits. In the one case two and in the other one ship sank after the first hits within several hours but five of the total of 12 ships hit remained afloat at first, one with two hits.

These five ships were sunk the next day in underwater attacks by the U-boats following the convoy—four of them as a result of five hits by *U 91*. Five more firings from three U-boats against three targets cannot be entirely clarified. Possibly one attack was aimed at the wreck of the *Fort Cedar Lake* from SC.122. In addition, a U-boat missed a corvette with a single G 7e to the stern of the convoy.

THE DAYLIGHT ATTACKS ON HX.229 ON MARCH 17
On the second day some 20 U-boats came into the vicinity of the convoys: six of them reported contact with HX.229 and six with SC.122.

In the case of HX.229 74 contact and other signals sent by U-boats could not be used for HF/DF bearings because the *Volunteer* had to use her radio personnel for other duties. In the good visibility of eight miles the surfaced U-boats could be sighted visually as they came within range at distances of 11,000–14,000 meters before they could be located by radar in the state 3–4 sea. In this way four boats were forced by the escorts to submerge; three of them were attacked with 45 depth charges and one hedgehog salvo in six approaches. Two U-boats made underwater attacks: of their 6–8 torpedoes fired in two salvoes against four targets, there were three hits on two ships, both of which sank. The attacking U-boats were not found by the escorts with asdic either before or after the attack.

In the evening all six boats were sighted as they advanced on the starboard side by the only covering aircraft on the scene and were forced underwater. One of them was attacked with four, another with two depth charges and two with gunfire.

THE DAYLIGHT ATTACKS ON SC.122 ON MARCH 17

In the case of SC.122 one escort used its HF/DF. Seventy-two bearings in "series 8" were taken. The rescue ship with HF/DF was to the stern of the convoy. The three fast escorts were repeatedly deployed against some of the bearings, but with a visibility of 14 miles the U-boats saw the approaching escorts so early that they were able to submerge before they were sighted or located by radar. Although they were not seen, their attempts to get ahead of the convoy were sometimes frustrated. Only one U-boat, again *U 338*, made an underwater attack. It was not recognized until it fired, then an escort sighted a torpedo breaking surface and the boat was attacked by two escorts with 18 depth charges in three approaches. Of the four torpedoes fired at two targets, one hit. The ship, which was hit, sank. Two aircraft repeatedly attacked in the morning and afternoon two U-boats sighted in the process of maneuvering forward. In two attacks four depth charges and in one two depth charges were dropped. In the fourth the release mechanism failed. Because of the good visibility all the U-boats with HX.229 and SC. 122 were able to submerge in time before the air attacks.

HX.229'S SECOND NIGHT

In the second night HX.229 was spared attacks. The temporary loss of contact was due to the fact that just before dusk the nearest six U-boats were forced underwater by an aircraft. The only U-boat which attempted an attack was located by the *Volunteer* when it sent its contact signals and it was forced underwater before it could fire.

SC.122'S SECOND NIGHT

Although at least five U-boats were driven off in the afternoon by the naval and air escort, contact was maintained. Two U-boats attempted surface attacks in the night. With good visibility—six miles—and increasing wind and sea—from force 2–3 to 6—the U-boats could again see further than the escorts were able to locate with their 271 M radar. *U 305* was located by the *Pimpernel* at 3,600 meters only after some time when the range was already increasing and not at all by the *Swale*, although, at times, the range must have been barely 1,000 meters. As the boat had reached its firing position at that moment, the attack could not be frustrated. In the second case, *U 338* wanted to send a contact signal again shortly before firing, but was this time located by the *Havelock* herself at position A and was forced underwater by an immediate sortie before it could fire. In the first case, asdic locations could not be obtained; in the second, they were impossible because of defective equipment.

Of the intended two salvoes of two G 7es, one torpedo operated defectively in the tube, the three others hit two ships, one of which sank and the second of which remained afloat after two hits. She was then finished off with a torpedo. A second torpedo to finish her off from the other U-boat came too late. The first boat was sighted by a corvette in its approach but no asdic contact was obtained.

HX.229'S THIRD DAY
The convoy had only four escorts by day. The only HF/DF ship had to use her radio personnel for other purposes. The result was that the contact signals sent off in the morning were undetected. Thirty-two to thirty-three signals in "series 8" were intercepted from both convoys. In the storm, albeit abating, and the sea of state 5–6, radar locations could not be obtained. But the U-boats were also greatly impeded by visibility of two miles which only slowly improved. Consequently, only one U-boat made an underwater attack. One fired four torpedoes at two targets at excessive range and they missed. The second with a stern firing and a mixed salvo of four FATs and G 7es obtained three hits on two ships, both of which sank.

Both U-boats were undetected before the attack. The second was recognized by ships in the convoy from its periscope. Then it was located on asdic by a corvette and attacked with six depth charges.

In the prevailing weather the air escort was unable to find the convoy. Two U-boats were sighted to astern of it by two aircraft and one was located by radar. One of the boats sighted was attacked with six depth charges.

SC.122'S THIRD DAY
After temporary loss of contact the U-boats again came into the vicinity of the convoy after midday. In the meantime the weather had become calmer and the convoy entered an area of clearer visibility. The three aircraft, which arrived in the afternoon, in part guided by HF/DF bearings from the *Havelock*, sighted six U-boats and four of them were attacked with a total of 13 depth charges as they submerged.

There were no U-boat attacks.

HX.229'S THIRD NIGHT
Because the convoy gave a false position of some 30–40 miles, the *Highlander*, which was closing up, did not reach the convoy before dusk and assume tactical command. It was not possible to make use of her very successful HF/DF team which had picked up many bearings in the afternoon. However, the escort was increased to five ships.

The radar range was limited by the state 3–4 sea. It only exceeded the visual range of the escorts operating against the U-boats in rain squalls when the normal seven mile visibility was temporarily reduced to 500 meters. In the night at least eight U-boats came into the vicinity on the convoy; three reached or came close to their firing positions. Of these two were recognized visually at about 3,600 meters before they could fire. The first was attacked by two escorts in five approaches with 29 depth charges and two hedgehog salvoes; 18 and 20 respectively of these hedgehog charges failed. The second boat fired 3–4 torpedoes at the approaching destroyer which had also picked up the boat with radar at 3,500 meters. The torpedoes missed; one possibly exploded in the wake. The destroyer attacked the submerged U-boat in four approaches with 38 depth charges and a hedgehog salvo, but 22 of the hedgehog charges failed.

A third boat came up to attack undetected. It fired five torpedoes which, however, missed (faulty settings), then it dived and was later located by a corvette with asdic and attacked with six depth charges.

Three other U-boats, including probably one of those visually located, were found by radar at 1,200–2,000 meters, when visibility was sharply reduced by rain squalls. All the boats were able to submerge. Two of them were engaged, one in two approaches with eight depth charges (there was a shortage of depth charges) and one in 11 approaches with 53 depth charges. The latter received damage in the fuel tanks.

SC.122'S THIRD NIGHT

This convoy now had eight escorts; two of these and the rescue ship were fitted with HF/DF. They heard 44 U-boat signals in "series 8." Four boats came into the vicinity of the convoy in the night. In three cases their contact signals were picked up by the leader *Havelock* with HF/DF; two of them were able to submerge in time as the escorts approached before they were found by radar or the human eye. One was located by a corvette with radar at a range of 3,000 meters and then attacked by two corvettes in three approaches with 20 depth charges. *U 666* came twice in the night undetected to a firing position and fired nine torpedoes in all. The first approach failed because of faulty settings, but was quite undetected. In the second, one torpedo hit. The boat was located with radar at a range of 3,650 meters by an escort immediately after it fired. It submerged close to the convoy and was attacked with 14 depth charges in one approach.

THE FOURTH DAY WITH BOTH CONVOYS

On the fourth day the naval escort of both convoys was increased to eight ships each by the evening. But no U-boat came close enough to be in contact with the escort.

Of the 16 aircraft deployed, one with HX.229 and four with SC.122 sighted seven U-boats in all. Of these, four U-boats were sighted visually by the aircraft, three were also sighted visually after the aircraft had followed HF/DF bearings. Four attacks were made in which a total of 12 depth charges were dropped. In a further case, the depth charges got stuck. One U-boat was damaged.

THE FIFTH DAY WITH BOTH CONVOYS

In the night contact signals were sent by U-boats only from great range after obtaining sound bearings. The escorts were not deployed on the basis of D/F bearings. Nineteen signals were intercepted by HX.229 and 23 by SC.122.

By day six U-boats were located by the air escort with SC.122. Only one was sighted visually after HF/DF bearings, the other five were sighted sometimes at a great distance from the convoy. Four attacks were made with 14 depth charges. One U-boat was destroyed.

## CHAPTER 14

Conclusion: The Convoy Battle of March 1943

RADIO CONTROL AND LOCATING THE CONVOYS

On the Allied side it was the aim of the Command Headquarters to reroute the convoys round the German U-boat formations. The most important method of recognizing these formations, after the "black out," was the shore-based automatic shortwave D/F network round the Atlantic with which practically every U-boat radio message could be picked up and located.

This technique was known to the Germans in principle but, as a result of the experiences of the first war years, its precision was greatly underestimated. The U-boat command repeatedly urged the U-boats to maintain radio silence until contact was established with the enemy. But after that stage there were hardly any limitations: the result was that the Allied D/F stations received very good indications from the signals about the strength of the groups operating against individual convoys.

The first indications about formations for convoy operations could be obtained from the approximate number of U-boats at sea, known from agents' reports from the German operational bases in France and from what was known to be the basic operational pattern. Despite the orders about radio silence, reports by U-boats of traffic sighted, of aircraft and damage sustained, often provided hints of the movement of groups which were sufficient to prompt large-scale evasive action.

The compromising of their own ciphers, which was feared so much by the U-boat command, played little part at this stage. Also, the danger the Germans saw of U-boat formations being located by radar-equipped reconnaissance aircraft was exaggerated.

On the German side radio intelligence played a primary role in finding the convoys in view of the lack of other intelligence sources. At this time the German "B" Service was frequently able to decipher the course instructions concerning the routing of the convoy, transmitted by radio, early enough for it to affect operations. Occasionally, the deciphering of the radio traffic of the convoys' air cover played a part.

217

RADIO CONTROL IN THE PERIOD OF CONTACT

In the phase between the locating of a convoy by a U-boat and the beginning of the actual attack, radio control played a decisive role. The first contact signal from the boat with the convoy gave the U-boat command a priceless opportunity to organize its U-boats to attack. At the same time, this signal was located by the Allied shore-based D/F stations and indicated that the convoy was threatened. If there were suitable naval or air units within range, support measures could be taken.

The Commander U-boats also reckoned with this possibility but he did not know that, at this time, practically every convoy had at least one, and usually several, escorts, including the rescue ship, equipped with shortwave D/F. When this equipment was operated by an experienced team and if it had succeeded in intercepting the first contact signal, a skillful escort commander could often drive off the contact-keeping U-boat, have the convoy take sharp evasive action and so deprive the enemy of contact before other boats came up. When very many HF/DF bearings were received, the Escort Commander was soon faced with the problem—particularly when his group was numerically weak—of not being able to deploy sufficient ships to follow the bearings without cutting down his close escort too drastically.

Although at this time on the Allied side almost all escort ships were equipped with 271 M radar, it became apparent in normal conditions of visibility that the U-boats could regularly see further than the escorts could locate with their radar. This was especially the case when, with a moderate sea, there were strong wave echoes which caused the radar range in locating U-boats to fall rapidly. This meant that the U-boat could usually proceed past the convoy at the limit of visibility vis-a-vis the escorts, without being located. When they sent their contact signals, were located by D/F and then approached by an escort ordered to follow the bearing, the Germans were frequently under the impression that they had been detected by radar. But, in fact, the boats were often able to submerge before they were located by the radar equipment.

Air escort with the convoy, for which frequently one aircraft sufficed, could make it extraordinarily difficult for the U-boats to advance and, often, impossible. Best use could be made of aircraft when signal communication between the Escort Commander and the aircraft was good and the aircraft could be deployed against U-boats located by D/F, particularly before dusk. Although most aircraft were fitted with ASV III radar, in normal weather conditions visual sighting was clearly more important than radar in locating the U-boat.

THE U-BOAT ATTACKS

At this time the surface attack by night was in the forefront of German tactics. The U-boat tried, where possible, by exploiting weather and light conditions such as moonlight, to outmaneuver the escorts and to get into a favorable firing position ahead of the convoy, whether to port or starboard. In normal visibility and in the often somewhat stormy sea the U-boat could generally see the escorts and steamers which stood higher out of the water at a greater distance than the escorts could see the U-boats which lay low in the water against the dark background of the sea. The range of the 271 M radar usually exceeded that of the human eye only in poor visibility conditions—particularly in fog and smooth seas; then it could be decisive, as it was in the case of ONS.5.

Underwater daylight attacks were resorted to less frequently. If the U-boats had been successful in getting forward and were able to submerge in front of the convoy, there was a good chance of reaching a firing position. The small number of escorts and the limited range of asdic made it impossible to establish a continuous underwater location line in front of the convoy.

At this time the U-boats usually attacked on the surface and under water at ranges between 1,500 and 3,000 meters and fired their torpedoes as quickly as possible in salvoes from the sides of the convoys. An attack inside the convoys, such as had been practiced in particular by Kptlt Kretschmer in 1940 and as some of his followers (e.g., Kptlt S. Freiherr von Forstner, *U 402*) later attempted, seldom occurred.

THE ENGAGEMENT OF THE U-BOATS

When the escorts tried to find the U-boats the locating of contact signals with HF/DF played the major role. On the one hand, it provided the greatest range; on the other, the least precision in fixing the position of the boats. There was generally an even balance between those U-boats located visually and those by radar. Optical vision provided greater range than radar in good visibility and radar was better in poor visibility. On the other hand, U-boats were seldom first picked up by asdic. Asdic, however, played a big part in the engagement of U-boats which had been located by other means and then had submerged. When it came to engaging the U-boats the chief means at this time was the ordinary depth charge which was dropped down stern chutes or by means of throwers. The usual carpet of depth charges was supplemented by some heavy Mark X torpedo depth charges which had a devastating effect, particularly at great depths. In addition, most of the escorts were already equipped with the hedgehog thrower: but this was clearly still suffering from teething troubles.

THE RESULTS OF THE HX.229 AND SC.122 OPERATIONS

In the case of the two convoys there were, in all, 75 engagements between the ships of the convoy, the escorts and aircraft (not counting damaged ships and stragglers which were proceeding independently) on the one hand and U-boats on the other. Thirty-two of these were attributed to the air escort. Twenty-four U-boats were sighted by aircraft and 13 of them were attacked with depth charges. Seven more U-boats were sighted by aircraft deployed on HF/DF bearings and only one U-boat was located with radar. In 19 depth charge attacks, 65 charges were dropped. One U-boat was sunk and another damaged. Twenty-two U-boats were located by the escorts as they came up or before an attack; 11 boats were located by HF/DF, but ten of them were able to submerge before there was radar or visual contact. Only one of them was found by radar; it submerged and was then engaged with depth charges. Five U-boats were located by radar; they submerged and were then engaged with depth charges. Six U-boats were located visually and one of them subsequently by radar. All six were engaged with depth charges.

The U-boats attempted 20 attacks (not counting torpedo attacks on wrecks); nine surface and three underwater attacks were completely unde-tected. Two underwater attacks were observed after the torpedoes were fired and then there was an engagement with the help of asdic. Three U-boats sent signals, shortly before the attacks, which were located with HF/DF. In one case, the boat still attacked. Two attacking boats were located by radar, but one of them still succeeded in firing. One boat was located by asdic after the attack, another was seen by the convoy when making a surface attack. All observed boats submerged when the enemy attacked.

In all, in 19 cases U-boats were attacked by the escorts when located in coming up or attacking. In 37 approaches 276 depth charges were dropped and five hedgehog salvoes fired; but only 40 out of 120 projectiles were properly launched. Apart from slight damage on various U-boats, no suc-cesses were obtained with these attacks.

The U-boats made a total of 16 attacks on the two convoys in which once two, once three, eight times four and six times five torpedoes were fired. They were divided among eight salvoes of four, comprising 32 torpedoes, when 13 hits were obtained, three salvoes of three comprising 9 torpedoes when three hits were obtained, nine salvoes of two comprising 18 torpedoes when nine hits were obtained; and eight single firings when one hit was obtained. In all, therefore, there were 28 separate approaches with 67 tor-pedoes and 26 hits (i.e., 38.8%).

In addition, five attacks with two single firings, two salvoes of three and one salvo of four were made on the escorts, all of which missed.

There were six single firings, three salvoes of two and two salvoes of three directed at damaged ships in which a total of nine hits was obtained. They sunk 21 ships (140,842 tons) and possibly *Clarissa Radcliffe* of 5,754 tons.

THE ROLE OF HF/DF

If we analyze the great convoy battles between June 1942 and May 1943—including both those operations which the Germans regarded as successful and those which ended as either minor successes or failures—the remarkable fact is that the outcome of the operation always depended decisively on the efficient use of HF/DF.

Even the analysis of operations which brought great losses to the Allies, e.g., against convoys SC.118 and ON.166 in February and against SC.121, HX.229 and SC.122 in March, reveals, when the details are investigated, that a not inconsiderable number of U-boats could be driven off as the result of HF/DF bearings; and that very heavy losses occurred particularly when this equipment could not be properly used, as in the first stages of the operation against HX.229. Consequently, at night, only a few boats successively approached the convoys to attack and not, as in 1940, half or even the majority of the boats involved.

The actual successes achieved in the first months of 1943 were exaggerated by the Germans because the U-boats put the number of ships hit too high, the result of frequently mistaken interpretations of what was observed, rather than deliberately false reports. This meant that the German Command did not fully recognize the constantly worsening ratio between the number of boats deployed and those actually achieving success. It was, of course, apparent that it was becoming ever more difficult for the U-boats to attack a convoy and achieve success. The war diary of the Commander U-boats reflects the concern with which the Germans observed the increasingly effective Allied defense and the great efforts they made to trace the reasons for it. Almost all conceivable possibilities were investigated. The question was repeatedly asked whether treason possibly played a part or whether the enemy had succeeded in breaking the ciphers. These questions were, however, always answered in the negative. The conclusion was invariably reached that the enemy must have at his disposal an effective, and not yet easily identifiable, weapon with which he could locate the U-boats from ships and, especially, aircraft. The most likely hypothesis, was, of course, the existence of radar, which was also known to the Germans. It was appreciated that the Germans' own search receiver, with which they tried to determine the enemy radar contact, emitted a detectable signal. But they mistakenly assumed that the enemy could operate on such emissions.

Then, when a British bomber was shot down in Rotterdam, a new radar equipment, which worked on a 9cm wavelength, was found. In the summer of 1943 it seemed obvious that this equipment was the main reason behind the Germans' devastating reverses. In addition, the question was also looked into whether the enemy was working on an infrared location device.

It is remarkable that during these months, and for a long time afterward, it did not occur to the Germans that the enemy, particularly in convoy operations, might be taking bearings on the very heavy shortwave radio traffic, not only from his shore-based stations but also from the escorts themselves and using them for direct tactical deployment. Evidence to this effect was always rejected because there was a more obvious technical explanation, radar. The warning given to Grand Admiral Raedar by the French Admiral Darlan on January 28, 1942, about the German U-boats' excessive use of radio, was associated with the dangers of shore-based stations taking bearings: this was regarded as less dangerous than had been expected. Reports from contact-keeping U-boats which were approached by enemy escorts making straight for them shortly after they sent their signals and which suggested the use of radio D/F, were not investigated because they could be equally, or better, explained by the British use of radar. In this connection it should be remembered that Oblt Otto Ites, the Commander of *U 94* who was the first to be heavily attacked with depth charges after a HF/DF bearing, had voiced this suspicion in June 1942.

In the comprehensive analyses and appreciations of the situation drawn up by the Commander U-boats in May 1943, after the U-boat campaign had been broken off in the North Atlantic, there is no word about the possibility of radio bearings being used. Attention was completely absorbed by radar. This appeared to be the device with which the constantly increasing naval and air forces were being deployed in the war against the U-boats.

It was possible to mistake the causes despite the fact that, at the latest, ever since the spring of 1943, the Germans had clear proof of the presence of shortwave D/F equipment on the escorts. In April the German "B" Service had deciphered a radio message of April 9 according to which the American Coast Guard cutter, *Spencer*, as leader of Task Unit 24.1.9, escorting convoy ON.175, was equipped with a High Frequency Direction Finder. Nor was this the only report. Another report on April 24 said that among the escorts for convoy HX.235 the destroyer *Churchill* and another unit were equipped with HF/DF. Three days later it was ascertained that the leader of Escort Group 24.1.15 was also equipped with HF/DF.

In the weekly reports of the "B" Service, where these details were to be found, no particular reference was made to their importance nor is there any apparent reaction to these hints in the war diaries of those departments mentioned on the distribution lists of the "B" reports. The directors and officers of these departments when questioned after the war could not remember any such hints at the time in spite of their often provenly clear recollections.

In addition, hints coming from another source were incorrectly interpreted. German agents, who were able to photograph Allied warships and merchantmen in the roads of Gibraltar from a house near Algeciras, succeeded in July and September 1943 in photographing British destroyers on which the Adcock aerials of the HF/DF could be clearly recognized on a tall after-mast. In a memorandum by the relevant department of the Naval High Command on July 24, 1943, these aerials were considered with some other "special aerials on enemy ships." The following observation occurs: "This equipment consists of a series of upright metal rods which are positioned like the edges of a six-sided prism. These are subdivided three or more times by cross-rods, 1 to 1.5 metres high with sides 60 cms to 1 m long. It is assumed that this is the aerial of the radio-locating device which the British call *Radar* and which probably serves to identify U-boats. It is a device about which we still have no precise information."

It must be remembered that the term "radar" had only just been introduced in Britain at this time and was beginning to replace the abbreviation used until then for such equipment, RDF. Clearly no one had concerned himself further with these photographs. Subsequently they were used chiefly for information about types of ships and, in this way, they survived the war as part of the estate left by the German expert on ship classification, Erich Gröner.

Had the existence of HF/DF on ships been recognized from the deciphered radio messages and photographs of the summer of 1943, the German U-boat Command would have surely taken immediate countermeasures. Certainly, it would not have been possible to forgo radio traffic altogether. But, doubtless, the number of radio signals and messages which the U-boats with the convoys transmitted without inhibition, "because their presence was already known to the enemy," would have been greatly reduced, had it been known that their transmission betrayed not merely their presence but also, with considerable accuracy, the position in relation to the convoy.

The knowledge of this enemy technique would also have provided the Germans with tactical possibilities. Had the control techniques been further developed, it would have been possible by specially detailing U-boats for radio work and possibly using radio buoys, to draw some of the escorts away from the convoy and so facilitate the attack for the remaining boats.

An analysis of the convoy operations from SC.107 in November 1942 to SC.122 in March 1943 shows how soon after the attacks began the normal discipline of a not very strong escort group was upset, with the result that even intercepted bearings could hardly be used for deployment purposes. When in September 1943 there was a weapon available for use against the destroyers—the acoustic homing *Zaunkönig* torpedo—the knowledge of Allied HF/DF procedure might have been deliberately exploited to get an enemy destroyer to approach a submarine head-on, i.e., the best firing position. In fact, the first hit obtained with this torpedo on September 20 was made from this position, although it was neither intended nor observed as such.

APPENDIX 1

The Merchant Ships of the Convoys

Pos.	Nat.	Type	Name	Built	Tonnage	Knots	Fate
A.1	**Convoy SC.122 from New York**						
11	pan	MT	*Permian*	31	8890	8.5	arr. destin. Halifax, 8.3.
12	brit	MS	*Asbjörn*	35	4733	12.0	arr. destin. Halifax 8.3.
21	brit	SWh	*Sevilla*	00	7022	9.5	arr. destin. St. John's 12.3.
22	norw	SS	*Polarland*	23	1591	7.5	return. New York, 8.3.
23	brit	SS	*Livingston*	28	2140	8.0	return. Halifax, 9.3.
24	pan	SS	*Alcedo*	37	1392	10.0	return. Halifax, 8.3./HX.229A
31	norw	SS	*Askepot*	37	1312	9.5	arr. Loch Ewe (destin. Iceland)
32	amer	SS	*Cartago*	08	4732	13.0	arr. Loch Ewe (destin. Iceland)
33	amer	SS	*Eastern Guide*	19	3704	8.5	return. Halifax, 8.3.
34	norw	SS	*Gudvor*	28	2280	8.5	return. Halifax, 8.3.
41	pan	SS	*Granville*	30	5745	8.0	sunk by *U 338*, 17.3.
42	icel	SS	*Godafoss*	21	1542	11.0	arr. Loch Ewe (destin. Iceland)
43	brit	SS	*Carso*	23	6275	9.0	arr. destin. Loch Ewe
51	brit	SS	*Kingsbury*	37	4898	8.0	sunk by *U 338*, 17.3.
52	brit	SS	*King Gruffydd*	19	5072	8.5	sunk by *U 338*, 17.3.
53	brit	SS	*Empire Summer*	41	6949	8.0	return. Halifax, 9.3.
54	swed	SS	*Atland*	10	5203	8.0	arr. destin. Loch Ewe
61	dutch	SS	*Alderamin*	20	7886	9.5	sunk by *U 338*, 17.3.
62	brit	ST	*Empire Galahad*	42	7046	9.0	arr. destin. Mersey
63	brit	MS	*Innesmoor*	28	4392	8.5	arr. destin. Loch Ewe
64	brit	ST	*Beacon Oil*	19	6893	9.0	arr. destin. Glasgow
65	greek	SS	*Georgios P.*	03	4052	8.5	arr. destin. Clyde
71	brit	SS	*Baron Stranraer*	29	3668	8.5	arr. destin. Loch Ewe
72	brit	MT	*Christian Holm*	27	9119	9.0	arr. destin. Belfast
73	brit	SS	*Bridgepool*	24	4845	8.0	arr. destin. Loch Ewe
74	brit	SS	*Baron Elgin*	33	3942	8.5	arr. destin. Loch Ewe
75	brit	SS	*Aymeric*	19	5196	9.0	arr. destin. Loch Ewe
81	brit	MS	*Glenapp*	20	9503	10.0	arr. destin. Mersey
82	brit	MT	*Benedick*	28	6978	9.0	arr. destin. Clyde
83	brit	SS	*Clarissa Radcliffe*	15	5754	7.5	missing 7.3. Sunk by *U 663*: 18.3.?
91	brit	SS	*Vinriver*	17	3881	8.0	arr. destin. Loch Ewe
92	brit	SS	*Historian*	24	5074	7.5	arr. destin. Mersey
93	brit	SS	*Orminister*	14	5712	8.5	arr. destin. Loch Ewe
101	brit	SS	*Losada*	21	6520	8.5	arr. destin. Mersey
102	brit	ST	*Gloxinia*	20	3336	7.5	arr. destin. Mersey
103	brit	SS	*Filleigh*	28	4856	8.5	arr. destin. Mersey
104	amer	LST	*No. 365*	43	*1490*ts	10.0	arr. destin. Mersey
111	brit	SS	*Empire Dunstan*	42	2887	8.0	arr. destin. Mersey
112	brit	ST	*Shirvan*	25	6017	8.0	arr. destin. Belfast/Manchester
113	brit	SS	*Boston City*	20	2870	9.0	arr. destin. Belfast
114	amer	LST	*No. 305*	43	*1490*ts	10.0	arr. destin. Clyde
121	brit	MS	*Dolius*	24	5507	8.5	arr. destin. Belfast
122	amer	MT	*Vistula*	20	8537	9.5	arr. destin. Belfast
123	brit	SS	*English Monarch*	24	4557	8.5	return. Halifax, 9.3.
124	brit	SS	*Fort Cedar Lake*	42	7134	9.0	sunk by *U 338*, 17.3.
131	brit	SS	*Baron Semple*	39	4573	9.0	arr. destin. Loch Ewe
132	greek	SS	*Carras*	18	5234	8.5	sunk by *U 666* and *U 333*, 19.3.
133	pan	SS	*Bonita*	18	4929	8.0	arr. destin. Belfast
141	amer	SS	*McKeesport*	19	6198	9.5	return. New York 8.3.
142	dutch	MS	*Kedoe*	21	3684	9.5	arr. destin. Belfast

Pos.	Nat.	Type	Name	Built	Tonnage	Knots	Fate
A.2	**Convoy HSC.122 from Halifax**						
11	icel	SS	*Fjallfoss*	19	1451	11.0	arr. Loch Ewe (destin. Iceland)
12	icel	SS	*Selfoss*	14	775	8.0	straggler, arr. Iceland
42	brit	SS	*Ogmore Castle*	19	2481	8.0	arr. destin.
45	yugo	SS	*Franka*	18	5273	8.0	arr. destin. Loch Ewe
55	dutch	SS	*Parkhaven*	20	4803	10.0	arr. destin. Loch Ewe
65	brit	SS	*Drakepool*	24	4838	10.0	arr. destin. Loch Ewe
84	brit	SS	*Zouave*	30	4256	10.0	sunk by *U 305*, 17.3.
85	brit	SS	*P.L.M.13*	21	3754	10.0	return. St. John's
92	brit	SS	*Port Auckland*	22	8789	13.0	sunk by *U 305*, 17.3.
95	brit	SS	*Zamalek*	21	1567	13.0	arr. Londonderry (rescue ship)
104	brit	SS	*Badjestan*	28	5573	13.0	arr. destin. Clyde
114	swed	SS	*Porjus*	06	2965	9.0	arr. destin. Manchester
131	brit	SS	*Empire Morn*	41	7092	11.0	straggler, arr. destin.
133	brit	SS	*Helencrest*	41	5233	11.0	arr. destin. Belfast
A.3	**Convoy WSC.122 from St. John's**						
63	brit	MS	*Reaveley*	40	4998	9.5	arr. destin. Mersey
B.	**Convoy HX.229 from New York**						
11	brit	SS	*Cape Breton*	40	6044	10.5	arr. destin. Clyde
12	amer	SS	*Robert Howe*	42	7176	10.0	arr. destin. Mersey
13	brit	SS	*Empire Knight*	42	7244	10.5	arr. destin. Clyde
21	amer	SS	*Walter Q. Gresham*	43	7191	10.5	sunk by *U 221*, 18.3.
22	amer	SS	*William Eustis*	43	7196	10.5	sunk by *U 435* and *U 91*, 17.3.
23	amer	SS	*Stephen C. Foster*	43	7196	11.0	return. St. John's, 13.3.
31	brit	SS	*Fort Anne*	42	7131	10.0	arr. destin. Loch Ewe
32	brit	MS	*Kaipara*	38	5882	12.0	arr. destin. Mersey
33	brit	MS	*Canadian Star*	39	8293	12.5	sunk by *U 221*, 18.3.
34	amer	SS	*Mathew Luckenbach*	18	5848	11.0	straggl., sunk by *U 527*, *U 523*.
41	brit	SS	*Nebraska*	20	8261	10.5	arr. destin. Mersey
42	brit	MT	*Regent Panther*	37	9556	10.5	arr. destin. U.K.
43	brit	MS	*Antar*	41	5250	10.0	arr. destin. Mersey
51	pan	MT	*Belgian Gulf*	29	8401	10.5	arr. destin. Mersey
52	brit	MT	*San Veronica*	43	8600	12.0	arr. destin. Mersey
53	amer	ST	*Pan Rhode Island*	41	7742	11.0	arr. destin. Mersey
54	brit	MT	*Empire Cavalier*	42	9891	11.0	arr. destin. Mersey
61	norw	MS	*Abraham Lincoln*	29	5740	12.0	arr. destin. Belfast
62	amer	ST	*Gulf Disc*	38	7141	11.0	arr. destin. Clyde
63	amer	SS	*Jean*	18	4902	10.0	arr. destin. Mersey
64	amer	SS	*Kofresi*	20	4934	10.5	arr. destin. Mersey
71	brit	SS	*City of Agra*	36	6361	13.5	arr. destin. Mersey
72	brit	SWh	*Southern Princess*	15	12156	10.5	sunk by *U 600*, 17.3.
73	pan	SS	*El Mundo*	10	6008	12.0	arr. destin. Mersey
74	amer	SS	*Margaret Lykes*	19	3537	11.5	arr. destin. Mersey
81	amer	SS	*Irenée Du Pont*	41	6125	15.0	sunk by *U 600* and *U 91*, 17.3.
82	brit	SS	*Coracero*	23	7252	10.0	sunk by *U 384/U 631*
83	brit	MT	*Nicania*	42	8179	11.0	arr. destin. Mersey
84	brit	SS	*Tekoa*	22	8695	13.0	arr. destin. Greenock/Mersey
91	brit	SS	*Clan Matheson*	19	5613	10.0	return. Halifax 12.3.
92	brit	SS	*Nariva*	20	8714	10.5	arr. destin. Mersey
93	dutch	MT	*Magdala*	31	8248	10.0	arr. destin. Belfast
94	amer	SS	*James Oglethorpe*	42	7176	10.0	sunk by *U 758* and *U 91*, 17.3.
101	norw	MS	*Elin K.*	37	5214	11.0	sunk by *U 603*, 16.3.

Pos.	Nat.	Type	Name	Built	Tonnage	Knots	Fate
102	brit	MT	*Luculus*	29	6546	10.0	arr. destin. Belfast
103	dutch	SS	*Zaanland*	21	6813	11.5	sunk by *U 758*, 17.3.
104	dutch	SS	*Terkoelei*	23	5158	10.0	sunk by *U 384/631*, 17.3.
111	amer	SS	*Harry Luckenbach*	19	6355	10.0	sunk by *U 91*, 17.3.
112	amer	SS	*Daniel Webster*	42	7176	10.5	arr. destin. Belfast
113	amer	SS	*Hugh Williamson*	42	7176	10.0	straggler, arr. destin. Belfast

C.1   Convoy HX.229A from New York

Pos.	Nat.	Type	Name	Built	Tonnage	Knots	Fate
11	brit	SS	*Fort Amherst*	36	3489	13.0	arr. destin. Halifax
12	amer	ST	*Esso Baltimore*	38	7949	12.0	arr. destin. Halifax
13	dutch	MT	*Regina*	37	9545	12.0	arr. destin. Loch Ewe
...	amer	SS	*Shickshinny*	19	5103	.	return, Halifax
21	brit	SS	*Fort Drew*	43	7134	11.0	arr. destin. Loch Ewe
22	brit	SS	*Iris*	40	1479	12.0	arr. destin. Halifax
23	pan	MT	*Esso Belgium*	37	10568	12.0	arr. destin. Halifax
...	amer	SS	*Pierre Soule*	43	7191	11.0	return. Halifax
32	amer	SS	*Fairfax*	26	5649	13.0	arr. destin. St. John's
33	amer	SS	*Michigan*	19	5594	10.0	return. St. John's
41	amer	ST	*Pan Florida*	36	7237	12.0	arr. destin. Loch Ewe
42	brit	MT	*Daphnella*	38	8078	12.0	arr. destin. Belfast
43	pan	SS	*North King*	03	4934	13.0	return. St. John's
44	brit	SS	*Tortuguero*	21	5285	13.0	arr. destin. Belfast
51	brit	SS	*Esperance Bay*	22	14204	16.0	arr. destin. Liverpool
52	pan	MT	*Orville Harden*	33	11191	12.0	arr. destin. Clyde
53	brit	SS	*Empire Airman*	42	9813	11.0	arr. destin. Mersey
54	amer	SS	*Lone Star*	19	5101	10.0	damage by ice, detach.
61	amer	ST	*Pan Maine*	36	7232	12.0	arr. destin. Mersey
62	amer	ST	*Esso Baytown*	37	7991	13.0	arr. destin. Belfast
63	brit	MT	*Clausina*	38	8083	12.0	arr. destin. Belfast
64	brit	SS	*Port Melbourne*	14	9142	13.0	arr. destin. Clyde
71	amer	ST	*Socony Vacuum*	35	9511	13.0	arr. destin. Manchester
72	brit	SS	*Empire Nugget*	42	9807	11.0	arr. destin. Belfast
81	brit	SWh	*Svend Foyn*	31	14795	12.0	sunk by ice damage 19.3.
82/3	amer	SS	*Henry S. Grove*	21	6220	11.0	arr. destin. Mersey
91	amer	SS	*John Fiske*	42	7176	11.0	arr. destin. Manchester
92/3	brit	SS	*Tactician*	28	5996	13.0	arr. destin. Clyde

C.2   Convoy HHX.229A from Halifax

Pos.	Nat.	Type	Name	Built	Tonnage	Knots	Fate
11	brit	MS	*Belgian Airman*	42	6959	11.0	damage by ice, detach.
12	dutch	SS	*Ganymedes*	17	2682	11.0	arr. destin. Loch Ewe
14	pan	SS	*Alcedo* (ex. SC.122!)	37	1392	10.0	arr. destin. Reykjavik
22	brit	SS	*Lady Rodney*	29	8194	14.0	arr. destin. St. John's
22	brit	MS	*Taybank*	30	5627	14.0	arr. destin. Mersey
23	brit	SS	*Bothnia*	28	2407	10.0	arr. destin. Loch Ewe
24	brit	SS	*Manchester Trader*	41	5671	11.0	arr. destin. Manchester
31	brit	SS	*Akaroa*	14	15130	15.0	arr. destin. Belfast
32	brit	SS	*Tudor Star*	19	7199	12.0	arr. destin. Manchester
34	brit	SS	*Fresno Star*	19	7998	13.0	arr. destin. Belfast
73	pan	MS	*Rosemont*	38	5002	16.0	arr. destin. Mersey
74	brit	SS	*Arabian Prince*	36	1960	12.0	arr. destin. Mersey
82	brit	SS	*City of Oran*	15	7323	12.0	arr. destin. Clyde
84	brit	MS	*Lossiebank*	30	5627	14.0	arr. destin. Mersey
92	brit	MS	*Tahsinia*	42	7267	11.0	arr. destin. Mersey
94	brit	SS	*Norwegian*	21	6366	11.0	arr. destin. Clyde

Merchant ships of convoys SC.122, HX.229 and HX.229A, lost and damaged later in the war.

1	20. 4.43	*Michigan* (HX.229A/33) sunk by *U 565* at 35°59′ N/01°25′ W
2	26. 4.43	*Empire Morn* (SC.122/131) damaged by mine from *U 117* at 33°52′ N/07°50′ W
3	29. 4.43	*McKeesport* (SC.122/141) sunk by *U 258* in convoy ONS.5 at 60°52′ N/ 34°20′ W
4	5. 5.43	*Dolius* (SC.122/121) sunk by *U 584* in convoy ONS.5 at 54°00′ N/43°55′ W
5	7. 5.43	*Aymeric* (SC.122/75) sunk by *U 657* in convoy ONS.7 at 59°42′ N/41°39′ W
6	18. 5.43	*Fort Anne* (HX.229/31) damaged by *U 414* in convoy at 36°35′ N/01°01′ E
7	16. 7.43	*Kaipara* (HX.229/32) damaged by *U 306* at 13°30′ N/17°43′ W
8	2. 8.43	*City of Oran* (HX.229A/82) sunk by *U 196* in convoy CB.21 at 13°45′ S/ 41°16′ E [1]
9	6. 9.43	*Fort Drew* (HX.229A/21) sunk by mine at 35°52′ N/14°47′ E
10	1.10.43	*Tahsinia* (HX.229A/92) sunk by *U 532* at 06°51′ N/73°48′ E
11	2.11.43	*Baron Semple* (SC.122/131) sunk by *U 848* at 05°S/21°W
12	18.11.43	*Empire Dunstan* (SC.122/111) sunk by *U 81* at 39 24′ N/17°40′ E
13	5.12.43	*Clan Matheson* (HX.229/91) damaged by Japanese bombs at Calcutta
14	10. 1.44	*Daniel Webster* (HX.229/112) sunk by air torpedo at 36°07′ N/00°11 W
15	8. 4.44	*Nebraska* (HX.229/41) sunk by *U 843* at 11°55′ S/19°52′ W
16	25. 8.44	*Orminister* (SC.122/93) sunk by *U 480* at 50°09′ N/00°44′ W
17	3. 9.44	*Livingston* (SC.122/23) sunk by *U 541* in convoy ONS.251 at 46°15′ N/ 58°05′ W
18	10.11.44	*Godafoss* (SC.122/42) sunk by *U 300* in convoy UR.142 at 64°08′ N/22°45′ W
19	10.11.44	*Shirvan* (SC.122/112) sunk by *U 300* in convoy UR.142 at 64°08′ N/22°45′ W
20	4. 1.45	*Polarland* (SC.122/22) sunk by *U 1232* at 44°30′ N/63°00′ W
21	28. 2.45	*Alcedo* (HX.229A/14) sunk by *U 1022* in convoy UR.155 at 64°07′ N/ 23°17′ W
22	14. 4.45	*Belgian Airman* (HX.229A/11) sunk by *U 879* at 36°05′ N/74°05′ W
23	18. 4.45	*Filleigh* (SC.122/103) sunk by *U 245* in convoy TAM.142 at 51°20′ N/ 01°42′ W

APPENDIX 2

Escort Vessels of Convoys SC.122 and HX.229

Nat.	Name	pend. No.	group	commiss.	C/O	fate	
Destroyers							
HMS	Havelock	H.88	B.5	10. 2.40	Cdr. R. C. Boyle, RN.	31.10.46	scrapped
HMS	Highlander	H.44	B.4	18. 3.40	Cdr. E. C. L. Day, RN.	27. 5.46	scrapped
HMS	Vimy	I.33	B.4	9. 3.18	Lt. Cdr. R. B. Stannard, RNR.	. 2.48	scrapped
HMS	Volunteer	I.71	B.4	7.11.19	Lt. Cdr. G. J. Luther, RN	. 4.48	scrapped
HMS	Witherington	I.76	Supp.	10.10.19	Lt. Cdr. M. H. R. Crichton, RN.	20. 3.47	scrapped
HMS	Mansfield (ex USS Evans)	G.76	Supp.	11.11.18	Lt. Cdr. L. C. Hill, RN.	21.10.44	scrapped
HMS	Leamington (ex USS Twiggs)	G.19	Supp.	28. 7.19 / 23.10.40	Lt. A. D. B. Campbell, RN	16. 7.44	UdSSR: Žgucij
USS	Babbitt	DD.128	Supp.	24.10.19	Cdr. S. F. Quarles, USN.	25. 2.46	scrapped
USS	Upshur	DD.144	Supp.	23.12.18	Cdr. G. McCabe, USN.	16.11.45	scrapped
HMS	Beverley (ex USS Branch)	H.64	B.4	26. 7.20 / 8.10.40	Lt. Cdr. Rodney Price, RN.	11. 4.43	sunk by U 188
Coast Guard Cutter							
USCGC	Ingham	WPG.35	Supp.	. 36	Capt. A. M. Martinson, USCG.	now USCG-Cutter	
Frigate							
HMS	Swale	K.217	B.5	24. 6.42	Lt. Cdr. J. Jackson, RN.	26. 2.55	scrapped
Corvettes							
HMS	Anemone	K.48	B.4	12.10.40	Lt. Cdr. P. G. A. King, RNR.	.50	mercantile
HMS	Pimpernel	K.71	B.5	9. 1.41	Lt. H. D. Hayes, RNR.	.10.48	scrapped
HMS	Abelia	K.184	B.4	3. 2.41	Lt. Cdr. F. Adern, RNR.	.48	scrapped
HMS	Lavender	K.60	B.5	16. 5.41	Lt. L. G. Pilcher, RN.	.48	mercantile
HMCS	Sherbrooke	K.152	B.4	15. 6.41	Lt. J. A. M. Levesque, RCNR.	5.47	scrapped
HMS	Saxifrage	K.04	B.5	6. 2.42	Lt. M. L. Knight, RNR.	.47	RNorw.N.
HMS	Godetia	K.226	B.5	23. 2.42	Lt. M. A. F. Larose, RNR.	.47	scrapped
HMS	Pennywort	K.111	B.4	5. 3.42	Lt. O. G. Stuart, RCNVR.	2.49	scrapped
HMS	Buttercup	K.193	B.5	24. 4.42	Lt. Cdr. J. C. Dawson, RNR.	.45	RNorw.N.

Technical data:

Highlander, Havelock (built for Brazil as *Jaguaribe* and *Jutahy*, acquired 1939)
Displacement: 1,340 tons
Dimensions: 323 (oa) x 33 x 8½ ft.
Machinery: 2 shaft geared turbines, S.H.P. 34,000 = 35½ knots.
Bunkers and radius: 450 tons, 5,000 miles at 12 knots.
Armament: Three 4.7 inch, one 3 inch. AA, four 20mm AA, four 21 inch
TT, one ATW (Hedgehog), [four DCT, DCs.
Radar, etc.: Type 271M, HF/DF.
Complement: 145

Vimy, Volunteer (rebuilt 1/41–6/41 and 8/42–1/43 as Long Range Escorts)
Displacement: 1,090 and 1,120 tons
Dimensions: 312 (oa) x 29½ x 10¾ ft.
Machinery: 2 shaft geared turbines, S.H.P., 18,000 = 24½ knots.
Bunkers and radius: 450 tons, 5,000 miles at 12 knots.
Armament: One 4 inch (Vol. 4.7), one 3 inch AA, four 20mm AA, three 21
inch TT, one ATW [(Hedgehog), four DCT, DCs.
Radar, etc.: Type 271M, HF/DF.
Complement: 125

Witherington (Short Leg Escort)
Displacement: 1,112 tons
Dimensions: as *Vimy*
Machinery: 2 shaft geared turbines, S.H.P. 27,000 = 34 knots.
Bunkers and radius: 365 tons, 2,380 miles at 12 knots.
Armament: Three 4.7 inch, one 3 inch AA, two 20mm AA, DCs.
Radar, etc.: Type 271M
Complement: 125

Leamington, Mansfield (Short Leg Escort)
Displacement: 1,090 tons
Dimensions: 314 (oa) x 30½ x 8¾ ft.
Machinery: 2 shaft geared turbines, S.H.P. 26,000 (25,200 MAN) = 35 knots.
Bunkers and radius: 290 tons, ca 2,000 miles at 12 knots.
Armament: Three (MAN one) 4 inch, one 3 inch AA, four 20mm AA, six
(MAN three) 21 TT, four DCT, DCs.
Radar, etc.: Type 271M
Complement: 146

Babbitt, Upshur
Displacement: 1,090 tons
Dimensions: as *Leamington*

Machinery: 2 shaft geared turbines, S.H.P. 26,000 (24,900 BAB) = 35 knots.
Bunkers and radius: 290 tons, ca 2,000 miles at 12 knots.
Armament: Six 3 inch AA, five 20mm AA, six 21 inch TT, DCT, DCs.
Radar: US-type radar
Complement: 150

Beverley (rebuilt as Long Range Escort)
Displacement: 1,190 tons
Dimensions: 314¼ (oa) x 30¾ x 9¼ ft.
Machinery: 2 shaft geared turbines. S.H.P. 13,500 = 25 knots.
Bunkers and radius: 430 tons, 5,000 miles at 12 knots.
Armament: One 4 inch, one 3 inch AA, four 20mm AA, three 21 inch TT, one ATW (Hedgehog), DCTs, DCs.
Radar, etc.: Type 271M
Complement: 146

Ingham (US Coast Guard Cutter)
Displacement: 2,216 tons
Dimensions: 327 x 41 x 12½ ft.
Machinery: 2 shaft geared turbines. S.H.P. 6,200 = 20 knots.
Bunkers and radius: 572 tons, 8,270 miles at 12 knots.
Armament: Three 5 inch DP, three 3 inch AA, five 20mm AA, DCTs, DCs.
Radar, etc.: US-type radar
Complement: 201

Swale (Frigate "River"-class)
Displacement: 1,370 tons
Dimensions: 301¼ x 36½ x 9 ft.
Machinery: 2 shaft reciprocating 4cyl. S.H.P. 6,500 = 20 knots.
Bunkers and radius: 720 tons, 9,600 miles at 12 knots.
Armament: Two 4 inch, ten 20mm AA, one ATW (Hedgehog), DCTs, DCs.
Radar, etc.: Type 271M, HF/DF.
Complement: 140

Corvettes ("Flower"-class)
Displacement: 940 tons
Dimensions: 205 (oa) x 33 x 14¾ ft.
Machinery: 1 shaft reciprocating 4 cyl. S.H.P. 2,750 = 16 knots.
Bunkers and radius: 200 tons, 4,000 miles at 12 knots.
Armament: One 4 inch, one 2pdr. AA, two 20mm AA, one ATW (Hedgehog), four DCTs, DCs.
Radar, etc.: Type 271M
Complement: 85

APPENDIX 3

U-boats Operating against SC.122 and HX.229

U-Boat	commiss.	C/O.	patrol/	dep./return.	group		fate
Type VIIB							
U 84	29. 4.41	KL Uphoff	7th	17.2.- 3.5.43	Raubgraf	24. 8.43	sunk at 27°09'N/37°03'W by A/C from USS Core
Type VIIC							
U 89	19.11.41	KK Lohmann	4th	23.1.-28.3.43	return.	12. 5.43	sunk at 46°30'N/25°40'W by A/C from HMS Biter and D/C by HMS Broadway and HMS Lagan; convoy HX.237
U 91	28. 1.42	KL Walkerling	3rd	11.2.-29.3.43	Raubgraf	25. 2.44	sunk at 49°45'N/26°20'W by HMS Affleck, HMS Gore, HMS Gould; 1st Escort Group
U 134	26. 7.41	OL Brosin	6th	6.3.- 2.5.43	Stürmer	24. 8.43	sunk at 42°07'N/09°30'W by Wellington, RAF-Sq. 179
U 221	9. 5.42	OL Trojer	3rd	27.2.-28.3.43	Dränger	27. 9.43	sunk at 47°00'N/18°00'W by Halifax, RAF-Sq. 58
U 228	12. 9.42	OL Christophersen	1st	6.2.-29.3.43	return.	26. 1.45	decomm. at Bergen, bomb damage 4.10.44
U 230	24.10.42	OL Siegmann	1st	4.2.-30.3.43	return.	21. 8.44	blown up off Toulon
U 305	17. 9.42	KL Bahr	1st	28.2.-12.4.43	Stürmer	17. 1.44	sunk at 49°39'N/20°10'W by HMS Wanderer and HMS Glenearn
U 333	25. 8.41	OL Schwaff	5th	2.3.-13.4.43	Dränger	31. 7.44	sunk at 49°39'N/07°28'W by HMS Starling and HMS Loch Killin; 2nd Escort Group
U 336	14. 2.42	KL Hunger	2nd	2.3.-11.4.43	Dränger	4.10.43	sunk at 60°40'N/26°30'W by Liberator, USN-VB-128; convoy HX.258
U 338	25. 6.42	KL Kinzel	1st	22.2.-24.3.43	Stürmer	20. 9.43	sunk at 57°40'N/29°48'W by Liberator, RAF-Sq. 120; convoy ON.202/ONS.18
U 373	22. 5.41	KL Loeser	8th	25.2.-13.4.43	Dränger	8. 6.44	sunk at 48°10'N/05 31'W by Liberator, RAF-Sq. 224
U 384	18. 7.42	KL v. Rosenberg-Gruszczinski	2nd	6.3.-20.3.43	Stürmer	20. 3.43	sunk at 54°18'N/26°15'W by Sunderland, RAF-Sq. 201; convoy HX.229/SC.122
U 406	22.10.41	KL Dieterichs	5th	22.2.-29.3.43	Dränger	18. 2.44	sunk at 48°32'N/23°36'W by HMS Spey
U 435	30. 8.41	KL Strelow	6th	18.2.-25.3.43	Raubgraf	9. 7.43	sunk at 39°48'N/14°22'W by Wellington, RAF-Sq. 179
U 439	20.12.41	OL v. Tippelskirch	2nd	22.2.-28.3.43	Stürmer	3. 5.43	sunk at 43°32'N/13°20'W after collision with U 659
U 440	24. 1.42	KL Geissler	4th	22.2.-11.4.43	Dränger	31. 5.43	sunk at 45°38'N/13°04'W by Sunderland, RAF-Sq. 201

U-Boat	commiss.	C/O.	patrol/dep./return.	group	fate
U 441	21. 2.42	KL Hartmann	22.2.-11.4.43	3rd	Dränger	18. 6.44 sunk at 49°03'N/04°48'W by Wellington, Pol. Sq. 304
U 468	12. 8.42	OL Schamong	28.1.-27.3.43	1st	Raubgraf	11. 8.43 sunk at 12°20'N/20°07'W by Liberator, RAF-Sq. 200
U 590	2.10.41	KL Müller-Edzards	22.2.-12.4.43	6th	Dränger	9. 7.43 sunk at 03°22'N/48°38'W by A/C USN-VP.94
U 598	27.11.41	KL Holtorf	6.3.-13.5.43	3rd	Stürmer	23. 7.43 sunk at 04°05'S/33°23'W by 3 Liberator, USN-VP 107
U 600	11.12.41	KL Zurmühlen	11.2.-26.3.43	3rd	Raubgraf	25.11.43 sunk at 40°31'N/22°07'W by HMS Bazely and HMS Blackwood
U 603	2. 1.42	KL Bertelsmann	7.2.-26.3.43	2nd	Raubgraf	1. 3.44 sunk at 48°55'N/26°10'W by USS Bronstein
U 608	5. 2.42	KL Struckmeier	20.1.-28.3.43	3rd	return.	10. 8.44 sunk at 46°30'N/03°08'W by Liberator, RAF-Sq. 53 and HMS Wren
U 610	19. 2.42	KL Frhr. v. Freyberg-Eisenberg-Allmendingen	8.3.-12.5.43	3rd	Stürmer	8.10.43 sunk at 55°45'N/24°33'W by Sunderland, RCAF-Sq. 423, convoy SC.143
U 615	26. 3.42	KL Kapitzky	18.2.-20.4.43	3rd	Raubgraf	7. 8.43 scuttled at 12°38'N/64°15'W after damage by 4 A/C USN-VP 130, 204, 205, USAAF-10, 1 Blimp.
U 616	2. 4.42	OL Koitschka	6.2.-26.3.43	1st	return.	14. 5.44 sunk at 36°46'N/00°53'E by 3 A/C and USS Nields, Gleaves, Ellyson, H. P. Jones, Macomb, Hambleton, Rodman, and Emmons
U 618	16. 4.42	KL Baberg	21.2.- 7.5.43	3rd	Stürmer	14. 8.44 sunk at 47°22'N/04°39'W by Liberator, RAF-Sq. 53 and HMS Duckworth
U 621	7. 5.42	OL Kruschka	1.2.-23.3.43	3rd	return.	18. 8.44 sunk at 45°52'N/02°36'W by HMCS Ottawa, HMCS Kootenay, HMCS Chaudière
U 631	16. 6.42	OL Krüger	6.3.-10.5.43	2nd	Stürmer	17.10.43 sunk at 58°13'N/32°29'W by HMS Sunflower, convoy ON.206
U 638	3. 9.42	KL Bernbeck	4.2.-30.3.43	1st	return.	5. 5.43 sunk at 53°06'N/45°02'W by HMS Loosestrife, convoy ONS.5
U 641	24. 9.42	KL Rendtel	20.2.-11.4.43	1st	Stürmer	19. 1.44 sunk at 50°25'N/18°49'W by HMS Violet
U 642	1.10.42	KL Brünning	20.2.- 8.4.43	1st	Stürmer	5. 7.44 sunk by air-raid in Toulon
U 653	25. 5.41	KL Feiler	28.1.-30.3.43	6th	return.	15. 3.44 sunk at 53°46'N/24°35'W by HMS Starling, HMS Wild Goose, A/C of HMS Vindex. 2nd Escort Group

U-Boat	commiss.	C/O	patrol/dep./return.		fate
U 664	17. 6.42	OL Graef	3rd	14.2.-27.3.43	Raubgraf	9. 8.43 sunk at 40°12'N/37°29'W by A/C USS *Card*
U 665	22. 7.42	OL Haupt	1st	20.2.-22.3.43	Stürmer	22. 3.43 sunk at 46°47'N/09°58'W by Wellington, RAF-Sq. 172
U 666	26. 8.42	OL Engel	1st	25.2.-10.4.43	Stürmer	10. 2.44 sunk at 53°56'N/17°16'W by A/C HMS *Fencer*
U 663	14. 5.42	KL Schmid	2nd	10.3.- 4.4.43	Seeteufel	7. 5.43 sunk at 46°33'N/11°12'W by Liberator, RAF-Sq. 58
U 758	5. 5.42	KL Manseck	2nd	14.2.-29.3.43	Raubgraf	decomm. at Kiel

Type IX/C

U 523	25. 6.42	KL Pietzsch	1st	9.2.-16.4.43	Stürmer	25. 8.43 sunk at 42°03'N/18°02'W by HMS *Wallflower* and HMS *Wanderer*

Type IX/C-40

U 190	24. 9.42	KL Wintermeyer	1st	20.2.-29.3.43	Stürmer	10. 5.45 surrendered at St. John's
U 526	12. 8.42	KL Möglich	1st	11.2.-14.4.43	Stürmer	14. 4.43 sunk at 47°30'N/04°45'W by mine
U 527	12. 8.42	KL Uhlig	1st	9.2.-12.4.43	Stürmer	23. 7.43 sunk at 35°25'N/27°56'W by A/C USS *Bogue*
U 530	14.10.42	KL Lange	1st	20.2.-22.4.43	Stürmer	10. 7.45 surrendered at Mar del Plata (Argentina)

Technical data:

Type VIIB
Displacement: 753/857 tons.
Dimensions: 218¼ x 20¼ x 15½ feet
Machinery: 2-shaft diesel/electric motors BHP/SHP. 2,800/750, 17.2/8.0 knots.
Bunkers and radius: Oil fuel 108, 2 tons, 9,700/130 miles at 10/2 knots.
Armament: One 3.5 inch, two 20mm AA guns, five 21-inch TT (four fwd, one aft), twelve torpedoes
Complement: 44

Type VIIC
Displacement: 769/871 tons.
Dimensions: 220¼ x 20¼ x 15¾ feet
Machinery: 2-shaft diesel/electric motors BHP/SHP. 2,800/750 17.0/7.6 knots.
Bunkers and radius: Oil fuel 113, 5 tons, 9,400/130 miles at 10/2 knots.
Armament: One 3.5 inch, two 20mm AA guns, five 21-inch TT (four fwd, one aft), twelve torpedoes
Complement: 44

Type IXC
Displacement: 1,120/1,232 tons.
Dimensions: 252 x 22¼ x 15½ feet
Machinery: 2 shaft diesel/electric motors BHP/SHP, 4,400/1,000, 18.3/7.3 knots.
Bunkers and radius: Oil fuel 208, 2 tons, 16,300/128 miles at 10/2 knots.
Armament: One 4.1 inch, two 20mm AA guns, six 21-inch TT (four fwd, two aft), nineteen torpedoes
Complement: 48

Type IX/C-40
Displacement: 1,144/1,257 tons.
Dimensions: 252 x 21¾ x 15¼ feet
Machinery: 2 shaft diesel/electric motors BHP/SHP. 4,400/1,000, 18.3/7.3 knots.
Bunkers and radius: Oil fuel 214, 0 tons, 16,800/128 miles at 10/2 knots.
Armament: One 4.1 inch, two 20mm AA guns, six 21-inch TT (four fwd, two aft), twenty-two torpedoes.
Complement: 48

APPENDIX 4

The Appreciation of the Situation by the Commander U-boats on March 5, 1943

Source: The Commander U-boats' War Diary of March 5, 1943

GENERAL

1/A 1 The systematic evaluation of the British U-boat situation reports of January and the beginning of February (i.e. comparisons of the U-boat positions suspected by the British and the evidence available to them in the form of radio bearings, sightings, U-boat attacks and aerial location, including cases when a number of U-boats have returned to base, etc., has, to some extent, allayed strong suspicions that the enemy has succeeded in breaking our ciphers or in obtaining some other unusual information about our operations.

With the exception of two or three unclarified cases, the enemy's information is based on evidence available to him about U-boat positions and on the plotting of their courses, as well as on entirely reasonable deduction.

The most important thing that has emerged is the virtual certainty that the enemy has been able, with the assistance of airborne radar, to find the U-boat formations with sufficient precision to permit his convoys to take successful evasive action. As always in the case of new enemy methods, our counter-measures have lagged some weeks behind because:

His evasive measures only became apparent after repeated instances and after British radio messages had been deciphered ("B" reports) and made available weeks later.

b Reports about established radio location in U-boat formations came in very infrequently by radio; its constant use by the enemy only became apparent when the U-boat situation reports were evaluated and the commanders had been able to render oral accounts.

c The technical possibilities of ASV location (simultaneous observation of several targets at great ranges and with it the simultaneous location of several U-boats in a formation) were still unknown.

1/A 2 The indisputable fact, which is established by the frequent use of the phrase "radio located" in the British situation reports, that U-boat formations have been discovered by airborne radar unfortunately makes our existing method of finding convoys by patrol lines more difficult. Since, with our still inadequate U-boat numbers, we cannot generally abandon the idea of the patrol line, the following orders have been issued:

  a The boats are at once to submerge for some 30 minutes when airborne radar contact is established in the patrol line. For this measure to be successful it is necessary to have a search receiver constantly outside and in working order. The present search receiver aerials in use at the front cannot, however, be employed in all weather conditions. Changes will be made at the beginning of March when the boats are equipped with firmly fitted search receiver cables and round dipoles.

  b All unnecessary waiting in the patrol line before the expected passage of a convoy is to be avoided. The *Neptun, Ritter, Burggraf* and *Neuland* groups were formed to comb the convoy routes in a western to south-west direction as far as the area of the Newfoundland Bank. In the generally unfavourable weather conditions prevailing the speed of the advance has been very slow. The formation could almost be said to be stationary in view of the great range of the ASV equipment and the high speed and action radius of the British aircraft.

  At present no better procedure has been tested. All other kinds of formation, for instance, arbitrary and haphazard dispersal, suffers from the disadvantage of creating too large gaps between the individual boats.

  When a convoy is not found by such a formation the question arises as to what is then to be done. There is not the certainty which exists in straightforward linear formations, except perhaps in periods of bad weather and fog, that the convoy has not passed through the area and that, in consequence, a change of position or procedure is necessary.

1/B 1 The engagement of Africa-bound supply ships from North America in the area north and south of the Azores has brought no success. It has not been possible to catch a UGS or GUS convoy with patrol and reconnaissance lines, such as *Rochen* and *Robbe.* The possibilities for the enemy to take evasive action north or south of the great circle without substantially lengthening the convoy route are very great, given the total distance.

1/B 2   The difficult situation confronting the defenders of the Tunis bridge-
         head compels us, however, to engage the African supply traffic.
         Since, on the one hand, the engagement of convoys in the area of
         the Gibraltar run does not promise much success in view of the
         strong defence and, on the other, as explained in (1) there is little
         prospect of finding the convoys in mid-ocean because of the size of
         the area, the only thing that remains is to try: to deploy the U-boats
         off the American departure harbours, to find the convoys there and
         to pursue them into the open sea. Here it must be said:
   a   The air defence in the coastal area is probably very strong, so the for-
         mation can only be stationary.
   b   The information about the departure harbours and sailing times is
         very incomplete, so a certain number of boats will be required.
   c   The defence will make it necessary to carry out a distant operation by
         moonlight outside the coastal area.

         If we take these facts into account, it means we must insist on a suf-
         ficient number of boats, some of which can operate as stationary
         reconnaissance boats outside the harbours and others of which can
         be stationed further back as an "interceptor" group that can operate
         and move on the basis of the reports from the reconnaissance boats.

         Because of the long approach route and the small number of U-
         boats, only type IX boats are at present suitable for these duties. The
         boats originally envisaged for deployment in the Cape Town area—*U
         172*, *U 515*, *U 513*—as well as *U 167*, *U 130*, *U 106*, *U 159* have been
         detached for this purpose (see also War Diary of February 27).

         The reports of *U 333* of March 5 and *U 156* of March 6 confirm the
         suspicions that have existed for some weeks that the enemy is using
         new locating devices which cannot be found with our present search
         receiver equipment. The boats have reported from sea and at com-
         manders' conferences, at first sporadically and then more frequently,
         that they were attacked by aircraft at night (particularly in the Bay of
         Biscay and off Trinidad) and that suddenly an aircraft searchlight
         illuminated the area without any previous locating having been estab-
         lished. The following new locating devices appear possible on the
         basis of present observations and considerations:
   a   The enemy is operating with very high or very low impulse frequen-
         cies which are therefore inaudible or virtually so.

         This possibility is confirmed by the observations of *U 214* in the
         Caribbean Sea. Radio Petty Officer Bruster, after encountering
         scarcely audible impulse frequencies, built the magic eye of the Ela
         10/12 receiver into the Metox receiver to make the inaudible

impulse frequencies visible and has apparently in this way established a radar contact. After an oral exposition by Radio Petty Officer Bruster with the Head of the Naval Signals Service and the Signals Weapon Office the installation of the magic eye has been ordered in all receivers of outward-bound boats. In addition, a number of oscillographs were sent off by courier to the west on March 6. They are also to be fitted on to the Metox receivers on the boats, so as to establish as soon as possible whether the enemy is in fact operating with inaudible impulse frequencies.

Boats have orders to report, if necessary, any observations at sea by radio.

b The enemy is operating on carrier frequencies which lie outside the frequency range of the present search receiver. The shooting down of an enemy aircraft over Holland, which apparently had on board a device using a frequency of 5.7 cm, is at the moment the only evidence to support this hypothesis.

The possibility that the enemy is trying, with his locating frequency, to get outside the frequency range of our search receiver, is, however, strong enough for this to be anticipated and frustrated.

c The enemy is using his equipment to search and range for only very brief periods (2–3 seconds). This procedure marks a further stage in the development and perfection of the economical use of radar, already observed. In such cases it would be very difficult and perhaps only possible by accident for an operator with the present search receiver to establish the radar contact.

Theoretically it seems desirable to counter all three possibilities in the following way: an aperiodic i.e. fixed frequency receiver with a visual indicator should be used in which every radar impulse, whether carrier or impulse frequency, should immediately become visible. A second variable frequency receiver should also be used to make further detailed observations of established radar contacts.

Whether this is technically possible remains to be seen. Further steps in this direction will be set in motion with the appropriate authorities without delay.

The Sailing Telegrams of Convoys SC.122 and HX.229

Sailing telegram of convoy SC.122

Text:

From: PORT DIR NYK

For action: ADMIRALTY

For information: NSHQ, FONF, CTF 24, COMEASTSEAFRON, CTG 24.6
NOIC SYDNEY CB, COMINCH C-R ALL INFO;
FROM PORT DIR NYK COMEASTSEAFRON PASS TO COAC FOR INFO.

PART 1 2130Z/5   NCR 5472
PART 2 2136Z/5   NCR 5547

SAILING TELEGRAM
PART 1

THIS COMPLETES MY 041800.

SC 122

7. 14 COLUMNS: 2 4 4 3 4 5 5 3 3 4 4 4 3 2

8. CONVOY COMMODORE S N WHITE RNR IN GLENAPP
VICE COMMODORE F R NEIL MASTER IN BOSTON CITY

14. ALL SHIPS HOLD SP 272 (22) (23) AND SP 2406, 220
ALL U.S. SHIPS HOLD CSP 1321 GH FOLLOWING SHIPS
HOLD SP 2413:

CARTAGO	208
BEACON OIL	1644
VISTULA	256
PERMIAN	1122
SHIRVAN	1739
GLOXINIA	1191
CHRISTIAN HOLM	434
POLARLAND ISSUED ONLY	SP 2406, 220

15. TQ

Text:

From: PORT DIR. NEW YORK

For action: ADMIRALTY

For information: COMINCH C & R, NSHQ, COMEASTSEAFRON, C.T.F.24,
FONF, NOIC SYDNEY FOR INFO;
FROM PORT DIR. NEW YORK. COMEASTSEAFRON PASS TO COAC.

PART 1 2228Z/05   NCR 5549
PART 2 2230Z/05   NCR 5520

(1) SAILING TELEGRAM SC-122. PART 2

	(10)	(11)	(12)	
PAN	PERMIAN	8.5	FUEL OIL	HALIFAX
BR	ASBJORN	12	BALLAST	HALIFAX
NOR	SEVILLA	9.5	GENERAL	ST. JOHNS
NOR	POLARLAND	7.5	GENERAL	ST. JOHNS FOR

240

BR	LIVINGSTON	8	GENERAL	ST. JOHNS FOR
PAN	ALCEDO	10	GENERAL	ICELAND
NOR	ASKEPOT	9.5	ARMY SUPPL.	ICELAND
US	CARTAGO	13	REEFER	ICELAND
US	EASTERN GUIDE	8.5	AMMU, ARMY GENERAL	ICELAND
NOR	GUDVOR	8.5	GENERAL	ICELAND
PAN	GRANVILLE	8	GAS, GENERAL 350 MAIL	ICELAND
ICE	GODAFOSS	11	GENERAL 2 PASSENGERS	ICELAND
BR	CARSO	9	MINERALS	LOCH EWE
BR	KINGSBURY	8	BAUXITE GENERAL 2 PASSEN.	LOCH EWE
BR	KING GRUFFYDD	8.5		LOCH EWE
BR	EMPIRE SUMMER	8	EXPL. GENERAL 8 PLANES	LOCH EWE
SW	ATLAND	9	IRON ORE	LOCH EWE
NETH	ALDERAMIN	9.5	GENERAL	LOCH EWE
BR	EMPIRE GALAHAD	9.5	GENERAL REEFER 1 PASSEN.	U.K.
BR	INNESMOOR	8.5	WHEAT	LOCH EWE
PAN	BEACON OIL	9	POOL DIESEL OIL	CLYDE
GR	GEORGIOS P.	8.5	SUGAR	CLYDE
BR	BARON STRANRAER	8.5	IRON ORE	LOCH EWE
BR	CHRISTIAN HOLM	9	FUEL OIL	U.K.
BR	BRIDGEPOOL	8	LINSEED	LOCH EWE
BR	BARON ELGIN	8.5	SUGAR	LOCH EWE
BR	AYMERIC	9	IRON ORE	LOCH EWE
BR	GLENAPP	10	AFRICAN PRODUCE 24 PASSEN. 500 MAIL	MERSEY
BR	BENEDICK	9	AD FUEL	CLYDE
BR	CLARISSA RADCLIFFE	7.5	IRON ORE	LOCH EWE
BR	VINRIVER	8	SUGAR	CLYDE
BR	HISTORIAN	7.5	GENERAL	MERSEY
BR	ORMINISTER	8.5	IRON ORE	LOCH EWE
BR	LOSADA	8.5	GENERAL 1 MAIL	MERSEY
BR	GLOXINIA	7.5	LUBE OIL	MERSEY
BR	FILLEIGH	8.5	GENERAL 17 MAIL	MERSEY
BR	LST 365	9		U.K.
BR	EMPIRE DUNSTAN	8	SUGAR	MERSEY
BR	SHIRVAN	8	GAS	BELFAST
BR	BOSTON CITY	9	GENERAL EXPL	BELFAST

BR	LST 305	9		U.K.
BR	DOLIUS	8.5	BAUXITE GENERAL 172 MAIL	BELFAST
US	VISTULA	9.5	PETRO PROD	BELFAST
BR	ENGLISH MONARCH	8.5	EXPL. GENERAL	BELFAST
BR	FORT CEDAR LAKE	9	EXPL. GENERAL	BELFAST
BR	BARON SAMPLE	9	GENERAL	BELFAST
GRK	CARRAS	8.5	WHEAT	BELFAST DOCKS
PAN	BONITA	8	STEEL TOBACCO	U.K.
US	MCKEESPORT	9.5	GRAIN GENERAL	U.K.
NETH	KEDOE	9.5	WHEAT ZINC ORE	BELFAST

M/FD/F GUARD SHIPS BRIDGEPOOL (R/T) DOLIUS.
ROVING FREQUENCY EMPIRE SUMMER (R/T) ESCORT OILER
    BENEDICK
STANDBY OILER CHRISTIAN HOLM

Sailing telegram of Convoy HX.229:
From: P.D. NEW YORK
For action: ADMIRALTY
For information: COMINCH C&R, COMEASTSEAFRON, CTF 24, CTG 24.6,
                NSHQ, FONF, COMEASTSEAFRON PASS TO COAC FOR INFO
Text:
THIS COMPLETES MY 072144
SAILING TELEGRAM PART 1 HX 229.
   (7)   11 COLUMNS DOUBLE 3 SINGLE 4 SINGLE 3
         6 COLUMNS 4 EACH SINGLE 3
  (13)   COMMODORE M J D MAYALL RNR IN ABRAHAM LINCOLN FOR
         BELFAST
         VICE-COMMODORE R J PARRY MASTER IN CLAN MATHESON FOR
         LOCH EWE
  (14)   ALL SHIPS HOLD RECODING TABLES 22 AND 23 AND SP 2406, 261.
         ALL US SHIPS HOLD CSP 1321 G H EXCEPT MARGARET LYKES HOLDS
         ONLY G
         ONLY FOLLOWING SHIPS HOLD 1 SHIP PADS LUCULUS 1194 NICANIA
         67
         EMPIRE CAVALIER 1182 SOUTHERN PRINCESS 56 SAN VERONICO
         1683
         BELGIAN GULF 179 PAN RHODE ISLAND 1569 MAGDALA 298 GULFDISC
         1598
         IRENEE DU PONT 1401.
  (15)   A Z

Text:
From: PORT DIR NEW YORK
For action: ADMIRALTY

For information: COMINCH C&R, NSHQ, COMEASTSEAFRON, CTF 24, FONF
　　　　　　　　COMEASTSEAFRON PASS TO COAC FOR INFO.
PART 1 2152Z/8 NCR 7725
PART 2 2240Z/8 NCR 7774
(1) SAILING TELEGRAM HX 229 PART 2 —
(10) (11) (12).

BR	CAPE BRETON	10-1/2	LINSEED 1 PASS CLYDE
US	ROBERT HOWE	10	GEN MERSEY
BR	EMPIRE KNIGHT	10-1/2	GEN CLYDE
US	WALTER Q. GRESHAM	10-1/2	FOOD 2 PASS CLYDE
US	WILLIAM EUSTIS	10-1/2	SUGAR CLYDE
US	STEPHEN C FOSTER	11	SUGAR GEN 2 PASS MERSEY
BR	FORT ANNE	10	LEAD PHOS LUMS LOCH EWE
BR	KAIPARA	12	REEFER GEN 15 MAIL MERSEY
BR	CANADIAN STAR	12-1/2	REEFER 22 PASS UKAY
US	MATHEW LUCKENBACH	11	GEN SOME MAIL UKAY
BR	NEBRASKA	10-1/2	REEFER MERSEY
BR	REGENT PANTHER	10-1/2	AV GAS UKAY
BR	ANTAR	10	GEN 21 MAIL MERSEY
PAN	BELGIAN GULF	10-1/2	LUBE OIL MERSEY
BR	SAN VERONICO ND	12	GAS MERSEY
US	PAN RHODE ISLAND	11	AV GAS MERSEY
BR	EMPIRE CAVALIER	11	AV GAS MERSEY
NOR	ABRAHAM LINCOLN	12	EXPL GEN BELFAST
US	GULF DISC	11	AD FUEL CLYDE
US	JEAN	10	GEN 56 ARMY PASS SOME MAIL MERSEY
US	KOFRESI	10-1/2	ARMY STORES MERSEY
BR	CITY OF AGRA	13-1/2	GEN EXPL 46 PASS MERSEY
BR	SOUTHERN PRINCESS	10-1/2	FUEL OIL 26 PASS CLYDE
PAN	EL MUNDO	12	VAL GEN SOME MAIL MERSEY
US	MARGARET LYKES	11-1/2	GEN GRAIN MERSEY
US	IRENEE DU PONT	15	OIL GEN 9 PLANES MERSEY
BR	CORACERO	10	REEFER 1 MAIL MERSEY
BR	NIGERIA	11	GAS MERSEY
BR	TEKOA	13	REEFER GEN 442 MAIL MERSEY
BR	CLAN MATHESON	10	GEN 1 PASS 6 MAIL LOCH EWE
BR	NARIVA	10-1/2	REEFER MERSEY
DU	MAGDALA	10	AV GAS BELFAST
US	JAMES OGLETHORPE	10	GEN PLANES FOOD MERSEY
NOR	ELIN KONG	11	MANG WHEAT 339 MAIL BELFAST DOCKS
BR	LUCULUS	10	GAS OIL BELFAST
DU	ZAANLAND	11-1/2	REEFER WHEAT ZINC BELFAST
DU	TERKOELEI	10	ZINC WHEAT 7 MAIL BELFAST
US	HARRY LUCKENBACH	12	GEN UKAY
US	DANIEL WEBSTER	10-1/2	GEN BELFAST
US	HUGH WILLIAMSON	10	GEN 6 PLANES BELFAST

M/FD/F GUARD SHIPS CORACERO, NARIVA, NEBRASKA, SOUTHERN
PRINCESS, ROVING FREQUENCY TEKOA, KAIPARA, ALL GUARD SHIPS
PLUS FOLLOWING HAVE R/T BELGIAN GULF, EMPIRE CAVALIER,
ABRAHAM LINCOLN, ESCORT TANKER GULF DISC 62 STANDBY ESCORT
TANKER SOUTHERN PRINCESS 72.

U-boat Attacks against Convoys SC.122 and HX.229

Legend

U-boat
1 number of U-boat attacking

time
1 date of attack
2 time of firing (GMT)

weather
1 wind direction and force (Beaufort scale)
2 sea
3 sight in miles

convoy
1 convoy number
2 number of escorts present

observation
1 attacking U-boat not observed by convoy or escorts
2 HF/DF-beam of attacking U-boat
3 RDF (RADAR)-location of attacking U-boat
4 optical sighting of U-boat
5 ASDIC (SONAR)-location of U-boat

target
1 type of attacked ship
2 gross tonnage estimated by attacking U-boat

attack
1 surface attack
2 submerged attack
3 surfaced coup de grace
4 submerged coup de grace
5 number of torpedoes fired in one attack
6 type of torpedo used

distance
1 distance to target as estimated by U-boat
2 running time of torpedo in minutes and seconds
3 real distance to target

success
1 hit on target
2 hit on other vessel
3 miss

U-boat	time 1	time 2	weather 1	weather 2	weather 3	convoy 1	convoy 2	observation	target 1	target 2	attack	attack 5	attack 6	distance 1	distance 2	distance 3	success	remarks
U603	16	2200	N-2	1	9	HX.229	4	x	S/S:	6000	x	3	FAT	3000	4'..."	4000	x	one hit on Stb. side of No. 101 *Elin K.*, sunk in 4 min.
U758	16	2323	NzE3	3	5	HX.229	3	x	S/S:	6000	x	1	FAT	?	?	—	x	one hit on Stb. side of No. 93 *James Oglethorpe*, damaged.
	16	2324							S/S:	7000	x	1	G7e	?	?	—	x	one hit on Stb. side of No.
	16	2325							S/T:	8000	x	1	FAT	?	?	—	x	103 *Zaanland*, sunk 1h 30min.
	16	2332							S/S:	4000	x	1	G7e	?	?	—		

U-boat	time	weather	convoy	observation (1 2 3 4 5)	target (1 2)	attack (1 2 3)	no.	torpedo	distance (4 5 6 / 1 2 3)	success (1 2 3)	remarks
U 435	17/0022	NE3	3 5 HX.229 1	1: x	S/T: 7000	x	2	FAT / FAT	? 13'46" 12000 / —	x (3)	one hit on Bb. side on No. 22 William Eustis, damaged
U 338	17/0205	W2-3	212 SC.122 7	2: x, 4: x	S/S: 5000	x	2	G7e 1500 1'50' 1600 / G7e 1500 1'50' 1600		x (2)	one hit each on Stb. sides of No. 51 and 52 Kingsbury and King Gruffydd, both sunk
	17/0206				S/S: 8500	x	2	G7e 860 1'00' 800 / G7e		x (1), x (2)	two hits on Stb. side of No. 61 Alderamin, sunk
	17/0207				S/S: 4000	x	1	G7e 600 ? 6000		x (3)	one hit on Bb. side of No. 124 Fort Cedar Lake, sunk?
U 435	17/0230	NE3	2 5 HX.229 2	1: x	S/S: 7000	x	2	FAT 3500 ? 3500 / FAT		x (1), x (3)	detonations at 8'19 and
	17/0232			x	S/S: 6000	x	1	G7e 3500 ? 3500		x (3)	9'12 from hits by U 91!
	17/0233			x	S/S: 4500	x	1	G7e 3500 ? 3500		x (3)	attack from Bb. side
U 91	17/0237	NE3	2 5 HX.229 2	1: x	S/S: 8000	x	2	FAT 1860 — ? / FAT		x (1), x (3)	
	17/0238			2: x	S/S: 10000	x	2	G7e 1500 1'23' 1280 / G7e 1'23'		x (1), x (3)	two hits on Stb. side of No. 111 Harry Luckenbach, sunk
U 435	17/0255	NE3	2 5 HX.229 2	1: x	S/T: 7000	x	1	G7e ? — ?		x (3)	
U 616	17/0418	NNW3	4-5 5 single	1: x	destroyer	x	4	G7e 1500 — ? / G7e — / G7e — / G7e —		x (1), x (2), x (3)	attack on Beverley, missed
U 600	17/0456	NNE4	3 6 HX.229 3	1: x	S/S: 7000 / S/S: 5000 / S/S: 5000 / S/S: 5000	x	4	FAT 3000 ? 2800 / FAT 3600 / FAT 3600 / FAT		x (3)	one, two, one hits each on No. 91, 81, 72 Nariva, Irenee Du Pont, Southern Princess. 91, 81 dam., 72 sunk
	17/0457			4: x	S/S: 5000	x	1	FAT 3000 ? 4200		x (1)	
U 228	17/0534	NNE4	3 6 single	1: x	destroyer	x	3	G7e 2000 — 1240 / G7e / G7e		x (1), x (2), x (3)	attack on Mansfield, missed

U-boat	time	weather	convoy	observation	target	attack	5 6	distance	success	remarks
U91	17/0739	NNE5	4 8 straggler	x	S/S:5000 S/S:6000	x	3	G7e 3200 3'30" 3200; G7e 3200 3'30" 3200; G7e 3400 3'40" 3350	x x x	two hits on *James Ogle-thorpe*, one hit on *William Eustis*, both sunk later
U228	17/0958	NNE4	3 7 straggler ?	x	S/S:6000	x	2	G7e ? ? ?; G7e ? ? ?	x x	one hit assumed, but missed
U616	17/1033	NNE4	3 6 single	x	destroyer	x	1	G7e ? ? ?	x	attack on *Anemone*, missed
U665	17/1057	NW	2 10? single ?	x	S/S:5000	x	2	G7e ? ? ?; G7e ? ? —	?	one hit possible on damaged *Fort Cedar Lake* (?)
U616	17/1210	NNE4	3 6 straggler	x	S/S:5000	x	1	G7e ? ? —	x	attack on *Nariva/Irenne Du Pont*, missed
U384	17/1305	NNE5	3-4 8 HX.229 3	x	S/S:6000 S/S:4000 S/S:2500	x	3	FAT ? ? ?; FAT ? ? ?; FAT ? ? ?	x	two hits on Stb. side No. 91 *Terkoelei*, sunk
U631	17/1306	NNE5	3-4 8 HX.229 3	x	S/T:7000	x	4	FAT ? ? ?; FAT ? — —; FAT — —; FAT — —	x x x	one hit on Stb. side No. 81 *Coracero*, sunk later
U338	17/1352 17/1354	NW2	3 14 SC.122 7	x x x	S/S:10000 S/S:5000	x x	1 3	G7e 1200 — —; G7e 2000 2'30" 2300; G7e; G7e	x x x	attack on *Cartago*, missed; one hit on No. 41 *Granville*; one torpedo surface runner
U91	17/1508 ?		? ? straggler / straggler	x	S/S:4000 S/S:7000		1 1	G7e ? ? ?; G7e ? ? ?	x x	coup de grace *Irenee Du Pont*; coup de grace *Nariva*
U305	17/2208	NW5	3-4 6 SC.122 7	x	S/S:8400 x	x	2	G7e 1500 3'47" 3500; G7e 1500 5'07" 4700	x x	one hit Stb. side No. 92 *Port Auckland*, dam.; one hit Stb. side No. 84 *Zouave*, sunk

U-boat	time	weather	convoy	obs.	target	attack	no.			distance			success	remarks
	17/2209				S/S: 6000	x (1)	2		G7e	1500	58'	3700	x (2)	hit on *Port Auckland* or depth charge from *Pimpernel* not fired
									G7e	—				
U 305	17/2341	NW4	2-3 6 straggler	x	S/S: 6000	x (3)	1		G7e	1450	1'34	1450	x (3)	coup de grace *Port Auckl.*
U 338	18/0155	NW6	6 2 straggler	x	S/S: 6000	x (3)	1		G7e	?		—	x (3)	*Port Auckland* sunk before torpedo reached ship
U 663	18/1435	NW7	6 2 straggler	x	S/S: 6000	x (1)	3		G7e	?	—		x (1)	starboard side
									G7e	—			x	
									G7e	—			x	
	18/1440				S/S: 6000	x (2)	1		G7e	?			x (1)	poss. hit *Clarissa Radcliffe*
U 221	18/1543	NW7	6 2 HX.229 4	x	S/S: 5495	x (1)	1		G7e	3000	2'51	2600	x (2)	one hit on Bb. side of No.21 *Walter Q. Gresham*, sunk
	18/1549			x	S/S: 6843	x (1)	4		FAT	600	0'30"	500	x (2)	two hits on Bb. side of No. 33 *Canadian Star*, sunk
									G7e		0'32"		x (3)	
									G7e					
									FAT	—				
U 666	19/0017	NW3	2-3 6 SC.122 6	x	S/S: 4000	x (1)	4		G7e	3000		4000	x (1)	attack on port side
					S/S: 5000				G7e	—			x (1)	
									G7e	—			x (1)	
									G7e	—			x (1)	
	19/0034				S/S: 4000	x (1)	1		G7e	3000		?	x (1)	one detonation heard
U 441	19/0450	NNW4	3 7 HX.229 3	x	S/S: 7000	x (1)	4		FAT	?	?	?	x (1)	attack on starboard side
					S/S: 5000				FAT	?	?	?	x (1)	
									G7e	?	?	?	x (1)	
									G7e				x (1)	
	19/0500				S/S: 5000	x (1)	1		G7e	?	?	?	x (1)	three detonations heard
U 608	19/0506	NNW4	3 7 HX.229 3	x (4)	destroyer	x (1)	3		G7e	2000	5'34"	5150?	x (1)	two detonations heard, actually depth charges from *Highlander*
									G7e				x (1)	
									G7e				x (1)	

U-boat	time	weather	convoy	observation	target	attack	distance	success	remarks
		1 2	1 2 3	1 2 3 4 5	1 2	1 2 3 4 5 6	1 2 3	1 2 3	
U 666	19/0541	NW3 2-3	6 SC.122 7	x	S/S: 3000 x	4 G7e	3000 —	x	one hit on stb. side of No. 131 Carras, damaged two
					S/S: 4000	G7e	3'15" 3000	x	more detonations heard
					S/S: 7000	G7e	3'20"	x	
					S/S: 4000	G7e	3'20"		
U 527	19/0947 ?		4 romper	x	S/S: 8000 x	3 G7e 1200	4'16" 3950	x	one hit on romper from HX.229 Mathew
						G7e	—	x	Luckenbach, damaged
						G7e	—	x	
U 523	19/1908 ?		?? straggler	x	S/S: 6000	x 1 G7e	2'19" 2150	x	coup de grace Mathew Luckenbach
U 333	19/2028 ?		?? straggler	x	S/S: 5000	x 2 G7e 2000	— ?	x	coup de grace missed
						G7e	2'18" 2100	x	coup de grace Carras, sunk

Attacks on U-boats by Escorts of Convoys SC.122 and HX.229

Appendix 7: Attacks on U-boats by Escorts of Convoys SC.122 and HX.229

Date/Time	(convoy) escort	position of esc. relative to convoy, metres distance	position of U/B relative to convoy, metres distance	detection first, metres	detection second, metres	detection third, metres	No	time	number type	depth	results/observations
16/2355	Anemone (HX.229)	astern of port columns, 8300 m	astern 10650 m	Sighting 2750 m	Asdic 2000 m		1	0009	5 D/C MkVII	15/ 15	no result
							2	0048	10 D/C MkVII	30/ 70	fired prematurely
							3	0108	10 D/C MkVII	45/ 90	one heavy explosion
							4	0126	Hedgehog	—	only 4 fired, no explos.
							5	0147	10 D/C MkVII	45/120	no result
17/0201	Glenapp commodore No. 61 (SC.122)	—	ahead of No. 61 300 m	Sighting 300 m			1	0201	M/G fire		during attack of U 338 / 4 ships in convoy torpedoed
17/0517	Mansfield (HX.229)	Sweeping down port quarter port side		Asdic ?			1		D/C's		no details known (contact no U/B ?)
17/0635	Beverley (HX.229)	starboard beam 3650 m	on starboard quarter, 5550 m	Radar 2750 m	Asdic 1100 m		1	0645	7 D/C MkVII	15/ 45	no result
17/1120	Anemone (HX.229)	astern 50 miles	astern 50 miles	Sighting 11000 m	Asdic 1830 m		1	1154	10 D/C MkVII	45/120	no result
17/1352	Beverley (HX.229)	starboard bow	starboard bow 15750 m	Sighting 15750 m	Asdic 1550 m		—	1453	1 D/C MkVII	— 120	no result
							—	1502	1 D/C MkVII	— 120	Hedgehog attack called off
							1	1521	Hedgehog		no explosions
							2	1548	10 D/C MkVII	45/ 90	no result
							3	1635	10 D/C MkVII	45/105	failure to explode
							4	1657	1 D/C MkX		no result
							5	1718	5 D/C MkVII	165	no result
17/1352	Godetia	port beam 3650 m	port bow	torpedo	Asdic		G1	1407	10 D/C MkVII	30/ 70	no result/attack by U 338
17/1407	Upshur (SC.122)	port quarter 3650 m		track sighted 2750 m	1000 m	600 m	U2	1420	8 D/C		no result/No. 31 sunk
17/.. ..	Mansfield (HX.229)	astern, rejoining astern	?	?			1	...	D/C's		no details known

Date/Time	Escort (Convoy)	Position of esc. relative to convoy metres distance	Position of U/B relative to convoy metres distance	Method of detection first metres	second metres	third metres	No	time	Number type	depth	results/observations
17/2206	Pimpernel (SC.122)	starboard bow 3650 m	starboard bow 2750 m	Radar 3650 m	Sighting 2750 m		—				U/B dived, no asdic contact, U 305 attacked, No. 92 torpedoed
17/2215	Reaveley No. 63 in (SC.122)	Pos. 63	between 7th & 8th column	Sighting			—				Periscope sighted, no contacts by escorts
17/2356	Godetia (SC.122)	astern 22200 m	astern	Radar 2750 m	Sighting	Asdic	—	0003	1 D/C MkVII	30	during rescue operations asdic was defect
18/1555	Pennywort (HX.229)	port quarter Op. Raspberry		Asdic 1000 m			1	1637	6 D/C MkVII	45/ 90	no result
18/2144	Lavender (SC.122)	Port bow 4570 m	port bow 7400 m	Radar 2920 m	wake sighted	Asdic 1550 m	1	2220	10 D/C MkVII MkX	30 70	no result
							2	2231	3 D/C MkVII	45 90	oil slick, explosion
19/0404	Anemone Volunteer (HX.229)	astern of port col. 3650 m	astern 5550 m	Sighting 3650 m	Asdic 2200-2300 m		A1	0410	10 D/C MkVII	45 120	no result
							V1	0425	10 D/C MkVII	45 90	no result
							A2	0438	Hedgehog		only 6 fired, no result
							A3	0452	9 D/C MkVII	150/165	no result
							A4	0514	Hedgehog		only 4 fired, no result
19/0420	Pennywort (HX.229)	starboard quarter 3650 m	starboard quarter	Asdic 900 m			1	0428	6 D/C MkVII	30/ 30	no result
19/0447	Highlander (HX.229)	port bow 6000 m	port bow 7400 m	Sighting 3650 m	Radar 3500 m	Asdic 2200 m	1	0457	10 D/C MkVII	30/ 70	no result
							2	0505	14 D/C MkVII	45/ 60	no result
							3	0527	Hedgehog		only 2 fired, no result
							4	0542	14 D/C MkVII	60/120	explosion 8 min 30 sec later
19/0515	Anemone (HX.229)	astern	astern 16 miles	Radar 2000 m Radar 3000 m	Sighting 450 m	Asdic sehr nah	1	0532	4 D/C MkVII 4 D/C MkX	15/ 45 45/105	no results, two U/B's sighted, only one attack not attacked as other U/B was nearer
19/0530	Babbitt (HX.229)	port beam 10 miles, joining	port beam	Radar 2000 m	Asdic		11 att.		53 D/C's		oil seen after attacks —
19/0548	Svale	starboard beam	starboard bow	Radar	Asdic		1	0557	14 D/C MkVII MkX	15/ 70	no results

Allied Aircraft Reports and the Decoding of the German "B" Service

Aircraft report		Position of U-boat relative to convoy (in miles)	Method of detection	Weapons used	German decoding		Text of decoded report
Date /Time	Aircraft				Day /Time	Position	
17/0822	Liberator M/86	20m pt. beam SC.	Sighting	4 D/Cs.	17/1035	5223N/ 45W	Submerging U-boat, 200°, 8 knots.
17/0935	Liberator M/86	10m pt. bow SC.	Sighting	2 D/Cs.	17/1115	5225N/ 59W	Submerging U-boat, 100°, 6 knots.
	(Liberator M/86)				17/1437	5132N/3010W	Submerging U-boat, Eastern course.
17/1336	Liberator G/120	10m pt. beam SC.	Sighting	4 D/Cs., D/C fail	17/1548	5128N/2932W	Periscope, 330
17/1448	Liberator G/120	10m stb. bow SC.	Sighting	2 U-boats	17/2006	5119N/3019W	U-boat, 45°, 10 knots.
17/1908	Liberator J/120	25m stb. beam HX.	Sighting	5 D/Cs. 3 U-boats	17/2008	5121N/3000W	Submerging U-boat, 45°, 10 knots.
17/1947	Liberator J/120	25m stb. quart. HX.	Sighting	1 D/Cs.	17/2151	5118N/3031W	3 submerging U-boats, 20°, 10 knots.
17/1956	Liberator J/120	25m stb. quart. HX.	Sighting	—	17/2156	5113N/3020W	Submerging U-boat, 20°, 10 knots.
18/1328	Liberator E/120	10m stb. quart. SC.	Sighting	4 D/Cs.	18/1428	5331N/2745W	U-boat
18/1640	Liberator N/120	60m astern HX.	Sighting	—	18/1750	5310N/2925W	Submerging U-boat, 70°, 7 knots.
18/1712	Liberator B/120	22m astern SC.	Sighting	2 D/Cs.	18/1812	5308N/2612W	U-boat
18/1722	Liberator X/120	35m stb. quart. SC.	Sighting	—	18/1822	5302N/2750W	Submerging U-boat, 70°, 12 knots.
18/1757	Liberator B/120	8m stb. quart. HX.	Sighting	4 D/Cs.	18/1845	5320N/2752W	U-boat
18/1811	Liberator N/120	50m astern HX.	Radar/Sight	—			
	Liberator X/120	10m stb. bow SC.	Sighting	3 D/Cs.			
18/2005	Liberator M/120	40m stb. quart. HX.	Sighting	6 D/Cs.	18/1945	5302N/2732W	U-boat, 360°
					18/2106	5312N/2840W	U-boat, 45° 10 knots.
18/2038	Liberator B/120	22m stb. quart. SC.	Sighting	—	18/2128	5335N/2913W	U-boat, 90° 4 knots.
					18/2136	5315N/2800W	U-boat
19/0824	Fortress B/206	30m Bb. quart. HX.	Sighting	4 D/Cs.	19/0924	5435N/2530W	U-boat Eastern course.
19/0914	Fortress M/220	16m stb. quart. SC.	Sighting	4 D/Cs.	19/1014	5355N/2331W	Submerging U-boat, 330°
19/1045	Sunderland E/423	26m stb. bow SC.	Sighting	—	19/1155	5403N/2246W	Periscope over U-boat (Aircraft as 1155) Eastern course, 5 knots
19/1232	Sunderland E/423	5m pt. beam, SC.	Sighting	2 D/Cs.	19/1316	5440N/2548W	Submerging U-boat, 10°
19/1216	Sunderland V/228	48m astern HX.	Sighting	4 D/Cs.	19/1318	"	(same aircraft)
					19/1333	"	Submerging U-boat (same aircraft) Depth charge attack. over U-boat
19/1925	Liberator J/120	45m pt. quart. SC.	Sighting	2 D/C.	19/2026	5424N/2319W	Submerging U-boat (same aircraft) Eastern course, 10 knots
					19/2028	"	(same aircraft) Depth charge drop.

19/2330	Liberator J/120	9m stb. quart. SC.	Sighting	D/C fail	20/0030	5417N/2114W	Submerging U-boat, 90°, 11 knots.
20/0750	Sunderland Z/201	18m stb. quart. SC.	Sighting	2 D/Cs.	20/0855	5438N/1921W	Submerging U-boat, 220°, 10 knots.
20/0835	Sunderland H/423	35m astern SC.	Sighting	—	20/0938	5427N/1950W	Submerging U-boat
20/0855	Sunderland F/423	110m stb. quart. SC.	Sighting	5 D/Cs.	20/1003	5404N/2157W	U-boat
					20/1004		(same aircraft), depth charge drop.
					20/1015	,, 2035W	U-boat
20/1327	Sunderland F/423	60m stb. quart. SC.	Sighting	1 D/C.	20/1430	5422N/1910W	U-boat
					20/1427	,,	(same aircraft), low-level attack.
20/1613	Sunderland T/201	250m astern	Sighting	—	20/1445	5530N/1930W	Submerging U-boat, 270°, 10 knots.
					20/1716	5438N/2450W	Submerging U-boat.
					20/1800	5447N/2303W	U-boat
20/1744	Sunderland T/201	210m pt. quart. SC.	Sighting	6 D/Cs.	20/1910	5530N/2315W	U-boat, probably 2 hits.

APPENDIX 9

The Summing up of the Commander U-boats on March 20, 1943

The convoy operation against the HX convoy bound for Britain lasted four days, from March 16 to March 20, 1943. In a very strong westerly wind the convoy was found on the morning of March 16 in BD 1491. The fact that it was early in the day meant that nearly all the *Burggraf* boats in the patrol line could get there by the evening of the same day in order to make a surprise attack on the convoy that night. As with so many convoy operations, this surprise attack by many boats in the first night achieved the greatest success.

In all, 38 boats were deployed. They were all on the scene by the second day and during the second night. Including outward and homeward-bound boats, an average of about 20 were in the vicinity of the convoy each day.

The operation was very much affected by bad visibility on the second day with the unfortunate result that at the beginning of the second night only a few boats were in the area of the convoy. Then at 0300 hrs in the morning of the second day a second convoy was found, probably the SC convoy, which was in the same area, only 120 miles ahead. Because the Command did not know their precise positions, the individual boats were given freedom to manoeuvre and were able to operate against the convoy nearest to them. Consequently, some of the boats were withdrawn from the main convoy and operated against the new one.

Contact with both convoys could be maintained—with brief interruptions. But on the second day there was strong air defence—land and sea-based aircraft. The surface escort was also strengthened with the result that from the second day onwards the boats had a very hard struggle. This was made even more severe on the last two days of the operation because of the particularly calm weather in the area of the convoy. Despite the deteriorating situation, the boats were constantly able to register further successes after the first attack: some of these were underwater daylight attacks. A total of 32 ships of 186000 tons and a destroyer were sunk; in addition, another nine hits were obtained on ships. This is the biggest success so far in a convoy battle. It is all the more gratifying because nearly 50% of the boats participated in the success.

After the first surprise attack the enemy's defence became perceptibly stronger. Nevertheless, it is probable that no boat was lost in the operation.

It is possible that the *U 384* was found by the enemy air force after the operation had been broken off. This boat has not since reported. Two boats were badly damaged by aircraft depth charges with the result that the operation had to be abandoned. Nearly all the boats were attacked by depth charges from ships and aircraft, but, apart from the two severely damaged boats, there were no serious consequences.

Notes on the Security of the German Decoding Systems*

Translated by Lt. Col. A. J. Barker

Shortly after the manuscript of this book had been sent to the publishers, the author learned that three new books dealing with Allied code-breaking operations in World War 2 had appeared in Poland, France and Britain respectively. (1) Published in Britain, Group Captain F. W. Winterbotham's book caused a sensation as he had held an important post at the British Code and Cipher School at Bletchley Park. Because until 1975 code-breaking techniques were considered to be a classified subject, Winterbotham's account was based solely on personal recollections. But his book stimulated interest which led to the publication (2) of a number of articles, some of which were critical (3) of Winterbotham's claims—the criticism stemming mainly from circles associated with the Royal Navy. Because of the controversy that had been aroused, the British Government reviewed the security classification of wartime deciphering activities and sanctioned the publication of certain files on the subject in the spring of 1976.

During the past twelve months the author has been studying the problems associated with the World War II code-breaking operations—in particular those related to the German Navy's radio traffic. For this study it was necessary to reproduce the sequence of development for the *Kriegsmarine*'s decoding machine, and on the basis of declassified information available this appeared to be a formidable undertaking. Fortunately it was found that some gaps in the story could be closed with information provided by experts who had worked on the original projects. For this information and other help the author is indebted to the following: Dr Erich Hüttenhain, formerly employed in the Coding Section of the German High Command; Captain Hanns Singer of the German Navy who was concerned with the development of cipher equipment for the *Kriegsmarine*; and Captain Hans Meckel, also of the German Navy, who was responsible for telecommunications in the German U-Boat Command. On the Allied side the help and cooperation afforded by the naval historian Captain S. W. Roskill; Vice-Admiral B. B.

---

*The figures in parentheses which appear in this text refer to the References section.

Schofield, Director of the Trade Division; Commander Patrick Beesly, Acting Head of the Admiralty's Submarine Tracking Room; Mrs. Mary Z. Pain, wartime assistant to the Royal Navy's Liaison Officer at the Code Centre Bletchley Park; Commander M. G. Saunders; Captain Kenneth Knowles, Chief of the Convoy Routing Section—Washington's equivalent to the British Submarine Tracking Room, is gratefully acknowledged. Their efforts facilitated access to the relevant documents in the Public Records Office, and made possible the correct interpretation of their contents. This, then is the background to the brief survey of German cipher systems and the British code-breaking operations which follows.

THE DEVELOPMENT OF THE CIPHER SYSTEMS BASED ON THE CIPHER MACHINES *ENIGMA* AND "M"

Radio traffic in war is an important source of intelligence, as radio waves cannot be limited to specific receivers and military transmissions are picked up by the enemy. A listening watch is maintained on enemy radio frequencies, and all transmissions are monitored. The evaluation process of such transmissions then begins by three different methods.

The *evaluation of contents* system takes clear texts and using them in comparison attempts to decode or decipher the encoded texts by analytical or technical methods one of which is code-breaking. Even without being able to understand the contents of the messages, however, a good deal of information will already have been revealed. An *analysis of the traffic*—its overall density and the relationship of transmissions to particular stations—will indicate the deployment of the enemy's forces and hence his Order of Battle. It may also indicate that he is concentrating units for an operation; this is important information of current interest. Additionally, *direction finding techniques* enable the geographical location of a transmitter to be plotted. This information, together with that gleaned from the traffic analysis, enables conclusions to be drawn to the positioning and movement of enemy units and vessels.

Thus, from one or more of the three components of the radio-monitoring process it is possible to gain a fairly accurate picture of the deployment of enemy radio transmitters [and hence of units and vessels]. Consequently [in World War 2], in order to make the construction of the intelligence jigsaw more difficult, army and air force units would employ telephone and teletype communications for as long as possible and until they were actually operationally deployed. Ships in port would also use the shore telephone links, and vessels at sea would preserve radio silence for as long as possible before an operation or until their presence had been detected by the enemy.

If the three components of the radio-monitoring process appear to be overshadowed by interest in code-breaking procedures, it must be stressed that traffic analysis and direction finding always played a major role in wartime intelligence—often supplementing the information disclosed by the code-breakers, and facilitating the proper evaluation of such information.

There are two methods of encoding a text. The simplest is to substitute different letters and figures for those appearing in the original. This substitution process may range from the replacement of one letter by another, producing a form of code easily cracked, via complicated exchange systems requiring the use of manually serviced exchange tablets, to mechanical systems in which the exchange of letters is effected in such a way that a specific letter or figure of the original text is replaced by the same substitute letter only after long periods. The second method involves the use of a form of dictionary termed a Code Book by means of which groups of letters in the text—words, phrases, or sentences—are replaced by arbitrarily assigned signals known as a code group. A combination of both methods is of course possible—code groups being reencoded by a letter exchange system.

Because it increased the length of periods in the letter substitution system the invention of the cryptographic cylinder was an important advance. Rows of figures or letters of the alphabet are inscribed on an adjustable ring and during an encoding operation this ring is automatically rotated when a letter of the text has been exchanged for the appropriate symbol on the cylinder. Thus, in a word of the uncoded text in which the same letter appears twice, the same symbol is not repeated. This automatic rotation— the symbol shunting which rearranges the encoding alphabet—is known by cryptographers as a "Caesar" series, and a message encoded in this method, while more difficult to solve than messages encoded by the two simpler methods, is still relatively easy to decipher. However, the cryptographic cylinder continued to serve as the basis of many sophisticated machines, but in power-driven machines the contacts on the starting symbols were linked electrically to contacts on other symbols arbitrarily selected as the end symbols of the message; the effect was to upset the continuity of the symbols.

During the 1920s a number of inventors developed cipher machines with cryptographic cylinders, and some of these machines were produced and marketed with varying degrees of commercial success. (4) One of the inventors was a certain Hugo Alexander Koch, who registered a patent in Holland in 1919. Four years later Koch transferred his rights to a German, Arthur Scherbius, who embodied Koch's patent and his own ideas in the *Enigma—A* coding machine, which was produced that year. While other cipher machines employed three to five cylinders rotating in the same direction, the *Enigma—A* was unique in having four cylinders—three rotating in one direction causing a fourth to counter-rotate, with the counter-rotating roller transferring a secondary movement back to the other three. By this means a double encoding effect was obtained, and decoding could be performed with the same setting on the machine.

The somewhat clumsy *Enigma—B* was developed from the original *A* model, and in 1926 Scherbius produced the *Enigma—C*, a smaller and more compact version of the earlier machines. On February 9 1926 a modified version of this machine was taken into service by the German Navy (then the *Reichsmarine*). (5) The modified *Enigma—C* had a keyboard similar to that of a typewriter (29 letters A–Z and the ä, ö, ü vowel variations). Above this keyboard there was an illuminated panel carrying an arrangement of 29 letters and a cylinder housing for an entry roller on the right, a return roller on the left, and three coding cylinders in the middle. These coding cylinders, which were interchangeable, could be inserted into the machine or removed at will; each of them carried 28 disks, inscribed with letters or numbers, which could be rotated and arranged in different ways in regard to each other, and to the other cylinders.

This machine was employed by the German Navy until 1933 when it was replaced by an improved version. (6) In the meantime, however, Scherbius had produced a series of *Enigma* machines for commercial exploitation.

In 1923 prototypes of the *A* and *B Enigmas* were exhibited at an International Postal Congress, but no orders of any consequence were forthcoming and Scherbius was on the verge of bankruptcy when he died. At this point the patent rights were bought up by two Berlin firms, Heimsoth and Rinke, and Konski and Kröger; moreover Scherbius's commercial enterprise was beginning to show dividends, as several machines had been sold abroad—to customers in Sweden, Poland and the USA. (7) In 1934 a model of the *Enigma* was sold to Japan, and three years later modified versions of this machine went into service first with the Japanese Navy and later with the Japanese Foreign Ministry. Top secret messages were encoded by these machines, and the *Enigma* system of letter-jumbling became widely known when the code-cracking successes of the US cryptologists William F. Friedman and Captain Lawrence F. Safford were publicized in the Pearl Harbor Committee of Inquiry. (7) In 1939 Friedman, whose studies began with the *Enigma* purchased by the USA earlier in the 1930s, started work on breaking the highest code of the Japanese government, "Code Purple"; and by August 1940 the type of circuitry the Japanese were using in their Code Purple machine had been reconceived. Three machines embodying the duplicated circuits of the Japanese original were then built—one going to the US Navy, and another which was shipped from Britain in HMS *King George V* in January 1941, to Singapore to monitor Japanese diplomatic and military radio traffic in South East Asia. Subsequently other machines were built and sent to Pearl Harbor and Manila. (8)

Meantime development work on the *Enigma* machines used by the German Army and Navy had continued. On October 1, 1934 the *Reichsmarine* replaced the "C" coding system with the "M" system. The main differences were that the new system had an additional key board with 26 double contacts—giving a maximum of a further 13 linkages; and the vowel modifications, which had been source of confusion in the "C" system, were omitted from the new key board. By this time also improvements had been incorporated in the Army's equipment and the modified version of the *Enigma—G* was now called the *Enigma—I.* On June 27, 1935 this machine was formally adopted as the "Army Encoding Machine" for the passage of intelligence information between Army, Navy and Air Force and other government departments. (10)

The fact that the Army and Air Force issued new instructions for the encoding procedure at this time is indicative of changes in technique. (11) The Navy's *Enigma—M* and the Army's *Enigma—I* machines each had five interchangeable coding cylinders, three of which were inserted in the machine at any time. This gave the machines a "code-period" of $26^3 - 26^2 = 16,900$. Only when this number of letters had been encoded did the symbols start to repeat themselves on the same cylinder settings. Thus to avoid the presence of pairs of symbols which enable cryptanalysts to crack a code it was essential never to code more than 16,900 consecutive letters without changing the coding key. By doing so, the code-period could be extended by several milliards.

Several alternative methods of effecting key changes were available. To begin with, as only three cylinders could be used at any one time, five cylinders offered a choice of *120 different cylinder inserts.* Secondly, as there were 26 disks on each of the three cylinders 26^3 *(i.e., 17,576) different disk settings* were available. With the selected cylinders in position in the machine there was the same number of 17,576 possible settings of the basic position for the symbols visible in the encoding windows. Thirdly the machine's electrical connections allowed further alternatives. In theory, by inserting the plugs in the control panel in different ways, 1,547 alternative circuits were possible. In effect only six to ten of the available plug positions in the panel were used.

The development of the *Kriegsmarine*'s *M* machine continued through 1938 and 1939 with the number of key cylinders being increased from five to seven. This gave a reserve of four cylinders with three in use. Initially the *M* cylinders I to V and the five *Enigma—I* cylinders were identical, so that—if the key settings were known—it was possible to decode *Wehrmacht* signals with a Navy code book. (13). Cylinders VI and VII, and eventually a new cylinder VIII which was introduced at the beginning of the war, were reserved for naval use, and naval signals encoded with these cylinders could not be deciphered by an *Enigma—I* machine. This fact was to be of considerable importance in the light of subsequent events. With seven cylinders the number of alternative cylinder-insert positions on the *Enigma—M* was increased to 210, and later, when the new cylinder was introduced, to 336.

The staff of the German telecommunications department was well aware of the danger of a coded message being deciphered because of the repetitive use of the same settings on a particular cipher machine, and efforts were made to prevent this happening. Instructions were issued that either the "inner adjustment" (i.e., the cylinder and disk positions) or the "external adjustment" (i.e., the cylinders to be used and the plug panel contacts) or both should be changed daily. Initially there were three alternative systems with the *Enigma—M*: "M—General," "M—Offizier" and "M—Staff." According to which system was in use the "inner adjustment" was supposed to be changed at irregular monthly intervals (M—General), or every day (M—Staff), while the "external adjustment" was changed daily for all three systems.

Even with the foregoing daily changes however, many symbols could still be repeated if the encoding of each message started from the same basic setting. So a separate coding key was used for every message processed by both the *Enigma—I* and *Enigma—M* machines. Messages of more than 180 letters had to be broken down into groups, each of which was encoded with a different coding key. The methods of doing this varied according to the machine that was used. With the *Enigma—I* the cryptographer made a random selection of three of a given set of letters, and these were tapped twice on to the machine in its basic encoding setting of the day. The six symbols delivered by the machine were then set as a prefix to the message. To identify the coding key which was to be used it was now necessary to consult the current key-table; this contained four basic groups, each of three letters. Having selected one of these groups the cryptographer would then add two other designated letters to form a five figure group. This was superimposed on the basic setting to become the enciphering base of the five letter groups into which the text of the uncoded signal was broken. Apart from the code-key information which prefixed a message when it was transmitted, the signal started with a date-time group and a figure quoting the total number of letters in it—including the message key.

In the case of the *Enigma—M* the groups which were needed to identify the system and the code-key in use were picked from a book of radio callsigns and recognition groups. As with the *Enigma—I* the selected group was tapped twice on to the machine in its basic setting. Another letter, chosen at random, followed the message text. At the end of the text the final group comprised the last three letters of the message, preceded by the random letter which denoted the start of the message. In this case the group taken from the radio call sign book constituted the key by which the message was encoded in four letter groups. In its encoded form the message was preceded by a date-time group, and—up until the outbreak of war—a four symbol group taken from the call sign book, indicating the address and the designation of the originator; the total number of groups in the message was also given. During the war, in order to make the work of the enemy cryptanalysts more difficult, addresses and designations were omitted unless they were incorporated in the text; in their place at the beginning of the message a current "guide" number would be transmitted. (15)

For technical reasons, to reduce the amount of material enciphered on any particular day—and hence using the same basic day code, the units and stations transmitting coded messages were grouped into *communication circuits* to which special frequencies were allotted, and into *code-circles* with their own codes.

Operational, tactical and geographical considerations dictated the composition and organization of the communication centers. In the case of the German Navy the limits of the so-called "circuits" extended as the war progressed and there were special frequencies for the Navy's different components—for the main battle fleet; for the cruisers, light cruisers and their supply vessels operating in distant regions; for the patrol boats and so on. Solely for the U-boats, eight operational circuits (*Schaltungen*) were kept for transmissions to and from submarines operating in close proximity to the enemy shores. These were dubbed the "Atlantic," "Ireland," "America I," "America II," "Africa," "Norway," "Mediterranean" and "Black Sea" *Schaltungen* and were in fact four-fold, in as much as they covered communications in one or two shortwave, the medium and the long wave bands.

Code-circles were organized wholly according to operational requirements. At the beginning of the war there were two simple traffic divisions: "M-Home Waters" and "M-Foreign Waters," and toward the end of 1942 these divisions were codenamed "Hydra" and "Aegir." Subsequently, for security reasons and because the amount of signal traffic had increased so much, it was found necessary to subdivide Hydra and Aegir. So "Triton" was created for the U-boats operating in the Atlantic, "Potsdam" for units deployed in the eastern half of the Baltic, "Süd" for surface vessels operating in the Mediterranean, "Neptune" for ships of the main battlefleet, "Medusa" for U-boats exercising in the Baltic and Home Waters. All the units concerned could, of course, use either the "M-General," "M-Offizier" or "M-Staff" coding systems. In 1943, at the height of the war, the German Navy alone had no less than 40 different code-circles, 24 of which operated the "M" machine—the others working with less complex manual systems.

To lessen the risk of surface vessel and U-boat locations being given away by their radio transmissions, a special "short signal" procedure was introduced during the winter of 1939–40. With the aid of a special "Short-Signal book" the text of a message was reduced by compressing sentences and phrases into single words or syllables; these were then coded by the standard method and transmitted on the appropriate "M-General," "M-Offizier" or "M-Staff" channel. Short signals were invariably prefixed by two Greek letters.

Several modifications were made to the *Enigma* machines to improve the security of the codes. The most important of these were *switch gaps* on the coding cylinder and the development of a new "M-4" machine. The introduction of the switch gaps did not interfere with the rotation of the disks on the cylinders in the normal course of operation, but they did stop the disks slipping and "jumping" to positions which were not programmed. It has not so far been possible to determine the date when this particular modification was effected; in all probability it was rather late in the war—the beginning of 1944 at the earliest. The *Enigma-M4* went into production in 1941 and was issued to units in that year and in 1942. The main difference between the M4 and its predecessors "M" (old model), MI, M2, and M3 was that the new machine had four coding cylinders instead of three. As before, the operating "entry" cylinder was on the right, the operating "return" cylinder on the left. The position of the three main coding cylinders was also as before; and these were selected from the same cylinders I to VIII used in the earlier machines. On the left of these, however, there was a housing for one of the new so-called "Greek" cylinders. When the M4 was first introduced there was only one of these new cylinders—the "Beta," which was used with the disks in one fixed position. This gave the same series of settings on the M4 as were possible on the obsolescent machines, and so allowed the M4s to operate with them. When all the machines of a code-circle had been replaced by M4s, however, it became possible to utilize the full capacity of the Beta cylinder, and in case of the "Triton" area, the extended system came into service on March 8, 1943. The introduction of the fourth cylinder meant that the number of possible cylinder positions was increased to 1,344 and the disk settings, with all four cylinders operating, were increased to 26^4, i.e., 456,976. Other modifications and new machines were still being developed when the war ended; among the latter was an "M5" model for the *Wehrmacht*, and an "M10" for the Navy. The latter had ten coding cylinders initially, and would subsequently have had twelve. But none of these machines were ever used operationally.

CRACKING THE *ENIGMA* CODE

The Poles began work on decoding German radio messages during the Weimar Republic in 1928, and when a certain Colonel Langer realized the

Germans were using coding machines a number of gifted German-speaking mathematical graduates were recruited. (1928 was the year that an *Enigma-G* coding machine, manufactured by the Berlin firm of *Chiffriermaschinen A G* went into service with the Reichswehr). In 1932, after a security check and a short course to familiarize them with ciphers and coding techniques, the graduates were set to work. In all probability their efforts were helped by the famous Polish spy, Rittmeister J. V. Sosnowski, who acquired a commercial version of the *Enigma*. In any event the Poles managed to crack the early *Enigma* code within a few months. (16)

Meantime, in France, interest in the Reichswehr coding machine had been stirred by a 28-year-old employee of the German War Office, who offered his services to the French *Deuxieme Bureau* in 1930. Between the spring of 1931 and the summer of 1938 this spy, "Asche," met French Army intelligence officers no less than 19 times at different places in Europe, and handed over a total of 303 documents. An *Enigma* instructional handbook, a code-key manual, consecutive key files relating to codes and coding techniques from 1931 to 1934, and a good deal of material from the Luftwaffe Research Institute were among these documents. (17)

In 1931 the Polish and French Intelligence Services started to cooperate on *Enigma*, and in the middle of October 1932 the French passed on a package of the material supplied by Asche. This package contained the service manual and coding instruction for the *Enigma-G*. Soon afterward—at the end of 1932 or the beginning of 1933—the Polish cryptanalysts cracked the *Enigma-G* system, and by 1934 the Poles had begun to manufacture *Enigmas* in the AVA telecommunications factory in Warsaw. They then went on to develop mechanical and electromechanical aids, like the *Zyklometer* (Cyclometer) to help the deciphering process. (In essence the function of the *Zyklometer*, which resembled a combination of punched stencil and slide rule, speeded up the work of locating matching symbols in encoded messages). The AVA firm ultimately produced six facsimile *Enigmas*, which were connected together to form a single machine called *Bomba*. With the use of *Bomba* the deciphering process was partially automated with considerable savings in time and effort. However the modifications and new types of coding machines introduced by the Germans inevitably created fresh problems for the cryptanalysts, which interrupted the continuous sequence and decoding of German radio traffic. (In January 1935 when *Enigma I* went into service, and again in October 1938, there were long breaks until the new coding systems were cracked.)

Anglo-French cooperation in the deciphering field began toward the end of 1938. Following preliminary discussions in Paris early the following year, British, French and Polish experts met in Warsaw on 24–25 July 1939, when the Poles, led by Colonel Langer, demonstrated the reconstructed version of the *Enigma* and their *Bomba*, to Captain Alistair Denniston and Mr. Alfred Dilwyn Knox of Britain and Major Bertrand and Captain Braquerie of France. Then in August, shortly before the outbreak of war, the Poles transferred one of their *Enigma* machines to Paris and another to London.

The whirlwind campaign in Poland precluded the effective use of the Polish decoding service, and masked the achievements of their cryptanalysts. However Colonel Langer's team of 14 experts, which escaped to France by way of Romania, was absorbed by the deciphering department of the French Intelligence Service. With the knowledge they had already acquired themselves, combined with the experience of the Poles, the French cryptologists now began to show a record of mounting success. Between October 28, 1939 and the start of the Norwegian campaign no less than 25 daily codes were cracked, enabling 947 radio messages to be deciphered. Most of these messages were originated by or transmitted to the *Luftwaffe*, the rest were Army signals. Between April 11 and May 12, 1940, 768 intercepted messages were deciphered, and during the campaign in France, between May 20 and June 14 the record was 3,074 messages. All in all from October 28, 1939 to June 14, 1940 a total of 121 of the daily codes employed in several code-circle areas were reconstructed. (18) However only half of them were cracked in sufficient time to allow any operational use to be made of information disclosed. Furthermore the Allied High Command does not appear to have had much confidence in this source of intelligence.

In Britain, Colonel Stewart Menzies of the British Army's intelligence service had had his attention drawn to the existence of *Enigma* by a report from Prague in 1938. Shortly afterward British intelligence managed to get hold of an engineer who had worked for the *Chiffriermachinen AG* in Berlin; this individual had fled from Germany to dodge the consequences of racial discrimination and had gone to Poland. From Poland he was taken to Paris where, under British orders, he supervised the building of a facsimile *Enigma*. (19)

Meanwhile British cryptanalysis of foreign code systems was continuing under Denniston's direction at the Government Code and Cipher School in London, and at the end of 1938 the efforts of the mathematicians and cryptographic specialists working there were concentrated on the *Enigma* system. A "Universal-Machine" was specially developed by the mathematician Alan S. Turing—one of Alfred Knox's assistants, for this research. In 1939, when the school moved from London to Bletchley Park, the knowledge and experience of the Poles and French was put to use, and a more complex deciphering machine was built to replace the "Universal." This new machine, which was named "The Bomb," was based on the Polish *Bomba*, but it also incorporated elements of the Turing design.

When "The Bomb" went into service at the beginning of April 1940 the first useful results emerging from radio intercepts related to *Luftwaffe* personnel problems. The fact that most of the messages originated with the *Luftwaffe* was probably due to its heavy dependence on radio communication while flying, and to the fact that *Luftwaffe* radio discipline was inferior to that of the *Wehrmacht*. Moreover the *Wehrmacht* was generally able to make far more use of land line communications, which, of course, were relatively secure. Not until 1940, when orders to the Panzer formations rapidly advancing deep into France had to be relayed by radio, was it possible to collect sufficient material to enable the *Wehrmacht*'s code to be broken. Just how the *Wehrmacht* codes were in fact cracked is a matter of conjecture. The painstaking efforts of the cryptanalysts may well be wholly responsible; on the other hand their work may have been simplified when a German armored car was captured by the Allies. This vehicle, which was being used as the command post of one of the Panzer columns, was carrying an *Enigma* machine and it must be supposed therefore that the coding instructions fell into Allied hands. (20)

Winterbotham, who was responsible for the security of the cryptography projects—now called *Ultra*—and the passage of information gleaned from the deciphered intercepts to Churchill, claims that deciphered *Luftwaffe* messages had great operational significance in the Battle of Britain. (21) In effect the information that was forthcoming was probably of greater strategic value than tactical importance. One fact that certainly emerged from the intercepts decoded early on was that the aim of the German air offensive was to engage the Royal Air Force and to destroy it prior to Operation Sea Lion—the invasion of Britain. Radar stations along the south coast of Britain gave early warning of the approach of *Luftwaffe* formations however, and Air Marshal Dowding was able to thwart the German aim by husbanding his forces and keeping losses to a minimum. As Winterbotham tells us (22), the deciphering of intercepted *Deutsches Afrika Korps* messages prior to Rommel's attempt to outflank the British positions at Alamein by way of Alam Halfa was of decisive importance. So too was the cryptanalysts' work during the campaigns in Sicily and Italy, and during the preparations for the Normandy landings. However, because of the restrictions that were imposed on German air traffic and improved security precautions, *Ultra*'s value diminished in the later phases of the war. Indeed, much of the surprise attained at the start of the Ardennes offensive, can be attributed to paucity of information provided by *Ultra*.

The British Code Centre speeded up in 1943 when an improved decoding machine, "Colossi," was introduced to Bletchley Park. It was one of the first computers and its components included two thousand thermionic valves. It was used to solve primarily the settings of the Siemens-teleprinter cipher machine that encoded *Funk Fenschreiber* (wireless teleprinter messages) which were used from 1942–3 for high-level communications.

WORK ON THE *KRIEGSMARINE* "M" CODE

The main effort of the Polish and French cryptanalysts was concentrated on the *Enigma-I* codes, and the British specialists at Bletchley Park followed suit. Elsewhere Royal Navy cryptanalysts were also trying to crack the German cipher system; these individuals at first worked independently but maintained contact with Bletchley Park through an RN Liaison Officer, Lieut Commander M. G. Saunders. Bletchley Park began working on the *Kriegsmarine* "M" code and recruited new personnel.

In the spring of 1941, when the naval cryptanalysts had made no progress, the Admiralty ordered all operational units at sea to try to capture enemy coding machines and coding equipment, (25) and the first complete coding machine was captured on May 8 1941 when *U-110* surrendered. Two months earlier, on March 3 1941, five code cylinders had been found aboard the patrol vessel *Krebs*. All this equipment was of the greatest importance; the cryptanalysts now had a lead and could start work on the "M" code in earnest. However, while the actual deciphering work was done at Bletchley Park, the naval experts insisted on evaluating the results themselves—much to the disgust of some of the pundits at Bletchley Park. It was best, argued the naval men, to evaluate deciphered messages at the Admiralty's Operational Intelligence Centre, where other naval intelligence from a variety of sources was available; furthermore any results that were forthcoming could then be quickly translated into action. (26)

The first positive results came soon after the capture of the *U-110*'s coding machine and coding documents found aboard the weather ship *München*. With this material the cryptanalysts were able to crack the "M" code and decipher radio communications between units in the code-circles "M-Home Waters" and "M-Foreign Waters." When Operation Bismarck was launched about a fortnight after the capture of *U-110*, this was not yet possible, but the benefits deriving from the deciphering of "M" Code communications began to be apparent about the end of May. (27) In June the organization of sea-borne supplies for naval units operating in the Atlantic which the Germans had built up for the Bismarck operation was completely disrupted by operations which brought the first fruits of the work of the Royal Navy's cryptanalysts and intelligence staff. In the course of these operations the coding equipment aboard the supply ships *Gedania* and *Lothringen,* the patrol ship *Gonzenheim,* and the weather ship *Lauenberg* fell into British hands. With the help of records taken from the *U-110,* convoys directed by the staff of the Admiralty's Submarine Tracking Room were able to dodge the German U-boat packs in the North Atlantic, and U-boat sinkings declined drastically.

Although the Germans did not know precisely what the *U-110* and the *München* had yielded, they were aware that some coding equipment had probably fallen into British hands when the four supply ships were captured. (28) So security was tightened and the two main code-circles were divided into smaller circles. However, it was some time before this could be done and the new arrangement probably did not start to become effective until the beginning of 1942. Communications with U-boats were concentrated in one code-circle area "Atlantic Front U-Boats" (code-named "Triton" at the beginning of 1943). Despite these changes, however, even when the captured code-books were time-expired and no longer applicable, the British were still able to decipher German radio-intercepts. Their success was due to the experience they had gained, and the new decoding machine which came into service at Bletchley Park during the second half of 1941. But the deciphering process took longer now. The new code-circle area for U-boats operating in the Atlantic was not working at this time and so it was possible to read the instructions and other communications radioed to them; time was the problem.

Let us assume that the maximum time needed to decipher a particular day-code—be it weeks initially, days later, or hours in the end—is 100 units. With luck a solution might be forthcoming after a lapse of only 5 units; on the other hand there were instances when it took 95 units to crack the code. Now, if one sets this time factor against U-boat communication timings, as in the theoretical example given below, it will be apparent which of the deciphered signals were of value for operational or tactical exploitation: In general the U-boats [operating in the North Atlantic] were given their instructions only after they had put to sea and negotiated a passage through the Iceland–Faeroe Ridge or had reached a longitude 20° West of the Bay of Biscay. A radio message then gave them the coordinates of a square of sea on to which they were to converge. To conserve fuel in getting to their square however, the instructions had to be radioed at least a week in advance. Consequently if such a message could be deciphered within five days the Admiralty was able to divert convoys away from the area where the U-boats were concentrating.

To counter this the commander of a U-boat pack would deploy his force across the path of an approaching convoy. How this was done depended on the information available at the time—and most of the information came from German radio-intercepts. In this instance orders were usually issued two to four days in advance and the time for the British to react was limited accordingly. More often than not it was insufficient for a diversionary maneuver. Only when the deciphering process was completed in 5, 10 or 15 units of the maximum was it possible to lead the convoy away from the U-boat concentrations.

This situation changed early in 1943. By then the Germans were able to decipher Allied messages directing convoys so quickly that the Commander U-boats was able to redeploy the submarines across the new course of the convoys, and the Allies rarely had time for further countermeasures.

The following example of what happened is taken from the records of the German deciphering service. In the first 20 days of March 1943, there were 35 Allied convoys in the North Atlantic. The presence of 30 of these convoys was disclosed by radio-intercepts, and 175 position reports and orders to change course were deciphered. Of these, however, only 10 could be passed to a U-boat pack commander in sufficient time for him to make use of the information.

The position on the British side was probably much the same during the second half of 1941; otherwise it is scarcely likely that the U-boats would have sunk so many ships in the North Atlantic. From British files recently made accessible to the public we now know that it was not possible to decipher messages from U-boats in the operational area between February and December 1942. On the other hand it seems that it was still possible to decode "M-Home Waters" (Hydra) communications. Why this black-out occurred has yet to be cleared up. The most likely reason is that U-boats in the North Atlantic ceased to be part of the "Hydra" code-circle and communicated on the newly created "Triton" code-circle area for which special regulations applied. It is also possible that at some time in January 1942 the new coding cylinders with switch gaps (mentioned earlier in this appendix) were taken into service in the "Triton" area.

There were two reasons why the effects of the blackout were limited for quite some time. To begin with it was still possible to decipher messages intercepted on the "Hydra" net, on which the escort vessels in Norwegian waters and the Bay of Biscay were communicating. As many of these messages were concerned with U-boat deployments, the Submarine Tracking Room could at least assess the number of submarines at sea and from radio bearings get an approximate picture of their distribution. From January to July 1942, however, the bulk of the U-boat force was scattered along the east coast of the United States, in the Caribbean and in the Gulf of Mexico. During this phase of the war at sea the U-boats operated singly, attacking lone, unescorted merchantmen. The operations were conducted in a vast area, and the fact that the Allied ships were not marshaled in convoys made it virtually impossible on the German side to direct the U-boats to their targets. Similarly on the Allied side it was difficult to utilize the intelligence emerging from the deciphered messages and apply it as was done later in the battle between U-boat packs and convoys. The operation of the *Hecht* group in May and June 1942, when—with only six submarines—the Germans intercepted five consecutive Allied convoys in the middle of the North Atlantic, illustrated what might have happened on the Atlantic route if the British had *not* been able to decipher radio-intercepts.

In the event Bletchley Park cracked the "Triton" area code in December 1942 and from then on all U-boat radio messages could be deciphered. In January 1943, when there was a pronounced decrease in the number of convoys sighted by the U-boats, the Germans believed that bad weather at the time was responsible. In actual fact the main reason for the decrease stemmed from the British ability to decipher messages to and from the U-boat packs and steer the convoys away from them. During January 1943 this was relatively easy as there was only a limited number of German submarines in the North Atlantic that month. But as the number of submarines increased, it became progressively more difficult for the convoys to make detours through safe waters. Moreover after February so many U-boats were at sea that it was possible to deploy two or three packs in patrol lines as early warning stations to report the approach of an Allied convoy. The fact that the Germans were also able to decipher Allied signals and pass on the information gleaned from them to the U-boats was another important factor. This intelligence was of direct operational value; the realization that the Allies were able to pinpoint U-boat locations was of indirect significance but no less important as it suggested that the German codes had been compromised. To clear this up the Navy's High Command ordered the Naval Signal Branch to undertake a thorough investigation, and the views expressed by the subsequent Court of Inquiry were recorded in the War Diary of the U-Boat Command for March 5, 1943. (See App. 15.4) After reviewing the different sources of intelligence available to the enemy, the conclusion was that codes had not been compromised. Nevertheless, from then on, to ensure that there should be no question of the location of the squares to which the U-boats were directed being disclosed, the symbols denoting the coordinates of the squares were encoded separately in a special cipher. This meant that the Admiralty Submarine Tracking Room had to rely on other sources to establish the location of the squares. (29)

One improvement in the coding system which facilitated the security of German transmissions about this time derived from the introduction of the fourth code-cylinder in the "M4" machine, as this increased the coding period from 26^3 to 26^4. Security was further enhanced when changes in code-keys were announced orally [over the air]—so doing away with code-files. (When code-files were lost or captured the inevitable time-lag which occurred before new code-files could be issued and the system changed meant that the messages were vulnerable to the enemy cryptanalysts. Oral announcements were, of course, disguised and passed on a prearranged code.)

Against these improved security measures must be set the gains in knowledge and experience acquired by the British experts at Bletchley Park. The existence of the "M4" was known and the British cryptanalysts were awaiting the employment of its fourth coding cylinder with some trepidation. The first indication came on March 8, 1943 when the key-word ordering units to change to four coding cylinders appeared in a German intercept. Rear Admiral Edelsten, Director of the Admiralty's Anti-Submarine Warfare Division, reported gloomily to Admiral of the Fleet Sir Dudley Pound. ". . . The expected has happened," he wrote in a letter dated March 9, 1943, "The Director of Naval Intelligence announced yesterday that information on U-boat movements is unlikely to be forthcoming for some time—perhaps even months . . ." (30) The erstwhile Director of the Economic Warfare Division, Vice Admiral B. B. Schofield recalls that this news—coming at a time when the U-boat war was at its peak—was extremely depressing. (31)

From reports and copies of the weekly U-Boat Situation Reviews published by the Submarine Tracking Room which are now accessible at the Public Records Office, we know the extent of intelligence information extracted from German radio-intercepts concerning the operations which took place during the passage of convoys HX229 and SC122. (32) As early as March 22, it seems, the Admiralty was in possession of deciphered versions of all messages passed between March 15 and 19 to the U-boats lying in wait for these two convoys. It is clear therefore, that the cracking of the German code systems was a crucial factor in the convoy battles of April and May (1943) which were seen later to have been the turning point of the U-boat war. Because the Allies had forewarning, many of the planned U-boat operations were never executed. Sudden realization by the British Office of Operational Intelligence that the Germans had cracked the British code then in use proved to be another disaster for the Germans at this time. When the British changed their code systems on June 1, 1943, the German cryptanalysts were faced with problems of tremendous complexity, many of which they never succeeded in solving before the war ended. Meanwhile their British counterparts were going from strength to strength as improved versions of "Colossi" steadily reduced code-cracking times, and deciphering times were correspondingly shortened.

By the end of the war the time taken to decipher traffic intercepted on the busy "M-Hydra-General" and "M-Triton-General" nets was usually only marginally greater than the time taken by the Germans to transmit the messages. Times varied according to circumstances, of course. For example, during the final operation of the *Scharnhorst* on December 25–26, 1943, from the time of transmission to the time the deciphered message arrived by teletype from Bletchley Park at the Operations Intelligence Centre, between 5 and 31 hours had elapsed if it had been sent by Admiral "Nordmeer," 8 to 12 hours if it had been sent by U-Boat Command Norway, 4 to 18 hours on the Battle Fleet net, and 3 to 8 hours if it had been transmitted from one of the *Luftwaffe* stations. As a general rule more time had to be spent on deciphering messages from the communication circles which were used least frequently, and the "M-Offizier" and "M-Staff" channels needed more time than "M-General." A few codes, such as those used in the "Neptune" area were never cracked.

Finally, to get a true appreciation of the value and effect of the British code-cracking activities, a good deal of research has still to be done. By reconstructing the circumstances from original records of transmissions—including the codes employed at the different communication circles on the German side, together with the British response, starting at the radio-intercept phase and continuing through the deciphering process to the ultimate operational application of the intelligence gained—it should be possible to get a precise picture from which the proper conclusions may be drawn. A summary judgment here would be quite out of place.

REFERENCES

1 Kozaczuk, Wladyslaw: *Bitwa o tajemnice.* Ksiazka i Wiedza. Warsaw 1967.
    Bertrand, Gustave: *Enigma ou la plus grande enigme de la guerre 1939–1945.* Librairie Plon. Paris 1973
    Winterbotham F. W.: *The Ultra Secret.* Weidenfeld & Nicolson. London 1974
2 Articles in various journals and magazines, and
    Brown, Anthony Cave: *Bodyguard of Lies.* Harper & Row. New York 1975
    (The German version, published by Desch, Munich 1976 was entitled: *The Invisible Front: Was the Outcome of the Second World War Decided by the German Secret Service?*)
3 e.g., Articles by Captain S. W. Roskill in the *Naval Review* of 1975, 185–88; and by Patrick Beesly also in issues of the *Naval Review* (for the months of July and October 1975 and January 1976) entitled "The Operational Intelligence Centre of the Admiralty." (The latter has been reprinted in *Marine-Rundschau* 1976, 147–64, 368–83)
4 Kahn, David: *The Codebreakers: The Story of Secret Writing.* Weidenfeld & Nicolson. London 1967, 420–23
5 *Code-key C.*; Secret Naval Service Instruction No 21, issued by the German War Office (Navy Command). Berlin 1926

6   *Code-key C.*; German War Office Instruction No 21. Navy Command. Berlin 1933

7   Kahn, loc. cit. 10, 18–23, 565

8   Kahn, loc. cit. 23

9   *Code-key M (Instructions)*; Naval Command Secret Instruction No 32. Naval Command. Berlin 1934

10   *The Army Code-key.* Instructions for the Use of Codes and Coding-Methods in Communications between the Army, Navy, Air Force and Departments of the Civil Administration. Issued on 27.6.1935. Wehrmacht Instruction No 11, Navy Instruction No 390, Luftwaffe Instruction No 11. Printed by the German Stationery Office. Berlin 1935

11   *Instruction for the Use of the Coding Machine ENIGMA.* Issued on 12.1.1937. Printed by the Government Stationery Office Berlin 1937. Army Instruction No 13, Luftwaffe Instruction No 13

      Keying Instruction for the ENIGMA code-machine. Issued on 8.6.1937. Army Instruction No 14, Navy Instruction No 168, Luftwaffe Instruction No 14. Printed by the Government Stationery Office Berlin 1937

12   Navy Instruction No 32, 7

13   *Code-key M. Instructions for encoding.* Naval Command Instruction 32/1. Issued by the *Kriegsmarine* High Command. Berlin 1939

14   *Encoding Instructions for the ENIGMA Code-Machine.* Issued on 13.1.1940. Army Instruction No 14, Naval Instruction No 168, Luftwaffe Instruction No 14. Printed by the Government Stationery Office. Berlin 1940, 8–9

15   *The M-key. 'M-General' Procedure.* Naval Instruction No 32/1. Issued by the *Kriegsmarine* High Command 1940, paras 46–51

16   Kozaczuk, loc. cit, (German translation: *ENIGMA.* How the Code of the Fascists was cracked. Published in the journal *Horizont* 1975, issue Nos 41–49)

17   Bertrand, loc. cit., 27–35

18   Bertrand, loc. cit., 79

19   Brown, loc. cit., 17–21

20   Winterbotham, loc. cit., 28

21   Winterbotham, loc. cit., 40–55

22   Winterbotham, loc. cit., 64–82. See also Spiller, Roger J, "Some Implications of *ULTRA.*" Published in *Military Affairs*, April 1976, 49–54

23   especially Brown, loc. cit., 432–643

24   amongst others: Roskill, loc. cit. and Beesley, loc. cit.

25   see also among others: McLachlan Donald, *Room 39.* Weidenfeld & Nicolson, London 1968

      and also Beesly in *Marine-Rundschau*, loc. cit.

26   Beesly, loc. cit.

27   In this context it is important to note that the "Special Intelligence" files now available in the Public Records Office contain only the deciphered and translated German intercepts. Their code-area numbers and originators' time-groups are given but no mention is made of the time they were passed on to the Operational Headquarters. In any assessment of the value of the deciphering work this time factor must be taken into consideration.

28   SK1/MND: Operational Secret. Berlin 24.7.1941

      1.SK1. I.K.: Investigation into the losses following Operation Bismarck Berlin 13.7.42 as reproduced in Brennecke, Jochen: *Schlachtschiff Bismarck.*

(Battleship Bismarck) Climax and End of an Epoch. Koehlers, Jugenheim, 1960, 516–21

29 Beesly, loc. cit.
30 Gretton, Sir Peter: *Crisis Convoy,* Cassell, London 1974, 20
31 Vice Admiral Schofield: Letter to the author
32 ADM. 223, Vol. 16, 73–80 (Public Records Office Files)
33 ADM. 223, Vol. 15, 22.3.1943 (Public Records Office Files)

N.B. Nos 5, 6, 9, 10, 11, 12, 13, 14, 15 and 28 can only be found in the original German, under German titles. These are the English translations of these titles.

Bibliography

UNPUBLISHED SOURCES

Germany

Those German naval documents of the Second World War, which reached the naval archives, transferred from Berlin to Tambach, up to the beginning of 1945, survived. Following an agreement between the victorious powers they were assigned to Great Britain and handed over to the Naval Historical Branch of the Admiralty which set up a Foreign Documents Section to deal with them. Here, under the direction of Commander M. G. Saunders, RN, and with the help of Amtsrat Pfeiffer from the German Naval Archives Office, they were rearranged and provided with new PG numbers.

As the result of an agreement between Great Britain and the Federal Republic of Germany, the papers of the naval archives have since been handed back to the Federal Republic and entrusted to the Federal Military Archives Office in Freiburg. Certain special documents were however excluded, inter alia, the U-boat documents of the Second World War which remain in the custody of the Naval Historical Branch and have not yet been made available for source research.

However, the complete text of the War Diary of the Commander U-boats 1939–45 and a large number of excerpts from the war diaries of individual U-boats have been made available to the author.

From the documents in the Federal Military Archives Office particular use was made of:

—*Oberkommando der Kriegsmarine, Seekriegsleitung,*

1. Abteilung Kriegstagebuch, Part A, 1939–1943, particularly No. 43, 1.–31. March 1943.

—*Oberkommando der Kriegsmarine, Seekriegsleitung, Chef Marine Nachrichten Dienst X-B-Berichte 1939–1943,* particularly No. 9–15 from 4, 11, 18, 25.3., 1, 8, and 15.4.1943.

Great Britain

With the lapse of the 30-year rule, the military documents of the Royal Navy and Royal Air Force concerning the Second World War, which until then could only be used by the official historians in the Naval Historical Branch and the Air Historical Branch, were handed over to the Public Records Office and made available for general use. The following documents could be used:

—Admiralty, Naval Staff, Operations Division

—Pink Lists 1939–1945, particularly March 1st, 1943, April 1st, 1943.

—War Diary Summaries: Sitreps, particularly vols 126, 127, 128 March 1–8, March 9–15, March 16–23, 1943.

—Daily Summary of Naval Events, particularly vol. 12, Jan.–June 1943.
—Admiralty, Naval Staff, Trade Division
—British and Foreign Merchant Vessels Lost or Damaged by Enemy Action during Second World War. From September 3rd, 1939 to September 2nd, 1945. London: Admiralty 1945 (printed for official use only).
—Convoy Lists, particularly vol. 6, September 17th, 1942 to June 30th, 1943.
—Convoy Organization. Size, Cycles, Routeing, etc.
—Reports of Proceedings by Commodores of Convoys, particularly SC.122 (March 22nd, 1943), HX.229 (April 12th, 1943), HX.229A (March 29th, 1943), ON.168 (March 17th, 1943), ONS.169 (March 24th, 1943), ON.170 (March 24th, 1943), ONS.171 (March 29th, 1943), ON.172 (March 30th, 1943).
—Admiralty, Naval Staff, Anti-Submarine Division
—Analysis of U-boat Operations in the Vicinity of Convoys, particularly vol. 43, KMS.10, OS.44, XK.2, SL.126, vol. 44, SC.121, HX.228, SC.122, HX.229. (April 15th, 1943).
—Convoys and Escorts. Routeing of Convoys in North Atlantic.
—Enemy Submarine Attacks on H.M. Ships (3 vols.).
—H.M. Ships lost or damaged Reports.
—Submarine Attacks on Convoys and Counter-attacks by Escorts (3 vols.).
—Anti-Submarine Attacks and Operations, U-Boat Sighting Signals and MkXXIV Mine Attacks.
—Frustration of U-Boat Attacks: Grouping of HF/DF Stations to give quicker and more accurate information to Convoy Escorts.
—Installment of Radar, HF and DF equipment in destroyers and escort vessels.
—Western Approaches Command
—War Diaries, particularly vol. 1943.
—Reports of Proceedings by Senior Officers of Escort Groups of Convoys, particularly S.O.E. SC.122 (March 22nd, 1943), S.O.E. HX.229 (March 30th, 1943), S.O.E. HX.229A (April 13th, 1943), S.O.E. ON.168 (March 8th, 1943), ONS.169 (April 10th, 1943), S.O.E. ON.170 (March 16th, 1943), S.O.E. ON.171 (April 13th, 1943).

The Naval Historical Branch provided additional details about the composition of the convoy Escort Groups on the Britain–Gibraltar route and the personnel of individual ships in the Escort Groups. A number of contradictions in the wartime documents could be cleared up with the help of the Naval Historical Branch.

The Air Historical Branch provided excerpts from the Coastal Command Order of Battle for March 1943 and the summaries of the flights carried out by RAF Coastal Command in defense of convoys SC.122 and HX.229 and also answered particular queries.

Canada

The Directorate of History in the Department of National Defence answered numerous questions and provided the following details:

—Naval Service Headquarters Ottawa, Operations Division
—Daily State I of HMC ships, HM and Allied ships, operated by RCN authorities, March 1st, March 4th, March 6th, March 10th, March 23rd and March 30th, 1943.
—Information sheets incl. track charts of convoys SC.121, HX.228, SC.122, HX.229, HX.229A, ON.168, ONS.169, ON.170.

—Royal Canadian Air Force Headquarters
—RCAF Organization Newfoundland, March 1943.
—Summary of Operations March 10th to March 15th, 1943.

USA

The Division of Naval History in the Navy Department provided numerous individual documents concerning the convoy operations in March 1943, including in particular:
—Convoy information sheets (harbors and times of departure, composition of convoy and escort groups, ships with cargo and destination, data on losses and stragglers, etc.) for convoys: SC.122, HX.229, UGS.5A, UGF.6, UGS.6, UGS.6A, GUS.4, GUS.5, GUS.5B, GUF.5, GUS.5A.
—Sailing telegrams of Port Director New York for SC.122, HX.229, UGS.6.
—Report of Proceedings by S.O.E. of Convoy UGS.6, COMTASKFOR 33.

BOOKS AND ARTICLES

Adams, H. H., Lundeberg, Ph. K. & Rohwer, J. Der U-Bottkrieg—Die Schlacht im Atlantik 1939–1945. In: *Seemacht. Von der Antike bis zur Gegenwart.* Munchen: Bernard & Graefe, 1974. 521–50.

Andreev, Vasilij Ivanovich. *Borba na okeanskich kommunikatsivach.* Moskva: Voenizdat 1961.

Anrys, Henri. L'attaque du convoi TM.1. In: *Revue Maritime* 1967. No. 248, 1281–97.

———. Bataille pour le SC 122. In: *Revue Maritime* 1969. No. 462, 452–65.

The Battle of the Atlantic. London: H. M. Stationery Office 1946.

Bekker, Cajus. *Radar, Deull im Dunkel.* Oldenburg/Hamburg: Stalling 1958. 2nd ed. 1964.

———. *Verdammte See- Ein Kriegstagebuch der deutschen Marine.* Oldenburg/ Hamburg: Stalling 1971.

Bogolepov, V. P. *Blokada i kontrblokada. Borba na okeansko-morskich soobshcheniyach vo vtoroj mirovoj vojne.* Moskva: Voenizdat 1966.

Bonatz, Heinz. Die deutsche Marine-Funkaufklärung 1914–1945. In: *Wehrwissenschaftliche Berichte.* Darmstadt: Wehr und Wissen 1970.

Brennecke, Jochen. *Jäger—Gejagte. Deutsche U-Boote 1939–45.* Biberach: Koehler. 2nd ed. 1956. Engl. transl. by R. H. Stevens: *The Hunters and the Hunted.* London: Starke 1958.

Buchheim, Lothar-Günther. *Das Boot.* Hamburg: Hoffmann & Campe 1974.

Busch, Harald. *So war der U-Bootkrieg.* Bielefeld: Dt.Heimat-Verlag 2nd ed. 1954. Engl. transl. by L. R. P. Wilson: *U-Boats at War.* London: Putnam 1955.

Chalmers, William S. *Max Horton and the Western Approaches.* London: Hodder & Stoughton 1954.

Churchill, Winston Spencer. *The Second World War.* Vol. 1–6. London: Cassell 1950–54.

Creighton, Sir Kenelm. *Convoy Commodore.* London: Kimber 1956.

Cunningham, Viscount Andrew Browne. *A Sailor's Odyssey: An Autobiography.* London: Hutchinson 1952.

Dönitz, Karl. *Essay on the conduct of the war at sea.* Washington: Office of Naval Intelligence 1946.

————. *Zehn Jahre und zwanzig Tage*. Bonn: Athenäum 1958. Engl. transl. by R. H. Stevens and David Woodward: *Memoirs*. London: Weidenfeld & Nicolson 1959.

————. Die Schlacht im Atlantik in der deutschen Strategie des Zweiten Weltkrieges. In: *Marine-Rundschau* 61 (1964), S.63–76.

Easton, Alan. *50 North. An Atlantic Battleground*. London: Eyre & Spottiswoode 1963.

Eremeev, L. M. (&) Shergin, A. P. *Podvodnye lodki inostrannych flotov vo vtoroj mirovoj vojne*. Moskva: Voenizdat 1962.

Farago, Ladislas. *The Tenth Fleet*. New York: Obolensky 3rd ed. 1962.

Frank, Wolfgang. *Die Wölfe und der Admiral*. Oldenburg/Hamburg: Stalling 1953. Engl. transl. *The Sea Wolves*. New York: Rinehart 1955.

Freyer, Paul Herbert. *Der Tod auf allen Meeren: Ein Tatsachenbericht zur Geschichte des faschistischen U-Boot-Krieges*. Berlin (Ost): Dt.Militärverlag 1970.

————. *German, Italian and Japanese U-Boat Casualties during the War*. London: H.M. Stationery Office 1946.

Gallery, Daniel V. *Twenty Million Tons under the Sea*. Chicago: Regnery 1956.

Giessler, Hellmuth. Der Marine- Nachrichten- und Ortungsdienst. In: *Wehrwissenschaftliche Berichte*. München: Lehmanns 1971.

Goodhart, Philip. *Fifty Ships That Saved the World. The Foundation of the Anglo-American Alliance*. London: Heinemann 1965.

Gretton, Sir Peter. *Convoy Escort Commander*. London: Cassell 1964.

————. *Crisis Convoy: The Story of the Atlantic Convoy HX.231*. London: Davies 1974.

Hasselwander, Gerald E. Der US-Zerstörer Greer und *U 652* am 4.September 1941. In: *Marine-Rundschau* 59 (1962), 148–60.

Herlin, Hans. *Verdammter Atlantik: Schicksale deutscher U-Bootfahrer*. Hamburg: Nannen 1959.

Herzog, Bodo. *U-Boote im Einsatz 1939–1945*. Dorheim: Podzun 1970.

Hudson, J. L. *British Merchantmen at War 1939–1945*. London: H.M. Stationery Office 1944.

Jeschke, Hubert. U-Boottaktik. Zur deutschen U-Boottaktik 1900–1945. In: *Einzelschriften zur militärischen Geschichte des zweiten Weltkrieges 9*. Freiburg: Rombach 1972.

Joubert de la Ferté, Sir Philip B. *The Third Service: The Story Behind the Royal Air Force*. London: Thames & Hudson 1955.

Kahn, David. *The Codebreakers: The Story of Secret Writing*. London: Weidenfeld & Nicolson 1967.

Kemp, Peter K. *Victory at Sea, 1939–1945*. London: Muller 1957.

Kent, Sherman. *Strategic Intelligence for American World Policy*. Princeton University Press 1949.

Kerr, George F. *Business in Great Waters*. London: Faber & Faber 1951.

King, Ernest J. & Whitehill, Walter Muir. *Fleet Admiral King: A Naval Record*. New York: Norton 1952.

Lagevorträge des Oberbefehlshabers der Kriegsmarine vor Hitler 1939–1945. Ed. by Gerhard Wagner. München: Lehmanns 1972.

Land, Emory Scott. *The United States Merchant Marine at War*. Washington: U.S. Government Printing Office 1946.

————. *Winning the War with Ships*. New York: McBride 1958.

Lenton, H. T. & Colledge, J. J. *Warships of World War II*. London: Ian Allan 1963–64.

Lenton, H. T. German Submarines. Vol. 1–2, In: *Navies of the Second World War*. London: Macdonald 1965.

————. British Fleet and Escort Destroyers. Vol. 1–2, In: *Navies of the Second World War*. London: Macdonald 1970.

————. American Fleet and Escort Destroyers. Vol. 1–2. In: *Navies of the Second World War*. London: Macdonald 1971.

————. British Escort Ships. In: *W.W. 2 Fact Files*. London: Macdonald & Jane's 1974.

Lewis, David D. *The Fight tor the Sea: The Past, Present, and Future of Submarine Warfare in the Atlantic*. New York: World Publ. Co. 1961.

Lincoln, F. Ashe. *Secret Naval Investigator*. London: Kimber 1961.

Lohmann, Walter & Hildebrand, Hans H. *Die deutsche Kriegsmarine 1939–1945: Gliederung, Einsatz, Stellenbesetzung*. Bad Nauheim: Podzun 1956–1964.

Lund, Paul & Ludlam, Harry. *Night of the U-Boats*. (The story of S.C.7). London: Foulsham 1973.

Macintyre, Donald. *U-Boat Killer*. London: Weidenfeld & Nicolson 1956.

————. *The Battle of the Atlantic*. London: Batsford 1961.

McLachlan, Donald. *Room 39. Naval Intelligence in Action 1939–45*. London: Weidenfeld & Nicolson 1968.

Mallmann Showell, J. P. *U-Boats under the Swastika: An Introduction to German Submarines 1939–1945*. London: Ian Allan 1973.

Medlicott, William Norden. The Economic Blockade. Vol. 1–2. In: *History of the Second World War. U.K. Civil Series*. London: H. M. Stationery Office 1952–1959.

Monserrat, Nicholas. *H.M. Corvette*. New York: Lippincott 1943.

Morison, Samuel Eliot. The Battle of the Atlantic. In: *History of United States Naval Operations in World War II, Vol. 1*, Boston: Little Brown & Co. 1948.

————. The Battle of the Atlantic Won. In: *op. cit., Vol. X*. Boston: Little Brown 1956.

Morsier, Pierre de. *Les corvettes de la France libre*. Paris: Ed. France-Empire 1972.

Noli, Jean. *Les loups de l'amiral: Les Sous-marins Allemands dans la bataille de l'Atlantique*. Paris: Fayard 1970.

Pertek, Jerzi. *Wielkie dni malej floty*. Poznan: Wydawnictwo Poznankie 3rd ed. 1967.

Peillard, Leonce. *Histoire générale de la guerre sous-marine 1939–1945*. Paris: Laffont 1970.

Poolman, Kenneth. *The Catafighters and Merchant Aircraft Carriers*. London: Kimber 1970.

————. *Escort Carrier 1941–1945: An Account of British Escort Carriers in Trade Protection*. London: Ian Allan 1972.

Preston, Anthony. *V and W Class Destroyers 1917–1945*. London: Macdonald 1971.

Preston, Anthony & Raven, Alan. Flower Class Corvettes. In: *Ensign 3*. London: Bivouac Books 1973.

Price, Alfred. *Aircraft versus Submarine: The Evolution of the Anti-submarine Aircraft 1912–1972*. London: Kimber 1973.

Radar. A Report on Science at War. Washington: U.S. Government Printing Office 1945.

Raeder, Erich. *Mein Leben. 2 Bde.* Tübingen: Schlichtenmayer 1956–57. Engl. transl. *My Life*. Annapolis: U.S. Naval Institute 1960.

Reuter, Frank. *Funkmess. Die Entwicklung und der Einsatz des RADAR-Verfahrens in Deutschland bis zum Ende des Zweiten Weltkrieges*. Opladen: Westdeutscher Verlag 1971.

Richards, Denis & Saunders, Hilary St George. *Royal Air Force, 1939–1945*. Vol. 1–3. London: H.M. Stationery Office 1953–1954.

Riesenberg, Felix. *Sea War: The Story of the U.S. Merchant Marine in World War II*. New York: Rinehart 1956.

Robertson, Terence. *Walker R.N.: The Story of Captain Frederic John Walker.* London: Evans 1956.

———. *The Golden Horseshoe: The Story of Otto Kretschmer.* London. Pan Books 1966.

Rohwer, Jürgen. Der Kearny-Zwischenfall am 17.Oktober 1941. In: *Marine-Rundschau* 56 (1959) 288–301.

———. Der U-Bootkrieg und sein Zusammenbruch 1943. In: *Entscheidungsschlachten des Zweiten Weltkrieges.* Frankfurt/Main: Bernard & Graefe 1960. 327–94. Engl. transl.: The U-boat War against the Allied Supply lines. In: *Decisive Battles of World War II.* London: André Deutsch 1965. 259–312.

———. La radiotélégraphie auxiliaire du commandment dans la guerre sous-marine. In: *Revue d'histoire de la Deuxieme Guerre Mondiale,* 1966, 42–66.

———. The last Triumph of the U-boats. In: *Purnell's History of the Second World War.* London: Purnell 1967. Vol. 4/4, 143–46.

———. Vor 25 Jahren: Die grösste Geleitzugschlacht des Krieges: HX.229 SC.122 (März 1943). In: *Wehrwissenschaftliche Rundschau* 18 (1968), 146–58.

———. *Die U-Booterfolge der Achsenmächte 1939–1945. Dokumentationen der Bibliothek für Zeitgeschichte 1.* München: Lehmanns 1968.

———. Die Funkführung der deutschen U-Boote im Zweiten Weltkrieg. Ein Beitrag zum Thema Technik und militärische Führung. In: *Wehrtechnik* 1969. 324–28, 360–64.

———. Die erste Geleitzugschlacht des zweiten Weltkrieges. In: *Koehlers Flottenkalender* 1970. 172–76.

———. Kriegsmarine U 107. In: *Profile Warships No. 8.* Windsor: Profile Publications 1971.

———. Die zweite Geleitzugschlacht im November 1939. In: *Koehlers Flottenkalender* 1971. 128–31.

Rohwer, Jürgen & Hümmelchen, Gerd. *Chronology of the War at Sea 1939–1945.* Vol. 1-2. London: Ian Allan 1972–74.

Rössler, Eberhard. *Geschichte des deutschen Ubootbaus.* München: Lehmanns 1974.

Roscoe, Theodore. *United States Destroyer Operations in World War II.* Annapolis: United States Naval Institute 1953.

Roskill, Stephen W. *The War at Sea 1939–1945.* Vol. 1, 2, 3/1, 3/2. In: *History of the Second World War.* United Kingdom Military Series. London: H.M. Stationery Office 1954–1961.

———. *The Secret Capture: The Story of U 110.* London: Collins 1959.

Ruge, Friedrich. *Der Seekrieg 1939–1945.* Stuttgart: Koehler 1954. Engl.transl. *Der Seekrieg: The German Navy's Story 1939–1945.* Annapolis: United States Naval Institute 1957.

Salewski, Michael. *Die deutsche Seekriegsleitung 1935–1945.* Vol. 1–3. Frankfurt/Main-München: Bernard & Graefe 1970–75.

Schofield, Brian Betham & Martyn, L. F. *The Rescue Ships.* Edinburgh: Blackwood 1968.

Schull, Joseph. *The Far Distant Ships: An Official Account of Canadian Naval Operations in the Second World War.* Ottawa: Cloutier 1952.

Seth, Ronald. *The Fiercest Battle: The Story of North Atlantic Convoy ONS.5, 22 April–7 May 1943.* London: Hutchinson 1961.

Ships of the Esso Fleet in World War II. New Jersey: Standard Oil Company of New Jersey 1946.

Slessor, Sir John. *The Central Blue: Recollections and Reflections.* London: Cassell 1956.
Smith, Peter C. *Destroyer Leader: The Story of H.M.S. Faulknor.* London: Kimber 1968.
Sohler, Herbert. U-Bootkrieg und Völkerrecht. *Marine-Rundschau,* Beiheft 1. Frankfurt/Main: Mittler 1956.
Steen, Erik Anker. Marines operasjoner fra baser i Storbritannia m.v. juli 1940 til December 1943 (vol. 1) and m.v. Januar 1944 til juni 1945 (vol. 2). In: *Norges sjökrig 1940–1945.* Vol. 6, 1/2. Oslo: Gyldendal Norsk Forl. 1963–69.
Tucker, Gilbert Norman. *The Naval Service of Canada: Its Official History.* Vol. 1–2. Ottawa: Cloutier 1952.
Ubaldini, U. Mori. I sommergibili negli oceani. In: *La Marine Italiana nelle Seconda Gurra Mondiale.* Tom. 12. Roma: Ufficio Storico della Marina Militare 1963.
U-Boote. Eine Chronik in Bildern. Ed. by Jürgen Rohwer. Oldenburg/Hamburg: Salling 1962.
United States Naval Chronology, World War II. Prep. by the Historical Division, Office of Naval Operations, Navy Department. Washington: U.S. Government Printing Office 1955.
Waters, John M. *Bloody Winter.* Princeton: Van Nostrand 1967.
Watson-Watt, Sir Robert. *Three Steps to Victory.* London: Odhams Press 1957.
Willoughby, Malcolm F. *The U.S. Coast Guard in World War II.* Annapolis: United States Naval Institute 1957.

ADDENDA
Unpublished Sources
Great Britain
—Admiralty, Naval Staff, Operational Intelligence Centre
—Operational Intelligence Centre Special Intelligence Summary, Convoys HX.229 and SC.122 (March 1943).
—Operational Intelligence Centre Special Intelligence Summary, U-Boat situation Reports, 4., 11., 18., 25.1., 1., 8., 15., 17.2., 1., 8., 15., 22., 29.3.1943.

USA
—Folders on Convoys HX.228, HX.229, SC.121, SC.122, UGS.6 etc., containing signal files for these convoys.
—Daily Situation Maps Atlantic with noon positions of Allied Vessels and Forces and German U-Boats (based on "special intelligence," D/F locations and other observations) January 1st to March 31, 1943.

Books
Beesly, Patrick. *Very Special Intelligence: The Story of the Admiralty's Operational Intelligence Centre 1939–1945.* London: Hamish Hamilton 1977.
Middlebrook, Martin. *Convoy: The Battle for Convoys SC.122 and HX.229.* London: Allen Lane 1976.

Index

Page numbers in italics indicates maps and tables.

Stackpole Military History Series

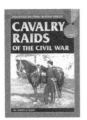
CAVALRY RAIDS OF THE CIVIL WAR

IN THE LION'S MOUTH

WITNESS TO GETTYSBURG

DOUGHBOY WAR

AFTER D-DAY

AIRBORNE COMBAT

ARMOR BATTLES OF THE WAFFEN SS

ARMOURED GUARDSMEN

ARNHEM 1944

B-24 IN CHINA

THE BATTALION

THE BATTLE OF FRANCE

THE BATTLE OF SICILY

BATTLE OF THE BULGE

BATTLE OF THE BULGE

BATTLE OF THE BULGE

BEYOND THE BEACHHEAD

BEYOND STALINGRAD

BLACK BULL

BLITZKRIEG UNLEASHED

BLOSSOMING SILK AGAINST THE RISING SUN

BODEN-PLATTE

BREAKING POINT

THE BRIGADE

CANADIAN ARMY AND THE NORMANDY CAMPAIGN

CRITICAL CONVOY BATTLES OF WWII

DANGEROUS ASSIGNMENT

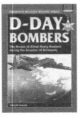
D-DAY BOMBERS

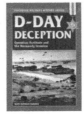
D-DAY DECEPTION

D-DAY TO BERLIN

Real battles. Real soldiers. Real stories.

DECISION IN THE UKRAINE
German Panzer Operations on the Eastern Front, Summer 1943

THE DEFENSE OF MOSCOW 1941
The Northern Flank

DESTINATION NORMANDY
Three American Regiments on D-Day

DIVE BOMBER!
Aircraft, Technology, and Tactics in WWII

EAGER EAGLES
The U.S. Eighth Air Force in Europe, 1941–43

EAGLES OF THE THIRD REICH
Men of the Luftwaffe in WWII

THE EARLY BATTLES OF EIGHTH ARMY
Crusader to the Alamein Line, 1941–42

EASTERN FRONT COMBAT
The German Soldier in Battle from Stalingrad to Berlin

EUROPE IN FLAMES
Understanding WWII

EXIT ROMMEL
The Tunisian Campaign, 1942–43

THE FACE OF COURAGE
The 98 Men Who Received the Knight's Cross and the Close-Combat Clasp in Gold

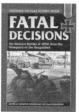

FATAL DECISIONS
Six Decisive Battles of WWII from the Viewpoint of the Vanquished

FIST FROM THE SKY
Japan's Dive-Bomber Ace of WWII

FLYING AMERICAN COMBAT AIRCRAFT OF WWII
1939–45

FOR EUROPE
The French Volunteers of the Waffen-SS

FORGING THE THUNDERBOLT
History of the US Army's Armored Forces, 1917–45

FOR THE HOMELAND
The 31st Waffen-SS Volunteer Grenadier Division in WWII

FORTRESS FRANCE
The Maginot Line and French Defenses in WWII

GERMAN DEFEAT IN THE EAST
1944–45

GERMAN ORDER OF BATTLE
Volume One: 1st–290th Infantry Divisions in WWII

GERMAN ORDER OF BATTLE
Volume Two: 291st–999th Infantry Divisions, Named Infantry Divisions, and Special Divisions in WWII

GERMAN ORDER OF BATTLE
Volume Three: Panzer, Panzer Grenadier, and Waffen-SS Divisions in WWII

THE GERMANS IN NORMANDY

GERMANY'S PANZER ARM IN WWII

GI INGENUITY
Improvisation, Technology, and Winning WWII

GOODBYE, TRANSYLVANIA
A Romanian Waffen-SS Soldier in WWII

THE GREAT SHIPS
British Battleships in WWII

GRENADIERS
The Story of Waffen-SS General Kurt "Panzer" Meyer

GUNS AGAINST THE REICH
Memoirs of a Soviet Artillery Officer on the Eastern Front

HITLER'S FINAL FORTRESS
Breslau 1945

Stackpole Military History Series

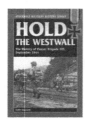

Real battles. Real soldiers. Real stories.

NO HOLDING BACK
Operation Totalize, Normandy, August 1944

OPERATION MERCURY
The Battle for Crete, 1941

PANZER ACES
German Tank Commanders of WWII

PANZER ACES II
Battle Stories of German Tank Commanders of WWII

PANZER COMMANDERS OF THE WESTERN FRONT
German Tank Generals in WWII

PANZERGRENADIER ACES
German Mechanized Infantry in WWII

PANZER GUNNER
A Canadian in the German 7th Panzer Division, 1944–45

PANZER LEGIONS
A Guide to the German Army Panzer Divisions of WWII and Their Commanders

PANZER WEDGE
Volume One: The German 3rd Panzer Division and the Summer of Victory in the East

PANZER WEDGE
Volume Two: The German 3rd Panzer Division and Barbarossa's Failure at the Gates of Moscow

PANZERS IN WINTER
Hitler's Army and the Battle of the Bulge

THE PATH TO BLITZKRIEG
Doctrine and Training in the German Army, 1920–39

PENALTY STRIKE
The Memoirs of a Red Army Penal Company Commander, 1943–45

POLAND BETRAYED
The Nazi-Soviet Invasions of 1939

RED ROAD FROM STALINGRAD
Recollections of a Soviet Infantryman

RED STAR UNDER THE BALTIC
A Soviet Submariner in WWII

RETREAT TO THE REICH
The German Defeat in France, 1944

ROMMEL RECONSIDERED

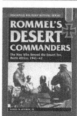

ROMMEL'S DESERT COMMANDERS
The Men Who Served the Desert Fox, North Africa, 1941–42

ROMMEL'S DESERT WAR
The Life and Death of the Afrika Korps

ROMMEL'S LIEUTENANTS
The Men Who Saved the Desert Fox, France, 1940

SAVAGE SKY
Life and Death on a Bomber over Germany in 1944

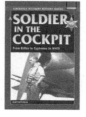

THE SEEDS OF DISASTER
The Development of French Army Doctrine, 1919–39

SHIP-BUSTERS
British Torpedo-Bombers in WWII

SIEGE OF BREST 1941
The Red Army's Stand against the Germans during Operation Barbarossa

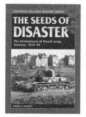

THE SIEGE OF KÜSTRIN
Gateway to Berlin, 1945

SIEGFRIED LINE
The German Defense of the West Wall, September–December 1944

SOLDIER IN THE COCKPIT
From Rifles to Typhoons in WWII

SOVIET BLITZKRIEG
The Battle for White Russia, 1944

SPITFIRES & YELLOW TAIL MUSTANGS
The U.S. 52nd Fighter Group in WWII

Stackpole Military History Series

STALIN'S KEYS TO VICTORY
The Rebirth of the Red Army in WWII

SURVIVING BATAAN AND BEYOND
Colonel Irwin Alexander's Odyssey as a Japanese Prisoner of War

T-34 IN ACTION
Soviet Tank Troops in WWII

TANK TACTICS
From Normandy to Lorraine

TIGERS IN THE MUD
The Combat Career of German Panzer Commander Otto Carius

TRIUMPHANT FOX
Erwin Rommel and the Rise of the Afrika Korps

THE 12TH SS
The History of the Hitler Youth Panzer Division: Volume One

THE 12TH SS
The History of the Hitler Youth Panzer Division: Volume Two

TWILIGHT OF THE GODS
A Swedish Volunteer in the 11th SS Panzergrenadier Division "Nordland" on the Eastern Front

TYPHOON ATTACK
The Legendary British Fighter in Combat in WWII

THE WAR AGAINST ROMMEL'S SUPPLY LINES
1942–43

WAR IN THE AEGEAN
The Campaign for the Eastern Mediterranean in WWII

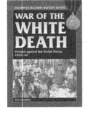
WAR OF THE WHITE DEATH
Finland against the Soviet Union, 1939–40

WARSAW 1944
An Insurgent's Journal of the Uprising

WINTER STORM
The Battle for Stalingrad and the Operation to Rescue 6th Army

WINTER WAR
The Soviet Attack on Finland, 1939–1940

WOLFPACK WARRIORS
The Story of WWII's Most Successful Fighter Outfit

ZHUKOV AT THE ODER
The Decisive Battle for Berlin

CYCLOPS IN THE JUNGLE
A One-Eyed LRP in Vietnam

EXPENDABLE WARRIORS
The Battle of Khe Sanh and the Vietnam War

Real battles. Real soldiers. Real stories.

 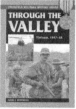   

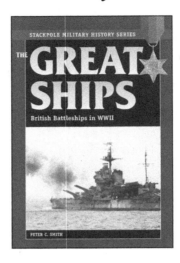

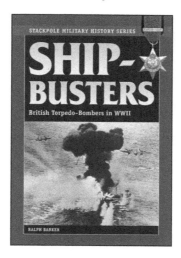

Stackpole Military History Series

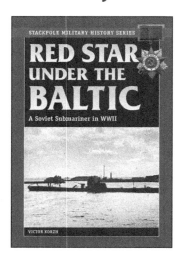

RED STAR UNDER THE BALTIC
A SOVIET SUBMARINER IN WWII
Viktor Korzh

Submarines were uninviting enough, with dank, claustrophobic conditions and little hope of escape if disaster struck, and the relatively shallow waters of the Baltic Sea only compounded the dangers. That's where Soviet submariner Victor Korzh served during World War II, hunting and sinking German ships. His memoir unfolds as a heart-pounding series of sonar pings, depth-charge explosions, and last-second evasions. Somehow Korzh and his comrades survived their frightful ordeal and witnessed the victory over the Germans.

Paperback • 6 x 9 • 224 pages • 1 map, 22 b/w photos

WWW.STACKPOLEBOOKS.COM
1-800-732-3669